Beauty is in the Street

Beauty is in the Street

Protest and Counterculture in Post-War Europe

JOACHIM C. HÄBERLEN

ALLEN LANE
an imprint of
PENGUIN BOOKS

ALLEN LANE

UK | USA | Canada | Ireland | Australia
India | New Zealand | South Africa

Penguin Books is part of the Penguin Random House group of companies
whose addresses can be found at global.penguinrandomhouse.com

First published in Great Britain by Allen Lane 2023

001

Copyright © Joachim C. Häberlen, 2023

The moral right of the author has been asserted

Set in 12/14.75 pt Dante MT Std
Typeset by Jouve (UK), Milton Keynes
Printed and bound in Great Britain by Clays Ltd, Elcograf S.p.A.

The authorized representative in the EEA is Penguin Random House Ireland,
Morrison Chambers, 32 Nassau Street, Dublin D02 YH68

A CIP catalogue record for this book is available from the British Library

ISBN: 978-0-241-47937-7

Contents

Contents

Introduction

The history of post-war Europe is full of protests, large and small. Across the continent, from Paris to Prague, from Wyhl in southwest Germany to Wrocław in Poland, ordinary people took to the streets, challenged established orders and demanded political, social and cultural change. City dwellers struggled for access to affordable and decent housing. Women campaigned for the right to abortion, gay men for the decriminalization of homosexuality, and migrants without legal status for the right to remain in their adopted homelands. In the 1970s and 1980s, hundreds of thousands of protestors participated in demonstrations against nuclear armament and what they understood to be the militarization of society, while committed activists set up protest camps against military bases and occupied construction sites to stop the building of nuclear power plants. From 1968, when students and – in some places – workers revolted all over the continent in an attempt to democratize universities, workplaces and society more generally, to 1989, when immense crowds brought down communism in Eastern Europe, these were decades of massive protest.

What can we learn from this history? Why does it matter for our world today?

Studying these protest movements provides a unique and enriching perspective on post-war European history. It shows how ordinary people who had the courage to take to the streets made history, not only those – usually men – in power; it gives a sense of how profoundly contested political decisions, cultural norms and expectations and ultimately entire societal orders were. But most importantly, we can learn about the alternatives to the status quo that people envisioned and tried to build. For activists went beyond organizing protests *against* something – nuclear power plants, the militarization of society, laws prohibiting abortions, even capitalism and communism themselves – to imagining something else, something better. They longed for a different world, a world in which nationality would no longer matter, which would be free of sexist and racist discrimination, where people would live and work together in solidarity, liberated from the constraints of traditional morals; a world in which it would be possible to enjoy an 'authentic' life, true to humans' longings and desires, untrammelled by the falsity of consumer capitalism.

This was more than just dreaming. Militants strived to put their visions of a better world into practice. They formed communes where they hoped to escape from conventional family life; they set up self-managed businesses where they worked without a boss, seeking to overcome the feelings of alienation they associated with work under capitalism. Not least, they tried to change their personal lives by exploring different forms of intimacy and sexuality, developing novel understandings of masculinity and femininity (and questioning those very categories) and living in harmony with nature. All of this was part of the struggle for a better world.

There is thus something utopian to the history of protesting: it illuminates people's dreams, the futures they hoped for and the means by which they tried to achieve them.

These past struggles remain part of our contemporary reality.[1] Conservative politicians frequently blame these movements for what they consider a devastating decline in patriotism and family values, or even a collapse of any moral standards. 'May '68' – the moment when the international student movement reached its apogee in France and the country seemed to be on the verge of revolution – 'has inflicted intellectual and moral relativism on us,' said French presidential candidate, later President, Nicolas Sarkozy at a rally in April 2007. 'The heirs of May '68 have imposed the idea that everything has the same value, that there is no difference between good and bad, truth and falsehood, beauty and ugliness . . . They have proclaimed that anything is permitted, that authority, civility, and respect are finished, that nothing is great, sacred or admirable any longer.' France, Sarkozy claimed, needed to 'liquidate' the 'inheritance of May '68'.[2] Similarly, German conservative politician Alexander Dobrindt called in 2018 for a cultural counter-revolution to strengthen traditional, patriotic values, values that had been under attack by the media and cultural institutions where, Dobrindt claimed, leftists had gained undue influence since the revolts of 1968.[3]

At the other end of the political spectrum, these protest movements of the past continue to provide a source of inspiration for present-day activism. There is, argues historian Timothy Scott Brown, 'unfinished business' left over from the 1960s: the radical and participatory democracy students struggled for then is yet to be brought into being. Such protest histories, seeking to reproduce the enthusiasm of the past for the present, sometimes read as a call to arms for activism. Victorious struggles of the past, when movements succeeded to bring hundreds of thousands to the streets, can, it seems, provide blueprints for today's activism.[4]

Indeed, many political and social movements today can trace their roots to the second half of the twentieth century. Current queer politics, the fight against sexism, against homophobia and transphobia: they all have their origins in the women's and gay movements of the 1970s. Campaigns against racism and for the support of refugees and migrants similarly build upon earlier solidarity movements for the 'Third World', while the ground for today's climate activism was prepared by the environmental movements of the 1970s and 1980s. If we are fully to understand today's political movements and cultures, we must explore their past.

Telling the history of these struggles for a better world in the form of a single narrative is impossible. They were too varied, too contradictory, too complex. To do justice to their richness, we need a more microscopic approach. This book thus tells their story through a series of deep dives into various movements at different places and moments in time.

Part I begins in the 1950s and early 1960s, years that don't have a reputation for upheaval. It was a time of rebuilding Europe after the destruction of the Second World War, of so-called economic miracles, of the rise of consumer capitalism, of political and cultural conservatism – all under the shadow of the early Cold War confrontation between the Western bloc of democratic, capitalist countries, organized into NATO (founded in 1949), and the Soviet Eastern bloc of communist countries, organized into the 1955 Warsaw Pact as NATO's Eastern equivalent. Yet in places like Amsterdam, West Berlin and Milan, a countercultural scene emerged that prepared the ground for future protests, while a group of critical artists formulated a radical critique of society that helped inspire the famous uprisings of 1968.

The book then turns to the revolts of 1968 in four countries – West Germany, France, Czechoslovakia and Italy – exploring how the rebels of 1968 hoped to radically transform their societies. These revolts set the agenda for activism in the years to come. They challenged the authority not only of the state, but also of the old labour movement, of communist parties and trade unions. They called for a rethinking of international solidarity, they made personal relations and questions of sexuality a central issue of oppositional politics and they fundamentally changed how activists thought about the workings of power in society, and hence the forms, methods and places of struggling.

Looking at the efflorescence of protest cultures, Part II explores different ways people fought for a better world. Such struggles took many forms, ranging from the extreme, deadly violence of terrorism to demonstrations and riots in the streets, to the playful staging of 'happenings', fluid and impromptu performances intended to disrupt public order. These struggles also had an intellectual dimension. Wanting to understand how power works in modern society, many activists were avid readers of intellectuals such as Italian Marxist Mario Tronti, Czechoslovak dissident Václav Havel and French philosopher Michel Foucault, thinkers whose ideas profoundly influenced opposition movements. But as interesting as reading books in lonely chambers could be, this hardly made standing up against an oppressive order emotionally appealing. Music did: bands like West German Ton Steine Scherben, the British Sex Pistols and Czechoslovak Plastic People of the Universe expressed outrage, gave hope, brought people to the streets – and scared authorities.

From different forms of protest, we move to the changing activist landscape in the wake of 1968, the subject of Part III. It begins by exploring how activists related to struggles outside of Europe, whether by calling for international solidarity or by engaging in human rights activism. However, these attempts to foster connections with activists from other parts of the world notwithstanding, protest movements in those years were a predominantly white affair. Indeed, for a long time, scholarship of protest movements has all but ignored questions of race. Struggles by migrants, who came to Western Europe in the wake of decolonization or as so-called guest workers, tended to be overlooked – which is why this book devotes a chapter to how migrants fought against racist violence, demanded the right to stay when facing deportation and campaigned for better working conditions, while forging fragile alliances with white comrades.

We then reach the largest protest movements of the post-1968 years: the closely connected peace and environmental movements of the 1970s and 1980s, whose marches attracted hundreds of thousands of citizens. Of particular interest are the various protest camps that dedicated activists set up as experimental places for building a better world in the here and now. While these protests often took place in the countryside, countercultural scenes typically emerged in urban spaces. Here, protestors fought for a 'right to the city'. They demanded affordable living space, occupied vacant buildings and sought to transform cities that critics deemed boring and monotonous into enjoyable places. Whereas these urban activists sought to change everyday life by intervening in the public space of the city, the women's and gay movements turned their gaze to the private sphere, thereby questioning its separation from the sphere of politics: 'The personal is political,' feminists famously argued. Private matters, most importantly reproductive rights, but also more generally sexual desires, feelings and the body, gained a profoundly political meaning, in the process challenging patriarchal and heteronormative norms.

As important as such campaigns were, many activists also believed that building a better society could not wait until the political battles were won. Change had to happen here and now, and it was them, the activists, who had to make a start with living a different life. Part IV explores how activists did this: by setting up urban and rural communes, where they hoped to escape from both the loneliness of modern cities and the constraints of conventional family life; by working in small, self-managed businesses without bosses; and by hitch-hiking across countries in search of feelings of freedom and community. For many activists, living a different life also meant that they had to change themselves: they joined consciousness-raising and therapy groups of all kinds to reflect on their feelings and sexuality. And, last but not least, they looked for ways of comprehending the world besides rationality and science, finding enlightenment in spiritualist teachings that promised a more holistic understanding of the universe. Changing the world, they believed, would only be possible if people developed an almost bodily sense for the inner connections of the universe that remained hidden from the scientific gaze.

Our journey ends with another pivotal moment in the history of protest: the peaceful revolutions of 1989 that brought down communism in Eastern Europe. These revolutions were a moment of tremendous hope for rebuilding societies in a more democratic, more humane way – hopes that, as so often, did not materialize.

At the heart of the story are the 1970s, years that saw the most vibrant protest movements emerge, whose ideas and practices proved immensely influential for activist milieus in future years. Those were tumultuous and eventful years, not only because of the protest movements. Many historians now consider the decade to be formative for our present. The optimistic belief in never-ending economic progress and stability collapsed, as did the belief in the ability of governments to effectively intervene in the economy in times of crisis. In 1972, the Club of Rome published its report on *The Limits to Growth*, stressing the limited natural resources of the earth; a year later, the oil crisis shocked the world and resulted in rapidly rising energy prices (though nothing compared to today). And in 1975, the American retreat from Vietnam drastically demonstrated the weakness of Western imperialism based on military might (though post-colonial exploitation, of course, has not ended). As the old world was fading away, a new one emerged. A third industrial revolution, characterized by automation and computerization, vastly increased productivity, but also destroyed old working-class milieus. Values changed, as people came to cherish personal development, creativity and cultural participation rather than material wealth. It was a time, many felt, of dramatic change, of old certainties disappearing without them being replaced by anything. The protest movements examined in this book can be understood as a search for alternatives to these fading certainties.[5]

The stories this book tells are full of hope and disappointments. As someone who was himself involved in protest movements at a younger age, I can well recall exhilarating moments of enthusiasm when chanting in the streets, of listening to famous protest songs, of feeling a sense of community when singing along with comrades. We certainly had a good time when we were squatting in vacant buildings to campaign for an independent youth club and ended up dancing in decaying factory halls. But I also recall the moments of frustration and sadness, the quarrels about political differences that destroyed friendships. When I now observe protests, sometimes with sympathy, sometimes with neutral curiosity, sometimes with sceptical irritation, I can sense the hopes for a better future among those in the streets.

Protests still inspire, and so does their history. I could see this when teaching at my old university. Many students, twenty years younger than I, felt that the issues that brought protestors to the streets in 1968 still haunt us today. Universities, they said, are a mere training ground for a job market that has nothing in common with the democratic spaces for learning that radical students of the 1960s envisioned. Social media, they argued, is nothing but a spectacle of fake self-representation; no wonder some told me how much sense Guy Debord's 1967 *Society of the Spectacle* made to them. And, of course, the visions of feminist and anti-racist movements also resonated with many students. But perhaps most interesting of all is that my students expressed a slight sense of nostalgia. In the 1970s, they felt, it was possible to try out new ideas and lifestyles, to experiment and make mistakes (and granted, this might be too romantic an image of the 1970s); this, they claimed, has now become impossible, with every mistake, everything they ever say, recorded for eternity on social media.

In a way, this book is a response to my students' feeling that something has been lost. It will, I hope, inspire readers. But it's not meant as a call to arms, a call to return to some unfinished business. It doesn't provide blueprints for protesting today. Rather, the book is an invitation to imagine alternatives, to have the courage to struggle, to experiment, risk failure and try again. At the same time, I hope the book will also make readers pause and critically reflect on the difficulties activists have encountered, on the forms of power and oppression they (re)created when trying to live a free and 'authentic' life. It's a book that, I hope, fires readers' imaginations, but also evokes a healthy dose of scepticism.

PART I

Setting the Scene

Rocking the Miracle Years: Rebellious Youth and Critical Intellectuals from the 1950s to the 1960s

Post-war Western Europe is often depicted as quiet and unremarkable. After the political extremism of the interwar years and the devastation of the Second World War, Europeans longed for political stability and economic recovery. People worked hard to rebuild the continent, and with stunning success. Driven by the American-funded Marshall Plan, countries such as West Germany, Italy, France, Belgium and the Netherlands saw impressive economic growth rates that allowed Western Europeans to enjoy the riches of consumer society, which they eagerly did. Citizens typically voted conservative parties into government, though even on the left, parties that had previously rallied for radical if not revolutionary change, notably communists, gave up on those demands. In countries such as France and Italy, where communists achieved consistently over 20 per cent at the polls, they effectively became integrated into the political mainstream.[1] In West Germany, where the Communist Party (KPD) was banned in 1956 due to its close relations with the GDR, the Soviet-backed East Germany, the moderate Social Democrats eliminated all traces of Marxist rhetoric from their programme, supporting the new 'social market-economy', private property and the constitution of the Federal Republic.[2] And, not least, people held traditional family values in high regard after what many considered a moral collapse in the interwar years that had led to the abyss of Fascism and Nazism.[3] The immediate post-war years, then, were not a time of rebellion – or so it seemed to many contemporary observers who expressed concern about the younger generation's political apathy, which troubled them, as they believed stable democracies needed political commitment and active engagement.[4]

With closer scrutiny, however, we can see signs of rebellion everywhere. Teenagers rebelled against the constraints of a society that praised orderly behaviour and hard work. Looking for meaning in life beyond working and consuming, non-conformist youngsters experimented with different ways of living that promised both personal autonomy and excitement in ways that contrasted sharply with the sterility and orderliness of post-war society; meanwhile, a group of radical artists and writers that became known as the Situationist International developed a critique of consumer society, calling for a 'revolution of everyday life'.[5] In multiple ways, rebellious teenagers, political activists and intellectuals imagined and experimented with alternatives to the status quo. In doing so, they also developed alternatives to traditional working-class leftist politics that were focused on improving workers' material lot. To them, the Soviet Union, with its bureaucratic socialism that looked as sterile, grey and boring as Western consumer capitalism, was no longer a role model to be emulated.

The Wild Ones: Rock 'n' Roll and Unruly Teens in 1950s West Germany[6]

In January 1955, the American movie *The Wild One* came to cinemas across West Germany. Starring Marlon Brando, the film painted a disturbing picture of the United States: two motorcycle gangs invaded a small American town, where they fought each other and the town's residents, while gang leader Johnny Stabler, played by Brando, fell in love with the daughter of a local policeman.[7] For many West German reviewers, the movie was depicting real social conflicts in the United States – luckily, they felt, Germany did not face such problems. But one anonymous reviewer, writing in West Berlin's daily *Kurier*, was less optimistic: West German teenagers, he feared, might well look up to Marlon Brando, take him as a role model and start acting in a similarly rowdy fashion.[8]

In the summer of 1955, his nightmares became true. West Berlin newspapers reported about a gang of bikers riding their motorcycles to the outskirts of the city, where they provoked customers of the Big Window café, located next to the River Havel in the west of the city, with 'skinny dipping and noisiness'. Inspired by the movie, the young rowdies referred to themselves – as one report claimed – as 'The Wild Ones of the Big Window', while another paper called them simply 'The Marlon Brandos'. A year later, a gang called Totenkopfbande (Skull and Crossbones Gang) by the media – according to them, the symbol was a reference to *The Wild One* – made the news in the working-class neighbourhood of Wedding, where they hung out in front of a local bar. Annoyed by their noisy behaviour, residents regularly called the police. But police intervention didn't pacify the situation, as young gang members refused to follow the officers' orders, and clashes ensued. The situation escalated on the evening of 12 July 1956, when some 200 adolescents gathered in front of a bar. Watched over by a crowd of about 5,000 spectators, including entire families equipped with strollers, they stopped cars and disrupted the traffic. Only with great effort did the police reimpose order; when the crowd reassembled a week later, police even used water hoses to clear the streets.[9]

These confrontations in West Berlin were no isolated events. In the second half of the 1950s, clashes between teenagers, whom the press came to call *Halbstarke* (literally 'the semi-strong'), and the police occurred throughout the Federal Republic, often after rock 'n' roll concerts or movie screenings. At times several thousand teenagers battled the police. The immediate triggers for such riots varied. Sometimes, youths gathered to provoke passers-by and stop traffic. In other instances, teenagers queuing unsuccessfully for tickets to see celebrated stars like Bill Haley or Elvis Presley started riots. In October 1958, some 200 teenagers without tickets for Haley's show *Rock Around the Clock* stormed West Berlin's Sportpalast. Inside the venue, they smashed chairs and forced an unpopular support act to leave the stage. Haley and his band didn't last much longer. Facing the riotous audience, they fled backstage, abandoning instruments as they went. A day later, the band performed in Hamburg. When Haley came on stage, the crowd went wild. Stewards and even Haley himself asked them to stick to the rules, remain seated and stop dancing, but to no avail. Young couples danced in the narrow aisles, while dozens of *Halbstarke* were 'excitedly throwing their arms into the air'. One of them, as a journalist wrote, even banged his head against the floor of the stage 'like a madman'. Again, the concert was cut short, leading to further riots outside the venue.[10]

Violent altercations with the police were the most visible sign of this growing frustration. Not only in West Germany, but across the entire continent – and on both sides of the Iron Curtain – increasing numbers of teenagers rebelled against the conservative norms and values of their parents' generation, disturbing, as the title of a book by West German psychologist Curt Bondy put it, the public order.[11] And a disturbance they were, if we believe the recollection of this former *Halbstarke*: 'When we came home on a Sunday morning, we put our bloody T-shirts, torn to pieces, on our cars' antennas; then we roamed through the streets in the early morning. People went to church, all well-behaved, and we were still wasted, bleary-eyed, full of blood, scarred, topless, driving through the streets.'[12] Roaming the streets on their mopeds in gangs of fifty must have been a thrilling feeling. 'You have to imagine, what kind of intoxication that was, when the pack was together.'[13]

What was this raucous teenage rebellion about? The *Halbstarken* had neither a political manifesto nor any clear vision of how to change society for the better. Theirs was a rebellion of the body, against gendered norms and styles, that functioned without written statements or political theory. Taking movie stars such as Marlon Brando and James Dean as role models, young men dressed in tight blue jeans and T-shirts, combined with short black leather jackets and boots. They greased their hair to form great ducktail plumes, tellingly known as *Elvis Quiff* or *Elvis Tolle* in German.[14] Even their movements were a provocation, as to this journalist of the West Berlin daily *Die Welt*, who wrote: 'The typical image: hands in the pockets, sloppy posture and clothes, marcelled hair – nothing stiff, no purposeful posture, soft and gawky.'[15] He was not a lonely voice. Curt Bondy similarly noted that teenagers avoided any 'jerking and stiff movements', instead accentuating 'elastic movements of the entire body'.[16] But perhaps most worrisome for parents and educators alike was the wild and excessive dancing to rock 'n' roll music: a music that was loud and fast, and a dancing that followed no rules, that did not require formal dancing lessons and that was full of sexual connotations that violated, as historian Sebastian Kurme writes, 'norms of female grace and male chivalry'.[17] No surprise that conservative observers feared a reversal of gender roles and considered such dancing 'erotic excesses'.[18]

Today, such behaviour might not sound particularly rebellious. In the 1950s, it frequently caused bitter conflicts with parents, teachers and other authority figures. They were appalled by young men spending hours in front of the mirror styling their hair, something that made them look dangerously effeminate.[19] The wild, artistic dancing of young men challenged ideals of masculinity that celebrated soldierly qualities like self-restraint, discipline, steadfastness and sacrifice.[20] Cultural critics were profoundly concerned. They went so far as to see a form of primitivism at work in the *Halbstarke*'s behaviour that they had witnessed in Nazism; such teenagers, they feared, would be easily seducible by political extremists. Just like the Nazis, the wild music, whether it was jazz or rock 'n' roll, seemed to appeal to the lower instincts of the masses, which made it profoundly dangerous for the young democracy. 'Who knows to what intricacy and audacity these mass highs, like the orgies of jazz fans, could grow, if at the critical moment certain motives were introduced?' pondered Walter Abendroth, former cultural editor of *Die Zeit*.[21] For education expert and high-school teacher Hans Muchow, the rebels' behaviour was a regression into a 'wild form'. And while the majority were simply biologically 'incapable of moving beyond menial labor', there was also a dangerous minority, an 'avant-garde of nihilists', who, he feared, would lead the 'primitive' and seducible youth into a war on existing values and against law and order.[22]

Politicians, though, reacted in a much more conciliatory manner, accepting the *Halbstarke*, their music and dancing, as long as they did not break any actual laws. In July 1956, West Berlin's Christian

Democratic deputy mayor Franz Amrehn, for example, decided to meet with some of the young rioters. Apparently, members of the Totenkopfbande who had caused so much trouble brought flowers and apologized for their behaviour. In return, the city government provided the teenagers with a place to meet, along with a jukebox, and paid for a concert that was attended by a crowd of 6,000 adolescents, all riding, as a report in the *Hannoversche Presse* noted, 'motorbikes with racing saddles and wearing Texas pants' – a somewhat derisive term for jeans.[23] By the late 1950s, the 'hot rhythms' of rock 'n' roll had lost their menace, and Defence Minister Franz-Josef Strauß benignly decreed jazz appropriate music for the newly formed West German army, the Bundeswehr.[24] The Federal Republic was on the way to becoming a liberal and democratic society.[25]

The Poverty of Everyday Life: The Situationist International

While teenagers in West Germany and elsewhere rebelled against the restrictive social mores of post-war society, a group of avant-garde artists from across Western Europe formed what would become famous for its biting critique of both consumer-capitalist society and the traditional left: the Situationist International, founded in July 1957 in the small Italian village of Cosio di Arroscia.[26] It was a small group, numbering over the course of its existence perhaps seventy individuals, though frequent splits and expulsions meant that its actual strength at any given time rarely exceeded twenty-five members.[27] Nevertheless, the pamphlets and articles published in the group's journal *Internationale Situationiste* and the books by its leading figures, notably *The Society of the Spectacle* by French writer Guy Debord and *The Revolution of Everyday Life* by Belgian Raoul Vaneigem, both published in 1967 (when both authors were, it should be noted, in their mid-thirties: Debord thirty-six, and Vaneigem thirty-three!), became immensely influential in leftist circles and are still widely read today.[28]

In contrast to the raucous *Halbstarke*, the Situationist International pursued an explicitly revolutionary project. 'First of all, we think the world must be changed. We want the most liberating change of the society and life in which we find ourselves confined,' the group's manifesto *Report on the Construction of Situations* read. The revolution it imagined radically differed from the kind of revolution typically called for by communist parties. Revolution, Debord argued in the manifesto, had to go beyond the question of who was to own the means of production. 'It must abolish not only the exploitation of humanity,' he wrote, 'but also the passions, compensations and habits which that exploitation has engendered. We have to define new desires in relation to present possibilities.' Modern capitalism, Situationists believed, produced false desires for superficial consumption, but suppressed real, authentic human passions. A genuine revolution hence had to change all aspects of everyday life to revitalize these buried passions. The way to do so was constructing 'situations' – hence the name of the group: 'Our central idea is the construction of situations, that is to say, the concrete construction of momentary ambiences of life and their transformation into a superior passionate quality,' the manifesto proclaimed in somewhat obscure language. In other words, Situationists hoped to create situations that would disrupt the frozen normalcy of everyday life and produce emotionally intense – 'passionate', in the Situationist parlance – experiences. 'The passions have been sufficiently interpreted; the point now is to discover new ones,' Debord concluded with a nod to Marx's *Communist Manifesto*.[29]

In the Situationists' analysis, the social developments of the post-war period, the economic boom and the rise of consumer capitalism, called for such a rethinking of the revolutionary project. Despite great technological advances, they wrote in 1958, 'the real possibilities of everyday life' had not increased correspondingly.[30] For Debord, life seemed to be empty: 'Someone posed the question, "What is private life [*vie privée*] deprived [*privée*] of?" Quite simply of life itself, which is cruelly absent. People are as deprived as possible of communication and of self-fulfillment; deprived of the opportunity to personally make their own history.'[31] Despite the material riches of modern society, people effectively had no chance to write the script of their lives, he argued. Modern society had 'atomized' people into 'isolated consumers', unable to communicate with each other and living, in the words of Vaneigem, with 'nothing in common except the illusion of being together'.[32] What remained was, he wrote, 'emotionally dead survival', made possible by the welfare state. And though physically surviving, people were 'dying of boredom' if not actually committing suicide.[33]

Situationists held modern consumer society responsible for this poverty of everyday life. The obsession with consumer goods, argued Vaneigem, substituted 'authentic life with things'. It was impossible for people to feel genuinely 'attached to these things, precisely because they have to be *consumed*, i.e., destroyed'. And those who produced these objects had no meaningful relationship with them, for it was 'useless to expect even a caricature of creativity from the conveyor belt'.[34] There was neither time nor space for creativity, adventure and play in this consumerist society. Every activity, Vaneigem wrote in his *Revolution of Everyday Life*, had a designated time: 'This is the temporality of work, progress, productivity, production deadlines, consumption and planning: time for a kiss, snapshot time.'[35] Likewise, every activity had its designated place. A 'rigid division between work zones and residence zones,' Debord noted, characterized modern cities.[36] Anticipating critiques of urban planning that became common in the 1970s, Dutch Situationist Constant Nieuwenhuys complained in 1959 that the streets of older neighbourhoods had 'degenerated into freeways, and leisure-time activities are being commercialized and corrupted by tourism. Social relations become impossible'. The new cities, rapidly built in the wake of the Second World War, were 'cemeteries of reinforced concrete', where 'masses of the population are condemned to die of boredom'.[37]

Yet, the Situationists believed there was hope. 'In the heart of each human being', wrote Vaneigem, there was a 'hidden room', a secret place to which only 'the mind and dreams' had access. There, in a 'magic circle', the 'world and the self are reconciled', and 'every childish wish comes true. The passions flower there, brilliant, poisonous blossoms clinging to and thriving on air, thin air.'[38] The task was to bring these hidden desires and dreams to the fore.[39] Deprived and impoverished life, in other words, had to be enriched, and fragmented relationships made whole. This was at the heart of the idea of the *dérive* (roughly meaning 'drift'), a way of exploring urban landscapes for which the Situationist International became famous. In the words of Debord: 'In a *dérive* one or more persons during a certain period drop their relations, their work and leisure activities, and all their other usual motives for movement and action, and let themselves be drawn by the attractions of the terrain and the encounters they find there.' Strolling through the city in a 'passionate journey out of the ordinary', it would become possible to overcome the strict divisions of the city into spaces for work and spaces for leisure and thereby to create a situation of genuine intensity that was otherwise missing in everyday life.[40]

With their celebration of radical subjectivity and playfulness, the Situationist International would set the agenda for countercultural movements in the years to come. In the early 1960s, however, few people took notice of their tracts. Their vision of constructing situations that would disrupt the normal structures of everyday life and make way for alternative adventures remained just that: a vision, barely put into practice.

In November 1966, this changed. In May that year, a group of six radical students at the University of Strasbourg had run for the local student union with a radical programme: they simply wanted to destroy the union, which they considered an utterly useless organization. And as most of their fellow students hadn't bothered to vote – thereby tacitly proving the radicals' point about the uselessness of the organization – they had won the election. Having no idea how to make use of their new powers, they had reached out to the Situationist International. In response Debord had instructed fellow Situationist and Strasbourg student Mustapha Khayati to pen a radical critique of student life and politics. His text was to finally make the Situationists famous: *On the Poverty of Student Life: A Consideration of Its Economic, Political, Sexual, Psychological and Notably Intellectual Aspects and of a Few Ways to Cure It.* Using the student union's funds, the radicals printed 10,000 copies of the pamphlet, which they distributed during the opening ceremony of the academic year on 22 November in the Palais Universitaire. As they took their seats, the local dignitaries, from university rector Maurice Bayen to the local bishop and prefect, found the pamphlet. They were not amused. The next day, the radicals handed out more copies in front of university cafeterias across campus. Khayati, and the Situationists, were front-page news.[41]

Khayati's pamphlet was both a polemical depiction of the student as a deeply despicable creature, and a radical critique of current but outdated revolutionary Bolshevik politics. Khayati had nothing but contempt for students: 'The student is a stoical slave: the more chains authority binds him with, the freer he thinks he is.' Students, he charged, immersed themselves in the latest fashionable intellectual trends, from existentialism to structuralism, while remaining passive consumers who followed debates between the intellectual celebrities of the day – Althusser, Sartre, Barthes and so on – without any genuine passion and, preparing for their careers as 'low-level functionaries', without any independent thought. Although students had some liberty with regard to how they used their time, they avoided 'adventure and experiment, preferring the security of the straitjacketed daily space-time organized for [their] benefit by the guardians of the system'. Instead of rebelling against the misery of student life, the student, in Khayati's indictment, 'is so stupid and so miserable that he voluntarily submits himself to the University Psychological Aid Centers, those agencies of psycho-police control established by the vanguard of modern oppression and naturally hailed as a great victory for student unionism.'[42]

Khayati's condemnation of student politics was equally scathing. Students, he wrote, continued 'to participate blithely in the most laughable demonstrations that never draw anybody but students'. In their 'utter political ignorance', they were prey to political agitators of 'dying bureaucratic organizations' such as the Communist Party. Yet, while he acknowledged that socialism and Stalinism had been defeated in Western Europe, he was certain that revolution would nonetheless come, albeit in a very different form: 'Proletarian revolutions will be *festivals* or nothing, for festivity is the very keynote of the life they announce. *Play* is the ultimate principle of this festival, and the only rules it can recognize are to live without dead time and to enjoy without restraints.'[43]

Unsurprisingly, the publication quickly became a massive scandal, with newspapers across France reporting on the radical anarchists. University authorities were outraged. By mid-December, a local court shut down the student union, seized the remaining funds and banned the radical executive committee from campus. The public outcry over the pamphlet only helped with its success. Reprinted the following March, it reached students across France, with groups supportive of Situationist ideas forming at many universities. Soon it was translated into multiple languages, giving the text a truly global audience. It has become one of the most famous texts of the Situationist International, with hundreds of thousands if not millions of copies reprinted – there is no copyright on the text, so radicals across the world can simply reproduce it. And it set the tone for the revolts to come: the uprising of 1968 would indeed be an explosive festival.

The Art of Provocation: The Amsterdam Provos

While the Situationists largely confined their activism to visionary tracts, another group took action: the Provos in Amsterdam.[44] In the 1960s, the liberal-minded Dutch city had become a hotspot for countercultural activists, attracting thousands of young people from across Europe. Part of this countercultural scene was a performance artist by the name of Robert Jasper Grootveld. In the early 1960s, he launched a campaign against smoking, which he – rightly – deemed a major public health issue. Initially, he simply painted a *K* for *Kanker* (cancer) on tobacco advertisements – small acts that got him into prison when he couldn't pay a fine after being sued by advertisement companies. Out of prison, he continued with his campaign. Dressed as a woman, he walked into a tobacco store, asked to make a phone call and then dropped a bottle of acetone on the floor. The fumes made the tobacco in the store tasteless; this again landed him in prison. But Grootveld's most successful campaign was a series of protests against the statue of a small boy called the *Lieverdje*, which he chose because it had been donated by the Hunter Tobacco Company. From June 1964 to September 1965, a small crowd gathered at the statue around midnight as he gave speeches against smoking, chanting some of the slogans he had invented such as the 'coughing chant': 'ugge, ugge'.[45]

One of those in the crowd that gathered in front of the *Lieverdje* statue was a young man named Roel van Duyn. Since he was a teenager, he had been politically active on the left, first joining the anti-nuclear armament movement and then working for the anarchist newspaper *De Vrije* (The Free). But neither activity satisfied him. The demonstrations of the peace movement were pointless rituals, and the anarchist newspaper was too old-fashioned, he felt. It was time to 'renew anarchism . . . the most direct rebellion against all authority, whether it be democratic or communist'. Thus van Duyn and two comrades announced the foundation of a new magazine called *PROVO*, to be launched in July 1965 (with individual issues called *Provokatie*, meaning provocation); it was to become the name of an entire movement.[46]

Like the Situationists, van Duyn and his comrades were deeply disappointed by the working-class movement. They hence looked for a new class of people to overthrow the existing order, which they found in what they called the 'Provotariat', the new revolutionary subject, as van Duyn argued in February 1966: 'Provos, beatniks, pleiners, nozems, teddy-boys, rockers, blousons noirs, hooligans . . .' – all names for unruly teenagers like the *Halbstarke* in West Germany.

Those who don't want a career and who lead irregular lives; those who come from the asphalt jungles of london, paris, amsterdam, new york, moscow, tokyo, berlin, milan, warsaw and who feel ill-adapted to this society . . . the Provotariat is the last element of rebellion in our 'developed' countries. The Proletariat is the slave of the politicians.

Watching TV. It has joined its old enemy, the bourgeoisie, and now constitutes with the bourgeoisie a huge grey mass. The new class opposition in our countries is the Provotariat against this mass. But the Provotariat is not a class – it is too heterogeneous for that.[47]

The name was programmatic: Provos sought to 'provoke' the state, its authorities and society in general. But unlike teenagers such as the *Halbstarke* who provoked authorities with their riotous behaviour, the Provos initially did so in a more mundane, even benign way, addressing a genuine problem Amsterdam was facing – traffic. Drawing on Grootveld's anti-smoking rhetoric, they wrote: 'Human sacrifices are made daily to this latest idol of the idiots: car power. Choking carbon monoxide is its incense, its image contaminates thousands of canals and streets.' The Provos suggested a radical remedy: while the city's centre should be closed to cars, an armada of bicycles, all painted in white, should flood the city. Remaining unlocked and therefore freely accessible to residents, they would provide the 'first free communal transport'. And for the Provos, this was more than solving a traffic problem: 'The white bicycle is a provocation against capitalist private property, for the white bicycle is anarchistic!'[48]

The idea did not go down well with the authorities. On 28 July 1965, Grootveld gave a speech at the Lieverdje, condemning 'the asphalt terror of the motorized masses'. In the background, Provos painted bicycles in white. Police were present, but no confrontation ensued as the crowd did not disrupt car traffic. Yet the police began confiscating white bicycles throughout Amsterdam, arguing that 'the bicycles were not locked and therefore invited theft' – the Provos' point was, of course, that anyone could take a bike without this being theft.[49] The following Sunday, 31 July, the crowd gathered as usual at the Lieverdje around midnight. But Grootveld did not show up. Police ordered the crowd to disperse; when van Duyn painted another bicycle in white, an officer hit him with a truncheon. But the crowd held its ground. Outnumbered, the police were forced to retreat, and traffic came to a halt, much to the annoyance of drivers. It was the first of many confrontations.

In the following weeks and months, police attacked both bystanders and protestors during similar happenings, and arrests became more frequent. Meanwhile, the Provo movement gained notoriety and support. And the Provos became more daring: on 7 October, they painted the residence of Amsterdam's mayor, Gijsbert van Hall, white.[50]

But the climax of Provos' attempts to provoke society was yet to come: the royal wedding of Dutch crown-princess Beatrix with German diplomat Claus von Amsberg, scheduled for 10 March 1966. It was not a particularly popular marriage, and especially not in liberal-minded Amsterdam, as von Amsberg had been, like so many boys of his generation, a member of the Hitler Youth, something that did not fly well with Dutch citizens who well remembered the brutal German occupation during World War Two. Some protests were to be expected, but it took the Provos to turn the wedding ceremony into a public spectacle ridiculing royal authority. For weeks, they focused all their energies on preparing for the event. Newspapers, who had taken notice of the Provos by that time, reported wild rumours: the Provos were planning to frighten the horses of the royal carriage by using supersonic whistles; to play tapes with recorded machine-gun fire to confuse the police; or to contaminate Amsterdam's drinking water with LSD, a rumour that saw the police mount close watch over the water system and regularly test the water for drugs.[51]

Indeed, the Provos did contemplate similarly wild ideas, such as collecting lion faeces from the Amsterdam Zoo to spread along the route the royal carriage would take to frighten the horses. However, they finally settled on different plans: First, they called for a conventional demonstration on the wedding day, which was to gather at Amsterdam's Dokwerker Monument, built to commemorate the largest protest against the antisemitic laws during the Nazi occupation. Second, and more Provo-style, they conspired to disrupt the royal spectacle by setting off white smoke bombs as close as possible to the procession.

As the day of the wedding approached, tensions mounted. Provos were busy producing their smoke bombs, hiding from the police, who were constantly searching apartments, but always missing their elusive target. Then came the morning of 10 March 1966. Several hundred protestors flocked to the Dokwerker Monument, from where they started marching towards the city centre to intercept the wedding procession. Quickly, the crowd swelled to several thousand people, more than the Provos had dared to dream of. When police tried to disperse them, clashes ensued. In the meanwhile, Provo members carrying smoke bombs managed to infiltrate the city centre, where both supporters and opponents of the monarchy were lining the streets. First smoke bombs started going off; according to van Duyn, some 200 over the course of the day. As the wedding procession moved slowly through the streets, one Provo threw a white chicken at the newly-wed couple's carriage, making the horses bolt. Then, two Provos, Hans Tuynman and Peter Bronkhorst, let off their smoke bombs right next to the wedding procession. The smoke covered the golden carriage for several minutes. Chaos ensued, with police unsuccessfully trying to apprehend the two Provos. The next day, photos of the moment were on the front pages of newspapers around the world. It was an embarrassment for the Dutch monarchy – and a triumph for the Provos: certainly, anyone who opposed authority had to smile seeing the photos.[52]

The protest against the royal wedding was the apex of the Provo movement. Police and the judiciary increased pressure on the Provos, arresting them and sending them to prison for minor infractions. To give just one example, in April 1966, they arrested a female Provo for handing out raisins at the Lieverdje monument; when she refused to undress at the police station in front of a female officer, which was standard procedure for suicide prevention, three male officers stepped in and forced her to undress, leaving her in her underwear.[53]

Within the movement, a process of disintegration set in as Provos debated where to go next. Some, like Roel van Duyn, wanted to participate in local politics and ran in Amsterdam's municipal council election. 'Vote Provo for better weather', their main slogan read. With the help of various 'white plans', they hoped to transform Amsterdam into a cultural playground, with computers rather than human beings doing most of the work, and police dressed all in white, handing out candy and band-aids rather than beating up Provos.[54] Having gained national fame, other well-known Provos gave lecture tours, for sometimes handsome pay cheques: unsurprisingly, this met with resistance from purist Provos, who viewed this as selling out. Meanwhile, both authorities and businesses embraced Provo ideas, or at least aesthetics. The Dutch Milk Company appropriated the idea of 'white plans' and promoted a 'white glasses plan' on their adverts.[55]

All these developments – internal divisions, co-option by the establishment, police pressure and not least a second, much more brutal riot in Amsterdam in June 1966 – resulted in a gradual decline of the movement. Happenings and demonstrations continued throughout the autumn of 1966, but they began feeling dull and unimaginative. The time for playful creativity was over. By the winter of 1966/7, the Provos were dying, though it took until May 1967 for the group to officially announce its death, fittingly celebrated with a public burial ceremony in Amsterdam's Vondelpark.[56]

Though the Provos in the Netherlands disbanded, they had encouraged the emergence of similar groups across Europe: in cities such as Milan and Frankfurt, in Sweden and even across the Iron Curtain in Poland. In France, young student Daniel Cohn-Bendit, who was to play a leading role in the events of May 1968, and his anarchist group discussed the ideas and tactics of the Provos.[57]

What was it that made the Provos so fascinating and appealing for many non-conformists eager to challenge political and societal norms? Very much like the Situationists, the Provos provided an alternative to both the organizations and the ideas of the old left. They saw the working class, once identified as leading the charge in the revolutionary struggle, becoming absorbed into bourgeois society; as the Provos noted, the working class now watched TV. And like the Situationists, the Provos identified new rebellious subjects in their place: anyone who rejected stability and defined career paths, preferring instead fluid, unstable lives. If the Situationist International had proclaimed in theory that revolutions would be festivals, then the Provos' happenings proved that rebellions could be fun. The Provos provided an inspiring and practical alternative to sterile left-wing politics as much as to the monotony of post-war consumer society.

The Emergence of a Counterculture

One place where the Provos' message fell on fertile ground was Milan. From the mid-1960s, young Italians looking for an alternative way of life had started gathering in the centre of the northern Italian metropolis. They hung around in the streets and parks, their shabby clothes and long hair signalling their rejection of respectability. 'Every day, dozens of kids emerge out of the escalator from Cordusio metro station with their sleeping bags and backpacks on their shoulders, kids who have fled from their homes, from factories, prisons, political parties, from the morass of an existence they do not know how to accept,' the Milanese radical youth magazine *Mondo Beat* wrote in March 1967.[58] Founded the previous year, *Mondo Beat* was the first Italian counterculture underground paper. It gave voice to the ideas of the 'long-haired', as the Italian press liked to call these non-conformist youths: their critique of war and sexual oppression, their fascination with anarchism and East Asian philosophy as alternatives to Western society.[59]

The magazine's name alluded to a group of American writers known as Beat Poets, including authors such as Jack Kerouac and Allen Ginsberg.[60] Celebrating a life of constant movement and experimenting with drugs, a life in which the intensity of the moment rather than long-term, stable relations mattered, and in which intuition and not rational thinking counted, the Beats' work inspired countercultures of the 1960s on both sides of the Atlantic.[61] In Italy, one band that picked up these ideas was Nomadi, a name that captured the ideal of an unstable, itinerant life. In their song 'God is Dead', they expressed a radical dissatisfaction with the current world. God, they sang, was dead 'in the car paid with an instalment plan' but also 'dead in concentration camps, dead with racial myths, dead with the hatred of political parties'. Out of this decaying society, the band proclaimed, 'this, my generation, is ready for a new world and for a hope that has just been born, for a future that it already holds in its hands, for a revolt without weapons'. Italy's public radio station RAI promptly censored the song.[62]

The Milanese Beats, as the countercultural movement in the city became known, called for a radical break with society. Youth, a group by the name of Onda Verde (Green Wave) argued, was done with the older generation, their wars and political ideologies like fascism and Stalinism. 'We've had enough of authority, family, sexual repression, consumer economy, war, police, priests, culture, pedagogues and demagogues.' To make this break work, they called for mocking and provoking authorities, for example with constant demonstrations in the city centre. And most importantly, 'it's better if the thing [i.e., their rebellion] is fun (for those who do it) and fashionable,' Onda Verde's pamphlet concluded.[63]

Like so many other young radicals around Europe at that time, the Milanese Beat organized non-violent demonstrations against the American war in Vietnam. More creatively, they distributed flowers to the police – who assaulted some protestors in response – and even walked, hands up, into a police precinct only to have themselves arrested.[64] But such demonstrations in the streets were only one aspect of their protesting. Searching for a 'new quality of life', Milanese Beats sought to create alternatives that could exist in parallel to the existing society.[65] Thus, in May 1967, leading figures of the movement rented a field on the outskirts of the city where anyone who would accept the three obligations of the movement – no drugs, no violence, no theft – could set up a tent. Intended as an experimental space for communal living and pushing for a sexual revolution, the 'beat-nick camp', as Milan's *Corriere della Sera* called the project, quickly attracted young people from all over Italy, but also from Germany, France and even Australia.

For Milan's conservative press, the camp was a scandal. They alleged that the 'new Berber City' – another name given by the press in a racist reference to North African tribes – hosted sexual orgies involving drugs and minors, and served as a refuge for underage run-away boys and girls. 'The Beats played dice to sort who would have sex with underage girls,' one headline ran. Parents were reported desperately searching for their children among the long-haired deni-zens of the camp. With the media stirring a moral panic and Mondo Beat responding with banners and pamphlets against the local press, tensions were rising, even though there were no riots or violent altercations between the police and the Beats in Milan's streets. Then, on 10 June, police raided the tent city, beating and arresting the teenagers – most of them still in bathing suits, as the unofficial history of the movement notes, implying that they were not pre-pared to battle the police. Two days later, they shut the camp down permanently, much to the satisfaction of a jubilant press. Effectively, it was also the end of the Beat movement in Milan.[66]

Around the same time as Mondo Beat was making headlines in Italy, similar groups of youngsters appeared in West German cities such as West Berlin, Munich and Frankfurt, quickly dubbed *Gammler* by the press, the name deriving from the verb *gammeln*, meaning 'to bum around'. Like their Italian counterparts, the *Gammler* sought to develop alternatives to a life characterized by work and consump-tion. They hung out in parks, sometimes even sleeping there, or in front of public buildings such as the Kaiser Wilhelm Memorial Church in West Berlin.[67] Unlike the *Halbstarke* a few years earlier, *Gammler* provoked not with wild dances, loud music and careful personal grooming, but simply by bumming around and doing nothing. They longed for meaning outside the sphere of work and genuinely 'free time' (the German word for leisure, *Freizeit*, literally means 'free time') without following strict schedules or preparing for a career, which is what traditional pedagogues preached. And while most *Gammler* actually did go to school or had more or less stable jobs, some genuinely dropped out, hitch-hiking through Eur-ope and beyond: one sixteen-year-old runaway girl tried to make it to Kathmandu to attend an 'international *Gammler* meeting', reach-ing Istanbul via Munich and Marseille.[68]

Politicians, the tabloid press and many West Germans were enraged by the sight of *Gammler* in the streets. Where other people went to work or to pray, they bummed around, smoking weed and strumming guitars. In June 1966, Chancellor Ludwig Erhard declared during an election rally: 'As long as I'm in power, I'll do everything to smash this nuisance [*Unwesen*].' TV documentaries show ordinary Germans demanding that *Gammler* should be put into labour camps. Hitler would have dealt with such lazy tramps, one woman said, with a crowd in her back laughing in agreement. After the June 1966 riots in Amsterdam, the federal government commissioned a report about the danger to public order posed by the *Gammler*. Many state ministries charged with contributing to the report were, however, more sober in their assessment: there was, they declared, no danger at all: a democracy, the argument went, had to accommodate non-conformist lifestyles. Under pressure from local politicians to take harsh measures against the *Gammler*, Munich's police president retorted that 'boorish behaviour' was not a crime. Reactions to the *Gammler*, indeed, became a litmus test for West German democracy after Nazism. While *Gammler* were often arrested and sometimes beaten by the police, they never faced such an onslaught as the Milanese beats did when police cleared their tent city. Even those who abhorred the *Gammler* realized that a democratic society couldn't just send non-conformist teenagers to labour camps – and yearned for a dictatorship for exactly this reason: 'Only dictators can deal with such problems,' one unnamed commentator told leftist magazine *konkret*.[69]

West German *Gammler* were far less coherent a grouping than their Italian counterparts. While generally left-leaning and peace-loving, they refrained from formulating a political programme or engaging in political activism. *Gammler* were, as German historian Detlef Siegfried noted, 'life-style revolutionaries'.[70] In the words of Hans-Peter Ernst, a central figure of Frankfurt's countercultural scene, where a local Provo group had formed: 'Dude, we want to make a revolution! Why should we care about politics?'[71]

Rebels and the Politics of Everyday Life

Despite their differences, West German *Halbstarke* and *Gammler*, Dutch Provos and Italian Beats as well as the Situationist International all expressed a deep dissatisfaction with what they perceived as the sterility and monotony of everyday life, whether they 'danced out of line' like the *Halbstarke*, set off smoke bombs in Amsterdam or wrote about the *Poverty of Student Life*. They tried to find meaning beyond their careers, to live a more fluid life liberated from the spatial, temporal and bodily constraints of established society. For the most part, they did not seek to overthrow the entire societal order (the Situationists, of course, being the exception here). Rather, they carved out spaces, such as the tent city in Milan, where they might live according to their ideals – microcosms that would exist in parallel to mainstream society. However, doing so without provoking established authorities, intentionally or otherwise, was nearly impossible. The desire for a different life created the potential for revolt. With these forms of protest and critique, rebellious teenagers and radical thinkers alike paved the way for new forms of radical activism in the years to come.

At the heart of their rebellion were fundamental questions of everyday life: how to live together, how to dress, how to dance, how to have sex, how to express feelings in a world seemingly dominated by a cold, capitalist rationality. The old, socialist or communist working-class movements with their hierarchical political parties no longer offered appealing answers to these questions. The new forms of rebellion were thus as much a critique of this old left as of capitalist society. A full-scale revolution to overthrow the state and the capitalist system was no longer the way forward. Rather, these non-conformists tried to build alternatives here and now and mocked the authorities; if there was to be a revolution, it had to be fun.

All Power to the Imagination:
1968 in East and West

Paris, 10 May 1968. It was the first night of the barricades. Following a protest march, students, young workers and some local residents used cars, wooden beams, rolls of wire, breeze blocks and scaffolding to erect more than sixty barricades, some of them more than two metres high, throughout the Latin Quarter, home to the famous Sorbonne University. In the streets, people gathered around portable radios to listen to live news about the latest developments. Strangers talked about the protests, the occupation of the Sorbonne and what they hoped to accomplish. But what they said to one another somehow mattered less than the mere fact that they were talking to people they had never met before, using the informal *tu*. Anticipating an attack by the police, protestors piled up cobblestones, put on motorcycle helmets, prepared wet rags to protect their eyes from tear gas, and some even started bulldozers. 'There's a sort of laborious, almost meticulous exaltation. A contagious enthusiasm, almost a joy,' the Parisian newspaper *Le Monde* wrote two days later.[1]

Government and university representatives tried to negotiate with student leaders, but to no avail. At 2.15 a.m., the police advanced, shields and truncheons in their hands. They fired tear gas into the crowds. The students responded by igniting the barricades with gas and setting buses on fire, *Le Monde* reported. But the advance of the security forces could not be stopped. Protestors and police alike were wounded; at the end of the night, official police reports counted 367 injured in the hospitals, among them 251 policemen and 102 students (the rest were bystanders).[2]

The escalation of violence did not stop the revolt. When the Sorbonne, which had been closed in response to student protests, reopened three days later, rebellious students declared it a 'people's university'. Contrary to the government's hopes, the protests spread throughout France and beyond the student milieu to factories. Soon, hundreds of thousands of workers were on strike. Their demands weren't totally clear, but they were certainly asking for more than just wage increases: they rejected consumer society, and they questioned the authority of foremen, union officials and leftist parties alike. As a famous slogan on the Odéon theatre in Paris claimed, imagination was taking power.[3]

What happened in France that May was part and parcel of an entire series of uprisings around the globe in 1968 that reached from the United States and Western Europe across the Iron Curtain to Poland, Yugoslavia and Czechoslovakia, to the cities in the Global South such as Mexico City, Tehran and Dakar.[4] Usually, students played a crucial role, though in many places, such as France and Italy, workers, and particularly young workers, also participated in the uprising. No single political programme united the protestors. Their demands ranged from democratizing the university to ending the Vietnam War, from liberating sexuality to establishing workers' autonomy in factories. It was a cultural lifestyle revolt that built on youth protests in the previous decade and experimented with different ways of collective living; it was equally a political rebellion, reviving traditions of radical Marxism from the interwar years, calling for international solidarity against imperialism and demanding a radical democratization of society. It was, in short, an immensely complex event that had a profound impact on global protest movements in the years to come.[5] To shed light on these uprisings, the following pages look at four national cases – West Germany, France, Czechoslovakia and Italy – exploring how activists envisioned a better world and struggled for it.

West Berlin: Democratizing the University, Democratizing Society

'Comrades! Our goal is the organization of the permanence of the counter-university as the basis for the politicization of higher education,' declared West German student leader Rudi Dutschke at the 21st congress of the Sozialistischer Deutscher Studentenbund (Socialist German Student Union, or SDS), held in Frankfurt in early September 1966. It's a horrible sentence to read, even in the original German. But when Dutschke said it, it sounded 'magnificent, even terrifying', a reporter of the left-liberal weekly *Die Zeit* noted.[6]

Organizing a counter-university – this doesn't sound like a particularly radical goal, coming from a self-proclaimed revolutionary. It's nothing like the exuberant visions of a festival-like revolution the Situationist International had imagined; it lacks the playfulness of the Amsterdam Provos. But for the SDS, establishing a critical counter-university was the way to radically change society. It seemed to offer a chance to educate the masses, to radicalize students and ultimately to democratize society at large.[7]

Rudi Dutschke was the most famous spokesperson of the West German student movement. Born in 1940, he grew up in the newly created socialist German Democratic Republic (GDR). As a teenager, Dutschke joined a Protestant youth group in his native town of Luckenwalde near Berlin, where he became a dedicated pacifist. When the GDR formed an army in 1956, Dutschke refused to volunteer, citing his pacifist and religious beliefs while still affirming his commitment to socialism. As a result, he was barred from studying sports journalism in Leipzig. Dutschke thus moved to West Berlin to complete his high-school degree in 1961. Just three days before the Berlin Wall went up on 13 August 1961, he officially took residence in the West. In protest against the Wall, he registered as a political refugee; a few days later, at age twenty-one, he and a group of friends unsuccessfully tried to pull a piece out of the Wall and threw leaflets across into East Berlin.[8]

Clearly, Dutschke was no supporter of the East German regime. But he continued to believe in socialism. In West Berlin, he enrolled at the Free University to study sociology. There, he joined the Berlin section of Subversive Aktion, a group of radical activists mostly based in Munich and led by Dieter Kunzelmann, who had previously been part of the Situationist International. Kunzelmann and his group sought to criticize established authorities by making fun of them. Dutschke, however, was not known for his sense of humour. He was dead serious, with a quasi-religious zeal. The small circle of anti-authoritarian activists within Subversive Aktion, he quickly realized, would not be enough to build the kind of mass organization he deemed necessary for effective political action within the university. In January 1965, Dutschke and his comrade Bernd Rabehl, another refugee from East Germany, joined the SDS, where Dutschke quickly rose to prominence due to his understanding of Marxism and his qualities as an intense, charismatic speaker. What had been a rather traditional organization that valued earnest discussions now turned to radical and confrontational activism.[9]

Dutschke's star did not only rise inside the SDS. He became a public celebrity in West Berlin and beyond, admired by the radical left and hated by conservatives and the radical right. 'Stop Dutschke now, otherwise there will be civil war,' ran a headline by the right-wing *National Zeitung*. On 11 April 1968, a young worker by the name of Josef Bachmann (who, it turned out much later, had contacts among organized neo-Nazis) answered the call. Carrying an issue of the *National Zeitung* with him, he shot at Dutschke as he left the SDS office, hitting him twice in the head and once in the shoulder. Dutschke barely survived after emergency surgery. Eleven years later, on Christmas Eve 1979, Dutschke died in Denmark, where he and his family had settled, as a result of his brain injuries. He was thirty-nine.

Not without justification, radical students blamed the tabloid press for having created a witch-hunt atmosphere that had made the attack possible. During what became known as the Easter Uprising of 1968, around 50,000 protestors gathered in front of the offices of the Springer publishing house, which owned West Germany's most notorious tabloid paper, the *BILD Zeitung*. Some of those students, albeit only a minority, took violent action, smashing windows and setting delivery trucks on fire. It marked the dramatic apogee of the rebellious year in West Germany.[10]

For many of those joining the protests, democracy was at stake. Given that Nazism had been defeated only twenty years before, students worried that there might be a relapse into authoritarian nationalism. The passing of the Emergency Laws in 1968, designed to ensure the functioning of the state and its institutions in a situation of war or civil unrest, stirred fears of an authoritarian government not only in radical student circles, but also among trade unionists and left-leaning liberals.[11] The fact that the two major political parties in West Germany, the conservative Christian Democrats and the Social Democrats, had entered a grand coalition in 1966, which left only the small faction of the Liberal Democrats in opposition, further contributed to the sense of a fragile democracy. In part, then, the West German movement of 1968 was about ensuring that democracy stood a chance of survival in the aftermath of Nazism.[12]

For radical students, however, defending democracy was not enough. As they saw it, the parliamentary institutions of the Federal Republic did not constitute a genuine democracy. In a famous TV interview with Günter Gaus from 1967, Dutschke made this point. Neither the government nor the opposition parties, he argued, engaged in a real 'dialogue with the masses'. In his view, parties had ceased to be 'instruments to elevate the consciousness of all members of society', turning instead into 'instruments for stabilizing the existing order'. In parliament, the 'real interests of our population', he claimed, lacked representation, precisely because there was no 'critical dialogue' between the parties and the 'people were kept in immaturity'. Given this lack of dialogue and political awareness, democracy couldn't thrive. The kind of democracy Dutschke hoped for required people to grasp their social and political situation. What Dutschke said wasn't an elaborate political programme, but it indicates how he envisioned radical change might happen: through education and critical discourse that would emancipate those kept in ignorance. It was a classical programme of enlightenment, and it would be, as he was keen to emphasize, a long-term process.[13]

Students at West Berlin's Free University, a hotspot of radical activism in the Federal Republic, tried to put these ideas into practice. Founded in 1949 with American support and built in the comparatively rich neighbourhood of Zehlendorf in the southwest of Berlin, the Free University was intended as a model of a modern and democratically organized university.[14] With its modern degree programmes such as sociology and political science, and a relatively young staff, it quickly attracted liberal and left-leaning students from all over West Germany. Above all, the university's structures gave students an institutional weight unique not only in the Federal Republic but anywhere in Western Europe. Every year, they elected a student parliament known as the Konvent that was responsible for forming an executive steering committee, the Allgemeiner Studentenausschuß (AStA), a legally recognized body of the university representing students. Until the mid-1960s, conservative and right-wing factions enjoyed a majority in these elected student bodies. Then in 1963, a student referendum rejected the AStA-presidency of right-wing Eberhard Diepgen, despite students having elected a conservative Konvent. Left-wing politics at the Free University clearly had some potential. The situation changed decisively in 1965, when a left-leaning Konvent elected SDS member Wolfgang Lefèvre as president of the AStA.[15]

Lefèvre's election coincided with what became known as the 'Kuby Affair', the first in a series of events that galvanized student protest at the Free University. The origins of the affair went back to July 1958, when journalist Erich Kuby had dared to question just how free the Free University really was. Considering such remarks a grave insult, the university's rectors banned Kuby from talking at public events on campus. In May 1965, the now left-leaning AStA ignored the university policy and invited Kuby to speak during a podium discussion on 'Restoration or New Beginning: The Federal Republic Twenty Years On'. But rector Herbert Lüers would not have it: Kuby was still not allowed to speak on university grounds.[16]

The university's position had not changed, but the political context had. Locally, the left now enjoyed a majority in the Konvent;

internationally, the Free Speech Movement at Berkeley had set a template for students demanding free political discussions on campus.[17] Students were no longer willing to simply accept Lüers' decision. They relocated the discussion to the city's other major institution of higher education, the Technical University, and organized a protest march that attracted some 500 students; another 3,000 signed a petition demanding freedom of speech. A week later, student representatives of the political science department called for a lecture strike. It was a stunning success: only about 10 per cent of students showed up for classes. The university's administration insisted on its right to decide about the use of rooms at the university, while students defended what they viewed as their democratic right to stage discussions on university grounds. 'The idea that the democratic spirit of the university can be protected through the authoritative exercise of disciplinary power . . . betrays a mistrust of democratic supervisory bodies,' the Konvent stated. 'The student body demands no suspension of the rights of individual parts of the university, but the confirmation of its right to democratic self-government.'[18] With such arguments, historian Ben Mercer notes, the students 'successfully framed the struggle as one of democracy versus authority'.[19]

This struggle seemed all the more urgent given the strength of the right-wing fraternities, the *Burschenschaften*, and the support they received from university professors. Just a few weeks after the contested talk by Erich Kuby, law professor Karl August Bettermann addressed a national conference of fraternity students, to frenetic applause:

> *Meine Herren*, as long as the words 'Honour, Freedom, Fatherland' stand on your flags, you cannot expect that all students or the mass of the population celebrate them. (Applause). Who says honour, demands honour and defends honour in these times must know that he finds himself in the minority. (Applause). And he who takes the word Fatherland so strongly and dutifully must yet work decades until all Germans are infused by the love of Fatherland and are ready to sacrifice themselves for this Fatherland.[20]

Such profoundly nationalist rhetoric did not go unchallenged at the Free University, where a transcript of the speech circulated, even among academic staff. Politics professor Otto von der Gablentz, for example, criticized his colleagues' questionable commitment to democracy: 'Their mindset is characteristic of that "state conscious-ness" with which the Germans acquiesced in National Socialism because it was ostensibly legitimate and "maintained order",' he wrote in the daily *Die Welt* with an eye on Bettermann. Tellingly, the university denounced von der Gablentz, but not Bettermann, for besmirching the institution's reputation.[21]

From the perspective of increasingly rebellious students and sympathetic professors, the situation looked clear: West Germany's democracy, established in the ruins of Nazism, was still fragile; a return to authoritarian forms of government had to be prevented. Facilitating open and critical discussions was the means to do so, and by banning such discussions, the university administration acted in an anti-democratic way, students argued. And it was not merely about defending democracy at the university level. Trans-forming the university into an institution for critical and democratic thinking should change society at large by raising the people's consciousness.

The situation had not calmed down after the Kuby Affair. Stu-dents had continued protesting against university authorities, but also increasingly outside of campus, notably against the war in Viet-nam. Then, on 2 June 1967, the Persian Shah visited Berlin. Along with students from Iran, the SDS had called for demonstrations. In the evening, police tried to disperse a crowd that had gathered in front of the German Opera, where the Shah together with his wife and Berlin dignitaries were enjoying themselves. In an alley nearby, student Benno Ohnesorg was shot and killed by a police officer (an event explored in more detail in Chapter 7).[22]

Ohnesorg's killing, nearly a year before the attempted assassin-ation of Rudi Dutschke, galvanized the student movement. Across the Federal Republic, numerous students joined the SDS. But the new recruits' enthusiasm was also a problem for the organization.

For the first time, SDS militant Wolfgang Nitsch noted eleven days after the deadly shooting, students had 'overcome their isolation' and 'found classmates with whom they could work spontaneously in a spirit of solidarity'. Now, the challenge was not to let this 'experience of emancipation' degenerate into 'private forms', but to transform it into a 'cooperative movement' both 'within and outside the university'. To increase the effectiveness of their activities, students needed to enlighten the general population about their movement. Students, Nitsch urged his comrades, had to create institutions that would incorporate 'members of socially dependent classes – in particular young workers, apprentices, pupils, but also police officers – into the process of intellectual emancipation and self-organization'. This latter point was particularly important, Nitsch argued, for it showed that students were not only interested in improving their own situation, but wanted to help preserve and implement democracy in the entire society. To accomplish these goals, Nitsch proposed organizing a Critical University, a form of self-organized and anti-authoritarian teaching and learning.[23]

The proposal for a Critical University highlights how the 'student movement,' a term Nitsch himself used, wanted to transform society. Students demanded having a say about both the content and the form of their education. And this was not a matter from which merely a small elite of students should benefit, but everyone, especially workers. In that sense, they called for a democratization of knowledge that should no longer remain the privilege of a highly educated elite. Knowledge, or, more precisely, the critical analyses of societal conditions, should also have a democratizing effect. It would enable the masses to understand their situation and therefore make their own history, in Marx's famous phrase. To accomplish such goals, students promoted open discussion in which the 'better argument', as philosopher Jürgen Habermas put it in an essay from 1971, should prevail. Discussions, students believed, would help people to overcome attitudes, like hatred against their movement, that were based solely on prejudice and lack of information. Here, political influence or ideology wouldn't matter, only the force of critical analysis based on facts.[24]

In the winter semester of 1967/8, SDS activists put their plans for the Critical University into practice. Its educational programme included thirty-three working groups on topics ranging from higher education reform to the 'Cuban Model' and politics in Latin America, from 'Sexuality and Authority' to the economic and social situation in West Berlin. The groups were not supposed to merely study such topics, but to draw practical conclusions, that is, to turn insights into action. A seminar in German Studies, for example, proposed to analyse the 'fascistic jargon of the Springer newspapers' in order to provide 'expert opinion in a tribunal against these businesses'. Teaching methods, too, should radically change. Lectures were to be abolished, and seminars should work without a single, designated leader. Instead, the programme envisioned 'new democratic forms [of teaching] taken from practice: defences, tribunals, hearings, documentations'.[25]

The hopes for the Critical University, however, were disappointed. The programme for the summer term 1968 reported numerous problems. Enthusiasm had quickly waned. Many groups noted a strong fluctuation of participants; one group lost half its members by mid-November. The ideals of democratic teaching frequently failed to live up to the test of reality. Abolishing lectures altogether proved infeasible, as a group working on psychosomatic medicine explained, because 'varied levels of knowledge and interest necessitated holding short lectures'. Not surprisingly, students 'already acquainted with the material' took over the discussion, whereas 'the majority of the participants stayed silent, abandoning themselves to passive perception'. Another group, studying Keynesianism, quickly realized that their meetings resembled traditional seminars. 'Even the pressure to perform or rather the gladiatorial struggles reproduced themselves anew, just this time not mediated via the struggle for good grades.' Not least, the Critical University failed to appeal to young workers and school students the way radical activists had hoped. While some 20 per cent of the participants were high-school students, likely to become students themselves in the near future, a mere 2 per cent were workers. The topics the Critical University addressed did not speak to their concerns, and its academic jargon was off-putting. As one worker put it, they were always talking about Vietnam, and yet 'on the White Circle [the removal of rent control] you don't say anything. For that we would participate.'[26]

The ideas informing the Critical University quickly spread beyond the campus of West Berlin's Free University. Taking on demands by the SDS, high-school students, too, called for the democratization of their education and challenged the authority of teachers and school administrators. Outside of Germany, student activists in Trento (Italy) and at Nanterre in Paris established Critical Universities.[27] Transforming society by means of critical education was an appealing idea. However, the experience in West Berlin also showed the problems radical students encountered in their reliance on rational discussions. As students quickly understood, authority did not disappear. Those who had the rhetorical and scholarly skills to dominate discussions did so. Rather than providing workers and apprentices with the means for self-emancipation, the latter simply found discussion circles repelling and frustrating. In a telling incident, activists of a leftist youth centre in West Berlin in 1974 issued a flat-out 'ban on discussions' (*Diskussionsverbot*) at their events, fearing that debates dominated by politically organized students would drive non-students away.[28]

Transgressing All Boundaries: Workers and Students in France

Radical students in West Germany had tried to engage with the working class, but by and large they had failed.[29] Their French comrades were more successful. What had started as a radical student protest on the new campus of Nanterre, a hotbed of activism somewhat akin to West Berlin's Free University, outside of Paris in March 1968, turned into a general strike that affected all of the country by the end of May. Students entered factories and talked to workers, convincing especially those of a younger generation to join the movement. At the peak of the strike movement, some seven million workers had walked off their jobs. France came to a standstill, and a genuine revolution seemed on the horizon. When, on 29 May 1968, President Charles de Gaulle flew by helicopter to southwest Germany to consult with General Jacques Massu, previously commander of the infamous French parachute division during the Algerian War, it looked like he had fled the country and was considering a military suppression of the uprising. Though he returned only a day later to dissolve parliament and call for new elections, the helicopter flight showed how tense the situation was.[30]

Yet, it would be a misunderstanding to simply view the general strike as the result of students agitating workers. There had been multiple strikes across France in the preceding years, meaning that student activism fell on fertile ground in factories. Even more importantly, the revolt challenged these categories themselves. In the words of Kristin Ross, May 1968 in France was a 'crisis in functionalism' as students ceased 'to function as students, workers as workers, and farmers as farmers'. It was an attempt to transgress and dissolve the boundaries that kept people in separate places and classes. 'The movement took the form of political experiments in *de*classification, in disrupting the natural "givenness" of places,' writes Ross.[31] While West German students endlessly discussed how to build a stronger democracy, their French comrades attempted to radically disrupt the very order of society.

A seemingly trivial matter provided the spark for the French student revolt. At the newly built campus of Nanterre, regulations banned male students from visiting dormitories for female students and vice versa. Most male students simply ignored these rules, entering the women's dormitories via open windows. On 16 March 1967, students turned their informal disregard of these rules into explicit defiance. 'The interior regulations imposed by the administration being antiquated, they will be considered as of today to be NULL AND VOID,' a student assembly declared. From now on, residents would have 'total freedom of meeting, information and circulation'. In addition, students called for mixed dormitories. Until they had been created, 'the freedom to visit the female buildings WILL BECOME A STATE OF FACT'. It was a bold challenge to the administration's authority over the use of space. Students went to places where they were not supposed to be – though it's telling that the demand focused on men visiting the female dormitory, but made no mention of women visiting fellow male students.[32]

University authorities negotiated with students in an attempt to quell the protests. It did not work. Four days after the passing of the resolution, on 21 March 1967, one student suggested taking action: 'Come on, let's go to the girls,' he told a crowd of fellow students.[33] Some sixty students followed him and occupied the girls' dormitory. At the dawn of 22 March, police arrived at the scene. Students, whose numbers had slightly declined during the night, blocked the narrow stairs and elevators, making it difficult for the police to forcibly clear the building. Police negotiated, with the help of official student organizations, and agreed to allow the occupants to leave as long as they could present a key card proving that they were, in fact, students and not outside intruders. There would be no other sanction, the university rector promised. But students now objected to the very intervention of the police. This, they argued, made the occupants look like a bunch of students pursuing some 'juvenile demands' but ignored the more general aims, such as freedom of assembly and information, that sought to 'democratize university life at every level'. The conflict was not over, not least because the university administration did not keep its word. In the aftermath of the occupation, twenty-nine students were sanctioned, despite the rector's assurances, some of whom had not even been present at the occupation. The sanctions only stirred fears that the university would keep 'blacklists' of unruly and oppositional students, ready to expel them as soon as possible.[34]

As the academic year 1967/8 passed, without any changes to the regulations, political tensions on campus grew. And students had learned how to provoke the authorities. On 8 January 1968, Minister of Youth and Sport François Missoffe visited the campus to inaugurate a new swimming pool. A bunch of radical students awaited him, including one Daniel Cohn-Bendit, 'a student of red hair, the collar wide, who seemed impatient to hold a rant', as a government official had described him during the dormitory occupation.[35] A son of Jewish refugees, Cohn-Bendit (b. 1945) had been born and grown up in France before moving with his family to Frankfurt in 1958. In 1961, when he had to choose between German and French citizenship, he opted for German citizenship to avoid French military service (in the Federal Republic, children of Jewish refugees were exempted from military service). In 1965, he moved back to France, where he studied sociology at the University of Paris-Nanterre.[36] By January 1968, he was a spokesperson of the anarchist student faction.

When Missoffe gave his speech, Cohn-Bendit delivered a masterclass in provocation. Standing in a crowd of students waiting for the minister, Cohn-Bendit suddenly approached Missoffe. The university's dean, Pierre Grappin, recognized him, grabbed him by the collar and tried to push him back into the crowd. But by accident or intentionally, Cohn-Bendit ended up not in the crowd, but standing right next to the minister. Missoffe turned pale, while Cohn-Bendit kept his cool. He asked him for a lighter and lit a cigarette. Then, noting that Missoffe had just published a 'White Book about Youth', Cohn-Bendit wondered: why had the minister not written a single word about the question of sexuality? He was in Nanterre to talk about sports, not sexuality, Missoffe responded. But Cohn-Bendit insisted: 'Why don't you talk about sexuality?' Missoffe had had enough. If Cohn-Bendit found dealing with sexual problems difficult, then perhaps he should jump into the newly opened swimming pool to cool off. 'Heil Hitler,' Cohn-Bendit rebuffed, implying that the minister's attitude to sexuality resembled that of the Nazis. Predictably, this got him into trouble. The university administration had already tried to have him transferred to the Sorbonne; now the minister of the interior, Christian Fouchet, suggested expelling the 'trouble-maker' – Cohn-Bendit was, after all, a German citizen – out of France altogether. For the moment, though, he stayed in France.[37]

Cohn-Bendit had ridiculed the minister. The next act in the unfolding drama was more violent. In February 1968, numerous activists travelled to West Berlin to attend the Vietnam Congress protesting against the American war.[38] Back in France, they were no longer content 'with the routine of nonchalant processions', as the paper of the Trotskyite Revolutionary Communist Youth noted.[39] On the evening of 20 March, a group of students took action. They headed to the offices of American Express, broke windows and threw a Molotov cocktail into the building. Police quickly arrested five protestors, all of them students at Nanterre. The next day, news began to spread on campus. Their comrades prepared demonstrations for 22 March. At first, the protests followed the usual formula: radicals disrupted lectures, urging fellow students to join the protest or to discuss the events. But this time, they went further. Anarchists proposed occupying university buildings, while Trotskyites called for a demonstration in central Paris. They resolved to leave the decision for a general assembly at 5 p.m.[40]

At the assembly, Cohn-Bendit rose to speak. 'The militants who are here, they have come, I believe, because they are determined to act against police repression in France.' He suggested occupying the sociology department. But his anarchist comrade Jean-Pierre Duteil had an even better idea: 'We must occupy the tower . . . the administrative building of the Faculty of Nanterre.' The assembly immediately agreed. Upon arrival, however, only 60 of the 500 students dared to enter the building. When they faced little resistance, the number of occupants slowly grew to 100. But they could not agree on how to proceed. Should they stay on the ground floor, or enter the offices upstairs? The majority pushed for the stairs, easily overcoming the few university officials in their way. Once upstairs, the disagreements did not end. The *enragés*, a group of Situationist-inspired radicals, proposed emptying the expensive bottles of whiskey the dean kept for special guests and destroying student files; anarchists wanted to search for the infamous blacklists the university allegedly kept; more serious-minded Trotskyite students were against further disruption. Cohn-Bendit then produced a bunch of keys. If one of them opened a drawer, they would search for blacklists. Students proceeded with a search, but with no results. In the meanwhile, news arrived that all arrested students had been released, which made a further occupation seem unnecessary. Eventually, students left the building, fearing a violent intervention by the police.[41]

Before they left, the occupants agreed to a manifesto. It signalled a radicalization of the protests: 'We must break with the techniques of contestation that cannot do anything!' And indeed, the movement rapidly gained a new dynamic. When the authorities tried to deal with the rebellious students by closing the University of Nanterre and arresting radicals, including Cohn-Bendit, students answered with more demonstrations. In early May, the movement reached the Sorbonne in central Paris, where, on Friday, 3 May, 500 students gathered to protest against the disciplinary measures their comrades at Nanterre faced. The rector of the Sorbonne, Jean Roche, immediately called the police to restore order, resulting in the arrest of 100 students. But far from calming the situation, the police intervention was the perfect provocation. Over the weekend, a couple of students were sentenced to prison terms, some without parole. The following Monday, some 3,000 students took to the streets for another demonstration. Over the course of the day, their number swelled; in the evening, up to 15,000 people engaged in an extremely violent battle with the police, leaving 500 wounded and 80 arrested.[42]

The protests quickly spread beyond universities and around France. Crucially, students made an effort to reach out to workers. They understood, historian Ludivine Bantigny notes, that standing alone would leave them powerless. They needed to convince workers that students were not simply the sons (and, to a lesser extent, daughters) of the bosses. On 9 June, Cohn-Bendit made this point on TV: 'The students refuse the function they are given by society, that is to say, they refuse to become the future managers of society who will exploit the working class and the peasantry.' Across French cities, calls for solidarity between students and workers appeared. Both faced, they declared, the same enemy: the bourgeoisie and the violent police. As one pamphlet put it: Students 'refuse to become the watch-dogs of the bourgeoisie'.[43]

Then came 10 May, the first night of the barricades in the Latin Quarter. Students and young workers alike battled the police. It was extremely violent. Riot police shot tear-gas grenades not only into the crowd, but also into the windows of local residents who supported injured rioters by providing water for their burning eyes. The confrontation with the forces of order facilitated encounters between people whose social worlds were usually separate – residents, students, workers. There was a sense of collective exuberance in the streets: 'I jumped for joy, and we all screamed: we're not alone,' a participant recalled.[44] The next day, unions reacted. Shocked by the extent of police violence, they called for a general strike, lasting for twenty-four hours, for 13 May. 'Workers are outraged! Solidarity with students,' Georges Séguy, general secretary of the trade union CGT, declared. Other unionists were even more explicit. In Saint-Nazaire, the leader of the Force ouvrière union assured students that 'workers, if necessary, will stand side by side with students in physical confrontations'. In Lyon, unionists of the car manufacturer Berliet compared the occupation of the Sorbonne by the riot police, known as the CRS, with the occupation of their factory during a strike the previous year. And in Rennes in Brittany, students and union activists distributed a pamphlet at the local Citroën factory, urging the workers to follow the students' example and occupy it.[45] The day after, workers at the Sud-Aviation factory in Nantes, some 100 kilometres south of Rennes, did exactly this: they occupied 'their' factory.[46]

Similar scenes took place all over the country as workers went on strike and occupied factories, often with the support of radical students. On 17 May, some 3,000 Parisian students marched to the Renault factory in Billancourt to support striking workers. 'From the fragile hands of students, workers will take the banner of the fight,' their banner read. Union delegates tried to close the factory gates, telling students that they appreciated their solidarity, but workers didn't need a lesson from students. But their attempt to keep workers and students separate failed. A resolution by workers published the next day praised 'the magnificent resistance of students facing the ferocious repression of the police forces', and, after a night of discussing at the picket lines, declared: 'A sense of sympathy, a mutual friendship between workers and students has been initiated. Those who weren't here tonight missed an unprecedented moment in history.'[47]

The strike brought people into places they were not supposed to be. Students went to factories to discuss with workers, much to the irritation of union officials; at the same time, they tried to make the university accessible to workers.[48] In Nantes, students planned to invite them to dining halls and cafeterias on campus, though it is unclear whether these plans were put into action. In Paris and Lyon, young workers belonging to local gangs joined students in occupying and physically defending university campuses, much to the concern of authorities (and eventually the students too, who worried about their violent inclinations).[49] Within occupied factories and on campuses, workers and students turned the shop floor, otherwise a detested space of labouring, into a space of solidarity, of joy and conversation. 'While we always have been denied the right to speak, we have now taken this right, we have learned how to speak, and this cannot be undone,' workers at the Rhône-Poulenc factory in Vitry declared.[50]

For a brief moment, the movement of 1968 in France turned the world on its head. This was more than mere rhetoric by Marxist students calling for an end to class hierarchy. Confrontations with the police and the general strike facilitated countless encounters between people whose social worlds rarely touched. As students left the grounds of the university to talk with striking workers on the picket line, they challenged the authority of the organizations of the working-class left – trade unions, the Communist Party – that sought to keep these worlds separate and confine politics to union committees and party meetings.

But the moment did not last. On 6 June 1968, the communist daily *L'Humanité* announced: 'Victorious return to work in the factory.' It was more an appeal than a description of reality. The same day, riot police cleared the Renault factory at Flins, which had hitherto been held by workers and students. Four days later, there were still a million workers on strike. And the struggle was yet to reach its violent climax: the death of high-school student Gilles Tautin, who drowned fleeing the police near Flins, and the death of two workers, Pierre Beylot and Henri Blanchet, at Sochaux during confrontations with the police. But effectively, announcing the end of the strike helped bring that end about.[51]

On paper, the outcome of the strikes might have looked like a victory. In what became known as the Grenelle Agreements, unions negotiated with employers and the government a 37 per cent increase in the minimum wage, while all other wages should increase by 10 per cent by 1 October 1968. The working week was reduced by half an hour, though only in those companies where it was longer than forty-five hours; in companies working forty-eight hours per week or more, it was to be reduced by another hour in the autumn of 1969. But promises on paper were not matched in reality, as many workers understood. Inflation quickly rendered wage increases meaningless, and the reduction in working time meant an increase in working intensity. At Renault, for example, the daily working time was reduced by a meagre twelve minutes, but the expected output remained the same as it had been before the strike: eighty cars per day.[52]

Above all, the end of the movement was a restoration of the old social order. People went back to where they supposedly belonged. Except for those that refused to do so. A famous scene in the documentary *La Reprise du travail aux usines Wonder*, depicting the return to work at a chemical factory in Saint-Ouen, shows one such refusal. On 10 June, as work is supposed to start again, a young woman called Jocelyn – her last name remains unknown – stands in front of the factory gates. She vigorously refuses to return to work, shaking her head repeatedly. 'No, I won't return, I won't go back for years. I won't set foot into that prison any more. You go back there, and you'll see what a nightmare it is.' Jocelyn's work conditions must have been horrendous. She had to work with tar and chemicals, without hot water to clean herself. In the scene, she is surrounded by men – the factory owner and personnel manager, but also unionists and a Maoist student – who all try to reason with her, explaining that 'it's important to know when to end a strike'. After all, 'it's a *victory*, don't you understand!' It might be a victory, but nothing would have changed for this stubbornly refusing woman.[53]

Socialism with a Human Face: The Prague Spring

Western European cities were not the only places where large student demonstrations took place. In March 1968, students in Warsaw protested against the cancellation of a play by Adam Mickiewicz, Poland's national poet of the early nineteenth century. Meanwhile, students in Yugoslavia briefly occupied the University of Belgrade and rioted in other cities such as Ljubljana, Zagreb and Sarajevo.[54] And already half a year earlier, on 31 October 1967, Prague students marched from their dormitories to the city's historical centre, chanting 'We want light!' and 'We want to study!' They were heading for Prague Castle, where official ceremonies to celebrate the fiftieth anniversary of the Russian October Revolution were taking place.

'We want light' might sound like a radical demand for enlightenment in a society kept in ideological darkness. But the issue was much more mundane. The lack of electricity, a common problem in Czechoslovakia's malfunctioning economy, made studying simply impossible. The police reacted with force, chasing protestors back to their dormitory and beating them up on the way. In the aftermath, the leadership of the ruling Communist Party praised the police and promised to persecute the protests' leaders. Yet, to the authorities' surprise, this harsh stance was met with open criticism, and not only by dissident students. The university's rector,

Oldřich Starý, declared the students' demands legitimate. Even the magazine of the state-run socialist youth organization, Mladá fronta, criticized the police. The protests, and even more so the public's reaction to them, showed that the authority of the regime under First Party Secretary Antonín Novotný (a hardliner who became first party secretary in 1953 and president of Czechoslovakia in 1957) was rapidly waning.[55]

Throughout the 1960s, parts of Prague's students had become critical of the regime and developed a non-conformist lifestyle that looked remarkably similar to its Western counterparts. Young people enjoyed Beat music, kept their hair long and had a casual attire. But under the communist regime, this could have more serious repercussions than in the West. Occasionally, security forces rounded up men with long hair and forcefully cut it. Men who in such ways demonstrated their contempt for socialist norms of (self-) discipline not only risked being thrown out of public transport or bars, but could also lose their jobs or places at university; and being without employment could result in criminal charges for 'parasitic behaviour'. Yet, such tough measures did not deter students. In 1964, a group called 'Clique of Oppositional Elements' won an election at Prague University's philosophy department for the committee of the Czechoslovak Youth Organization. They didn't campaign for political change as such, but demanded autonomy and truth. As one of the group's members, Jana Kohnová, said: 'Changing things is no priority for us. Above all, we want to be independent . . . Our conflict with power did not result from us being against it, but because we've behaved independently from it. We stopped playing its game and began calling a spade a spade.' They had a desire to speak the truth, which seemed (and was) impossible under communist rule.[56]

But change didn't happen only in the student milieu. Even more importantly, Novotný's authority was crumbling within the ruling Communist Party. Tensions had been mounting for some years by 1967. Reform-minded communists urged the party to come to terms with the legacy of the murderous Stalinist show trials of the 1950s. They also called for a 'fully developed political democracy', as politician Zdeněk Mlynář put it, which would protect citizens' rights regardless of their social origins. Finally, it became increasingly clear that reforms were necessary to deal with economic stagnation, for example, as economic expert Ota Šik proposed, by introducing market elements into Czechoslovakia's state-run economy.[57]

Novotný faced demands from multiple sides within the party. At a meeting of the party's central committee in October 1967, Slovak politician Alexander Dubček called for a reorganization of relations between the country's two major nationalities, Czechs and Slovaks. As a practical step he suggested separating the position of first party secretary and president. Novotný rebuffed him, accusing Dubček of promoting narrow-minded national interests, an accusation that alienated Slovaks within the party. Two months later, in December 1967, the party's central committee met again. This time, Novotný also faced a challenge from Šik, who criticized the 'immense concentration of power in the hands of a few comrades, in particular comrade Novotný'. With both reformers and Slovaks openly questioning his authority, Novotný's position became untenable. In January 1968, he gave in to the pressure and stepped down. He was succeeded by Alexander Dubček, a compromise candidate, as hardliners were keen to prevent leading reformers like Šik from taking power, and reformers demanded that Novotný wouldn't be replaced by another hardliner.[58] While student protests were challenging the regime's authority, it was a power struggle within the ruling party that set one of the most famous democratic reform movements in socialist Eastern Europe into motion: the Prague Spring.[59]

In his memoirs, Dubček claimed to have fought to democratize Czechoslovakia from the moment he came to power. To contemporaries, it looked otherwise. Dubček seemed to have stumbled into power somewhat by accident, without any clear political agenda. Indeed, after his election to the party's central committee, Dubček stressed that he had not expected this to be the outcome of the crisis.

If anything changed, then it was the style of leadership. Dubček seemed more authentic and humbler. He was willing to listen. When he met a delegation from Prague's Charles University, Dubček presented himself as 'a modest, decent guy', who told the scholars:

> I'm very aware that I'm here [in the position of first party secretary] more by chance, but I assure you that, as long as I'm in this position, I will treat you differently from my predecessors. While they endeavoured to prove to you how much you needed them, I will endeavour to convince you that I need you more than you need me.

Compared with Novotný, this was a dramatic change.[60]

But Dubček's political announcements remained ambiguous. In a February 1968 speech, he mentioned a particular Czechoslovak path to socialism, but also stressed the need to cooperate with the Soviet Union; he encouraged his compatriots to tread untrodden paths (without saying what exactly this meant, but this vagueness was the very point: experiment with new ways of doing things!), but also wanted to preserve 'all positive values of the past'; he wanted to expand the welfare state, but also spoke out against the 'deeply rooted evil of levelling and egalitarianism', which made no distinction between skilled and unskilled labour. This indecisive rhetoric allowed for a broad variety of interpretations and expectations for the future. Reformers saw an opportunity to push for their agenda, demanding, in the words of one reformist, Josef Smrkovský, a 'thorough and honest democratization' of politics and society.[61]

Then came an unexpected scandal. On 25 February, General Jan Šejna defected to the United States, taking his son and a twenty-two-year-old woman, sometimes believed to be the general's lover, sometimes his son's fiancée, with him. In the US, he provided the CIA with top-secret Warsaw Pact mobilization plans. The press eagerly reported the scandal and could do so more or less unhindered by state authorities. For the first time in Czechoslovakia, journalists could freely investigate and report. What they found undermined the authority of the old guard. Šejna had family ties to

Novotný and had benefited from a system of nepotism. Soldiers had, for example, built a villa for him for free. The revelations allowed reformers to now openly criticize the old leadership, something they had previously avoided. The reporting about the scandal set a precedent. Press censorship became untenable and was officially abolished on 4 March 1968.[62]

Only now did the Prague Spring really begin. What followed was an explosion of communication and reporting. As reform politician Čestmír Císař wrote, society was swimming 'on a wave of mass-drunkenness of democracy'. The participants of one TV debate in front of a large audience had the audacity to question whether socialism could be reformed at all; previously, even raising such a question in public would have been impossible. The press played an even larger role than TV shows. Freed from the constraints of censorship, journalists reported on the show trials of the 1950s and current political dramas.[63]

Ordinary citizens, too, could voice their thoughts. The Institute for Public Opinion Research, founded in 1965, conducted – with a small staff – twenty-three surveys in just a few months. For its head, Jaromíra Zapletalová, such surveys were nothing less than the 'science of democracy'. And in the absence of free elections, these polls legitimized the course of the new leadership. In January 1968, 73 per cent of those polled viewed the recent political developments in a positive light; a month later, the approval rate was even higher.[64]

Finally, mass gatherings took place in cities throughout Czechoslovakia, attracting thousands of participants who came to listen to politicians and public intellectuals debating past and present. On 20 March 1968, for example, some 15,000 people attended a seven-hour debate in Prague with reformers, including Josef Smrkovský and Ota Šik, as well as writers such as Pavel Kohout and Jan Procházka. The audience did not remain passive: they asked questions, and at the end of the event, which was broadcast live on radio in its entirety, they passed a resolution that demanded a 'genuinely enlightened humane and democratic socialism'.[65]

While the country was debating, the Communist Party developed a new 'action programme', made public on 5 April 1968.[66] For the first time, the programme gave a more precise sense of the direction Czechoslovakia was to take, outlining the vision of what became known as socialism with a human face. It breathed the spirit of a new beginning and democratic reforms. 'It is up to us to make our way through unknown conditions, to experiment, to give the socialist development a new look,' the concluding lines stated.[67] With stunning clarity, the programme admitted to the mistakes and crimes committed by the state in the past, recognized a lack of democracy within the party, criticized the accumulation of power in the hands of a few leading cadres, even naming Antonín Novotný personally, and bemoaned the party's economic incompetence: 'In economic life, independence, diligence, expertise, and initiative were not appreciated, whereas subservience, obedience, and even kowtowing to higher ups were.'[68]

The remedies the programme suggested were a thorough democratization of party and society, a commitment to transparency and open discussion without creating 'an atmosphere of distrust and suspicion' and an encouragement of market economies within the socialist framework.[69] In no ambivalent terms, the programme defended the abolishing of press censorship, affirmed the principle of freedom of thought and expression for all citizens and called for free artistic expression to make culture more than a mere ideological tool. It proposed economic reforms that would strengthen independent businesses, especially artisans and farmers, establish a free market and generally reward people according to their 'social importance and effectiveness'.[70] At the same time 'collective teams of workers' should be given a say in 'the management of production'. Reflecting a humanist ethos, the party would 'strive for the alleviation of extremely tiring jobs, the humanization of work, and the improvement of working conditions.'[71] This was a radically transformative programme – even though neither the alliance with the Soviet Union nor the leading role of the Communist Party was called into question.

The collective enthusiasm for reforms impressed party leaders.

The party under its new leadership was still able to inspire the country, despite its history of violence and oppression. But some of the reformers were worried. Dubček himself, for example, admitted that the Communist Party had not anticipated the 'wildness and complexity of the events' since January and had been forced to respond to the 'spontaneous activities of broad masses'. But now this situation had become untenable, Dubček argued. It was necessary to return to a path of 'organic change' that would result not in 'some kind of democracy' but in 'socialist democracy'. Reform politician Smrkovský agreed that such 'fierce and rapid change' could be a source of confusion and predicted that the next phase of change would be less turbulent, but more profound. And leaders had good reasons to use a more careful rhetoric in stressing, to different degrees, the role the Communist Party would play. In particular, they were keen to emphasize their loyalty to the Soviet Union and the other socialist countries of the Warsaw Pact. After all, the Soviet Union was closely monitoring events in Czechoslovakia. The democratic changes the reformers promised might bring the country closer to the West; and they might inspire similar demands within the rest of the Eastern bloc.[72]

Despite all the party's efforts to bring the situation under control, it remained turbulent. As the May Day celebrations of 1968 showed, the party enjoyed broad support. In previous years, these celebrations had been well-staged events that people were more or less required to attend. In 1968, it was different. This time, organizers did not pressure the population to come; and yet more people than ever gathered at the central Republic Square to greet Dubček, Smrkovský and other prominent party leaders. People asked them for an autograph, something that had not happened in the past. Even hippies, who had not long ago been persecuted by the police, joined the celebrations. But for all the sense of unity and hopes of a new beginning, there were signs of dissent. One banner, for example, proclaimed, 'For ever with the Soviet Union', an omnipresent slogan in Czechoslovakia, and added: '. . . but not a day longer'. Two days later, some 4,000 students marched through Prague. They broadly supported Dubček's reform efforts, but they also went further by denying the Communist Party its leading role and questioning the alliance with the Soviet Union. With such demands, they left the confines of political discourse the party leadership deemed acceptable.[73]

And despite appeals to unity, disagreements over the reforms mounted. Opponents of the reforms sent threatening and often antisemitic letters, usually anonymously, to leading reform politicians. Most of these letters remained private and unpublished. In late May, however, Eduard Goldstücker, professor of German studies at Prague University and leading reformist intellectual, decided to publish a letter sent to him in the party newspaper *Rudé právo* in an appeal for public solidarity. Goldstücker, who had been Czechoslovakia's first ambassador to Israel before being convicted in a show trial in 1951 and sent to work in a uranium mine (he was released in 1955), should have been hanged, the anonymous author wrote. There was no place for a 'hyena' like him in the Communist Party; he should establish his own party, 'perhaps an Israeli one'. After all, Jews were not real Czechoslovaks; in the pre-war years, they hadn't spoken Czech, but German, the 'language of the hyena Hitler'. The letter concluded with an unconcealed threat: 'The honest members [of the Czechoslovak Communist Party] and the people's militias have a plan. They will put an end to your machinations.'

He was familiar with such rhetoric, Goldstücker wrote in his published reply. It was the language of the old security apparatus that always talked about Zionist conspiracies when seeking to limit popular freedoms. The Communist Party, he urged, had to 'cleanse' itself of members of the old guard still expressing such Nazi ideas. His appeal was quickly answered: numerous people, both ordinary citizens and politicians, expressed their outrage.[74]

While the authors of such letters were hostile to any democratic reforms, others pushed for more radical democratization of the country. The most famous document in this regard was the 'Manifesto of 2,000 Words', written by renowned author Ludvík Vaculík on behalf of a group of scientists and published on 12 June 1968. The document was a provocation, rhetorically and in its content. Without any of the usual pathos, he wrote about the 'common cause' of Czechoslovakia, 'which has the working title of social-ism', implying that socialism might not be the final goal of history after all. Vaculík also had a proposal for how to move forwards. To stimulate political debate, he suggested forming citizen committees that would discuss 'questions which no one wants to know any-thing about'. In his mind, it would be 'simple: A few people convene, they elect a chairman, keep regular minutes, publish their findings, demand a solution, and do not let themselves be intimidated'. It was not a call for open rebellion or disobedience, but it questioned the political leadership of the party and invested ordinary citizens with authority. The fact that many members of the Communist Party signed and supported the text made it all the more problematic.[75]

Not surprisingly, the party's central committee rejected the mani-festo, though it had to concede that it showed 'consciousness and engaged civic behaviour'. But it also was, as Smrkovský put in his retort, the 'Manifesto of 1,000 words', a 'piece of political romanti-cism', based on 'insufficient information' and neglecting 'relevant internal and external aspects', a concealed reference to mounting pressure from Moscow to put an end to the democratization pro-cess. These attempts by the party leadership to contain the spread of the Manifesto did not succeed. It enjoyed too much support, even within the party, to be suppressed.[76]

Smrkovský had good reasons to mention 'external aspects'. He had just returned from Moscow and, unlike the Czechoslovak pub-lic, he was keenly aware of the increasing pressure regarding the reforms. For the Soviet leadership under Leonid Brezhnev, the Manifesto was another sign of 'counter-revolutionary' forces gain-ing strength. Dubček and his comrades understood that, without Moscow's tacit acceptance, the reforms would lead nowhere. Over the course of the summer, they tried to negotiate with the Soviet leadership. At the end of July, after negotiations in the border town of Čierna, it seemed as if a compromise that was acceptable for everyone had been reached. Interior Minister Josef Pavel, one of the most pronounced reformists, would step down, the formation of new political parties would be stopped and the freedom of the press would be revoked. But the situation was out of control. In Prague, young people gathered in parks giving anti-Soviet speeches; a petition calling for the dissolution of the party militias circulated; and it was impossible to bring the media back under state control.[77]

Ultimately, it was the Soviet Union that decided the struggle: on the night of 20/21 August 1968, a force half a million strong, mostly Soviet soldiers, but also troops from its Warsaw Pact allies Poland, Hungary and Bulgaria, entered Czechoslovakia. They arrested the Czechoslovak leadership around Dubček and brought them to Moscow. President Ludvík Svoboda also flew to the Soviet capital, where he first pushed Brezhnev to include Dubček and his government in any negotiations, but also convinced Dubček – who wanted to stand his ground even if that meant his death – to give in for the greater good of the country. Dubček signed an agreement stating that reforms such as the end of press censorship and the freedom of speech would be undone, though he asked for it to be kept secret. The public was only informed about a mutual commitment to 'normalizing relations' between the socialist countries with accompanying photographs of their leaders toasting with champagne. It was an utter charade.

At home, Czechoslovaks peacefully resisted the occupation force. Photos show ordinary citizens talking to Soviet tank crews, trying to reason with them about the wrongness of the invasion. Remembering the liberation of Prague from the Nazis a little over twenty years earlier, they still believed in the fundamental friendship between the two countries. But the time for reforms was over. The economy would not be liberalized along the lines Ota Šik had proposed, nor would the country be democratized. Young people and students felt the loss of their new freedoms most acutely. It was one of them who became the most famous, most tragic symbol of Czechoslovak bravery: on 16 January 1969, twenty-one-year-old history student Jan Palach immolated himself on Prague's Wences-las Square. Three days later, he died in hospital. It wasn't an act of radical protest merely against the Soviet occupation and the undo-ing of reforms, but also against the growing apathy taking hold of the country. 'As our country is on the verge of succumbing to hope-lessness, we have decided to express our protest in this way to stir up people.' For a moment, it seemed to work. On the day of his self-immolation, some 200,000 people flocked to Wenceslas Square to lay down wreaths; 10,000 people attended his funeral. And in the following months, more students burned themselves to death.[78]

But even if the Prague Spring did not result in the democratic transformation of the country people had hoped for, it had a lasting impact. It was, as Martin Schulze Wessel notes, a 'laboratory', an attempt to create a truly democratic form of socialism.[79] Though reform-oriented politicians had developed plans and proposals in the years before 1968, there was no clear and coherent reform pro-gramme to be enacted. Dubček's rise to power and the fall of press censorship created a situation in which it became possible to envi-sion and debate alternatives to the dictatorial rule of the Communist Party without simply copying Western capitalism. The Prague Spring had made another future visible. After that experience, it was clear that communism wouldn't have to last for ever.

We Want Everything: Workers' Autonomy in Italy

Turin, 3 July 1969. Trade unions had called for a day-long general strike in the city to push for housing reforms, an important issue in a country facing massive housing shortages. But workers, notably at the car manufacturer FIAT, reacted angrily to the unions' call for action. In the previous months, they had started forming independ-ent workers' committees that had challenged the authority of the unions to represent workers. They viewed the strike as an attempt to distract from work-related struggles on the shop floor, and more generally to bring workers back under union control. Yet, despite their discontent, workers gathered at 3 p.m. in front of the Mirafiori factory, FIAT's huge factory in the neighbourhood of the same name.

Police tried to disperse the workers, but to no avail. Other workers, teenagers and students from the area quickly joined the crowd. A demonstration formed, marching down the Corso Traiano. At the end of the road, protestors faced a police cordon, equipped with truncheons and shields. It was clear that they wouldn't let the protestors pass into the inner city, and it was clear that they were ready for a confrontation. The battle began when one of the protestors jumped on a car trailer and forced the driver to park it across the road, blocking the police. It was the first barricade of the afternoon.

The riot that ensued lasted for hours. It marked the beginning of what became known as Italy's 'hot autumn'. Workers in the streets that day wanted more than the rent controls the trade unions campaigned for. Their chant: 'What do we want? Everything!' The slogan, popularized by a novel by Nanni Balestrini, encapsulates the radical vision of the workers' movement in Italy. The workers were no longer content with demanding just a bigger piece of the cake; they wanted *everything*.[80]

In many ways, the protests in Italy around 1968 resembled those in West Germany and in France. In Italy, too, the movement originated with students who wanted to democratize university life.[81] And like their comrades in France, students went to factories hoping to establish contacts with workers. Medical students in Turin, for instance, organized meetings in factories and working-class neighbourhoods to discuss how working in a capitalist society damaged their health.[82] But the protests in Italy also differed in important ways from those elsewhere in Western Europe. For one thing, they lasted longer. In France and West Germany, the movement came to a rapid end following the dramatic events of spring 1968. In Italy, it reached its apex in 1969, and then lasted well into the 1970s. Here, workers came to play a central role in a manner not seen elsewhere. As in France, they demanded more than mere wage increases. They challenged the authority of employers to organize the labour process; they wanted to liberate life inside the factories. Autonomy became the rallying cry for radical Italian workers.[83] The protests around 1968 in Italy thus represent another attempt to rewrite the rules of social life.

The riot in Turin did not come from nowhere. Over the course of Italy's post-war 'economic miracle', a rapid period of recovery and growth, many young men had migrated from southern Italy to the industrial centres in the north, such as Milan and Turin, where they found work as unskilled factory labourers. These workers had not grown up as part of the communist working-class culture in northern Italy for which memories of the resistance against the Fascist regime played a central role. They cared little about Communist Party programmes and dismissed the discipline trade unions demanded. They came with different traditions and repertoires of struggling, more ready to use violence, to commit small acts of sabotage to disrupt the work process and to assault or mock foremen and scabs. Where the older generation of workers, well versed in communist theory, accepted the alleged social necessity of factory labour even while fighting against exploitation, these young workers from the south simply hated the place that kept them from what they really wanted to do, that is, enjoy the sun and meet their friends, only to produce metal parts they cared little about. These southern workers provided the backbone for the revolts in the late 1960s, not least because leftist student agitators idolized them and their unwillingness to collaborate with unions.[84]

As the student movement evolved in Italy in tandem with movements in France and West Germany, workers gained new confidence. Throughout most of the 1960s, they had shown little eagerness for activism. This changed in 1968. A first sign that workers were ready to confront their employers was a general strike on 7 March 1968, which was called after negotiations for a pension reform between unions and the government had collapsed. In Milan alone, some 300,000 engineering workers participated. 'There was something in the air that encouraged workers to take back what they had lost in the previous few years . . . the strike for pensions, that's what happened in 1968 that really changed things,' Rina Barbieri, an activist of radical leftist Avanguardia Operaia, recalled.[85] The mood among workers had radically changed. On toilet cubicles and in the corridors of factories, leaflets and pamphlets appeared that detailed multiple small acts of resistance, of sabotage and refusal in the workplace. Then, over the course of the spring of 1968, a movement developed in the FIAT-Mirafiori factories demanding a forty-four-hour-week. In itself it was not a particularly radical demand, but the tone was new. 'Working at FIAT is hell for the workers,' one pamphlet declared, 'now it's the moment when every day at the factory becomes hell for the management.'[86]

Throughout 1968 and into 1969, agitation on the shop floor continued under the influence of radical groups such as Lotta Continua (Permanent Struggle) and usually outside the established trade unions. An egalitarian spirit characterized workers' demands: they fought against piece rates that made workers compete with each other; against the so-called 'wage cages', which meant that workers in different parts of the country were paid differently; and against incremental wage increases, which benefited the highest-paid workers, instead demanding that all wages should rise by the same amount. Other demands addressed the organization of work itself: workers called for slowing the production pace, or permitting free movement within the factory so that workers could talk to each other. The conflicts culminated in the 'hot autumn' of 1969. Throughout the country, workers went on strike, sometimes occupying factories. Cities were full of strike pickets and almost daily demonstrations by students and workers, often erupting into violence.[87]

The labour unrest in Italy throughout 1968/9 was a challenge to the authority of both employers and trade unions. Despising unions for their willingness to negotiate and compromise with employers, radical workers organized in independent, shop-floor-based committees that became known as the Comitati Unitari di Base (Unitary Base Committees, CUBs). The first of these committees emerged at the rubber company of Pirelli in Milan. In early February 1968, the company and the country's three big trade unions had agreed to sign the national contract for the rubber sector. It stipulated a one-hour reduction in the working week and a 5 per cent increase in basic wages, but left the much-hated piece-rate system subject to unspecified 'further talks'.[88] This did not satisfy workers. In response, they formed a rank-and-file committee: the first CUB. Workers with previous experience in unionizing, held in high esteem by their colleagues despite their contempt for unions as organizations, took the lead. They fostered a general sense of unity among workers. Even though meetings were organized semi-clandestinely, they were 'far more crowded than those held by the unions', a March 1968 report noted.[89]

Initially, the committee's demands remained well within those of conventional trade unionism, for example by asking for higher piece rates. But it quickly radicalized when it called for 'the total abolition of health hazards, including piece-work, the elimination of the lowest grades and equal wage increases for all workers'. Whereas unions had traditionally demanded financial compensation for workers taking on dangerous jobs, the committee argued that the organization of the production process itself should be changed in a way that would protect workers' health. The CUB also went beyond traditional unionism by including student militants as full members. In the unions, students had merely helped out as 'distributors of leaflets and members of the picket line', but in the CUB, students could 'participate in the first person [i.e., as students with a political voice] in the workers' political activity'. This meant giving up on the old ideal of workers as the exclusive revolutionary avant-garde. And finally, it sought to overcome the distinction between economic and political struggles. 'It is workers' consciousness of their own inter-ests and rights in the workplace that leads to general struggle in society, and vice versa,' a pamphlet by the CUB proclaimed.[90]

The base committees, which spread from Pirelli to other fac-tories throughout Italy, also played a vital role in developing innovative protests that disrupted the production process more effectively than conventional strikes. The most famous was the *autoriduzione*, literally 'self-reduction', meaning that workers reduced the pace of work and hence productivity. They turned the piece-rate system to their advantage, as they did not have to go on an official strike for *autoriduzione*. Contemporaries were amazed by the practice. 'The reduction of work speed is a masterpiece of consciousness (*auto-coscienza*) and technical ability. It is as if an orchestra had managed to play a difficult symphony harmoniously without the conductor and at a tempo agreed upon and regulated by the players of the individual instruments,' wrote journalist Aniello Coppola in an article celebrating the 'victory for workers' inventiveness' taking place at Pirelli. The leftist daily *Il Manifesto* praised *autoriduzione* in a similar vein. The factory, it noted, 'functioned with the regularity of a clock, but the tick-tock is more spaced out in time; it has a slowness that exasperates the bosses who protest about the "irregularities" of this form of struggle. The workers, for their part, acquire consciousness of their power and learn to make the bosses dance to the rhythm of their music.' As these comments suggest, a reduction of work pace required, especially in large factories with complex production processes, a high degree of coordination which became possible only through the base committees that were closely connected with ordinary workers.[91]

Reducing the work pace obviously hurt companies financially without high costs for workers. But it was also, as student activists claimed, a way of 'practising the objective'. Workers demanded more humane working conditions in the factory; hence, they went ahead and implemented them. Taking over the organization of production, workers defied the authority of foremen, who were usually responsible for assigning tasks and tried to prohibit workers from talking to each other. And this was not the only means to create autonomy inside the factory. Another tactic was the 'check-board strike', meaning that specific groups of workers within the factory would strike for a short time; half an hour was enough to disrupt the production process for the entire day. Sometimes, this was arbitrary as striking by alphabetic order – to the frustration of employers and the amusement of workers. Such strikes not only confused authority at the workplace, but also liberated workers. 'When you strike, you go around as pleased as punch and you can't be stopped,' recalled Rina Barbieri. Once the power of foremen was broken and the rhythm of work disrupted, it became possible to socialize at work. The factory turned from a place of hated, monotonous work to a place where workers could debate, make friends and mock the authority of employers.[92]

While the practice of *autoriduzione* originated in the factory, it did not remain there. Already during the wave of protests in 1968/9, students and workers on their way to demonstrations had refused to pay for public transport; in 1971, youngsters in Milan threatened to sabotage pop concerts to enforce ticket price reductions. By the mid-1970s, such practices had become widespread in working-class neighbourhoods. Residents not only reduced rents, but also gas, electricity and telephone bills. If students had carried the struggle to factories, the movement now moved back from the factories to society, making use of the tactics learned at the workplace.[93]

The protests both inside and outside the factory gates stirred massive hopes among radical activists in Italy. It seemed like a revolution was on the horizon, that workers and students had really forged an alliance that might bring down capitalism. In November 1969, Lotta Continua wrote: 'The workers are slowly liberating themselves. In the factories, they are destroying all constituted authority, they are dismantling the instruments which the bosses use to control and divide them, they are overcoming the taboos which until now have kept them as slaves.'[94] But once again, such revolutionary expectations did not materialize. Workers were happy to engage in disruptive action and often rejected agreements unions had negotiated, but when it came to potentially revolutionary steps, calls for action fell on deaf ears. In May 1968, for example, the base committee of Pirelli suggested occupying the factory, taking French workers at Renault as a role model. But workers were not interested. Given their experiences on the shop floor, it didn't make sense. Why occupy a place they hated so much? In short, workers were less revolutionary than radical militants had imagined. On the other hand, Italian trade unions, unlike those in France, adapted to the situation and endorsed both demands and forms of struggle first promoted by the independent committees.[95]

And working-class militancy paid off. In December 1969, the metal workers' unions signed a new national contract that saw several central demands by workers fulfilled: wage increases would be the same for all workers; within three years, the forty-hour week was to be implemented; trade unions gained the right to hold mass meetings at the workplace and during regular working hours. A few months later, in May 1970, parliament voted on a Labour Charter that gave unions legal recognition and made it illegal for employers to sack or otherwise reprimand workers for their union activities. In addition, parliament voted for a general amnesty for all charges related to the protests. But neither the contract nor the legal reforms stopped workers' activism. At FIAT, workers immediately reduced the working week to forty-two hours. They continued agitating on the shop floor against piece-rates, for equal wage increases across the factory, and for recognizing their delegates.[96]

When the national contract came up for negotiation again in late 1972, employers found themselves, to their surprise, in a weak position. Once again, workers accomplished significant victories: employers agreed to a single wage scale for white- and blue-collar workers, and the distance between the highest and lowest points on the pay scale was reduced. Most interestingly, perhaps, workers also won the right to 150 hours of paid study leave per year, which gave workers the chance to complete the school degrees they needed for promotion, but also brought leftist union agitators and workers together. Workers wanted more than material benefits. They longed for education and a cultural improvement.[97]

What Was 1968?

Like few other moments in post-war European history, the protests around the year 1968 have captured the imagination of both scholars and the public. The year '1968' has become a cypher, if not a myth. The year invokes images of hope, of protest, of belief in the possibility of radical change. How are we to make sense of this year of rebellion around the globe? Scholars have debated at length the causes and consequences, the meanings and legacies of the protests. One way to think about them is through democratization. Evidently, revolutionary dreams did not become reality. Political institutions remained unchanged, capitalism in the West was not overthrown, and democratic socialism did not take root in Czechoslovakia. In that sense, it was a political failure. But nevertheless, scholars have argued that the protests have resulted in a more thorough democratization of societies (at least in Western Europe). It was, in the words of German sociologist Claus Leggewie, a 're-foundation of the [Federal] Republic' that strengthened democracy in West Germany after the catastrophe of National Socialism.[98] Historians approaching the protests with considerable sympathy go even further and see them as an attempt to build a radical 'participatory democracy', a project yet to be completed by future generations of activists.[99]

Other scholars are more sceptical. They highlight the totalitarian dimension of Marxist ideologies that informed much of student activism; in this reading, if Western Europe, and especially the Federal Republic of Germany, became more democratic, then it was in spite, and not because, of 1968.[100] Some have even questioned the very relevance of 1968. Did it have any political effects, or was it a brief episode with no lasting consequences?[101] After all, critics have argued, the processes of political democratization and cultural liberalization were well underway by 1968. Students, as one author put it, stormed barricades that had long been deserted.[102] And finally, there is an 'ironic' reading of 1968: by promoting values such as autonomy, individual fulfilment and playfulness, the protagonists of 1968 contributed to a renewal of capitalism that now relies on those values: just think of working conditions in the tech industry, which sometimes seem to model playgrounds for adults.[103] In this reading, 1968 did have profound consequences, albeit not the ones its protagonists had hoped for.

What tends to fade into the background in these debates is the experience of 1968 itself. Above all, '1968' was a year of radical imagination, of envisioning a different world: by facilitating communication and critical discussion, by overcoming social boundaries that kept people apart, by democratizing socialism, or by practically creating more humane and less alienating working conditions. It was a moment of hope and experimentation.[104] Whatever measurable results the movements might have had, they were a moment of empowerment, sometimes of a very personal nature. Chantal Cambronne-Desvignes, a thirty-two-year-old high-school teacher in France, pregnant with her fourth child, began talking to women in her neighbourhood in May 1968 about cheating husbands and sexual frustrations. For Chantal, the liberating divorce that followed is a 'direct consequence of May 68'. Jacques Guilhaumou, a first-year history student at Nanterre, finally settled the struggle with his authoritarian father, who got lost searching for his son amid the barricades at the Sorbonne. Standing in the crowd of students, the father, 'used to commanding others', suddenly 'became nothing, or rather someone ordinary'. As a worker in Nantes wrote in his diary, the strike had a 'moral result': 'Like or not, it will not be like before'.[105]

PART II

Forms of Protest

Terror and Violence: Red Army Faction, Red Brigades and Street Violence

'When will Berlin's department stores burn?' a pamphlet circulating in late May 1967 at West Berlin's Free University asked sardonically. Signed by the infamous left-wing commune Kommune 1, the pamphlet referred to a department store fire in Brussels two days before that had killed 322 customers and employees. German tabloid *Bild* had reported extensively about the catastrophe, including testimonies by witnesses that linked the blaze to anti-Vietnam War protests in the preceding days. Rainer Langhans and Fritz Teufel, the authors of the pamphlet, considered the tragedy an opportunity. Previously, they explained in the leaflet, student protestors had been 'plodding with banners through empty streets', occasionally throwing eggs. But now, their comrades in Brussels led the way: 'Our Belgian friends finally got the hang of how to really involve the population in the merry goings-on in Vietnam: They set fire to a department store, three hundred bourgeois cease their exciting lives, and Brussels becomes Hanoi.' If in future barracks blew up or a grandstand collapsed, nobody should be surprised, just as American forces bombing the city centre of Hanoi wouldn't be a surprise for anyone. 'Brussels gave us the only answer: burn ware-house burn,' they concluded (in broken English).[1]

Predictably, the media were outraged by the pamphlet. 'Whoever glorifies this catastrophe that was probably started by radical leftist arson' – a false allegation as it turned out – 'and recommends copying it, should be put behind bars,' *Bild* demanded.[2] And indeed, Langhans and Teufel were charged with inciting violence. After enlisting prominent literary scholars who testified that the pamphlet should be understood as a satire meant to shock and not an actual call for violence, their lawyers convinced the judge to acquit Langhans and

Teufel. Yet, less than two weeks after their acquittal, on 2 April 1968, Andreas Baader, a charismatic young man working precarious jobs and with no higher education, and students Gudrun Ensslin, Thorwald Proll and Horst Söhnlein, all in their mid to late twenties, set a department store in Frankfurt on fire. Luckily, nobody was hurt, and the material damage was minimal.[3] It was the first attack of a gang that was to become the Red Army Faction (RAF), the left-wing terror organization that engaged in what the terrorists called an 'armed struggle' against the West German state in the years to come.

Violence and terror, the subject of this chapter, might sound like an inappropriate theme for a book about attempts to build a better world, a world that would be, as many activists hoped, less violent. And yet, feeling that peaceful protests didn't lead anywhere, many protestors in 1968, particularly in West Germany and Italy, where the Brigate Rosse (BR) committed numerous murders, considered not just throwing rocks, but taking up arms. A significant minority opted to do so. Fighting an imperialist system that was waging a deadly war in Vietnam required equally deadly force, they believed. For contemporaries and historians alike, left-wing terrorist violence has come to characterize the (late) 1970s, often described in German and Italian as 'Years of Lead', referring both to bullets and a general sense of depression and confrontation. We need to understand how this violence related to the hopeful protests of 1968, why people felt that 'armed struggle' was a legitimate and appropriate choice, but also why many militants ultimately turned their backs on terrorist groups.[4] And we need to look beyond deadly terror. On many occasions, protestors engaged in street battles with the police, at times even celebrating the joyful rioting. What was it that made such violence seem not only legitimate, but emotionally appealing?

A Deadly Struggle: Terrorist Violence against the State

It didn't take long for the police to arrest the Frankfurt arsonists. In the autumn of 1968, they were put on trial. It turned into a political spectacle for the left. Ensslin, a highly talented student who had been involved in West Berlin's student movement, confessed to the crime, justifying it as a protest 'against the indifference with which people watch the genocide in Vietnam'. Peacefully protesting wasn't enough, she proclaimed. 'We have learned that talking without acting is unjust.'[5] Her lawyer, Horst Mahler, who would become a founding member of the Red Army Faction, presented Ensslin as a person acting out of deep, inner conviction, rebelling against the older generation of Nazi perpetrators and silent bystanders. On 31 October 1968, the court sentenced all four defendants to three years in prison. The student left were outraged. It was the most draconian verdict so far for activists involved in the 1968 protests, though three years of prison were, in fact, a rather mild punishment for an attack that had endangered human life. Only nine months later, in June 1969, all four arsonists were released on parole pending an appeal by their lawyers.[6]

Freed, Baader and Ensslin joined leftist students from Frankfurt working with runaway teenagers. Inspired by theorist Herbert Marcuse's belief that socially marginalized groups were the new revolutionary subject, these radicals had organized a network of communes for young people running away from foster homes; later, the RAF would recruit among these delinquent teenagers.[7] In November, their appeal was rejected. To escape imprisonment, the arsonists fled first to Paris, then to Italy. Meanwhile, lawyer Horst Mahler in West Berlin began recruiting leftist militants for an armed group he hoped to form, including among others renowned leftist journalist Ulrike Meinhof. Mahler also convinced Baader and Ensslin to return from Italy and join the gang. The core of the Red Army Faction was forming. But then, on 4 April 1970, the police arrested the charismatic Baader. Freeing him became the top priority for his comrades.[8]

Using her friendship with left-wing publisher Klaus Wagenbach, Meinhof managed to have Baader visit the library of the Dahlem Institute for Social Studies, allegedly to conduct research for a co-authored book. On 14 May 1970, Meinhof and Baader met in the library. They talked quietly, pretending to do research. Then the group of armed liberators arrived: Gudrun Ensslin, Ingrid Schubert, who had just completed her medical studies, Irene Goergens, a nineteen-year-old girl Meinhof knew from her journalistic work in a foster home, and an ex-convict, hired for support, whose identity has never been confirmed. Everything went to plan, until sixty-two-year-old library employee Georg Linke tried to stop the gang and was shot by the masked man; though badly injured, Linke survived. The group escaped with Baader, while Meinhof jumped out the window, going 'underground'. It was the founding moment of the Red Army Faction.[9]

Early on, Baader and his comrades had established contacts in Italy, where they encountered a spirit of militancy that deeply impressed them. Militant workers frequently attacked unpopular foremen and managers, damaged their cars or beat them up. Importantly, however, political violence in Italy wasn't limited to the extreme left. In the autumn of 1969, a series of bombings shocked the country. Most notoriously, a bomb at the Milan train station killed sixteen people and injured another eighty-eight on 12 December. The police and media initially held leftist anarchists responsible for those bombings, when in reality neo-fascists had committed the atrocities as part of a 'strategy of tension': violence, the right-wing terrorists hoped, would increase political tensions and make people long for a strong, authoritarian government willing to establish order by any means necessary – fascism, in other words.[10] Police arrested several leftists, among them anarchist railway worker Giuseppe Pinelli. Three days later, he was dead. During a police interrogation, he – the police said – 'fell' out of a window. The exact circumstances of this defenestration remain unclear to this day, but for the radical left, there was no doubt that he had been murdered by the state.[11]

It was in the context of these violent conflicts that the Brigate Rosse (Red Brigades) first appeared. Founded by Renato Curcio and Margherita Cagol – both students at the University of Trento, an epicentre of the student rebellion – Alberto Franceschini, a young communist from Rome, and Mario Moretti from Milan, the Red Brigades became the most important left-wing terrorist organization in

Italy.[12] Unlike the spectacular beginning of the Red Army Faction, the first attack by the Red Brigades was barely noticed: on 17 September 1970, arsonists torched the car of a leading manager of Sit-Siemens named Leoni. They left no explanation, but the same evening, Giorgio Villa, another engineer at Sit-Siemens, found a pamphlet put under his Ferrari's windshield wiper. 'How long will the little Ferrari last? Until we decide that it's time to put an end to the banditry.' The pamphlet was signed 'Brigate Rosse'.[13]

Similar attacks followed, but in the general climate of militant struggles and violence, these didn't generate particular attention either. This changed on 25 January 1971, when a commando of the Red Brigades placed incendiary bombs beneath car trucks belonging to the rubber-making company Pirelli, a hotspot of labour militancy, completely destroying three of them. Only then did Italy's mainstream press take notice, wondering about the clandestine organization and the threat it might pose.

The attack wasn't well received on the left. The radical left-wing newspaper *Lotta Continua*, for example, condemned it for being 'exemplary' and not supported by the masses. With the next attack, the Red Brigades gained more support. On 3 March 1972, they abducted Idalgo Macchiarini, an engineer at Sit-Siemens, too, who was particularly unpopular among workers for his 'dictatorial methods'.[14] His captors held a 'political trial'; after only twenty minutes, they released him with a placard around his neck saying: 'Macchiarini, Idalgo, Fascist manager of Sit-Siemens, tried by the BR. The proletarians have taken up arms, for the bosses it is the "beginning of the end".'[15] For radicals, the abduction was a cause to celebrate, as a demonstration of 'the masses' general willingness to pursue class war, even on the terrain of violence and illegality', as *Lotta Continua* wrote.[16]

With these attacks, both the Red Army Faction, or 'Baader-Meinhof Gang', as the press often called the group, and the Red Brigades gained fame and notoriety. But they still had to explain their violent means to their comrades in radical leftist scenes. Two weeks after freeing Andreas Baader, the Red Army Faction published its first statement in the West Berlin underground paper *agit 883*. 'Building the Red Army', as the text was entitled, directly addressed the group's 'comrades' in Berlin's radical left. Its authors saw no need to explain why they had freed Baader, or to justify the shooting of an unarmed library employee. Rather, they instructed their would-be comrades on what to do: they had to explain the coup, though not to 'chattering intellectuals or know-it-alls, shitting their pants in fear.' Instead, they should persuade the 'potentially revolutionary elements in the people'. 'Your job is to explain the liberation of Baader to the kids in Märkisches Viertel [a newly built high-rise neighbourhood in the north of Berlin],' they demanded. Freeing Baader marked a beginning: now, they were done with empty reformist promises, with the power of the police, teachers and other authorities. The kids would understand, the terrorists believed. Tell them that 'an end of the rule of cops is in sight. You have to tell them that we're building a Red Army, that's their army. You have to tell them that it's starting now.' It was time to escalate the conflict.[17]

Nearly a year later, the group published its second, much longer statement, *Das Konzept Stadtguerilla* (roughly 'The Strategy of the Urban Guerrilla'). By then, the group had robbed several banks to fund their activities, but also had to cope with the arrest of some founding members including Horst Mahler and Astrid Proll, the younger sister of the arsonist Thorwald Proll, who had turned his back on the gang. Once again, the document is above all a justification of armed struggle. Forming an urban guerrilla group, it emphasized, was not the result of an unrealistically optimistic evaluation of the situation in the Federal Republic. Clearly, the 'imperialist system', the pamphlet's author Ulrike Meinhof conceded, was not about to falter in West Germany. Why, then, take up arms? Because of a global struggle against imperialism, in which the Red Army Faction believed they were participating. After all, the student movement – and the Red Army Faction did not deny its origins there – had gained its strength because it considered itself part of an 'international movement' fighting the same 'paper tiger' as the Vietcong.[18] If 'American imperialism' was to be defeated, then it had to be fought everywhere, and there was no reason not to fight it in West Germany just because the 'powers of revolution' were weak there. Thus, Meinhof and her comrades entered a deadly struggle between two opposing forces: American imperialism and its allies, including the Federal Republic, and all those fighting it. There would be no turning back. Quoting French revolutionary Louis-Auguste Blanqui, Meinhof concluded: 'It is the duty of a revolutionary to always fight, to fight nevertheless, to fight until death.'

In Italy, the Red Brigades similarly imagined themselves in a constant struggle. However, where the Red Army Faction placed itself in the context of a global fight against imperialism, the Red Brigades focused more on class struggle in Italy itself. In a self-interview published in September 1971, they argued that 'revolutionary struggle often takes place through secretly organized direct actions', made necessary by the 'repressive organization of the bosses'. It was an existential struggle, as leading Red Brigades member Renato Curcio wrote in a letter to his mother from prison in November 1974:

> Seeking my path, I found exploitation, injustice, and oppression. People who meted them out and people who submitted to them. I was one of the latter. And these latter were in the majority. I therefore understood that my history was their history, that my future was their future . . . What more can I say? My enemies are the enemies of humanity and intelligence, those who have built and still build their monstrous fortunes on the material and intellectual misery of the people.[19]

Rather than envisioning a different world, the Red Brigades began to mirror the state, its language and institutions they hated so much. The first abduction of Macchiarini in 1972, though it lasted for only twenty minutes, was after all presented as an 'arrest', with a subsequent trial and release. Clearly, the Red Brigades used that language in an ironic way, reversing the usual power relations. But nevertheless, as Primo Moroni and Nanni Balestrini stress, such a tendency to build a 'counter-state' anticipated later 'people's prisons', 'proletarian trials' and very real executions. This was not an alternative to the state, but its 'reversed mirror image'.[20]

In the early 1970s, this was still in the future. For the moment, the Red Brigades continued to focus on ongoing conflicts between workers and employers in northern Italy, particularly at the FIAT-Mirafiori factories in Turin, known for its militant working force.[21] In cooperation with militants of Potere Operaio, a militant group that had formed during the 1968 struggles, the Red Brigades committed acts of sabotage and arson and assaulted unpopular foremen. Most dramatically, members of the Red Brigades also abducted further foremen and low-level managers with ties to the neo-fascist right. One victim at FIAT was Bruno Labate, who was taken hostage in February 1973. After being held captive for a day, the Brigades chained him to the factory gate at Mirafiori, half naked and with shorn hair – a practice that had been common among resistance movements in Nazi-occupied Europe to penalize and shame women accused of having relationships with Germans and collaborating with the enemy. To the amusement of workers watching the scene, or so reports claimed, it took an hour until he was freed.[22]

For the most part, the Red Brigades' attacks in this early phase remained non-lethal. This changed in June 1974, when members of Red Brigades raided the offices of the neo-fascist Movimento Sociale Italiano in Padua. They had not expected to find anyone there, but when they encountered two members of the movement, they did not hesitate to execute them with shots to the neck. The Red Brigades had not planned the murders and therefore described them as a 'work accident', a phrase that speaks volumes for the acceptance of deadly violence by the group.[23]

Meanwhile, in the Federal Republic, the Red Army Faction prepared for action. Throughout 1971, the group had robbed several banks to finance their activities. They were still hiding from the police, who were intensifying their efforts to catch members of the 'Baader-Meinhof Gang'. On both sides, people died that year. On 15 July, the police shot and killed twenty-year-old Petra Schelm after she had opened fire during an attempted escape. On 22 October, plain-clothes officers in Hamburg tried to arrest three members of the group, among them Meinhof. This time, the terrorists fired the first shots, killing thirty-two-year-old policeman Norbert Schmid. More shoot-outs followed, with more people killed or gravely injured.[24]

By spring 1972, the gang felt ready to launch a series of attacks. Between 11 and 24 May, eleven bombs went off. On 11 May, three bombs placed in the Frankfurt headquarters of the 5th US Army Corps killed one US soldier and injured thirteen. Attacks against police stations in Augsburg and Munich followed a day later. On 15 May, terrorists detonated a bomb beneath the car of federal judge Wolfgang Buddenberg, gravely injuring his wife, who was in the car, as her husband had walked to work. Then, on 19 May, a bomb exploded in Hamburg in the offices of the publisher Springer, owner of the tabloid paper *BILD*, injuring seventeen employees. Finally, on 24 May, a bomb hit the European headquarters of the US Army in Heidelberg, killing three GIs.[25]

If the terrorists had expected sympathy from the extra-parliamentary left, they were disappointed. Yet, they did successfully provoke the state. Making use of the latest computerized technologies and an unprecedented number of officers, the police managed to arrest most members of the Red Army Faction by July 1972. It looked like the state had put a swift end to left-wing terrorism in the Federal Republic.[26] Yet, the battle wasn't over. From now on, however, the Red Army Faction focused on itself.

The state feared the terrorists, even in prison. Worrying that they would continue to coordinate the group's activities from behind bars, the authorities went to great lengths to isolate group members from each other – they were spread out in prisons across the country – and to closely monitor their communication with the outside world. Prison authorities also kept the terrorists apart from the general prison population, fearing a 'politicization of the prison' that would end in revolts.[27] Conditions were harsh, particularly for Astrid Proll and Ulrike Meinhof in Cologne, who had to endure 'acoustic isolation', meaning they could not hear any of the normal sounds of prison life, and complete surveillance including nightly

illumination of their cells.[28] From the terrorists' and their supporters' point of view, this was a form of torture. Soon, with the support
of RAF lawyers, so-called Committees Against Isolation Torture
formed, drawing public attention to the situation.[29]

As a last resort in their struggle, the terrorists turned their
bodies – in their own words – into weapons, by going on collective
hunger strikes.[30] It was a way to continue the battle, and that's what
mattered. 'If fighting is your identity,' Ulrike Meinhof wrote in a
secret letter to her younger comrade Irene Goergens, encouraging
her to continue the hunger strike, 'if you've *grasped* that there's . . .
just *one* way to victory – namely, *this* hunger strike, now, for you
too – why "can't" you?' Similarly, Holger Meins, who was to die of
malnutrition, claimed that the 'only thing that counts is fighting . . .
Fight, get beaten, fight again, get beaten again, fight anew and so on
until the final victory . . . fight to the death.'[31] These hunger strikes
helped the group to present itself as victim rather than perpetrator.
More importantly, the rhetoric of relentless fighting encouraged
sympathizers outside of prison to join the 'armed struggle'. Volker
Speitel, briefly a member of the group, recalled how 'the death of
Holger Meins and my decision to pick up a gun, that was one'.[32]

The state was not wrong to assume that the terrorists would
continue to be a threat despite their imprisonment. All the efforts
to prevent them from communicating with the outside world notwithstanding, they managed, with the help of lawyers, to instruct
comrades who were still at large to work for their release.[33] An operation by another left-wing terrorist group, the Movement 2nd June,
gave reason to hope. On 27 February 1975, the group kidnapped conservative politician and mayoral candidate for West Berlin Peter
Lorenz. The authorities feared for Lorenz's life: a few months before,
the group had shot and killed judge Gunter von Drenkmann in a bun-
gled attempt to abduct him. This time, in exchange for Lorenz, the
group demanded the release of their imprisoned comrades, albeit,
with the exception of Horst Mahler, none of those charged with murder. They realized that such demands would have minimized their
chances for success. Eventually, the state gave in and released five

prisoners – Mahler, in fact, rejected the deal – who were flown to Yemen. Sticking to their side of the bargain, the kidnappers brought Lorenz to a park in Berlin and let him go, with just enough money in his pockets to make a phone call. It was a triumph for the group, not only because their demands were met, but also because it boosted the group's reputation. A small gang of armed rebels, it seemed, had humiliated the state.[34]

For the Red Army Faction, the Lorenz abduction showed that pressure could force the state to give in. On 24 April 1975, barely two months after Lorenz had been kidnapped, the group took action. A 'Commando Holger Meins', named after the terrorist who had died on hunger strike, entered the German embassy in Stockholm, taking eleven people hostage. They also placed TNT bombs in the building, ready to go off in case of a police assault. Swedish police quickly arrived at the scene. The terrorists told them to retreat; to underline their point, they shot military attaché Andreas von Mirbach. Then they announced their demands: the release of twenty-six prisoners in Germany, including Ulrike Meinhof, Andreas Baader and Gudrun Ensslin. This time, however, German chancellor Helmut Schmidt was resolved not to yield to force. It would have been too much of an embarrassment for the state. For the kidnappers, the refusal to even negotiate came as a shock. The Swedish authorities were ready to offer safe conduct if they would release their hostages. But the terrorists refused: 'Victory or death!' To exert further pressure, they put another hostage, Heinz Hillegaart, by the window, where they shot and killed him. The police were already preparing for an assault when what was in all likelihood an accident caused the TNT to go off. One of the terrorists died immediately, another succumbed to his injuries a few days later, and the remaining three kidnappers were arrested. The attempt to free the leading members of the Red Army Faction had failed.[35]

Meanwhile, court trials against the apprehended terrorists for their various crimes proceeded. It did not look good for the defendants. Then, on 9 May 1976, Ulrike Meinhof was found dead in her prison cell. RAF supporters rejected the official statement that her death was a suicide, and claimed the state had murdered Meinhof.[36] Outside of prison, remaining members of the RAF prepared for a new wave of attacks. What came to be known as the 'offensive '77' began on 7 April 1977 with the fatal shooting of Federal Attorney General Siegfried Buback, his driver Wolfgang Göbel and judicial official Georg Wurster.[37] The next attack followed shortly afterwards, on 30 July, when three terrorists entered the home of Jürgen Ponto, chairman of the Dresdner Bank board of directors. They had planned to abduct Ponto, but when he tried to push away the gun that terrorist Christian Klar was holding, shots were fired; Ponto died two hours later in hospital.[38]

These murders were only the prelude to the group's most spectacular operation. On 5 September 1977, an RAF commando consisting of Willy Peter Stoll, Stefan Wisniewski, Sieglinde Hofmann and Peter-Jürgen Boock ambushed the motorcade of Hanns Martin Schleyer, president of the Federation of German Industries. Schleyer's driver and three police bodyguards died in the hail of bullets. At first, the attackers thought they had accidentally killed Schleyer, their target, as well, but he had survived, unharmed. They dragged him to a Volkswagen minibus and drove away. Schleyer had become a 'prisoner of the Red Army Faction'.[39]

A day later, the kidnappers made their demands known: the release of ten imprisoned RAF members, including Andreas Baader and Gudrun Ensslin, by the morning of 7 September, as well as a million German marks per RAF prisoner. But just as in April 1975, the federal government was determined to stay tough. They trusted the police to locate Schleyer and tried to gain time. But, despite all their efforts, the police could not find him.

Trying to increase the pressure, RAF members who had travelled to Baghdad negotiated with a Palestinian group for a support operation: the hijacking of a German aeroplane. In return, the German terrorists promised the Palestinians a portion of the ransom money. On 13 October 1977 – after more than a month, Schleyer was still in the hands of his abductors – four members of the Popular Front for the Liberation of Palestine hijacked Lufthansa flight 181 on its way from Palma de Mallorca to Frankfurt. After stops in Rome, Larnaca (Cyprus), Dubai and Aden (Yemen), they forced the pilots to fly to Mogadishu. The 'Commando Martyr Halimeh' declared themselves in solidarity with the RAF and added their own demands: the release of two Palestinians held in a Turkish prison and a ransom of fifteen million dollars.

Still the federal government was not willing to comply. Instead, it sent the anti-terror unit GSG9 for its first deployment to Mogadishu. A few minutes after midnight of 18 October, the unit stormed the aircraft, freeing all ninety hostages (the pilot Jürgen Schumann had been shot in Aden) and killing all but one terrorist. When the imprisoned RAF members learned about the outcome of the hijacking, they knew that chances for their release were now nil. The very same night, Andreas Baader, Gudrun Ensslin and Jan-Carl Raspe committed suicide in a high-security prison in Stammheim near Stuttgart; Irmgard Möller survived badly injured. After receiving news of their comrades' death, Schleyer's abductors executed their prisoner with a shot to the back of his head. After forty-three days, the German Autumn, as the autumn of 1977 is often called, had reached its bloody end.

In Italy, the situation for the Red Brigades looked desperate in early 1976.[40] The police had killed or arrested most members, including Margherita Cagol, who had been killed in June 1975, and Renato Curcio, arrested in January 1976.[41] The group had effectively shrunk to around ten members who remained free.[42] But the small circle of militants succeeded with an attack so dramatic that it seemed to demonstrate the strength of the Red Brigades both to the general public and to potential new recruits. On 8 June 1976, the Red Brigades assassinated the public prosecutor of Genoa, Francesco Coco, and two of his bodyguards, just as the trial against founding members of the group, including Curcio and Alberto Franceschini, was to begin in Turin.[43] The assassination was, in the words of Gian Carlo Caselli and Donatella Della Porta, a 'criminal "bet"' that aimed to relaunch the Red Brigades. And the gamble worked: the group attracted new recruits, in part from other left-wing terrorist organizations that had dissolved during 1977 amid a new wave of youth unrest (to be discussed in the following chapter).[44]

After the killings in Genoa, a cycle of escalating violence began. No longer seeking to support workers in fighting their employers, the Red Brigades instead turned against what they simply called 'the system' and its representatives. In the first instance, this meant assassinating members of the judicial system such as Fulvio Croce, president of Turin's Bar Association, and Rosario Berardi, head of Turin's political police. To instil fear among low- and mid-ranking representatives of the state, the terrorists also assaulted no less than twelve municipal and regional councillors, all belonging to Italy's conservative party, the Democrazia Cristiana, between 1977 and 1978. 'Strike one, educate a hundred', as a slogan at the time put it.[45]

The wave of terror in Italy reached its apogee in Rome on 16 March 1978. Shortly before 9 a.m., a commando of the Red Brigades stopped the car of the former prime minister and leader of Democrazia Cristiana Aldo Moro. In a fierce firefight, four of his bodyguards were killed; a fifth died later in hospital. The assailants dragged Moro, who remained unharmed, into a car waiting nearby and drove away at high speed. Moro was in the hands of the Red Brigades. The attack strikingly resembled the kidnapping of Schleyer seven months earlier in Cologne: the stopping of the car, the swift killing of the bodyguards, even the photographs the terrorists produced of their captive. Just as Hanns Martin Schleyer had to pose with a sign showing him as 'prisoner of the RAF', so did Moro with a placard saying, 'prisoner of the Red Brigades'.

Like the terrorists of the RAF, the Red Brigades requested the release of imprisoned comrades, though they first interrogated Moro at length and issued no demands until 24 April. But the Italian government, too, refused to comply and did not even pretend to negotiate with the Red Brigades, despite personal letters Moro himself wrote during his captivity imploring friends and family to secure his release. With the government not showing any inclination to give in even when a letter by an increasingly desperate Moro suggested that releasing only one imprisoned terrorist might suffice to ensure his survival, the Red Brigades decided to kill their hostage. On the morning of 9 May, an anonymous caller told Moro's friend Professor Francesco Titto that Moro's body could be found in the trunk of a car in Rome.[46]

The killings of Schleyer and Moro did not mark the end of left-wing terrorism. Throughout the 1980s and into the early 1990s, more deadly attacks occurred both in the Federal Republic and in Italy. Yet, in both countries, the abductions marked a turning point. Any sympathy felt in radical leftist scenes completely vanished. Not that leftists had uncritically supported terrorism before, but many still felt that the terrorists of the Red Army Faction and the Red Brigades were part of a common struggle.[47] At Holger Meins' funeral in November 1974, Rudi Dutschke had famously declared, his left fist raised: 'Holger, the fight goes on!' That he had also described the murder of Berlin judge Drenkmann as a 'brutal insanity' was easily missed.[48] After the events of the German Autumn and the abduction of Aldo Moro in Italy, such attitudes disappeared. Rather than building a better world, the terrorists' deadly struggle, leftists realized, merely replicated the oppressive structures of the system they tried to overcome. Whereas leftists longed for collective joy, the confrontation with the state produced only bitterness.

A 'Call to All Women for the Invention of Happiness', written in early 1978 by a group of women from Frankfurt and widely circulated in West Germany's leftist scene, made the point in no ambivalent terms. Murder and abductions were not part of their search for happiness. 'We propose that the warring parties send their lords into a duel, so that they can settle the issue among themselves. But they should finally stop bothering us with it!' In the future, they – that is, the terrorists and the state alike – would have no legitimacy to engage in their struggles in the name of 'any right that needs to be defended'. The state and the terrorists, they felt, were both 'gravediggers', and part of a world they wanted to escape from. Terrorism brought only death, while they had 'a desire for life'.[49]

This leaves us with an important question: what is the relation between the hopeful protests of 1968 and the left-wing terrorism that followed? According to some scholars and political commentators, the terrorist violence of the 1970s is the true legacy of 1968.[50] It is hard to deny that the Red Army Faction, the Red Brigades and other, smaller terrorist groups emerged out of the student movements in 1968. Renato Curcio had played a crucial role in the student movement of Trento, and Ulrike Meinhof was one of the leading voices of the radical student left before she became a terrorist. Protestors in 1968 were certainly no pacifists who abhorred violence in principle. The rhetoric of struggle against a class of capitalists, against an oppressive state and its police, usually described as 'pigs', and not least against American imperialism had been common in both the Italian and West German movements of 1968.[51] It's therefore easy to see connections between the years of protesting from 1967 to 1969 and the years of violence in 1977 and 1978. In one important way, however, terrorism marked a distinct break with these protests. Whereas the rebels of 1968 had tried to imagine an alternative future and how they might accomplish it, for the terrorists, only the fighting mattered. They longed for victory, but had no vision of the better world they would build afterwards.[52]

Militant Cultures and the Appeal of Rioting

There were red flags on some of the barricades; on one there was a sign that said: *Che cosa vogliamo: tutto* [What do we want: everything]. People kept coming from all around. You could hear a hollow noise, continuous, the drumbeat of stones rhythmically striking the electricity pylons. They made this sound, hollow, striking, continuous. The police couldn't surround and search the whole area, full of building sites, workshops, public housing, fields. People kept attacking, the whole population was fighting. Groups reorganized themselves, attacked at one point, scattered, came back to attack somewhere else. But now the thing that moves them more than rage was joy. The joy of finally being strong. Of discovering that your needs, your struggle, were everyone's needs, everyone's struggle.

They were feeling their strength, feeling there was a popular explosion all over the city. They were really feeling this unity, this force. So every rock that was hurled at the police was hurled with joy, not rage. Because in a word we were all strong.

This is how Nanni Balestrini described the famous battle at Corso Traiano in Turin on 3 July 1969 in his novel *We Want Everything*.[53] It's a very different kind of violence compared with the terrorism of the 1970s. This was an open confrontation with the police that involved thousands of workers and residents, not a well-planned abduction, bombing or assassination. The police fought back, and for many of the protestors-turned-rioters, the night was bloody, though not deadly. But nevertheless, if we are to believe Balestrini, it was a moment of exuberance, rather than rage or even hatred. Whatever terrorist violence was, those practising it certainly did not celebrate it as a source of joy.

While the battle at Corso Traiano was an extraordinary event that became legendary, street demonstrations turning into riots were nothing unusual. This form of mostly non-lethal violence has received much less attention than terrorism. It is seen, somewhat ahistorically, as just an unfortunate by-product of street protests. However, in the 1970s and 1980s, militant protest cultures developed throughout Western Europe that embraced and sometimes even celebrated violent confrontations with the police. Unlike terrorism, which many on the radical left rejected in unambiguous terms, such street violence continued to have an emotional appeal. Let's turn therefore to one of the most violent episodes of protesting in postwar Europe: the urban revolts of the early 1980s.[54]

Zurich, 30 May 1980. Protestors had gathered in front of the local opera. They were outraged that the municipal council would spend 60 million Swiss francs to renovate the opera house, but remained unwilling to fund an autonomous youth centre. It was not a large crowd, perhaps 200 people, unlikely to have any impact. But they were a nuisance for the local elites who wanted to enjoy the performance. Police decided to disperse the demonstration, and to everyone's surprise, the situation turned violent, with the audience of a Bob Marley concert on its way home joining the confrontation. A day later, thousands hit the streets, and more riots ensued. The police had lost control. City authorities were shocked: they did not expect Swiss youth to rebel in such a violent manner. It was the beginning of what came to be called a 'hot summer' of constant protests and frequent riots.[55]

The revolt was not limited to Switzerland. Already in April, squatters in Amsterdam had battled the police. In early May, a protest against a public army recruitment ceremony in Bremen had turned violent. Then half a year later, the movement reached West Berlin, where activists had read about events in Zurich and Amsterdam full of admiration. On 12 December 1980, rumours circulated in the city's leftist scene that the police had evicted squatters at Fraenkel-ufer in the neighbourhood of Kreuzberg, a stronghold of the countercultural milieu. The rumours turned out to be false (police had, in fact, prevented the squatting of an empty house), but this didn't matter much. A crowd of angry protestors rallied around Kottbusser Tor. The atmosphere was tense, ready to explode. Not after long, squatters attacked the police with stones, windows were broken, stores were vandalized; it took the police almost six hours to regain control over the area. At the end of the night, fifty-eight people had been arrested, and one individual severely injured after being run over by a police van. The riotous night sparked not only a renewed squatting movement that resulted in at least 165 squatted houses by June 1981 (to which we'll return in Chapter 10), but also a series of extremely violent confrontations.[56]

Neither in Zurich nor in West Berlin were the rioters ashamed of the violence; they celebrated it as a liberation.[57] 'Spending ten years in hiding, we've built up a nice little package of anger and frustration while constantly running up against walls,' the Zurich underground magazine *Stilett* wrote in the aftermath of the May riots. 'Nothing happened until now, Thirtieth May: holy mackerel! How the eyes were glowing, but not full of hatred, no fanaticism – no, one could feel oneself, for once . . . The long years of darkening and dulled life rhythms loosened up, like a persistent cough that finally comes rumbling from the throat. One could breathe again.'[58] In West Berlin, a reporter of the moderate left-wing daily *die tageszeitung* noted that the 'long pent-up aggression, the result of a permanent meandering between threats and negotiations, the daily needling has created a situation that nobody can control'. Within a moment of looking at the scenery around Kottbusser Tor, he felt like entering a 'different reality ... A feeling of euphoria spreads, collectivization is well under way.'[59] The riot, as an author of *radikal*, the West Berlin magazine most closely associated with the radical squatting scene, wrote, had opened a 'hole in the wall', behind which the contours of something entirely different became visible.[60]

How can we make sense of this rioting and its celebration? For once, the issues at stake were intimate and local, not distant American imperialism. The evicted squatters were being deprived of their newly found homes and the personal connections they had built there. One squatter even compared the loss of their house with the death of a good friend. Smashing windows in response to an eviction just felt 'insanely good', as another squatter put it, because every destroyed window had a personal story.[61] In part, this might explain protestors' anger and their willingness to use violence. But rioting was about more than this. For protestors who had hitherto felt impotent and 'encaged', seeing the police lose control, if only for a few hours, was a sudden and unexpected experience of empowerment. As another author for *radikal* wrote, rioting generated a 'liberating feeling when you lose your fear and fight back, and the pigs run away from you, and not the other way round'.[62] It was something utterly new: 'Nobody, including us, could imagine that this might ever happen, but it happened, like a thunderstorm on a bright day,' *Stilett* noted.[63]

Was this an attempt to change the world in a lasting way? Certainly, militants tried to establish autonomous spaces in squatted buildings and youth centres. However, this is not what mattered for those who described confrontations with the police in such exuberant terms. In Zurich, *Stilett* mocked activists who worried that violence might hurt the movement: 'It might be unreasonable to throw rocks, but, at last, STOP BEING REASONABLE, because reasonable is a word of the others', the others being anyone outside the movement, anyone normal, rational, hard-working. Instead, the magazine urged its readers to 'only act according to your feelings. And if you are feeling enough hatred, then just smash the windows of the opera house . . . plunder, pillage, but don't discuss for ever whether this is reasonable or whether it hurts the "movement".'[64]

The moment of the riot itself, not victory or defeat, mattered. 'Why would I care for risk and strategy, gains or material damages given this feeling that all the armoured might [of the police] is at the whim of my ridiculous rocks! It should go on like this for ever. It was better than any revolution,' wrote self-proclaimed street fighter Tomas Lecorte in a widely read autobiographical novel, *We Dance to the End*.[65] And for a West Berlin group calling themselves 'Fighters of the Erupting Sado-Marxist International', rioting was a joyful event where they could meet old friends, 'in short: have some fun', as they wrote after one riot that had broken out during the visit of US Secretary of State Alexander Haig in September 1981. And it *was* fun, if we are to believe the somewhat idiosyncratically written pamphlet. After breaking through police barriers, the crowd 'killed time by throwing stones and lighting joyous fires, without bosses or any prior planning'. It was 'a game for the sake of playing', to joy-fully destroy anything that made life unpleasant: 'commodities, cars, traffic, concrete, fragmented time . . . One settled the score against the accumulated grey of work and daily boredom.'[66]

This was a radical politics of the present.[67] The idea of revolution as the point 'where freedom is supposed to start' was, militants from West Berlin argued, nothing but a 'consolidation for a distant paradise, but we live here, now and today. Perhaps freedom is only the brief moment, from the point when the cobblestone is picked up until it hits, that is, the moment of change, of transgression, of movement.'[68] Only the brief moment of transgression counted;

what came after was irrelevant. After all, the prospects for the future were bleak anyway. If there was 'no future', as a popular slogan claimed, then only today mattered.[69]

Violence and the Struggle for a Better World

It would be easy to dismiss such rhetoric as a mere mystification of violence akin to what terrorists said.[70] But rioting clearly had a profound appeal. Events like those of 30 May 1980 in Zurich or 12 December 1980 in Berlin became legendary in protest scenes for a reason.[71] In those moments, when the established order seemed to briefly dissolve, militants experienced a strength that contrasted with their usual sense of impotence; they gained a sense of community and overcame feelings of isolation. This is also what distinguished the rioting in the streets from deadly terrorist violence. Though terrorists emphasized the struggle, their struggle was anything but joyous. It required a lonely life in hiding that usually ended with imprisonment or a violent death. Terrorists didn't offer a 'better life', neither in the here and now, nor in some distant future; all they had to offer was fighting and dying.

Today, the deadly violence of left-wing terrorism has largely disappeared, and there is no sign that it will return, despite claims to the contrary by fear-mongering right-wing politicians (indeed, racist far-right violence has cost far more lives than left-wing terrorism in recent years). And protests-turned-riots, though they still occur, tend to be less intense, not least because the police are able to contain them more effectively due to both better equipment and smarter tactics. There are, of course, exceptions, such as the extremely violent protests against the G8 summit in Genoa in the summer of 2001 that resulted in the death of a young activist, but there has been a wider cultural shift.[72] By and large, violent protesting has been discredited, even among protesters themselves.

Mocking the Authorities: The Subversive Power of Laughter

West Berlin, summer 1981. It was the heyday of the squatting movement. For the last six months, squatters had regularly taken to the streets and engaged in bloody battles with the police. One hot day, it looked like another riot was about to start. Both protestors and the police had prepared for battle, the protestors with their black leather jackets, some even wearing helmets, the police in full riot gear. Everyone was sweating in the sun. But the battle didn't happen. The protestors had something else in mind. When they passed Lake Halensee, they undressed and went for a swim, most of them butt naked. The police, still in riot gear and still sweating, could only stand and watch. Clearly, the protestors had more fun that summer day. And more than that, they also made the police look a little ridiculous. It was a playful, non-violent way of disrupting order and defying expectations.[1]

A former squatter once told me this anecdote, with a huge smile on his face. His story points to a different way of challenging authorities: not through violent action, but by mockery – though the boundaries were by no means always clear, as some of those making fun of the police were equally happy to throw rocks at them in another situation. Humour is, of course, not a new tactic. Jokes about those in power, satire and carnivalesque performances have been part of the repertoire of collective action for a long time. In the protest movements that developed since the 1960s, ridicule gained new prominence – as we have already seen, with the Amsterdam Provos and their white chicken.

At first glance, it might seem as if such humorous activism was just that: a joke, without any real impact on politics and society. It

86

certainly didn't constitute a lethal threat as terrorism did. No surprise, perhaps, that scholars have paid much less attention to skinny
dipping than to the Years of Lead.[2] Yet such a perspective underesti-
mates the power of humour. The 'fun guerrillas', as a West Berlin
book from 1984 called those humorous activists, could tear down
the façade of authority and unmask its empty rituals.[3] They helped
ordinary citizens to overcome their fear of the police by making
them look ridiculous rather than threatening. In times that seemed
dull and hopeless, their joyful happenings offered brief, happy
moments of respite.

Staging a Media Spectacle: Kommune 1 in West Berlin

By late 1966, protests against the Vietnam War were frequently
attracting hundreds of students in West Berlin. On 10 December,
2,000 protestors turned out, but as they marched along rather empty
streets, barely anyone took notice. Such a demonstration, some felt,
would not achieve anything. Looking for a different way of protesting, about 200 radicals went to the central shopping street
Kurfürstendamm, where they walked among Christmas shoppers.
'Christmas wishes coming true, US bombs are brought to you,'
they chanted. They engaged in discussions with the shoppers, only
to disperse when the police approached. That afternoon, the police
arrested eighty-six people, mostly innocent bystanders who, facing
police violence themselves, took the side of the protesting students.
For Dieter Kunzelmann, *spiritus rector* of the group Subversive
Aktion, the 'walkabout demonstration' was a success. And it was
about more than raising awareness of US atrocities in Vietnam. The
tactic, the group argued in a leaflet calling for another walkabout
demonstration the following Saturday, 'seeks to deride the petrified
legality'. Provoking the authorities into taking drastic action without
distinguishing between actual protestors and harmless Christmas
shoppers would make the police look like fools, while radical students
felt energized by overstepping the boundaries of the legal order.[4]

Around the same time, the circle around Kunzelmann began discussing plans for a revolutionary commune. Living collectively, they believed, would allow them to radically transform everyday life, notably by overcoming the constraints of the conventional bourgeois family. And it would provide the basis for continuous subversive activism. In February 1967, after weeks of discussions, the group was ready: nine communards, including Kunzelmann and Fritz Teufel, moved into three different apartments in Berlin Friedenau; a month later, young radical Rainer Langhans joined too. Kommune I was born.[5]

At first, the communards spent hours discussing their upbringing, the emotional and sexual problems it had caused, and the personal relations within the commune. But some communards felt this endless soul-searching didn't lead anywhere except frustration. The solution to their internal problems, they argued, was collective activism, which might in turn help them deal with their emotional issues. After all, being arrested during a protest had made communard Dagrun Enzensberger realize, or so she claimed, the absurdity of her fears.[6]

Thus, the group began planning a spectacular protest against US Vice President Hubert H. Humphrey, an ardent supporter of the Vietnam War and hence an ideal target. He was scheduled to visit Berlin on 6 April 1967. 'Laughter must be on our side,' communard Hans-Joachim Hameister summarized the group's fundamental principle.[7] They considered various ideas, involving the use of crow's-feet to stop the motorcade or doing something with a fire extinguisher. Ultimately, the group settled on constructing smoke bombs to bring the motorcade to a halt, and then attacking Humphrey with flour, custard and high-jumping rubber balls. With the help of a chemistry student, they bought the ingredients for the smoke bombs. But then, on 5 April 1967, police arrested the entire group. In a bizarre coincidence, utterly unrelated to the group's activities, Western secret services had tapped the telephone line of one of their apartments, because Elisabeth Johnson, wife of German author Uwe Johnson, who owned the apartment, had once worked for the Czechoslovak secret service. According to most accounts, though details remain unclear and unconfirmed, Western services informed the German police about the group's plans to purchase chemicals that could be used to build a bomb. Just three and a half years after the shooting of John F. Kennedy, the prospect of an attack on an American politician in West Berlin called for swift action.[8]

The arrests and the subsequent press coverage were the best thing that could have happened to the communards. The next morning, the tabloid *Berliner Morgenpost* ran the headline: 'Police thwarts attack on Humphrey – Free University Students prepare bombs using explosives from Beijing'. Another tabloid, *Der Abend*, had: 'Mao's embassy in East Berlin provided the bombs against Vice President Humphrey.'[9] Kunzelmann and his comrades were charged with preparing a potentially deadly bomb, but once a technician had analysed the confiscated chemicals, the police quickly had to release the alleged terrorists.[10] Two days later, the communards held a press conference presenting their weapons: pudding powder and flour. The next day, they even took the press to Grunewald, where some of them had been arrested while practising how to throw the smoke bombs; now, they re-enacted their exercises for a television crew. Overnight, Kommune 1 had gained fame in West Germany's media. And laughter *was* on their side, at least for now.[11]

The commune's newly won fame also got them kicked out of their apartments in Friedenau, as their landlords realized who their tenants were. But the group were lucky. In May 1967, the communards found a new home in Charlottenburg near Stuttgarter Platz (ironically owned by a high-ranking judge, according to the lease as 'a boarding house', meaning a brothel).[12] Finally, they could all live together.

In their new domicile, the group's weapon of choice became pamphlets ridiculing the authorities and above all the tabloid press. We have already encountered scandalous 'burn ware-house burn' pamphlet in the context of emerging terrorism (see Chapter 3). In fact, it was part of a small series of leaflets all sardonically address-ing the deadly fire in Brussels. In another pamphlet, they depicted the catastrophe as a 'new' and 'unconventional' American advertise-ment gag, never seen before in a European city: 'A burning department store, full of burning people, conveyed a real sense of the sizzling Vietnam feeling (being there and being on fire) that we in Berlin have missed so far.' The final leaflet consisted of surreal and suggestive sentences arranged in a spiral: 'Revolution in rosé / revolution in red / through blazing red furs fly into the street / a mink for every housewife in Brussels . . .'[13]

Once again, it was the authorities' reaction to the pamphlets that ensured their success. The state attorney charged the pamphlet's authors, Fritz Teufel and Rainer Langhans, with 'public incitement for arson endangering human life'. On 6 July 1967, they had their first day in court. Understanding the theatricality of such trials, Langhans and Teufel turned the proceedings into a huge show: the 'Moabit Soap Opera', as the two defendants called their trial in ref-erence to the district where the court was located. The minutes of the proceedings (or at least the defendants' version), published by Langhans and Teufel in a small book tellingly called *Klau mich* (Steal Me), became legendary in the West German left. They provide a vivid account of how they made fun of the court. Apparently, both the judge and the state attorney had great difficulties dealing with the defendants, who didn't take their situation very seriously:[14]

State Attorney Kuntze: 'And what if someone had considered fol-lowing the pamphlets' advice, lighting a cigarette in a changing room of a department store?'
Teufel: 'I have to say, nobody considered really doing this – except for the state attorney. But he didn't do it either, and wrote an indict-ment instead.[15]

Though ostensibly the case dealt with the pamphlets, the polit-ical project of the commune was on trial as well. What did Langhans mean when he mentioned 'sexual difficulties' the commune wanted to address, Judge Schwerdtner enquired. 'It doesn't merely concern members of the commune,' Langhans explained, 'but you as well, it's not limited. It concerns everyone among us, that's a result of our upbringing: how to deal with girls, orgasm problems, attentiveness disorders and neuroses, the difficulty of dealing with oneself and others.' And how did such difficulties manifest themselves? Schwerdtner wondered. 'Can't you imagine that? Or don't you have any? That would be surprising.' The minutes in *Klau mich* note: 'The chairman turns pale and swallows.'[16]

What could the court do with these colourfully dressed defendants? (An officer of the court once tried to stop Langhans from entering the court because of his attire, until Langhans pointed out that he was the one on trial.) They seemed crazy. It was only logical that the court decided to have them psychologically evaluated. Their lawyer, future Red Army Faction member Horst Mahler, argued against such an evaluation, but Fritz Teufel said he consented – 'if the members of the court and the state attorney equally agree to being evaluated'. The audience applauded enthusiastically, until Schwerdtner had the courtroom cleared. Despite their protests, the court ruled to have Teufel and Langhans examined, and adjourned until March 1968.[17]

When the trial resumed, not much had changed. The defendants disrespected the court and made fun of the judge, who responded by excluding Teufel from the proceedings and imposed administrative penalties that put both Teufel and Langhans behind bars. Once, Langhans even yelled at the judge after being interrupted: 'I can't finish a single sentence without being interrupted. Now keep quiet until I'm finished.'[18] They happily admitted that they considered the entire trial an absurdity, and were treating it as such. That the judiciary hadn't been capable of grasping the pamphlets' satirical content, though, was no surprise, Teufel declared. Still, they found the indictment hilarious and such a great work of satire that they reprinted it themselves. Teufel offered to sell one to the judge for two marks.[19] Eventually, even Judge Schwerdtner showed a sense of humour. When Teufel asked him about the relevance of a particular witness, Schwerdtner replied that they had called them 'just for fun'.

> Teufel: 'This should be recorded.'
>
> Schwerdtner: 'That was satire! I thought you were a specialist?'
>
> Teufel: 'That's news to me, that you know something about that [satire]. It would be the first time that you've learned something from us.'
>
> Schwerdtner: 'For the record: the defendant says, the presiding judge has for the first time learned something.'[20]

But above all, it was the expert opinion by Obermedizinalrat (a title that probably exists only in German, meaning roughly senior medical officer) Dr Spengler that ensured the second act of Moabit's soap opera a lasting place in the 'annals of real satire'.[21] Based purely on observations of Teufel's and Langhans's demeanour in court, Spengler diagnosed a 'pathological personality', though without questioning their legal culpability.

It was up to Rainer Langhans to deliver closing remarks. He used the opportunity to analyse the trial from the defendants' perspective. To him, it felt like a 'puppet show', with all participants acting like marionettes: the state attorney, the defendants' attorneys and above all the presiding judge. During the trial, Langhans observed, he looked serious and powerful with his robe and thick books, quite literally sitting above the defendants. But when they met him after the proceedings on the floor, in his everyday clothes, he looked very ordinary, a 'small man with huge ears, and he was jumpy. You feel deceived.' They, the defendants, felt like spectators of an absurd play. They had seized the opportunity to become the play's directors. Still, the show had turned somewhat boring, 'sitting here and ridiculing the same people over and over'. Now, there were two options: acquittal, which he thought likely, or conviction. If they were acquitted, it would be difficult to justify the expense to taxpayers, not least because the public couldn't even enjoy the play. A conviction, though, would be even more absurd. 'We are curious to see what happens next, and we say thanks for the play,' he concluded. On 22 March 1968, the court acquitted Langhans and Teufel.[22]

By then, however, the commune was slowly disintegrating. As the student movement reached its violent apogee with the attack on Rudi Dutschke and the Easter Riots of 1968 which followed, some communards, including Teufel and Kunzelmann, turned to violence themselves. At the same time, the commune's fame resulted in fans from all over West Germany writing and visiting them. They became 'pop icons', as Kunzelmann's biographer Aribert Reimann notes, but not so much for their activism as for the 'cultural revolution' that was supposedly happening within the commune itself. By the end of 1969, Kommune 1 was history.[23] For Kunzelmann and Teufel, peacefully mocking authorities was no longer enough. They joined armed groups and spent time in prison, though they never became high-profile terrorists. In the meantime, Langhans turned to spiritualism and became a media star. The group's fame, however, lasted. The Moabit Soap Opera made Kommune 1 a legend among West Germany's radical left. They continue to be a source of inspiration for 'fun guerrillas'.[24]

Semiological Guerrillas: Metropolitan Indians and Radio Alice in Italy

Rome, 17 February 1977. For several weeks, the Italian capital had seen demonstrations and violent clashes between neo-fascists, leftist students and the police: On 1 February, a group of armed fascists had assaulted students at the university. A protest march by the left the following day had ended with an attack on the nearby headquarters of the fascist Movimento Sociale Italiano, which had been burned down, and a shoot-out with the police during which an officer and two students had been seriously injured. More demonstrations and counter-demonstrations had followed, while students had proceeded to occupy the University of Rome. On 15 February, members of the Communist Party – which was hostile to the independent leftist movement and called for 'the resumption of didactic and scientific activity' – had entered the occupied campus. They had proposed a public meeting two days later, where communist union leader Luciano Lama, a supporter of the government's austerity politics (following the Communist Party's 'historic compromise' with the governing Democrazia Cristiana), would speak. Though hostile to the Communist Party, the students had decided to allow him to speak and avoid using physical force; they wanted to defeat him by 'political means'.

The communist union hoped to restore order at the university. Several hundred cadres of its Servizio d'Ordine, mobilized at short notice, were told that they would liberate the campus from fascists. On the morning of 17 February, communist cadres proceeded to remove posters and graffiti mocking Lama: *I lama stanno nel Tibet* (The Lamas remain in Tibet). Then Lama finally spoke from the back of a lorry, surrounded by the union cadres, hoping to bring the rebellious students to reason. He faced a hostile crowd of more than 10,000, among them a group by the name of Indiani Metropolitani (the Metropolitan Indians). They had their faces painted for battle (like the Native American 'Indians' in popular western movies at the time), they were colourfully dressed and armed with plastic tomahawks and confetti. On the steps of the library, the Indiani had mounted a dummy of Lama. As he began his speech, they responded by chanting: 'L'ama o non L'ama? Non L'ama più nessuno' (Does anyone love him or not? Nobody loves him any more), a playful mockery of Lama's name. Another chant started up: 'Attenti: i Lama sputano' (Careful, Lamas spit). Then they sang, to the melody of 'Jesus Christ Superstar': 'Lama star, Lama star, we want to make sacrifices', an allusion to the austerity policies.

The teasing was too much for the communists. A melee ensued. The Indiani threw plastic bags filled with water at the communists, who responded with fire extinguishers. Ultimately, the Indiani and more militant occupiers of the university chased the communists from campus. The Indiani chanted: 'Please Lama, don't leave, we want more police.' But, as Maurizio Torrealta emphasizes, 'they do not take over the platform on the truck, and they do not seize the microphone'.[25] They ousted the famous communist speaker, but they didn't seek to replace him.[26]

The Indiani were part of a wave of leftist activism simply called the Movement of '77.[27] Like Kommune 1, the movement was known for its ironic and satirical forms of activism. Its origins can be traced to the mid-1970s, when groups of working-class teenagers known as Circoli del Proletariato Giovanile (Circles of Young Proletarians) struggled for a better life in a most direct way. Under the slogan 'stare insieme', meaning 'being together', they squatted empty buildings and established *Centri Sociale* where they could hang out, discuss and have fun at festivals – they could simply 'be together'. Drawing on practices of 'self-reduction' developed in 1968/9, they ate at expensive restaurants and went to cinemas without paying, took food from supermarkets ('proletarian shopping', as it was called), and famously stormed the Umbria Jazz festival in 1975, demanding free access and being treated as active participants rather than a passively consuming audience.[28]

At its heart, the movement was an attack on standard forms of political communication. The Indiani refused to engage in any meaningful debate, and instead made fun of leaders like Lama as well as any other organized political group. Take the opening statement of Olivier Turquet, wearing a 'top hat and theatrical make-up', at a press conference in 1977: 'My name is Gandalf the Violet' – violet being a colour that distinguished the movement from the red of the communist left, the black of anarchism and pink used by feminists at the time. 'I shall speak in a strictly personal capacity. As such, I speak in the name of the Elves of Fangorn Forest, the Coloured Nuclei of Red Laughter, the Absent Phantom Political Movement, the Dada-Hedonist Cells, Worker's Joy and Student Rejoicing, the Schizophrenic International, the Disturbed Clandestine Nuclei, the Chicory Tribe, the Cimbles and all the Metropolitan Indians', deftly skewering the names of leftist groups in Italy.[29]

The Indiani became famous for transforming protests into joyful and absurd happenings. Dressed up as Native Americans, carrying plastic weapons, playing music and dancing, they chanted slogans whose meaning was difficult to decipher: *eah, eah, eah, eah, eah eh-eh!* (an attempt to emulate what they took for Native American war chants, which would be considered racist today, but was not seen as problematic in the 1970s).[30] Equally playful were their graffiti and murals that appeared throughout Italian cities.[31] Some of them conveyed a distinct political message: one demanded zero work for full pay, and that all production should be automated. Others altered existing graffiti: the acronym *Fuan*, standing for a fascist student union, was turned into 'Va Fuan c . . .', meaning 'Lick my ass'. Someone came along after this and added: 'You should feel ashamed, children are reading this'; and a fourth person retorted: 'Buoni, i bambini' (Good children!). And finally, some graffiti were entirely self-referential: 'Questa scritta è bleu' (This inscription is blue); 'Voglio fare una scritta' ('I want to write something'); and some simply played with the meaning of words: 'dopo Marx, Aprile' and 'dopo Mao, Giugno' ('after Marx, April', 'after Mao, June'). As Klemens Gruber writes, such graffiti aimed at 'destroying the very order of signs'.[32]

Like the Frankfurt women calling for the invention of happiness, the Indiani promoted a politics of joy. In a 'verbal reversal', they replaced 'power', a key term for groups like Potere Operaio (Workers' Power), with 'enjoyment', *godere* instead of *potere*.[33] 'For a long time, we've danced around the totem of our insanity. We've danced and played around the fire of our humanity,' the *Declaration of War by Rome's Metropolitan Indians* read. The time of dancing in the rain was over; it was time for war (though, the Indiani never engaged in real violence).

The blue coats [in Italy, the police had blue uniforms] have destroyed everything that once was alive, they have smothered the breath of nature with steel and concrete. They have created a desert of death and called it 'progress'. But the people of humanity [Popolo degli Uomini] has rediscovered itself, its strength, its imagination and its will to victory, and louder than ever does it scream, full of joy and despair, of love and hatred: war!!![34]

Their demands were simultaneously highly pragmatic and absurd. They joined the Young Proletarians in calling for the state to provide empty buildings that teenagers could use as 'communication centres'. Here, teenagers might live a different life, away from parental authority. But they also demanded that 'youthful laziness' should be paid for, that any child able to escape from home, 'even crawling on all fours', should be declared legally mature, that imprisoned animals should be released, and zoos closed. Such demands set the Indiani apart from the Red Brigades and other terrorist groups engaged in a deadly struggle against the Italian state. Though they called for 'war', the Indiani did not seek death, but happiness, silliness and creative life.[35]

Making sense of the Indiani Metropolitani, their slogans and graffiti is difficult; after all, the very point of their absurd language was to defy meaning. How can this be a form of politics? In an article about the 'new barbarians' and their language, published in April 1977, writer Umberto Eco told a short fable to illustrate what was happening to academic researchers trying to understand the Indiani.

An American businessman, in reality of course a CIA agent, travels through space to visit faraway planets, hoping to build low-cost production centres for a future colonial expansion. The businessman is an expert in linguistics. He doesn't speak the language of the natives he encounters, and hence has to decipher their codes by observation. But one day, he reaches a planet where his well-established methods don't work. He learns their grammatical rules, he communicates with the natives, and finally he offers a contract. But when the contract is about to be signed, the natives ask him questions that don't make sense to him. Confused, the businessman studies their language again, finds new communicative codes and develops a new model; only to fail again. Finally, he realizes that he has encountered a civilization that is able to completely rearrange its communicative rules overnight. Frustrated, he returns home. The planet remains unconquered.[36]

Eco's tale points to the importance of language as the instrument of social order and governance. As much as a protest or demonstration might challenge the status quo, it also confirms it, precisely because demonstrations are an accepted way of expressing political opinions. There are certain expectations as to how a protest should look: protestors should carry banners and chant slogans with meaningful political messages. Even engaging in violence and breaking the law can be part of these informal rules of protest. After all, the police know how to respond. By making fun of authorities such as union leader Lama, dancing in the streets and chanting absurd slogans, however, the Indiani refused to play by the rules. Just like the inhabitants of the fictional planet (and Kommune 1 in the courtroom), they tried to remain ungovernable by refusing to engage in meaningful dialogue with politicians, journalists or academics.

Already a decade earlier, Eco had published a famous article that called for a 'semiological guerrilla'.[37] In the age of mass media, taking control of those media, of radio and TV stations, seemed vital for political power. Whoever was in control of the technical means and the message that was conveyed would stand a good chance of also being in control of governing institutions. This might be true with regard to political power, Eco argued, but it would not help liberate the people. After all, and this was Eco's crucial point, being in control of the message does not mean being in control of the reception of that message. For example, a banker in Milan watching a TV advertisement for a new fridge might react as the company had intended and consider buying the fridge. A landless rural worker in Calabria, by contrast, might view the same ad as an indictment of a world of consumption that remained out of reach for him. The task for a 'semiological guerrilla' was, argued Eco, to intervene at the point of reception, to produce misunderstandings of the original, intended message and thereby disrupt codes of communication.

In the mid-1970s, Eco's vision of the semiological guerrilla inspired Italian militants, most prominently the collective A/traverso from

Bologna. They summarized their programme as 'Mao plus Dada'. It was equally a mockery of the turn to Maoism among radical leftists across Western Europe, and an attempt to reconnect to artistic traditions from the early twentieth century that tried to overcome the distinction between art and everyday life.[38] Yet, unlike the original Dadaists, A/traverso did not look for radical change in art, but in language. They argued against viewing language as a neutral instrument for conveying information about a truth existing outside of language. Thus, they considered language not merely a means, but 'a practice, an absolutely material terrain that modifies reality, the balance of power between the classes, the forms of interpersonal relations, the conditions of the struggle for power'. In the struggle against 'codified language', it was not enough to insert 'new content into old models of communication'; instead, they wanted to smuggle 'a subversive desire into the organization of everyday communication'.[39]

Ironically, it was a court ruling that allowed the group to put these abstract ideas into practice. In 1975, the highest Italian court ruled the state's monopoly on radio stations unconstitutional. In the aftermath, a plethora of independent local radio stations formed, often with affiliations to radical and countercultural scenes. The militants of A/Traverso saw an opportunity. For a cheap price, they bought radio equipment and set up a studio in an apartment at Via Pratello 41, in the midst of the old Bolognese neighbourhood of Pradel.[40] On 9 February 1976, they went on air: Radio Alice (a homage to Lewis Carroll) was born. At 6.30 a.m., a female voice, with Indian music in the background, wished their listeners good morning. 'This is an invitation not to get up this morning, to stay in bed with someone, to build musical instruments and war machines.'[41] What was this supposed to mean, building war machines? (It was an allusion to the book *Rhizome* written by Gilles Deleuze and Félix Guattari, but this didn't make the invitation any less obscure.)

Radio Alice was an attempt to radically break with the usual mode of operation of radio stations. The unpaid staff worked with cheap equipment and avoided the common division of labour. They didn't have a well-organized programme either; what happened depended on who showed up at Via Pratello 41. There was space for realizing spontaneous ideas, but equally, it wasn't a problem either if someone put on a song and then went for a walk, and the radio remained silent for two minutes because they didn't come back in time. And if there was a programme scheduled for a particular time, it could easily be rescheduled if the presenter had missed the bus.[42]

The most radical innovation, however, was how the radio-makers interacted with their audience. A test show announced:

> Radio Alice broadcasts: music, news, flower gardens, rants, inventions, discoveries, recipes, horoscopes, magic filters, love, bulletins of war, photos, messages, messages, lies . . . Radio Alice broadcasts all sorts of things: whatever you want, whatever you don't want, whatever you think and whatever you think to think, especially if you come over and say it here or give us a call under the following number: 66 or 271428 or 80 and so on, in the heart of Bologna.[43]

The last bit was the crucial invention. Listeners could simply ring Radio Alice and say whatever they wanted. It was an attempt to radically democratize the radio and make it the 'voice of the excluded'. The distinction between sender and recipient of a message became meaningless. In the words of an advertisement for Radio Alice: 'Let's broadcast to ourselves' ('trasmettiamoci addosso').[44]

The result was a 'communicative delirium'.[45] State regulations restricted the reach of local radio stations to a radius of fifteen kilometres, but Radio Alice turned this limitation into an advantage by focusing on local issues, attracting an average of 30,000 daily listeners (in a city of nearly half a million).[46] Klemens Gruber describes a situation that was, he claims, common in Bologna in those days: someone comes with a small transistor radio to a *piazza* and sits down in front of a bar. He puts the radio down, perhaps scribbles *Radio Alice* on a piece of paper, sticks it on the antenna and tunes in.

Quickly, other people stop, start listening: 'So, that's Radio Alice!' Soon, there are two dozen people, carefully listening, as if something big had happened: perhaps a king has died, or a war broke out, or maybe wages had been doubled. They laugh, they discuss, and then someone there calls Radio Alice, 'because he wants to test the thing himself'.[47]

And indeed, people frequently came to the offices or called, from home or a public phone booth. Incoming calls were put on air straight away, with no prior vetting. 'We are female workers during a two-hour strike, we want you to broadcast music for us, and we want to talk about the thirty-five-hour week, it's time for this to be discussed in collective bargaining,' one caller said. Next call: 'Dirty communists, we're going to make you pay dearly for this radio station, we know who you are.' And the one after: 'We are from the antifascist committee of the Rizzoli hospital, don't worry and call us, if something happens, we are here, day and night.' The best call was someone who didn't say a word, just played the saxophone for a couple of minutes.[48]

The lack of structure brought a confusing plethora of topics on air, ranging from topical news to discussions about 'other potential worlds', from shows about Sardinian music to interviews with workers on strike. Someone read passages from Roland Barthes' *The Pleasure of the Text*, then another caller rang to say: 'Someone stole my bike, can you please say on air that he's a son of a bitch.' Listeners could learn about up-to-date drug prices, about a study of the Bologna dialect and about sexuality, a topic addressed without any of the usual taboos.[49] A small army of amateur reporters took portable tape recorders around the city to record social conflicts, like the police shutting down the small and informal 'red markets'. They recorded 'the pigs' yelling at 'comrades and housewives', but also the women demanding the closure of supermarkets, where the meat cost nearly twice as much.[50]

Did Radio Alice accomplish anything with its anarchic broadcasts? What did the radio activists actually want? Radio Alice's response: 'Blowing up the dictatorship of meaning, introducing delirium into the order of communication, making desire, rage, madness, impatience and refusal speak. This form of linguistic practice is the only adequate form of a comprehensive practice that blasts the dictatorship of the political . . .'[51] If that sounds obscure, then that was exactly the point. Did it work? All we can say is that Radio Alice had a tremendous appeal, in Bologna, in Italy and within the radical left in Western Europe. For the authorities, Radio Alice became a threat. After Francesco Lorusso, a militant member of Lotta Continua, was killed by the police on 11 March 1977, left-wing and conservative students clashed at the university.[52] Police then entered the area, beating students who responded by throwing rocks and Molotov cocktails. Radio Alice reported live on the events, calling militants to the scene, denouncing police violence and even coordinating the actions of the protestors. In the aftermath, police shut down Radio Alice, destroyed its equipment and arrested its staff.[53]

The Revolution of Dwarves: Orange Alternative in Poland

Łódź, Poland, sometimes in the early autumn of 1982. One evening, two young men called Waldemar Fydrych, known as Major, and Piotr Adamcio, known as Lieutenant Pablo, wandered around the city. They looked out for patches of fresh paint on the buildings, newly blank walls where members of the militia or hired hands had painted over anti-government graffiti. The country had just seen a massive strike movement, led by the independent trade union Solidarność against the communist regime. After the government had initially seemed to retreat, General Wojciech Jaruzelski had declared martial law on 13 December 1981. Three days later, police had shot at striking workers at the Wujek coal mine, killing nine; the following day, another protestor was killed in Gdansk. By the autumn of 1982, the movement was crippled. But the fresh patches of white on the walls reminded Poles of what had happened.[54]

That night, however, the two young men were not interested in slogans. They were painting little red dwarves on the walls of Łódź, a hundred of them. When they saw a large grey building with lots of available walls, they were thrilled and got to work immediately. Just as they were finishing up, a tall man approached them from behind. His uniform identified him as a member of the militia, as the country's main police force was commonly known. 'What are you doing?' the officer asked. 'We're painting,' the young men replied. 'What?' – 'A pompom with a hat.' – 'Do you have permission?' – 'Yes.' The answer astonished the militiaman. They clarified: 'From God.' That was enough. The painters would have to talk to the officer's superior. When he pointed to a door, it dawned on them that the large grey building was the militia's school for officer cadets.

After a brief interrogation, the two men were driven to the secret police, who would take over the investigation. An agent asked what they were doing. 'Don't you know?' Fydrych replied. 'No, I don't.' This time, the agent was shouting. There was a pause. 'I was painting a dwarf,' said Fydrych. Probably feeling that Fydrych was making fun of him, the officer threatened to have the militia beat him up. But Fydrych was not easily intimidated. 'Please don't talk like that to me, I'm a citizen.' What was the deal with these dwarves, the agent wanted to know. He was getting impatient. 'I'll tell you under one condition,' declared Fydrych: that the agent must keep it a secret. The agent agreed. Fydrych began to whisper; it was, after all, a secret. '*I want a revolution, a revolution of dwarves. It's a great secret.*' The agent wanted to make notes, but 'it was as if his ballpoint pen had begun to burn in his hand.' Instead, he asked Fydrych to draw a dwarf. The next day, both Fydrych and his comrade were released. A revolution of dwarves, that was just absurd. (That, at least, is how Fydrych himself tells the story in his autobiography.)[55]

It was not the first time that Fydrych, born in 1953, had challenged authorities by mocking them. At school, he had founded a 'secret organization', the 'Union of Bacchus'. According to his autobiography, the school functioned like a 'military camp', with strict dress codes; teachers even measured hair length. Fydrych developed a rebellious plan: he and his co-conspirators in the Union of Bacchus would all shave their heads to undermine the authority of the headmaster, the school and ultimately the entire educational system: 'a revolution of baldies'. But the plan did not work. His teachers treated him with politeness, and Fydrych ended up alone: his comrades had 'come to their senses' and kept their hair. 'You failed,' the headmaster told him. 'It isn't so easy to bring down a school. You're out of luck.'[56]

At university, first in Toruń, then in Wrocław, Fydrych became involved in the alternative student scene. They listened to bands such as the Plastic People of the Universe from Czechoslovakia (see Chapter 6), smoked weed and grew their hair and beards long. Their opposition was as much cultural as it was political. Within the student milieu, their anarchic and unconventional lifestyle brought them fame, but also hostility.[57] When students occupied the university during the strikes of 1980/81, the circle around Fydrych distributed a magazine called *Orange Alternative*, with the telling motto 'All Proletarians, Be Beautiful!' The magazine became the voice of the New Culture Movement. 'Kill reason! . . . Imagination lives in us, as long as it's free,' the manifesto announced.[58] For Fydrych and his friends, the liberated university was a 'revolution of imagination', disturbing 'the symmetry of bureaucratic life with its dogmas and institutionalized truths . . . The free university', they wrote, 'is the most wonderful game with plenty of ciuciubabcias [a word that doesn't exist in Polish, though Google Translate says it means "kisses" in Corsican, which would be a most fitting coincidence!] with thousands of old, sleeping bears and a waiting carousel.'[59] Employing a playful and non-sensical language reminiscent of the Situationist International and May '68 in Paris, they wanted to turn the university into a playground. One morning, Fydrych welcomed the militiamen who regularly came to campus to tear down banners and posters with a megaphone, instructing them: 'Put up the ladder! Climb up the ladder! Tear down posters!' Meanwhile, other members of the group with self-made helmets were standing at windows, taking photos and singing the Internationale. According to Fydrych, the militiamen then retreated.[60]

Not all students on strike were happy about the group's actions. Concerned about the humorous nature of *Orange Alternative*, the strike committee sought to intervene and banned the magazine's distribution on campus. It wasn't sufficiently serious for the struggle against the dictatorship, the committee felt. But when it transpired that the paper would be printed anyway, a compromise was agreed upon: before publication, the magazine would be subject to censorship (and the first thing one of the student censors did, Fydrych reports, was ask for weed). Realizing the absurdity of the situation, Fydrych asked the strike committee for a written summary. The committee obliged. 'The Strike Committee, bearing in mind the higher virtues of the strike, forbids the newspaper of the New Culture Movement to be published while the strike is still on. UKS [the University Strike Committee] also prohibits meetings of the New Culture Movement members with workers in the factories.' The next issue of *Orange Alternative* printed the entire decree on its front page. The state was not the only authority to be mocked.[61]

With the strike movement crushed by martial law, the New Culture Movement was also running out of steam by early 1982. This was when Fydrych developed the idea of painting little red dwarves on the walls to beautify the city. 'If a million dwarves get painted on a million walls, people will find strength and the government will fall,' he predicted grandly. And eventually, the paintings of dwarves on the walls would turn into 'armies of dwarves [that] will appear on the streets. There'll be the dwarves and the militia. The general [Jaruzelski] will surrender. If not to the cardinal, then he'll come out with a white flag and surrender to the dwarves.'[62]

It would take a few years for his prediction to become reality. By the mid-1980s, members of the Orange Alternative, as the group came to be known, began staging small happenings in the streets of Wrocław.[63] Those were boring times in Poland, Fydrych recalls, and hence any spectacle was likely to receive attention. For example, they gathered in the city centre with coloured tubes, lit them and disappeared before the militia could arrest them. It was fun to watch, but no major event.[64]

Then, Fydrych decided to return to his idea about red dwarves. He would literally create an army of dwarves. With the support of fellow students, he started producing little red paper hats they planned to distribute in the streets. A day was set to bring the army of dwarves to life: 1 June 1987, at 3 p.m., in central Wrocław. The group made posters, put them up in the streets and encouraged people to come. When authorities became aware, they stationed a police van nearby; a mistake that only attracted more people even before the actual event.[65]

While the officers were sitting in their van, burning under the summer sun, the members of Orange Alternative arrived, all wearing their red paper hats. They handed them out to passers-by, while Fydrych's comrade Krzysztof Jakubczak played the guitar. As he sang children's songs, people started dancing in the streets. A group of female high-school students, too, distributed hats and auctioned off supposedly enchanted objects. But then, officers of the militia arrested Fydrych and some fellow members of Orange Alternative. The crowd did not appreciate this intervention. People surrounded the van in which Fydrych and his comrades had been taken. Someone opened the door, Fydrych jumped out and threw candy into the air. Officers caught him and pushed him back inside. It was a cheerful atmosphere. 'Anyone who doesn't take off their special hat must show their ID papers,' an officer announced via megaphone. The crowd roared with laughter. 'Mum, why are they arresting the dwarves?' asked a child. 'Because dwarves belong to capitalism, and not to socialism,' the mum replied.

In the van, Fydrych could listen in to the militia's radio. Headquarters radioed in, asking whom they had arrested. 'They're dwarves.' – 'What?' – 'You know, dwarves. It's all right, we're arresting them.' 'Have you been drinking?' headquarters enquired. 'No, sir, we haven't touched a drop.' The officer clarified that they were students, dressed as dwarves. 'So, what are they doing?' – 'Singing.' – 'Singing what?' – 'We are the dwarves.' It's a famous Polish children's song:

> We are the dwarves
> hop sa sa, hop sa sa
> Our houses are under mushrooms

hop sa sa, hop sa sa
We eat ants and frog legs
Oh yes, oh yes, oh yes!
Red hats on our heads
Are our sign, our sign.

Eventually, the dwarves were brought to the station for questioning. It wasn't the kind of serious opposition the secret police agents were used to. An agent wanted to know what they had planned for the event. 'We were all meant to think up something funny,' a dwarf explained. 'What was your idea?' – 'Happy pills.' Finally, it seemed like there was a lead. They searched the dwarf's rucksack, even finding some pills. According to the witness, a militiaman was quick to try one; apparently, the prospect of a happy pill was tempting. They turned out to be mints.[66]

More cheerful happenings followed. In October, the group staged an event to distribute toilet paper, a notoriously scarce necessity in communist Poland. 'Who is afraid of toilet paper?' the flyer asked. 'Are lines of people queuing to buy toilet paper an expression of (a) drive to culture; (b) sexual desire; (c) the Communist Party's leading role in a fully developed socialist society? Circle the right answer.' The regime, which apparently was indeed afraid of toilet paper, had the participants arrested.[67]

For 6 November 1987, the anniversary of the October Revolution in Russia, and a day of many official celebrations, Orange Alternative decided to re-enact the revolutionary events. High-school students, the Orange Kids, used the 'finest cardboard' to rebuild the famous battleship *Potemkin*; another group from Szczecin made a model of the *Aurora*. They asked participants to 'dress in red for the celebrations!' Anything in red would do: 'If you don't have anything red, buy a baguette with ketchup,' the invitation advised. On the day, various 'units', named after famous revolutionary army units such as the Kronstadt sailors, tried to storm the 'Winter Palace' – a café named Barbara's Bar, known for the red borscht it served. Yet that day, the bar was closed, and when it reopened, borscht was taken off the menu. Once again, many people were arrested. But it was, said one participant, a 'great battle'.[68]

These events made the authorities look ridiculous. The police arrested people – for dressing like dwarves, for handing out toilet paper or for drinking red strawberry juice. People had to spend a few hours in jail; it might have been scary, but nothing serious happened. Above all, it was absurd. As a result, fear of detention 'evaporated', noted Fydrych. The happenings gave participants the confidence to then support more serious protests, like Peace and Freedom, an antimilitarist organization.[69] Writing in 1992, a young mother recalled that she tried not to miss any of their happenings:

> This is because I want sometimes not to fear the militia and their clubs. I come to convince myself that not every day must be depressive and dirty . . . I need this for my psychological health. I don't want always to think about the fact that there is no milk for my child. Such a happening, once every few months, is an orange alternative to reality.[70]

It might be difficult to say what kind of alternative society Fydrych and his comrades envisioned in the long term – certainly, they wanted to oust the communist regime under Jaruzelski – but they did create an alternative reality.

Such protests worked because they allowed ordinary people to participate with relative ease: all they needed was a red paper hat, and suddenly they were revolutionary dwarves. Orange Alternative's happenings enabled people to get to know each other, to exchange ideas and to make contact with other oppositional groups. Not least, they brought an older generation in touch with younger activists. An underground paper in a lathe factory, for example, first thanked the 'youth of Wrocław' for 'having helped smiles to bloom on the faces of the people of Wrocław', and then appealed 'to the workers of our factory to participate in these gatherings, which are creating a new climate, unheard of elsewhere; they

eliminate generational barriers. These gatherings give us HOPE –
because the youth is our hope.'[71]

What impact did Orange Alternative and the happenings they
organized have? Did they play a role in the eventual fall of communism in Poland (to be discussed in Chapter 15)? In the spring and
summer of 1988, workers in Poland went on strike in massive
numbers, and in February 1989, the unimaginable happened: the
government talked to members of the opposition, leading to a
round-table agreement in April that mandated national elections.
The regime was crumbling. Not surprisingly, the regime did not
choose to negotiate with Waldemar Fydrych and his comrades; they
could hardly be taken seriously. But arguably, their happenings had,
in some way, prepared the ground for peaceful revolutions. They
had helped people to overcome their fears of the regime, they had
created a space for imagining alternatives, and not least, they had
made the moderate members of the opposition, people like
Solidarność leader Lech Wałęsa, look reasonable and constructive.
With them, after all, the government could negotiate.

The Subversive Power of Laughing

Many other protests would make good use of humour in the years
to come. Activists formed entire political parties with absurd and
satirical programmes: the German Anarchist Pogo Party (APPD,
founded in 1981) organized protests demanding 'freedom for Easter
bunnies', the right to unemployment and a world of 'spending
the entire day in idleness under the sun', while the Kreuzberger
Patriotic Democrats / Realistic Centre (KPD/RZ, playing on the
acronyms usually referring to the Communist Party and the left-
wing terrorist group Revolutionary Cells, founded in 1988) in
West Berlin called for a curfew for men at temperatures above 30
degree Celsius and livelier melodies for police cars and fire trucks.[72]
This playful activism was not limited to mocking formal party politics. On the evening of May Day 1999, the KPD/RZ for example

organized a protest march against 'nightly disturbances and point-less violence' through Kreuzberg, with some 2,500 participants chanting 'We want to sleep' and 'I have to work tomorrow.' It was a peaceful demonstration, the left-wing daily *taz* reported, but nevertheless, the police used force to disperse the crowd. And in recent years, the Clowns Army became famous at protests through-out Europe. Dressed as clowns, they 'attack' police, not with rocks and Molotov cocktails, but with water pistols and soap bubbles, or clean police vehicles with feather dusters. Standing next to clowns, the police fully equipped in riot gear probably do look ridiculous.[73]

Given the very serious problems the world was (and still is) facing, is comedy the right response? Critics worry that the real politics beneath the joke can be lost. But activists and scholars have rightly argued that such forms of humorous activism can be highly effect-ive in demolishing the symbolic authority of those in power.[74] They can liberate people from their fears of the regime and its police, as the Orange Alternative has shown. They can facilitate communica-tion that cuts across the usual hierarchies and allows people to speak up in new ways, like Radio Alice. And perhaps most importantly, those happenings did create a better world, if only for a moment: they were a chance to forget how 'dirty and depressive' life was, as the woman from Wrocław put it.

5.

The Appeal of Theory: Criticizing Power and Imagining Alternatives

Huge demonstrations, barricades, fights with the police and anarchic squats were the most visible forms of protest. They attracted, and still do, the most media attention, always likely to produce spectacular images. But just as important as actions were the ideas that inspired them. The struggle for a better world required intellectual labour. Activists needed the conceptual tools to both analyse and criticize society and politics, and to imagine alternatives. On both sides of the Iron Curtain, critical thinkers such as Herbert Marcuse, Václav Havel, and Michel Foucault engaged in this work. They reinterpreted Marx's critique of capitalism with the help of psychoanalysis; they exposed the falsehood of official communist ideology in Eastern Europe; and they scrutinized microscopic forms of power that shaped subjectivities and bodies, to name but a few important lines of argument.

This theoretical labour wasn't only the work of famous intellectuals. In the aftermath of 1968, many activists became involved in the production and distribution of books and magazines. They set up publishing houses to make works available that would not sell on the mainstream market, they established alternative bookstores, organized reading circles, and founded countless magazines and journals: daily newspapers like *Libération* in France (founded in 1973), *Il Manifesto* (1969) and *Lotta Continua* (first as a monthly magazine in 1969, then a daily newspaper in 1972) in Italy, and the *tageszeitung* in West Germany (1978); theoretically ambitious journals like *Les Révoltes Logiques*, published by a group of philosophers and historians in Paris; the short-lived *Quaderni Rossi* (1961–6) that gained fame as the major forum for discussing autonomist

Marxism in Italy; *Kursbuch* in West Germany that served for many years as a major discussion forum for the extra-parliamentary left; the *New Left Review* that debated questions of leftist theory from Marxist perspectives for English-speaking readers; the philosophical journal *Praxis* in Yugoslavia that developed a humanist understanding of socialism; and not least countless countercultural magazines like *Re Nudo*, *L'Erba Voglio* and the feminist *Effe* in Italy, or *Pflasterstrand*, *Autonomie* and *Courage* in West Germany. On the Eastern side of the Iron Curtain, where the publishing of oppositional magazines was illegal, underground publications known as *Samizdat* (literally 'self-publishing') were secretly produced, often using simple typewriters and carbon paper.[1]

These publications created a counter-public sphere. They were forums for exchanging ideas across borders and allowed activists to connect. Indeed, the radical milieus of the 1960s and 1970s were very much reading and writing cultures. The leftist daily or the local alternative magazine on the kitchen table and the latest work of theory on the bookshelf signalled belonging to the radical scene.[2] Militant students in the 1970s devoured the difficult works of famous critical theorists ranging from Karl Marx to postmodern French thinkers such as Gilles Deleuze and Jean Baudrillard. But there was also a large appetite for 'alternative', often autobiographical literature written by activists themselves that is now largely forgotten: works like *Pigs Have Wings* (*Porci con le ali*) by Lidia Ravera and Marco Radice about the sexual and political struggles of two young leftists in Italy during the 1970s, or *The Death of the Fairytale Prince* (*Der Tod des Märchenprinzen*) by Svende Merian, depicting a souring love affair between a feminist woman and a militant male anti-nuclear activist in Hamburg.[3]

In fact, a word on gender is in order here, as all the thinkers examined in this chapter are men. This isn't simply an omission, nor does it imply that women played no role in these critical intellectual milieus. They had important positions as editors and practically facilitated the exchange of ideas; they published feminist magazines and founded exclusively female publishing houses; and of course, they were writers in their own right. Feminist thinkers such as Luce Irigaray, Hélène Cixous, Carla Lonzi, Gerburg Treusch-Dieter and others developed powerful critiques of patriarchal society and sexuality, discussed in Chapter 11.[4] Yet – and this is in itself telling with regard to how male-dominated these intellectual scenes were, and how profound the feminist challenge to them was – discussions around Marxism, intellectual dissidence and the microphysics of power were profoundly male enterprises. They all had very little to say about women and gender more generally.

With this limitation in mind, this chapter explores the intellectual dimension of activism. It examines the central ideas and texts widely read among activists, and what they had to say about power and the forms and possibilities of fighting oppression. These were difficult texts, hard to understand. Activists spent hours in study groups discussing classics of critical theory as well as the latest publication by fashionable authors. But theory wasn't merely demanding; it was exciting and inspiring. It mattered for those engaged in struggling for a better world.

Rediscovering Marx and the Working Class

In the wake of the Second World War, communism was not only at the zenith of its political power, but also enjoyed an immense intellectual appeal across Western Europe (with the notable exception of the Federal Republic of Germany). Major thinkers and artists joined communist parties or at least supported their cause during the early 1950s: people like French philosopher Jean-Paul Sartre, writer Louis Aragon, painter Pablo Picasso, or British historians such as Eric Hobsbawm, E. P. Thompson and Christopher Hill. Yet this pro-communist consensus began to crack in 1956, with revelations about Stalin's terror regime in Nikita Khrushchev's February speech 'On the Cult of Personality and Its Consequences', followed by the crushing of the Hungarian uprising in November that year by the Red Army. These seismic events made many supporters of communism question the official party line. At the same time, the integration of communist parties in France and Italy into mainstream politics meant that a proletarian revolution to overthrow capitalism was no longer on their agenda. In short, the Soviet Union and communist parties had joined the forces of order, oppressing rather than encouraging rebellions, an impression that harsh communist crackdowns in response to the 1968 uprisings would confirm.[5]

In light of these developments, the orthodox Marxism propagated by the party ideologues no longer appealed to critical intellectuals. They looked elsewhere for inspiration, often turning to thinkers from the Third World such as Frantz Fanon (see Chapter 7). But they also returned to Marx, especially the young Marx, and rediscovered dissident Marxists of the interwar years such as Wilhelm Reich, Karl Korsch, Antonio Gramsci and György Lukács.[6] What might their writings contribute to a radical critique of the post-war world on both sides of the Iron Curtain? How might Marx's *Capital* still be useful to analyse (and fight) the 'capitalism of today', as Mario Tronti wondered in 1962.[7] This rediscovery of Marx was a transnational development stretching across the Iron Curtain. Whether writers were associated with the British Communist Party Historians Group, with Italian journals such as *Quaderni Rossi* and *Operai e Capitale*, or with the Yugoslav *Praxis* group and its journal of the same name, they tended to share a critique of the ossified bureaucracies of the working-class movement and its lack of interest in the actual experiences and voices of workers. They were more interested in questions of alienation than in questions of exploitation, they developed a critical gaze on work itself, and they wanted to rediscover the revolutionary potential of Marx's writings.

As we've seen in preceding chapters, Italy was the site of particularly vibrant (and violent) protest cultures throughout the 1960s and 1970s involving – and that distinguished Italy from the rest of Western Europe – numerous workers. The most influential organizations of Italy's radical leftist scene during those years, groups such as Potere Operaio, Lotta Continua, Avanguardia Operaia and later

Autonomia Operaia, all drew their inspiration from a Marxist theory that became known as *operaismo*, translated somewhat clumsily as workerism.[8]

What was so novel and appealing about this theory? After all, the plight of workers and their organization into a political force had always been of central interest for socialists and communists alike. From a classical Marxist perspective, history is an epic struggle between antagonistic classes, between the proletariat and the bourgeoisie under capitalism.[9] In that sense, Marxism is inherently about workers. Yet theorists of *operaismo* such as Raniero Panzieri and Mario Tronti argued in the 1950s that traditional trade unions and especially political parties of the left had lost any interest in the realities of life for workers on the shop floor. All that mattered for them was gaining political influence by cooperating with bourgeois parties. In response, *operaismo* theorists turned their attention to workers, both politically by emphasizing the 'revolutionary autonomy of the proletariat' vis-à-vis political parties, and empirically by actually studying the situation of workers, their demands and actions.[10] Influenced by the French group Socialisme ou Barbarie and the American journal *Correspondence*, edited by Raya Dunayevskaya and C. L. R. James, Panzieri's comrades went to factories and talked to workers to learn about their experiences.[11]

What they learned from their French and American comrades and their own inquiries, laid the foundations for *operaismo*. At FIAT, noted Romano Alquati, the introduction of new technologies had resulted in the marginalization of skilled labour, something workers were acutely aware of. They quickly understood that any talk of career opportunities based on newly acquired skills was an illusion. Like their colleagues in the US and in France, workers at FIAT despised the very nature of their work, which they frequently described as 'absurd'. The rhetoric of the inherent dignity of work, popular among communists and trade unionists, had lost any appeal for these workers. Unions hardly grasped how workers rejected the 'capitalist organization of labour', but workers themselves found ways to resist this labour regime. At the petrochemical works of Porto Marghera in Veneto, Antonio Negri observed a 'dynamics of sabotage: in fact, no one had set out to commit sabotage, yet there existed a continuity of imperfect operations such that by the end the product was completely useless'. Workers, these findings suggested to the *operaisti*, were rebelling against work itself.[12]

This was also the central argument of Mario Tronti's widely read 1966 book *Workers and Capital*. Based on a critical reading of Marx's oeuvre, Tronti challenged one of the main tenets of traditional Marxism: that the working class was 'completely outside of capital and, as such, its general antagonist'. To the contrary, he argued, the working class was '*part* of capital'. The working class opposed not simply 'the machine, as constant capital', but 'labour-power itself, as variable capital'; in other words, it opposed 'itself as part of capital. Labour should see labour-power *as a commodity* as its enemy.'[13] This might sound like obscure Marxist jargon. But he made a crucial point: labour (to be precise: labour as a commodity) was itself part of capitalism. After all, workers were selling their labour-power on the market. As such, there was nothing to be celebrated about labour. Instead, labour, in its capitalist form, had to be the object of critique. Tronti's analysis had important implications. The old working-class movement had criticized capitalism from the standpoint of labour; *operaisti*, by contrast, criticized labour in capitalism, as Marxist historian Moishe Postone would later write.[14] And the workers weren't fighting merely for a bigger share of the cake, for higher wages that would allow them to purchase more consumer goods, but against their very status as workers. On the revolutionary agenda was the abolition of labour as a commodity itself.

Italian *operaisti* were not alone in this critique. Like their Italian comrades, radical students in France and West Germany after the upheavals of 1968 took jobs in factories to discover, and agitate, the working class.[15] But leftist authors also turned to the past, seeking to write about the experiences of workers beyond conventional histories of the working-class movement, its parties, trade unions and ideologies. Influenced and inspired by Italian *operaismo*, West

German leftist activist and historian Karl Heinz Roth published a 'history of the "other" [German] working-class movement' exploring the 'unknown struggles of unskilled workers'.[16] In the United Kingdom, E. P. Thompson famously wrote about how English working men (he didn't concern himself much with working women) 'came to feel an identity of interests as between themselves and as against their rulers and employers', thus 'making' a working class, by carefully paying attention to the voices of workers themselves.[17] And in France, Jacques Rancière studied early nineteenth-century workers who refused to be defined as workers by spending the night writing poetry and philosophical texts rather than recovering for more work. Rancière hardly qualifies as Marxist, yet there is a remarkable similarity between his line of inquiry and the Marxist theory of Italian *operaisti*. In a way, the workers Rancière wrote about had done what Tronti had proposed: considering daily work a 'robbery of time', they had rejected their own status as labourers, and had tried to be something else – albeit individually, rather than as a class.[18]

This critical rediscovery of Marx also reached beyond Western intellectual circles. Indeed, one of the most international projects rethinking socialism came out of Yugoslavia: the journal *Praxis*, first published in 1964, which appeared in a Serbo-Croatian as well as an international edition, the latter containing articles in English, French, German and, occasionally, Italian by celebrities of the international left such as Henri Lefebvre and Herbert Marcuse.[19]

Before 1956 and the awakening of their Western comrades, dissident Marxists in Yugoslavia criticized the dehumanizing regimes of both Soviet and Chinese socialism that utterly disregarded individual human feelings and experiences. If a humane society was the goal of communism, then the building of that society, here and now, had to be humane as well. Yet, argued Serbian philosopher Mihailo Marković, there was no space for authentic humane relationships in the existing socialist societies, ruled by bureaucratic state apparatuses. No matter where people stood on the political hierarchy, they related to each other based on their social position and hence as objects, rather than as real subjects. 'In this atmosphere of mistrust, insincerity, artificiality,' Marković wrote in 1965, 'many potentially human and intimate relationships between people die before they begin to develop.' The remedy for this 'political alienation' in bureaucracies would be self-management as a foundational principle for socialist organization. This would have to go beyond existing forms of self-management that remained limited to local government and factory production and had to entail 'the whole social life', including the 'central organs of the state'. That way, Marković argued, self-management might overcome 'the *permanent* and fixed division of society into the subjects and objects of history, into rulers and executors, into the cunning social mind and its physical instruments in human form'.[20]

The ideological and party establishment in Yugoslavia did not welcome such critical voices. From the very beginning, *Praxis* faced attacks both in the daily press and in the Party's Central Committee's official journal *Socijalizam*. Nevertheless, the journal survived for more than ten years until January 1975, when the Serbian parliament, under the control of communists, forced Belgrade University to dismiss eight leading members of the *Praxis* circle from their jobs in the philosophy department. A month later, *Praxis* ceased publication.[21]

Praxis's critique of the alienating, bureaucratic world had its equivalent in the West. There, famous intellectuals such as Herbert Marcuse but also less well-known authors such as Reimut Reiche and Dieter Duhm developed a critique of capitalist modernity that foregrounded its damaging sexual and emotional impact.[22] Such critiques weren't entirely novel. In the 1920s, Wilhelm Reich, whose works were rediscovered by French and West German student radicals in the 1960s, combined Freudian and Marxist thinking to argue that it was the social realities of capitalism – and not civilization as such, as Freud had claimed – that forced the suppression of sexual desires. A communist revolution that would put an end to capitalism would therefore also result in a 'sexual revolution' and the liberation of sexual desires.[23]

After the Second World War, Herbert Marcuse presented a similar critique of the 'administered world', albeit in a more philosophical way, and without any reference to Reich. As a leftist Jew, he was forced to flee Germany in 1933, first to Switzerland, then to the United States, where he joined Max Horkheimer and Theodor W. Adorno at the Institute of Social Research. There, he wrote *Eros and Civilization: A Philosophical Inquiry into Freud* (1955) and *The One-Dimensional Man: Studies in the Ideology of Advanced Industrial Society* (1964), both widely read by rebellious students around 1968.[24] While the latter provided a critique of the 'technological rationality' in both the capitalist West and the socialist East that had suffocated any form of dissent and opposition, the former offered both a critical and a utopian reading of Sigmund Freud. If the process of civilization required, as Freud had argued, the repression of desires to make people engage in (fundamentally unpleasant) work, then – countered Marcuse – technological advances such as the automation of production rendered some of this repression unnecessary: a 'surplus repression', as Marcuse put it. This opened the possibility for imagining a society that existed 'beyond the reality principle', a society no longer dominated by alienated labour, in which work could become play, desires could be fulfilled and the 'pleasure principle' could reign.[25]

Marcuse's philosophical inquiry into Freud was certainly miles away from Mario Tronti's analysis of class and capital, and the thick descriptions of nineteenth-century workers' lives by E. P. Thompson and Jacques Rancière had little in common with the theoretical reflections on alienation, bureaucracy and self-management by Mihailo Marković. But all these writers shared a disillusionment and dissatisfaction with traditional Marxism, with communist parties in Western Europe and communist regimes in Eastern Europe. They were all deeply sceptical of the celebration of hard, physical work (usually depicted as male, though this gender aspect wasn't of much interest to those authors) within the old working-class movement. And they viewed bureaucratic societies in the capitalist West and the communist East as profoundly alienating. A better world, these thinkers argued, would establish non-alienating social relations, and non-alienating forms of work; this required autonomy from large organizations and bureaucracies. It would be a more *humane* struggle for a more *humane* world.

Writing as Resistance: Intellectual Dissidents in Czechoslovakia

Imagine a greengrocer in communist Czechoslovakia during the 1970s. One day, alongside the usual vegetables, a poster is delivered to him: 'Workers of the World, Unite!', it says – the famous slogan from *The Communist Manifesto*. The greengrocer doesn't think much of it and puts the poster in the shop's window, with the carrots and onions. That's the famous parable of the greengrocer Václav Havel tells in his essay *The Power of the Powerless* (1978), one of the most influential texts by intellectual dissidents – though Havel and others were rather critical about the label, mostly used by Western media – in communist Eastern Europe after the crushing of the Prague Spring.[26] The essay offers a unique understanding of how power functioned in communist societies; even more importantly, it sheds light on how dissidents imagined opposition against these regimes.

Why would the greengrocer put the poster on display, Havel wondered. 'What is he trying to communicate to the world? Is he genuinely enthusiastic about the idea of unity among workers in the world?' He probably didn't even think much about the reasons; he simply did it, 'because it has been done that way for years, because everyone does it, and because that is the way it has to be'. And besides, if he wouldn't do it, he would be in trouble; 'someone might even accuse him of disloyalty'.

What, then, did he communicate with the poster? It signalled conformity: 'I, the greengrocer XY, live here and I know what I must do. I behave in the manner expected of me.' It was a message to those in power: 'I am obedient and therefore I have the right to be left in peace.' The true message of the poster was that the greengrocer was 'afraid', and 'therefore unquestioningly obedient'. But he couldn't say this openly. He would be too ashamed. Hence, he had to express his conformity behind the façade of ideology. The greengrocer's poster was one small part of an entire landscape of similar conformist acts. His customers, who would certainly be more interested in the quality of his tomatoes, might have put the very same poster up in their office. They might not even notice the slogan; its absence, however, amid countless other posters with exactly the same words, would speak volumes.

Havel used the tale of the greengrocer to critically analyse how power functioned in what he called the post-totalitarian societies of communist Eastern Europe. These weren't dictatorships that relied on the blunt force of a police state. Rather, they relied on a sort of ritualistic alternative understanding of the world detached from reality. In this alternative reality, the suppression of free expression and 'farcical elections' were presented as the highest forms of free-dom and democracy, while 'military occupation becomes fraternal assistance' – a clear allusion to the Soviet invasion that ended the Prague Spring. Ideology, that is, became an automatism in which everyone had to participate, whether they were small greengrocers or prime ministers. All had to follow the ideological rituals, which made power anonymous. Whether or not individuals believed in these falsities did not matter, they had to *behave* as though they did. Havel had a powerful name for such conformist behaviour: *living in a lie*.[27]

If ordinary people like the fictional greengrocer and his custom-ers more or less knowingly lived in a lie, what would be the alternative? What would it mean to dissent, to resist, to live differ-ently? The answer Havel gave is straightforward and simple: all it took was to stop participating in the lie, and instead to live 'within the truth'. Such a life within the truth would restore the 'authentic existence' that living in the lie had violated. For Havel, the 'real aim' of life was to express truth. Even if repressed, this desire for truth continued to exist in 'hidden spheres', which is why living openly in the truth was so threatening for the regime. Those who dared to refuse the lie might set an example for others, which, if enough people joined them, might ultimately make the entire ideological façade collapse.

These reflections had important consequences for how Havel thought about opposition and the potential of political change. The confrontation between the regime and those opposing it would not happen 'on the level of real, institutionalized, quantifiable power', he believed, but 'on the level of human consciousness and conscience, the existential level'. Living and acting in opposition to the regime thus wasn't merely the task of a small circle of intellectual dissidents; becoming a dissident was a moral choice every ordinary citizen could make.[28]

To give an example, Havel told another story, that of a beer brewer named Š, with whom he had worked in 1974. Š was dedicated to his job. All he wanted was to brew good beer, and this made his co-workers who cared much less about the quality of their product feel uncomfortable. He frequently made suggestions for improvements, but the brewery's managers, who all had politically influential friends, didn't show any interest. His efforts to do a better job became an annoyance for them. Eventually, brewer Š took a bold step and wrote a letter to the managers' superiors analysing the brewery's bad performance. Predictably, the regime did not react by making any improvements or even replacing the incompetent management, but by accusing brewer Š of being a 'political saboteur'. In the end, he lost his job and was transferred to another brewery, where he was given tasks that required no skills. 'By speaking the truth, Š had stepped out of line, broken the rules, cast himself out, and he ended up as a sub-citizen, stigmatized as an enemy . . . He had become the "dissident" of the Eastern Bohemian Brewery.' Importantly, he had not challenged the regime on political grounds, nor did he choose to become a political dissident. He had simply wanted to do a good job, and said so out loud. Yet, this wasn't acceptable in the 'auto-totality' of post-totalitarian Czechoslovakia.[29]

The Power of the Powerless is usually considered a brilliant critical analysis of the situation in communist Czechoslovakia after the crushing of the Prague Spring. Yet, according to Havel, communist Czechoslovakia was only a particularly drastic illustration of a challenge faced by the entire 'contemporary technological society', East and West: humanity had lost control over technology, he argued with reference to German philosopher Martin Heidegger. Rather than serving humanity's needs, technology had 'enslaved us and compelled us to participate in the preparation of our own destruction' – an argument many Western environmentalists would certainly have agreed with. The automatism he saw in Czechoslovakia, Havel continued, was 'merely an extreme version of the global automatism of technological civilization'. Western parliamentary democracies and their consumer societies could therefore hardly serve as a positive role model for communist Eastern Europe. More than political change was needed: a worldwide 'existential revolution' that would, he hoped, yield 'a new experience of being, a renewed rootedness in the universe, a newly grasped sense of "higher responsibility", a new-found inner relationship to other people and to the human community'.[30] This was a lofty goal, and one which no formal organization might achieve. But small grassroots communities from below, held together by a shared enthusiasm for a common cause, might work towards it: groups like the informal circles that constituted the backbone of the dissident scene in Czechoslovakia. Dissidence in the East might provide a role model for the West.[31]

Havel had a specific example in mind for such an authentic self-organization from below: Charter 77, an informal group in which Havel had played a leading role and which he discussed in *The Power of the Powerless*.[32] It had formed in the wake of a 1976 trial against members of the musical underground scene centred around the rock band the Plastic People of the Universe (discussed in Chapter 6), taking its name from the group's foundational document. According to its first publication, Charter 77 sought to call 'attention to various concrete instances of the violation of human and civil rights', to document them and to work for a better implementation of those rights in Czechoslovak society.[33] To that end, Charter 77 published a variety of reports detailing, for example, how the regime prevented students from attending high school or university because they or their parents had made critical political statements. Other publications addressed 'low work morale, unequal pay for women, and the failure of unions to support the rights of workers'.[34]

How can we understand Charter 77's resistance to the communist regime? The group's central activity was writing, whether it was documenting human rights violations or analysing communist forms of governance. Writing itself was a way of 'living in the truth', to use Havel's language. It was a moral, even existential act of resistance. 'The truth', wrote Havel, 'had to be spoken loudly and collectively', no matter the consequences.[35] In a similar way, Jan Patočka, one of the original three spokespeople of Charter 77, had refused to see the group as 'a basis for oppositional political activity'. The signatories of the Charter, he claimed, did 'not act out of any interest, but out of *obligation* alone', an obligation to a 'higher authority' of morality.[36] Speaking the truth gave people a chance to act morally and therefore be a person. The medium was the message.

But writing was about more than taking an individual moral stance. The secretly circulating texts of samizdat literature formed a community: an alternative public sphere in which information could be shared and ideas could be debated that weren't addressed in official media. Chartist philosopher Ladislav Hejdánek outlined this vision in a series of letters to a fictional student, widely read among fellow Chartists. Ostensibly, the major question was whether the student should sign Charter 77 and thereby take a public, moral stance – to openly live within the truth, as it were. Hejdánek argued against such a step, as it would put the student at risk. After all, the goal of Charter 77 was 'to convince as many people as possible that . . . they can and should behave toward their fellow citizens as friends, companions, comrades'.[37] But again, the medium, or, more precisely, the genre, was the message: the fictional letters (though he didn't write the students' responses) allowed him to develop and re-examine unfinished thoughts in a dialogue. With these letters, Hejdánek envisioned Charter 77 as a 'deliberating public'. Dissidents would become the core of what another Chartist, Václav

Benda, called a 'parallel polis', that is, alternative political and social structures that included samizdat literature as well as underground concerts and lectures given in private apartments.[38]

Sceptics might argue that these grand ideas about living within the truth or building a parallel polis existed in the abstract, without much of an impact on social and political life, at least in the case of Czechoslovakia, where no mass opposition existed. But such a critique misses the point of intellectual dissidence. For thinkers like Havel, Patočka, Hejdánek and Benda, the act of writing itself mattered in a way that was not the case for intellectuals in the West like Mario Tronti or Herbert Marcuse. It was a way of living a different, more moral life, and it helped to create a public sphere, no matter how minuscule it was. Speaking the truth was essential for shaping what we might call the dissident self. It wasn't only a struggle for a better world, but also, and perhaps even more importantly, a struggle for a better, more authentic self.

Not everyone agreed with this project, even in the dissident community itself. In *The Czech Dream Book: Dreams of the Year 1979*, Ludvík Vaculík presented a radical alternative. Vaculík had crafted three central texts of the Prague Spring – including the 'Manifesto of 2,000 Words' of June 1968 discussed in Chapter 2 – but had not been a particularly productive writer in the decade that followed, though he had participated in dissident activities, notably by running the publishing house Edice Petlice.[39] Then, in early January 1979, he ran into his friend Jiří Kolář, who told him to 'just write about why you can't write. Record what you see, hear, and what occurs to you.' The comment inspired Vaculík to begin three weeks later with writing a diary, recording his daily life and his nightly dreams from 22 January 1979 to 2 February 1980.[40]

The diary dealt with a broad range of topics, ranging from everyday chores to Vaculík's work for Petlice, to debates about Charter 77, dissident writing and other forms of political activism, and his marriage and two affairs (which his wife was fully aware of). Towards the end of 1979, Vaculík showed passages of the book to several of its protagonists, including Major Fišer, the police officer who interrogated him every month, to ask about their reactions (which he then also recorded). With its attention to the daily lives and quarrels of dissidents, the *Dream Book* – as Vaculík eventually called the published version of his diary – provided, in the words of theorist Jiří Pechar, a 'de-glorification of dissidence'.[41] As such, it was a radical contrast to the heroic 'life within the truth' Havel had called for. The dissident self Vaculík presented wasn't authentic and integrated, but fluid and constantly developing; it lacked consistency, and was profoundly fragmented. Vaculík was certainly a dissident, but at the same time, he rejected the label. And while Havel longed to restore a 'rightful dignity' and 'moral integrity', which he considered the 'essential aims of life', Vaculík found freedom in acknowledging and writing about his fractured, flawed self.

The *Dream Book* was, he commented in December 1980, 'actually my freest text. It's about sixty percent free.'[42] A book that is 60 per cent free – that certainly sounds less heroic than the ideal of a life within the truth. And yet, Vaculík's quiet irony was perhaps all the more subversive.

Under the Microscope: Foucault's Analysis of Power

'Maybe the target nowadays is not to discover what we are but to refuse what we are,' French philosopher Michel Foucault wrote in his famous article 'The Subject and Power' (1982). When, 200 years earlier, Immanuel Kant had asked, 'What Does Enlightenment Mean?', he had addressed the former question: who are we?[43] It was a profoundly historical question, Foucault argued, inquiring not about a universal, ahistorical human subject, but about who we are in this precise historical moment. Two centuries later, the question had to be flipped. The issue was no longer to figure out who we are at this moment in time; rather, the target was to refuse 'what we are', and by doing so imagine 'what we could be'. 'We have to promote new forms of subjectivity through the refusal of this kind of individuality which has been imposed on us for several centuries,'

Foucault noted. The historical situation had changed, and the struggle had to change with it.

To explain his point, Foucault distinguished between three different kinds of struggle: those 'against forms of domination', those 'against forms of exploitation which separate individuals from what they produce' – the struggles of the labour movement, one might say – and finally struggles 'against that which ties the individual to himself and submits him to others in this way (struggles against subjection, against forms of subjectivity and submission)'. And while the struggles against domination and exploitation had not disappeared, it was the third kind of struggle that Foucault saw prevailing by the early 1980s.[44]

Foucault's article, published in the academic journal *Critical Inquiry*, wasn't a call to action in the way that, for example, Mario Tronti had called on workers to fight against labour itself, or that Václav Havel had called for a life within the truth. Rather, it was an attempt to grasp at a conceptual level the demands that had emerged in the wake of 1968: 'opposition to the power of men over women, of parents over children, of psychiatry over the mentally ill, of medicine over the population, of administration over the ways people live'. According to Foucault, these weren't struggles against a political or economic elite, but against a 'technique, a form of power', a power that affected individuals in their everyday lives by categorizing them and imposing 'a law of truth' on them. 'It is a form of power which makes individuals subjects.'[45]

After Foucault's election to the Collège de France in 1969, where he held a chair for the 'history of systems of thought', he not only became a prominent intellectual in France (and, unlike most other intellectuals discussed in this chapter, had a lasting influence in academia), but also an activist involved in various political campaigns. Most prominently, he co-founded the Groupe d'information sur les prisons (GIP), which sought to shed light on the conditions French inmates faced.[46] Drawing on both his academic studies and his grassroots activism, Foucault developed a critical perspective on how the left had conventionally thought about power, and by implication about liberation and revolution, ideas he outlined in articles and interviews that were often translated and circulated in Western Europe's leftist intellectual milieus.[47] These writings, along with those of several other French writers such as Gilles Deleuze, Jean Baudrillard and, from a feminist perspective, Luce Irigaray, informed and inspired a reimagination of protest, in which questions of subjectivities, bodies and sexualities, wishes and desires became central.[48]

Power is at the heart of any political or social struggle: that much seems obvious. After all, such struggles challenge established orders and authorities. But what is power? Conventional understandings of power, which tend to be expressed in rhetoric rather than being fully theorized, imply a binary structure: those with power, the rulers or the bosses, oppress those without power, the ruled or the workers; and the latter 'fight the power'. Power appears to be an exclusively negative force, something that represses, forbids, excludes, censors. And opposed to power, as its radical opposite, stands freedom, always resisting the impositions of power, even if there are only limited opportunities for autonomy. Such binary understandings of power characterize a variety of protests: the class struggle of exploited workers standing up to their oppressive bosses; anti-colonial struggles against the domination of the colonizers; struggles for sexual liberation against an oppressive patriarchy; but also Havel's struggle for a life within the truth. Yet in this analysis, the actual 'mechanics of power', how power works and how it's exercised, remain uncomprehended. Such understandings of power are not only inadequate, argued Foucault, but also 'possibly dangerous'.[49]

The everyday battles that were fought in the wake of 1968, however, from households to factories, revealed the 'fine meshes of the web of power'. Here, 'the concrete nature of power became visible', in ways that had 'hitherto remained outside the field of political analysis'.[50] This attention to the 'microphysics of power' yielded important insights for Foucault. Perhaps most fundamentally, he argued that we should think of power not as something somebody could possess, like a commodity, but as a relation that 'exists only when it is put into action', as he wrote in 'The Subject and Power'.[51] Power was never localized, or held in anyone's hand, but circulating and exercised in an all-embracing net. This was a crucial point to make: there was no outside of power, 'no spaces of primal liberty between the meshes of its network', no brief snatches of true autonomy. Other kinds of relations, like those of production or love, are always interwoven with relations of power.[52] Trying to defend, or to extend, the realm of liberty against the oppressive forces of power would therefore be based on a misconception. Yet, any relation of power was also a form of struggle, as it involved resistance against exerting power, which might be best understood as a 'permanent provocation' of both sides. And if power was everywhere, then resistance, too, was possible everywhere; it could be 'multiple' and global.[53]

For Foucault, power is more than merely repressive, as a 'para-Marxist' like Marcuse assumed in his discussions of Freud.[54] Power also works by inciting and seducing, by prescribing certain actions: power doesn't simply repress sexual desires, but wants its subject to confess to them; it demands work on bodies to keep them beautiful and healthy. It's a never-ending struggle. Restrictions on children's masturbation, for example, made their bodies the object of control and surveillance. It made sexuality as such 'an object of analysis and concern', thereby at the same time engendering 'an intensification of each individual's desire for, in and over his body'. This might be described as the resistance of bodies. Yet, power's response to this resistance came swiftly. Instead of controlling 'by repression', power now worked 'by stimulation. "Get undressed – but be slim, good looking, tanned!"'[55] The effect of power was thus not merely to repress, but to produce certain bodies (healthy, beautiful, sexy), certain subjectivities and desires. The point was then not to submit to these stimulations, but to refuse them, to refuse 'what we are'.[56]

What did these examinations of the workings of power mean for protesters on the ground, in the streets of Paris or the squats of Berlin? Foucault has been accused of rendering their struggles conceptually impossible.[57] If power is everywhere, if there aren't any zones of freedom, how, then, is it possible to struggle against power and for liberation? Clearly, Foucault hardly provides the script for a grand, revolutionary emancipation that would end all struggles.

His analyses called for diverse, microscopic, yet connected acts. He urged his readers to recognize and resist the multiple ways in which power works, how it incites and seduces us to talk about ourselves, to work on our bodies, that is, to willingly govern ourselves and thereby become a subject. These would be never-ending struggles, always calling for new strategic positions of resistance, but lacking a firm ground, like those islands of liberty or the true aims of life, from which to operate.[58]

We might describe these diffuse struggles as *rhizomatic*. The term was popularized in another influential book which came out of France: *Rhizome* (1976), by Gilles Deleuze and Félix Guattari. The book was written as the introduction for the second volume of their work *Capitalism and Schizophrenia*, called *A Thousand Plateaus* (1980), but they published it as a little booklet ahead of the major work. It's a short, dense, obscure but also suggestive text. The book critiques systematic thinking that functions like a tree, with roots in the ground and branches growing from those roots, and a hierarchical society based on that model. The alternative Deleuze and Guattari proposed is the *rhizome*, a subterranean stem, a bulb or a tuber rather than a root. A rhizome lacks a foundation organizing everything, but instead consists of ever-evolving lines and assemblages. (Though Deleuze and Guattari also stressed that we shouldn't think about the tree model and the rhizome model as two opposing alternatives; this would only reintroduce the kind of dualism they wanted to move beyond.) This wasn't merely an abstract philosophical reflection, for, Deleuze and Guattari argued, nation states are built on the tree model: they require organization and settlement, whereas nomads with their constant movement resembled the rhizome, overthrowing and undermining the 'state apparatus' with their 'war machines'. 'Make rhizomes, not roots, never plant! . . . Be the Pink Panther and your loves will be like the wasp and the orchid, the cat and the baboon,' they cryptically proclaimed at the end of their booklet.[59]

In the 1970s, the ideas of Deleuze, Guattari and Foucault enjoyed tremendous popularity within parts of Western Europe's radical left. Supposedly a left-leaning bar in West Berlin during the early 1980s even named itself *Rhizom*.[60] More substantially, their writings offered a way to think differently about protest and activism. Gone were the days, Herbert Röttgen remarked in the Munich-based magazine *Das Blatt* in the wake of the German Autumn of 1977, when the left had dreamed of mobilizing the masses for a confrontation with the state. New struggles foregrounded autonomy and subjectivity. Rather than confronting the state, it was time to confront the self, to experiment with bodies and subjectivities in multiple different ways – in women's groups, in rural communes, in spiritualist men's groups, as the coming chapters discuss. These experiments would function like a rhizome, a term Röttgen used with reference to Deleuze and Guattari, pushing its multiple 'strands and webs' through the 'masonry' of the state.[61]

What Remains of Theory

In the radical scenes of the 1960s to the 1980s, theoretical questions were always subject to heavy and sometimes bitter controversy. How should Marx be interpreted? Did Foucault have anything to say that was of relevance for emancipatory politics? The thinkers discussed here offered radically different analyses. Some returned to Marx's writings to rediscover their revolutionary potential; others wanted to move beyond Marx altogether. Some searched for the true values of human life that both capitalism and socialism denied, while others dismissed the very notion of an authentic human existence. Yet, despite their differences, they also had something in common. Most notably, they all rejected the rigidities of orthodox Marxism and communist party politics. At the same time, they all took an interest in individual or collective autonomy, whether it was the autonomy of workers from unions and parties promoted by *operaisti* like Mario Tronti, the autonomy of individuals from the ideological apparatus of socialism, or the autonomy of refusing who we are supposed to be. In that sense, Foucault had a point when he described the struggles of the late twentieth century as being 'against forms of subjectivity and submission'. And theory was more than just descriptive. It was a source of inspiration for activists across the continent. In Italy, the ideas of Tronti and his comrades informed the protests and strikes in factories around 1968; in communist Czechoslovakia, writing theory was itself a mode of resisting, of living – in Havel's words – a 'life within truth'; and in the late 1970s and 1980s, Foucault's somewhat vague call to refute who we are and to imagine new forms of subjectivity became hugely popular among activists seeking to develop different intimate and sexual relations, an issue Chapter 13 returns to.

What has happened to these subversive reading and writing cultures of the 1960s and 1970s? What happened to the earnest dedication with which countless reading circles studied Karl Marx, to the enthusiasm with which readers devoured the latest works of authors like Tronti, Havel, Foucault, Deleuze, and many others? To be sure, these reading cultures have not completely disappeared. Publishing houses, magazines and newspapers established by leftist activists in the wake of the revolts around 1968 continue to exist, and authors like Foucault and Deleuze are still read, though perhaps more in (critical) university seminars within the humanities than within protest scenes. Their ideas inform contemporary identity politics, especially with regard to gender, sexuality and queerness. And of course, new books appear that provide analysis and inspiration. Yet, already by the 1980s, the lust for theory, the desire for conceptual tools with which to grasp the world, was waning, and so were the counter-publics that alternative media had built. In the world of social media, of blogs and Twitter, there are fewer theoretical magazines or even books that are 'must reads', serving as common points of reference, for members of protest scenes the way that texts like Marcuse's *One-Dimensional Man*, Tronti's *Workers and Capital*, Havel's *Power of the Powerless* or Deleuze and Guattari's *Rhizome* once functioned.

6.

Rebellious Sounds: The Music of Protesting

Protests have a sound. It might be people chanting slogans or singing stirring songs, or even marching in solemn silence. If protests turn into riots, then there's the sound of police sirens, of stones flying through the air and crashing into windows, of the yells and cries of the wounded. And many protest movements were closely connected with musical subcultures. Rebellious songs expressed protestors' frustration with society and politics, but also the promise of happiness and freedom not yet achieved. The experience of music could be a glimpse into the future. It made protesting emotionally appealing. Listening to rebellious music at concerts, dancing in the crowds or singing along with the lyrics of iconic political songs during demonstrations fostered feelings of belonging, of collective rebelliousness; at times, it could even inspire direct action in the streets. And music was about more than the explicitly political lyrics of songs. The very sound of rebellious music could be disruptive and threatening. It encouraged certain styles of dancing, dressing, piercing ears and noses, or dying and styling hair, that authorities have at times felt undermined the moral order.[1] But above all, music was, and of course still is, an aural and bodily experience. Readers of the following discussion of political rock concerts in West Berlin, the musical underground in Prague, punk in Great Britain, the techno scene post-unification Berlin, and French rap artists are thus encouraged to look up some of the songs (most are available on YouTube) and also enjoy the sound of protesting.[2]

Rock to Riot

In September 1965, the Rolling Stones were playing at West Berlin's Waldbühne stadium in front of a crowd of some 20,000 people.[3] It was a short concert; and for the audience, it was far too short. The Stones had just performed 'I Can't Get No Satisfaction' and were winding up, when the concert-goers started hollering and demanding an encore. But the organizers had other ideas and 'simply turned out the lights'. In the darkness, 'total chaos broke out at the Waldbühne', recalled Ralf Reinders, who had participated in the riots and later became a member of the terrorist group Movement 2nd June.[4] Earlier that day, fans without tickets, mostly young workers and apprentices, had broken through police lines trying to force their way in. Inside the stadium an echo of the earlier conflict resumed. Police used truncheons and water cannons to disperse the crowd, which in turn tore apart the stadium stands and threw debris at the police. Outside the stadium, the battle continued in trains of the local railway system known as the S-Bahn. At the end of the night at least eighty-seven people had been injured, including twenty-six police officers, eighty-five arrests had been made, and seventeen train cars were demolished. In total, the cost of repairs came to between 300,000 and 400,000 marks.[5] It was a pivotal moment for the development of the anti-authoritarian movement of 1968 that involved youngsters with less explicit political motivations.

The concert demonstrated, as historian Timothy Brown puts it, the 'insurrectionary potential of young rock fans' – and not just of the fans, but of rock music.[6] It is no accident that riots broke out at a concert by the Stones and not, say, the Beatles. Neither band's music was overtly political, and neither showed much sympathy for the political protests that were to come. But the Beatles' music was easy to listen to, a kind of 'entertainment music' (*Unterhaltungsmusik*), with little connection to rock 'n' roll, as Wolfgang Seidel, founding member of the German political rock band Ton Steine Scherben, explained.[7] Their sound was certainly not confrontational. Pieces like

'Yellow Submarine' were 'about a nice old man in a fairytale world telling beautiful stories', claimed photographer Jens Hagen. The sound of the Stones, by contrast, was rooted in blues. Songs like 'Satisfaction' expressed a fundamental dissatisfaction with the world, without naming a clear target. Arguably, this made the appeal for rebellion only more powerful. 'Leave me alone with your shit! And with a rhythm that goes into your bones – music to riot to,' declared Hagen.[8] There might be a good deal of nostalgia in such words, but they give a sense of how rock music could incite confrontations with the authorities, even without bands engaging explicitly with politics.

The Stones might have been popular among anti-authoritarian protestors, but they were never part of a particular political movement. By contrast, Ton Steine Scherben, a local band from West Berlin commonly known as the Scherben that became the most famous political rock band in West Germany during the 1970s, played a much more active role within the radical scene.[9] With songs that were easy to play on a guitar and catchy lyrics, their music became popular with leftist teenagers who listened to it in parks or youth clubs and helped foster a sense of a rebellious community. Formed in the summer of 1970 in Kreuzberg, West Berlin, back then a neighbourhood next to the Wall, the Scherben quickly attracted a huge fan base within the local scene. They were the first political rock band to sing in German, with a distinct Berlin slang. Far from making a nationalist statement, the Scherben tried to reach an audience of working-class kids who would not understand lyrics in English, the language most other bands preferred to perform in. And soon, the band's popularity reached far beyond West Berlin. Their songs such as 'Macht kaputt was euch kaputt macht' (Smash What Is Smashing You), 'Keine Macht für Niemand' (No Power for Nobody) and the 'Rauch-Haus-Song', named after a squat in Kreuzberg, became legendary in West Germany's protesting scenes. Listening to their song about a riot at Kreuzberg's Mariannenplatz could make leftist teenagers, like the author of these lines, dream of heroically battling the police.[10]

Indeed, the Scherben's music inspired people to take action in the streets. On 3 July 1971, the band played a concert at Berlin's

Technical University, a popular venue for leftist events. At the end of the concert, Rio Reiser, the lead singer, told the receptive audience made up of young workers, students, and other radicals to march to Kreuzberg, where developers were planning to tear down the old buildings to make space for new apartment blocks. Local activists had campaigned against these plans for a while, but Reiser's short speech galvanized the movement. Concert-goers readily answered his call for action, descending on and squatting an empty factory building at Mariannenstraße 13.

The occupation lasted only for a night, as police forces quickly evicted the squatters. But it set the stage for another, more lasting occupation. In December 1971, the Scherben returned for another concert at the Technical University. This time, their performance included short political speeches by the band members. At the end of the gig, they called for the crowd to head over to Kreuzberg once more. Some 600 activists answered the call and went to Kreuzberg, where they entered the former Bethanien hospital, a now empty building, and occupied it. They named the house the 'Rauch-Haus' in remembrance of the recently shot RAF member Georg von Rauch.[11] This time, squatters could stay, as they managed to negotiate an official lease with the Berlin Senate. To this day, the Rauch-Haus exists as a place for self-managed, communal living.

Documenting their involvement in the occupation, the Scherben dedicated a song to the house – the 'Rauch-Haus-Song' – with residents of the house singing the refrain for a recording: 'Das ist unser Haus, ihr kriegt uns hier nicht raus' ('This is our house, you won't get us out of here'). Collective singing could be a way to foster a sense of community, as a scene in a documentary of the house, shot by activists, shows: while the Scherben performed inside the squat, young residents chanted the chorus.[12] Yet, such scenes could also be misleading. In fact, the band was not on good terms with the activists in charge of the Rauch-Haus, who blamed the Scherben for having written a song that had 'nothing to do with reality'.

It was not the only conflict between the band and political activists. Expectations within the scene for the Scherben ran high. Not only did activists from around West Germany frequently ask them to perform at solidarity concerts for school strikes or for various leftist organizations, they also demanded the band adhere to the right kind of left-wing politics. The cadres of emerging communist groups but also the nascent Red Army Faction rejected the band's anarchist leanings. Others blamed them for playing good-time rock 'n' roll standards with no explicit political content, or engaging female backing singers who danced behind them on stage. Everyone felt that they had a say in the band's politics. As part of a political scene, the Scherben could not remain independent. Ultimately, these political pressures from within the West Berlin leftist scene led the Scherben to retreat from the city to a farmhouse in North Friesland, where they hoped to live and work together. They continued to produce music, but became less involved in political activism. 'The dream was over,' as a 1972 song put it.[13]

Dissident Sounds: The Plastic People of the Universe

While the Scherben gained fame in West Berlin, a musical and cultural underground movement developed on the other side of the Iron Curtain in Prague. Independent-minded artists gathered in bars to read poetry and novels to each other and organized underground concerts with psychedelic avant-garde bands. The most famous of these were the Plastic People of the Universe – the band Václav Havel wrote about in his *The Power of the Powerless*.[14] The band's origins go back to September 1968, when four teenage boys from Prague started playing together. It might be easy, as historian Jonathan Bolton notes, to link the formation of the band to the Prague Spring. Yet, the band members don't seem to have been thinking much about politics at this point. According to his own account, singer and bassist Milan Hlavsa was in fact surprised to see 'Russian soldiers on his way to rehearsal one day in the winter of 1968–1969'.[15] Complying with the rules for artists in Czechoslovakia, the band officially registered with the authorities and, after enjoying some initial successes – such as winning a prize at the Prague 'Beat Salon' in 1969 – managed to get hold of expensive equipment and rehearsal space at the prestigious Kinský Palace on Prague's Old Town Square. But with official support came expectations from the cultural authorities: cutting their hair short, wearing appropriate attire and singing in Czech instead of English. When the Plastic People refused to comply, they soon lost their official status. They had to find a new practice space, return their expensive instruments and look for regular work because they would no longer be employed as artists by the state.[16]

Initially, the Plastic People mostly played covers of English-speaking bands such as the Velvet Underground. Yet by 1973, the band were performing their own songs, sung in Czech rather than in English, though this wasn't enough to appease authorities. Just as the Scherben in West Berlin had hoped to reach local working-class kids by singing in German, the Plastic People believed, as their 'artistic director' Ivan Jirous put it, that 'contemporary music ought to speak to people in the language they understand'.[17] The years that followed defined the Plastic People, whose line-up then included Milan Hlavsa on bass, Jiří Števich on guitar, Vratislav Brabenec on saxophone and Jiří Kabeš on viola and violin. Additionally, Jirous as well as poet Egon Bondy, who occasionally sang with them, were sources of artistic and intellectual inspiration, writing lyrics and spending time with the band. Though not officially licensed, normally a requirement for bands in communist Czechoslovakia, the band performed fairly freely at registered concerts in Prague and other Czechoslovak towns and cities. Concerts usually attracted crowds of a few hundred people. At times, even government-sponsored organizations such as the Socialist Youth League hosted their concerts.

By the mid-1970s, the band was a focal point of an 'underground' – a term used by contemporaries – in Prague that resembled its Western counterpart in terms of clothing and hairstyles. Photos show long-haired artists wearing wide trousers, scruffy shirts and colourful sweaters.[18] The hair in particular frequently caused trouble as it made finding work difficult, and invited dangerous charges of 'parasitism'. For members of the underground, cutting hair short that had previously been long became a sign of defeat and giving in.[19] Appearances aside, the Plastic People of the Universe, and by extension the scene they represented, have been described as apolitical. Václav Havel, for example, wrote about their trial as prosecuting young people without a 'political past, or even any well-defined political positions'. In his reading, they were 'simply young people who wanted to live in their own way, to make music they liked, to sing what they wanted to sing, to live in harmony with themselves, and to express themselves in a truthful way'.[20] Yet these dismissals ignore the fact that the lyrics of the Plastic People did contain political allusions. A line such as 'Mír mír mír / jako hajzlpapír' ('Peace peace peace / like toilet paper'), as Jonathan Bolton remarks, 'satirized the language of Communist propaganda'.[21] Even more so, the entire underground culture, the styles and texts it produced, rested on a critique of consumerism in both the communist East and the capitalist West. Very much like their Western counterparts, members of the Czech underground longed for an authentic life: they idealized life in the countryside far away from the 'materialistic pursuits of the cities', celebrating primitivism and even madness as an alternative to modern rational and technological society.[22]

In the early years, this scene and the Plastic People were mostly left alone by the authorities, though clashes with the police were always a possibility. However, by 1974, such clashes were becoming increasingly common. The regime and the underground were edging towards confrontation, which came to a head on 30 March 1974. The Plastic People were about to play a concert at Rudolfov, just outside the city of České Budějovice, when police arrived and ordered the audience to leave. Officers pushed people out of the venue, using batons, and into the train station, where they were supposed to board trains back to Prague. The situation escalated when the crowd moved through an underpass, and even more people were badly beaten and arrested. Subsequently, numerous members of the underground scene were expelled from school or had to face other sanctions. A small number faced criminal charges and eventually convictions. Nobody had died, but the psychological effect was so devastating that people talked about the events as the České Budějovice massacre.

But this did not deter the underground. Barely half a year later, on 1 September 1974, a wedding at Postupice was turned into a large concert where the Plastic People and other bands performed; the wedding party would come to be known as the First Festival of the Second Culture, signalling how much the underground sought to distance itself from the official state culture machine. A year and a half later, on 21 February 1976, the Second Festival of the Second Culture took place in Bojanovice. Surprisingly, no police showed up, but it was a false lull. Within a month, security forces started taking action, raiding concerts and arresting members of the Plastic People and other notable people in the scene. The campaign culminated in September of that year with a trial against four leading members of the underground (the trial Václav Havel referred to in *The Power of the Powerless*), though only one of them actually played for the Plastic People of the Universe. In the end, all four defendants were convicted and sent to prison for eight to eighteen months.[23]

What was it about these young people, their dress codes and hairstyles, their ways of dancing and playing music, that posed a threat to the communist regime? Was it merely their ironic critique of official propaganda, or was there something about the *sound* of their music that felt dangerous? The answer isn't easy. Compared with the kind of rock music played by the Rolling Stones, the sound of the Plastic People is much less aggressive. Trying to solve the puzzle, I liked to do a small experiment with my students: I showed them video footage of Plastic People concerts and asked them why this music might sound dangerous; for comparison, I then played communist working-class songs of the kind the regime would have embraced.[24] My students were usually quick to note that the latter are marching songs; they have a clear and simple rhythm, they invite you to join the heroic community of the working class resisting the forces of capitalism and imperialism, singing as one chorus. On the other hand, the sound of the Plastic People of the Universe lacks a clear rhythm, it is disruptive and more melodic; those are no battle songs. The concert-goers shown in the video footage dance by themselves as individuals, they're not striving to be part of a community, and they certainly don't look like strong workers. For a regime that celebrated the building of a great, socialist future, such playful music that doesn't seem to lead anywhere must have sounded disturbing.

No Future: The Shock of Punk

November 1975, London's St Martin's School of Art. The Sex Pistols were playing their first show. Lead singer Johnny Rotten was performing the band's most famous song, 'Anarchy in the UK'. He was yelling into the microphone. 'Right now ha, ha, ha, ha, ha / I am an antichrist / I am an anarchist / Don't know what I want / But I know how to get it / I wanna destroy the passersby'.[25] The Pistols' music was a shock. 'What immediately strikes you is that *this is actually happening*. This is a bloke, with a brain on his shoulders, who is actually saying something he *sincerely* believes is happening in the world, saying it with real venom, with real passion. It touches you, and it scares you, it makes you feel uncomfortable,' mod guitarist Pete Townshend remembered on first listening to the Sex Pistols.[26]

And the Pistols continued to shock the public. On 1 December 1976, they appeared on television on Bill Grundy's show, *Today*. Grundy had planned to present Queen's latest single 'Somebody to Love', but when the band cancelled the interview at the last minute, the record company EMI sent the Pistols in their place. The band members, Johnny Rotten, Steve Jones, Paul Cook and Glenn Mattock, sat in the front row, drinking and smoking, with their feet on the table in front of them. Behind them stood some other members of their gang, among them Siouxsie Sioux. Live on air, they talked about receiving £40,000 from their record company, but it had all gone 'down the boozer', Jones explained. When Sioux told Grundy she had always wanted to meet him, he replied: 'We'll meet afterwards, shall we?' Jones added: 'You dirty sod. You dirty old man!' Grundy, in fact, encouraged Jones to continue. 'You dirty bastard,' he went on, 'you dirty fucker', much to the amusement of everyone standing behind him.[27] Watching the interview today, it feels rather tame. But in 1979, it caused national outrage. The day after, Elvis Costello recalled the mood on a train platform during his commute to work in London. 'God, did you see the Sex Pistols on TV last night?' people said. 'It was as if it was the most awful thing that ever happened. It's a mistake to confuse it with a major event in history, but it was a great morning just to hear people's blood pressure going up and down.'[28]

Though not the first punk band, the Sex Pistols had a profound impact on the punk scene that emerged in the UK and beyond in the late 1970s and throughout the 1980s. They 'tore open the cultural fabric, trashing the past and confronting the present to better refine the future'.[29] Spreading from London to the rest of the UK and then continental Europe, a distinct youth culture with bands, clubs, aesthetic styles and fanzines emerged that challenged . . . everything: 'No Feelings', 'No Fun', 'No Future', as famous punk slogans put it.[30] In August 1976, a first European Punk Rock Festival took place in Mont-de-Marsan in southwestern France, with bands from the UK, France and the United States performing. A second round of the festival a year later featured celebrities such as the Damned, the Clash and French Asphalt Jungle.[31] The first female punk bands formed that summer, such as the Slits or X-Ray Spex. Even the Iron Curtain did not stop punk, much to the dismay of socialist regimes. Punk appealed to youths in the GDR, in Poland, where thousands of teenagers flocked to the Jarocin punk rock festival, and in Yugoslavia, where a punk scene emerged in various cities, most famously in Slovenia's capital Ljubljana.[32]

Punk attracted a tremendous amount of attention from both the authorities and from a media that was equally worried and excited.[33] What is it about this loud, simple, rowdy music and lifestyle that so shocked and disturbed, that was so threatening and yet at the same time enthralling? Punk was a radical negation. Its sound was fast, aggressive and disturbing. Vocals were yelled rather than sung, and there was no need for musical virtuosity: songs relied on simple chords, with no elaborate guitar or drum solos. Any teenager could join a band. Punk rejected consumer society and hippie culture, as well as ideals of femininity and masculinity, not to mention conventional party politics. It painted the world in bleak terms without a sense of hope for the future.

With its anarchist rhetoric, punk is often considered a fundamentally leftist subculture. Many bands indeed embraced leftist politics. In Britain, numerous bands performed at concerts organized by the Rock Against Racism campaign in the late 1970s (see Chapter 8). Punk lyrics and fanzines critically addressed racism and sexism, but also the situation in Northern Ireland and, in the early 1980s, the Falklands War.[34] In West Germany, punk and its political message even made it to the highest constitutional court. During a minor protest march, activists had played the track 'Germany Perish!' ('Deutschland verrecke!'), with its chorus 'Germany must die so that we can live', by the band Slime. This was enough for a lower court to convict the activists for insulting the symbols of the state.[35] When the cases finally reached the Federal Constitutional Court, it not only overruled the conviction, but also argued that it was part and parcel of a long tradition of lyrical critiques of society that stretched back to Heinrich Heine's famous poem 'The Silesian Weavers' from 1842.[36] Since then, the court ruling has become a favourite story of the leftist scene, shared in bars and at parties, much to everyone's amusement – which is how I first heard it.

More politically committed bands such as Crass in the UK were closely tied to the structures of an alternative counterculture, living in squats and playing gigs at leftist venues.[37] However, punk bands and their fan base often refused to get involved with political parties on the left such as the Socialist Workers Party.[38] After all, running these groups effectively relied on discipline and organization, things that punks despised. And more than once, punks' anarchic lifestyle led to conflicts with other members of countercultural scenes: in squatted houses, punks – the charge went – did not help with creating a better home or better relations with neighbours, but quite literally destroyed everything.[39]

That said, punk music offered a biting critique of the social realities of the 1970s and 1980s. The lyrics of British bands addressed the bleak reality of mass unemployment, which averaged more than 3 million between 1982 and 1986.[40] 'Forgotten youth just waste away / Sniffing glue to face the day / Walking streets, singing on / Government schemes go on and on', the Abrasive Wheels sang.[41] The Exploited even predicted that unemployed youths would be conscripted into the army in a coming war.[42] At the same time, punks detested the monotony of work. In the lyrics of East German punk band Schleimkeim: 'Getting up early in the morning / standing all day at the machine / day by day the same kind of shit / every human being will get mad / going to a bar in the evening / always seeing the same people / eight, nine beers in the cell / a shot and then home'.[43]

Boredom was generally a central theme for punks: according to the Clash, 'London burned with boredom', while the Adverts portrayed 'bored teenagers' who looked for 'emotional rages' to 'fill the vacuum'. Other bands were bored with school, 'druggy hippies', media, conversations or just felt they had 'a boring life' (the Slits).[44] In particular life in suburbia was a 'dystopia' for punk: 'a panorama of tedium and banality wherein "your future dream is a shopping theme"'.[45] 'The Sound of the Suburbs' by the Members gave an account of this banality: 'Same old boring Sunday morning / old man's out washing the car / Mum's in the kitchen cooking Sunday dinner / Her best meal moaning while it lasts'. On Mondays, 'Heathrow jets go crashing over our home', while 'the woman next door / just sits and stares outside'. And so the song goes on, depicting a dull routine with 'family shoppers crowding out the centre of town', while 'young blokes' sit on the benches, 'shouting at the young girls walking around'. All the while, Johnny stands in the bedroom, stares into the dark and annoys the neighbours 'with his punk rock electric guitar'.[46]

Finally, punk was also a rejection of gender norms, for both women and men. Women such as Viv Albertine, Vivienne Westwood, Jordan and Siouxsie Sioux played a crucial role for the development of British punk. Fanzines in the early 1980s, at least in the UK, discussed sexism next to topics such as militarism and animal liberation.[47] Numerous punk bands either included female members or were exclusively female, challenging the stereotype of the masculine rock star. In their lyrics, bands such as the Slits, Ludus and the Raincoats sang about taboo-busting themes like rape, the pressure for young girls to conform to ideals of femininity or menstruation and female sexuality.[48] Ideals of strong masculinity were equally put into question. Consider Johnny Rotten with his sallow skin, the rotten teeth that gave him his name and the torn clothes 'hiding a skinny physique scarred by cigarette burns and cuts'.[49] Even the word 'punk' implied a rejection of 'rock's association with male virility', as its etymological origins refer to 'the worthless and degenerate, to male prostitutes and imprisoned young delinquents ready or forced to be fucked by the fellow inmates'.[50]

Rebelling against society in all its aspects, whether it was consumer capitalism in the West or state socialism in the East, punk had no vision of a better future. 'There's no future, no future, no future for you', Johnny Rotten famously sang in 'God Save the Queen'.[51] The future punk anticipated was a dystopia, characterized by nuclear war, destruction or total surveillance of society by then-novel computer systems.[52] They imagined society to utterly collapse into chaos and permanent violence.[53] Finding work, Chron Gen reasoned in the 1980s, made no sense, "cos pretty soon, all life will be void'.[54] Punk was the sound of pure rebellion, a scream into the void rather than a hopeful call for change.

Utopian Bodies: The Sound of Techno

Berlin, 1989. On 9 November, the Wall had fallen. In the streets, people were celebrating their freedom, they danced, they hugged each other (see Chapter 15). But music did not play a prominent role in that event. There are no famous revolutionary songs, despite bands such as the Plastic People of the Universe or the role that punk played in the GDR. If a song is popularly remembered to symbolize the moment, it's David Hasselhoff's 'Looking for Freedom', which he performed at the remnants of the Wall on New Year's Eve that year. But this is not the sound of the *Wende* (the 'turn-around', as the period is called in German). It's the deep bass line of techno music.[55]

Already before the Wall fell, East Berlin youngsters were listening to techno music on the West Berlin radio programme *SF-Beat*, hosted by Monika Dietl. When the Wall came down, a vibrant underground techno scene developed with improvised, semi-legal clubs opening up in East Berlin's many abandoned buildings and factory halls such as a former electric power station. But should we consider techno a rebellious sound? The Love Parades in Berlin during the 1990s, huge techno events that attracted up to a million participants, were officially registered as political demonstrations for peace and harmony. They weren't particularly rebellious. For sure, some 'Hate' or 'Fuck Parades', organized in response to these 'Love Parades', did result in minor clashes with the police. But techno wasn't music to riot to. Techno did not sound as disruptive as the psychedelic rock of the Plastic People, or the punk of the Sex Pistols. If punk was the music of 'no future', of radical rejection, then techno was the sound of envisioning and creating a better future. Perhaps more so than any other music, techno was utopian. Yet, the utopia of techno was not that of a better society achieved by revolutionary means, but a utopia of bodies and bodily pleasures.

When music critics in the early 1990s encountered techno, they felt uncomfortable. They were unconvinced that the harsh and monotonous rhythm of techno could make people feel good in their bodies. Techno was, journalists Falko Blask and Michael Fuchs-Gamböck wrote in 1995, the first youth culture 'in which sex plays at most a secondary role, or perhaps no role at all'.[56] Dancing to the sound of electronically produced music sucked party-goers into a 'maelstrom of aggressive monotony', another journalist, named Michael Pilz, claimed. In the artificial lights of fog machines and stroboscopes, 'the last natural movements freeze into mechanical tremors'.[57]

Yet, these outsider perspectives missed what techno artists sought to achieve. Techno was about expanding the potential of pleasure. It should affect the entire body, not only the ears of listeners. 'First the bass massaged the area around the tail. There you felt a sensation of warmth that crept up the spine and reached via the back of the head the entire skull. Then you got a big grin on your face,' was how Wolfram Neugebauer, formerly known as Wolle XDP, described the 'magic bass line' he used at the Tekknozid parties he organized in the early 1990s.[58] Club owners and party organizers arranged the interior of their locations to heighten these pleasurable sensations. Whereas the typical venues of punk concerts, leftist youth clubs and squatted houses had been minimalist, without any sense of cosiness, techno clubs either reduced visual impressions so that party-goers would entirely focus on the equally acoustic and haptic experience of music, or they introduced playful elements. Sabine Schelbert, for example, recalled a back room in the 90 Grad Club furnished like a playground, including swings. 'We were like little children,' she commented.[59] While punks had tried to escape the demand for constant self-improvement by acts of symbolic self-destruction – think of piercings with safety needles – techno sought to expand and improve the body by technological means, that is, through music that energized and accelerated bodies and brains.

Contrary to the perception of media observers, techno was not hostile to sexuality, but imagined a form of sexuality that broke with heterosexual norms. 'In the basement', one party-goer remembered, 'everyone was lying down, everyone caressed an arm, a leg. Heterosexuals and gays all in a tumble, and girls in between.'[60] Heterosexual men kissed gay men, women danced with bare breasts. In the 'smooching culture' of techno, recalled Inga Humpe, everyone could kiss everyone, without sexual connotations. 'Particularly as a woman, you could feel absolutely free,' she remarked.[61] The experience of music itself gained a sexual dimension. DJ 3-Phase, for example, described how creating a techno track required 'intention and dedication . . . and then, when you press the right button in the right moment . . . then you have sex with machines,

aural sex so to speak.'[62] Techno was promised technologically stimulated bodily pleasure without boundaries, disregarding gendered
sexual norms.

In the 1970s and 1980s, many activists had viewed the newly
invented computers as a massive threat, as a means of controlling
minds, bodies and nature, of potentially destroying the world.
Techno artists had a much more optimistic take on information
technology. In the words of DJ Mijk van Dijk:

> Punk was always an attitude of rejection. In Techno, you were for
> something, for the music, for the lifestyle. It was a time full of hope.
> So many things were gone: the Wall, the East–West conflict . . . In the
> 1980s, computers were seen as the epitome of the surveillance state,
> and suddenly it was a means of self-realization, of making new music.
> A machine of liberation, not a machine of surveillance.[63]

Some might question how political excessive dancing in techno
clubs, often with the aid of drugs, actually was. From a critical perspective, techno looks simply hedonistic at best. It could be seen as
the music of a neo-liberal age that required, and still requires, individuals to work until exhaustion, just as they party until exhaustion;
a music that subjects human beings to machines and the sounds
they produce. In short, wasn't techno more dystopian than utopian?[64] For techno activists at least, the party culture of the raves
had a fundamentally democratic dimension. The producer of the
music, the DJ, was no longer a star standing on a stage that separated him, and less often her, from the audience, but one more
person in the crowd. Talking about the Berlin club Ufo, Arne Grahm
recalled that 'the DJ just stood there. Not on a stage. At eye level. It
was like grassroots democracy, just great. Even in the [supposedly
egalitarian] GDR, DJs were standing on a stage, or least somewhat
separated. Knowing the DJ was considered a privilege. And this did
not happen at the Ufo. The DJs played, recorded and danced themselves.'[65] On the dance floor, the crowd could become one, any
distinction disappeared. In that sense, techno represented a vision

of an egalitarian and democratic community held together by music and collective joy.

Techno was not just a promise for a better future, but an attempt to create that future right here right now, on the dance floor. But did this work, or was this just the talk of utopian artists? Sure, there were those who lost themselves in the never-ending parties and drugs, who quickly exhausted their physical strength. But others described the positive effects that techno parties could have on people. At a trance party, Wolfram Neugebauer had installed a 'Mind Machine' that did not play distinct beats, the characteristic of techno, but only 'spherical' and more melodic soundscapes. During the fifteen minutes it played, 'many had closed their eyes, and all moved like an amorphous mass in tune. Others sat down and hugged. My girlfriend said that coming into the room was like the comforting feeling of a great dream.'[66]

And while the anarchic urban techno scene of the immediate post-Cold War period in Berlin has disappeared, the utopian vision of techno culture continues to live on during events such as the yearly Fusion Festival at a former military airfield in northeastern Germany, some 100 kilometres away from Berlin. Having started in 1997, it attracted in the years before Covid-19 up to 70,000 visitors. In the words of its leftist organizers, the festival seeks to create a 'parallel society of a special kind', free of social norms and constraints, 'a carnival of senses', which they tellingly describe as 'holiday communism'.[67] Whether that's true is, of course, another question. 'Just compare the toilets for ordinary visitors with those who have some function at the Fusion,' a friend said when I mentioned the festival's communist vision.

The Rebellious Republicanism of Hip Hop

'Stranger in my own country / no foreigner, but still a stranger', the hip hop crew Advanced Chemistry from Heidelberg rapped in 1992.[68] In the wake of a series of sometimes deadly attacks against shelters for asylum seekers and houses where Turkish immigrants and their descendants lived, the rappers – Torch, Toni L and Linguist – drew attention to the everyday realities of racism that people of colour in Germany were exposed to. The sons of Italian 'guestworker' (Toni L.), Afro-German (Linguist) and Haitian-German (Torch) parents all had German passports, as they emphasized in the track, but were still regularly confronted with racist violence and discrimination. Police picked them out for ID-checks when nobody else was stopped, and acquaintances enquired when they would return home – not to Heidelberg, but to their 'real' country of origin. In Germany, the assumption still was that a 'real German' had to be blue-eyed and blond-haired, while Germans liked to forget that it was foreigners who carried out unpopular labour. Their song, one of the first rap tracks in German, was both a vigorous critique of racism in Germany and an assertion of power: as German citizens with 'migrant backgrounds', they dared to speak up against injustice.[69]

From its origins in the United States in the late 1970s, rap had a political message.[70] It called out police violence and racism in the ghettos of American cities, it criticized the limited opportunities the state afforded their inhabitants. In Europe, rap music – whether American or home-grown – particularly resonated with marginalized youth, often from immigrant backgrounds, who used rap as a means of self-expression. In some cases, such as Advanced Chemistry, this took a distinctly political form, though the music became less politicized, at least in Germany, as it became more popular during the 1990s and 2000s. In France, the situation was different. In the infamous French *banlieues*, the suburbs of large cities such as Paris, Marseille and Lyon, popularly known for burning cars, riots, high levels of violence and unemployment, and home to many immigrants and their descendants from France's colonies (of course, a deeply problematic picture), rap found a receptive audience.[71] However, the celebration of material wealth, of luxurious cars and excessive parties so common in American rap music did not resonate among the youth of the *banlieues*. Despite all the problems they were facing, their situation was not comparable to that of Afro-Americans, as French rappers were keen to point out. In France, where by the 1990s the world's second-largest market for rap music had emerged, addressing political issues in rap lyrics was much more common than elsewhere in Europe. Politics and popular success were – and still are – not mutually exclusive.[72]

Unlike the utopian dreams of techno that functioned with sound alone, rap music celebrated lyrical complexity and intricacy. In their tracks, artists expressed the pride they took from 'coming from the neighbourhood'. They depicted a rough life, smoking marijuana and drinking beer all night, while also emphasizing solidarity among neighbours.[73] For the *banlieusards*, the marginalized inhabitants of the suburbs, rap music became a way of proudly asserting their identity. Tellingly, many rappers continued to live in the *banlieue* where they had grown up, even after they gained fame and money that would have allowed them to move out.[74] At the same time, rap artists frequently drew attention to the challenges of growing up in a *cité*: to the everyday racism, the common feelings of shame that come with being a marginalized outsider, the insults, the lack of money, the misery, the need to 'hold back the tears so as not to appear a weakling', as rap group KDD put it in one 1998 song.[75] Tracks encouraged parents to look after their children and expressed concern about the 'young brothers' exposed to the temptations of consumer culture and easily trapped in cycles of humiliation and violence.[76] The music turned into a means to engage with, to reject but also to creatively appropriate stigmas and prejudices about the 'savage' *banlieues*.[77] Rap, was, and still is, a way of claiming agency for those marginalized by the police and the state.

Rappers who speak openly about politics have often faced charges of propagating violence, homophobia, misogyny, antisemitism or radical Islamism, and (in the French context) of undermining republican values. Conservative and right-wing politicians frequently hold rappers and their aggressive songs responsible for stirring up unrest in the *banlieues*.[78] In November 1996, such accusations even resulted in the conviction of the rap group Suprême NTM (meaning the North Transmits the Message, referring to the northern districts of cities like Paris and Marseille, but also the insult *nique ta mère*, literally 'fuck your mother'), one of the most famous and most socially engaged rap groups. A year earlier, they had insulted police officers on duty during a concert, calling them fascist thugs and a danger to freedom. Three different police unions took offence and filed charges. Considering these insults an attack on public order, the district court in Toulon convicted two rappers to six months in prison, put three of them on probation and imposed a six-month ban on performances. Toulon had, in fact, just elected a local mayor from the right-wing Front National, and the judge had a reputation for extraordinarily harsh rulings. Following a public outcry over the limitation of the freedom of expression, an appeal court overturned the ruling and imposed instead a two-month prison term and fine of 50,000 francs; but the conviction itself stood.[79]

In some cases, such accusations are not without foundation. There are rappers who make homophobic and antisemitic comments. Most infamously, British Abdel-Majed Abdel Bary, known as rapper Jinn, and German Denis Cuspert, known as Deso Dogg, celebrated jihadist violence and eventually joined the Islamic State of Iraq and the Levant (ISIL) in 2013, where Jinn renamed himself Abu Kalashnikov. However, far from rejecting democratic society in favour of violence and or even Islamist terrorism, most European rap artists have critically engaged with liberal and republican values, charging society for not fulfilling its egalitarian promises. Advanced Chemistry, for example, emphasized that they were all German citizens, but were not treated as such. In another track, they explicitly referred to Article 3 of the German constitution, which bans discrimination.[80] The lyrics of French rap artists draw attention to the country's colonial history, which for a long time has been ignored in school curricula.[81] In his 2012 song 'Letter to the Republic', Kery James, for example, reminded French audiences of the country's colonial crimes in Africa and specifically Algeria: 'It's you who chose to tie your history with ours.' And now, he argued, it was time for

France to take responsibility: 'We, the Arabs and Blacks, we're not here by chance. Every arrival has its departure!'[82] Along similar lines, rapper Tunisiano brought a complaint to the police in a 2008 track, against police violence and racist laws: 'Nobody is below the law, because everybody has rights,' he charged.[83]

Rap, then, is, at least in its socially and politically engaged form, a self-empowering and potentially radical music. It's neither a total rejection of society, like punk, nor a utopian celebration of happiness, like techno. It depicts difficult social realities and encourages young audiences to find an alternative to crime and violence, to use language and art as a means to build a better life: 'Put down the gun, put down the knife, grab a book and teach your group,' Assassin rapped in English: 'Open a book, take a book and you're sure to find the truth.'[84] At the same time, rap appeals to the universalist values that liberal democracies like to uphold. Rap envisioned a form of citizenship that reaches beyond borders; it created a culture that is not tied to any nation or ethnicity, and that cherishes exchange and interaction.[85]

The Power of Music

Music played, and plays, an immensely powerful role in protest movements. It can incite direct action, up to rioting and violence; it can disturb existing orders and threaten established powers; it can express an utter rejection of existing society, or it can practically anticipate a better future. It can be a way to assert an identity, to gain a voice and to insist on universal rights. It can speak across national and cultural boundaries and unite people for common demands. It can generate hope. Audiences not only listen to songs, but they sing along and thereby appropriate the message when they join in at concerts, parties and street protests. The entire body is affected, when people gather and dance to the sounds of rebellious and utopian music. Music, that is, calls for an active engagement in many ways.

Music has not lost this power. Across the world, protestors express their hopes and demands by singing: in the Syrian revolution of 2011, crowds did not chant but sang about the end of Assad's regime. During the wave of protests in Lebanon in the autumn of 2019, protestors sang Beethoven's 'Ode to Joy', in Arabic; and in November of that year, the Italian Sardine movement mobilized thousands who gathered in the streets and squares across the country singing the old anti-Fascist song 'Bella Ciao', in opposition to the right-wing Lega Nord party.[86] In such moments, the collective experience of singing unites people. It connects them with traditions of past political struggles and expresses hope for the future.

PART III

A Better Future: Movements and Campaigns

7.

From International Solidarity to Humanitarian Help

'Ho, Ho, Ho Chi Minh,' radical students chanted at protest marches around the world in 1968. Photos of the protestors show them carrying placards with images of the heroes of global revolution: alongside Ho Chi Minh, the leader of the Vietcong fighting Americans in Vietnam, loom the now iconic portraits of Ernesto Che Guevara and Fidel Castro, both heroes of the Cuban Revolution (1953–9), and Chinese communist leader Mao Zedong. These student protestors inhabited what historian Christoph Kalter has called a 'shared space of imagination, communication and action' that connected the First with the Third World in what they believed was a common fight against the capitalist and imperialist order.[1] Revolutionary movements in the Third World would, activists in the First World hoped, lead the way in this struggle.

Some fifty years later, another wave of activism has crossed national boundaries: the movement in support of refugees coming from countries such as Syria, Afghanistan and Iraq to Europe; and though the movement saw its heyday during the so-called refugee crisis – a deeply problematic term – of 2015/16, it lives on, most recently providing help to Ukrainians fleeing the Russian war of aggression in early 2022.[2] Volunteer organizations run rescue missions on the Mediterranean Sea and provide first aid in overcrowded camps on the Greek Islands. In the countries of final destination, mostly Germany, France and Sweden, individual volunteers help refugees integrate into their new homes in all kinds of ways. It is an impressive movement driven by people's desire to express kindness towards strangers. This new movement comes with its own heroes, who are more often than not heroines. They are people like Pia Klemp and Carola Rackete, two German captains of rescue missions facing charges in Italy for breaking new and harsh immigration laws. If the name of any refugee is recognizable it is that of Alan Kurdi, the young Syrian boy who drowned together with most of his family while trying to reach Greece in September 2015.[3] The iconography of heroes, heroines and in particular of victims has thus fundamentally changed. The shift points to a deeper transformation of internationalist activism, which this chapter traces: from the early days of international solidarity to the emergence of humanitarian aid and a 'politics of pity'.[4]

International Solidarity

'Our growing political awareness is closely linked with the Algerian revolution,' wrote Jean-Philippe Talbo Bernigaud in the first issue of French leftist magazine *Partisans* in September 1961.[5] Bernigaud was part of a generation of leftist intellectuals and militants across Western Europe who felt profoundly alienated from traditional communist politics. Nikita Khrushchev's revelations about Stalin's terror regime in 1956 and the crushing of the Hungarian uprising that same year made once-dedicated communists break with their parties and engage in a rereading of Marx's writings, as we've seen in Chapter 5. In France, the Communist Party's failure to unambiguously oppose the French war against the Algerian independence movement only amplified this sense of alienation. When these intellectuals looked for revolutionary movements that might give reason to hope, they found them outside of Europe: first in the Cuban Revolution of 1959, then in the defeat of the French in Algeria and the country's subsequent independence, events that both demonstrated that the historically weak could overcome the strong on the international stage. If revolution in the so-called advanced countries of the West had become impossible, and the communist East did not provide a convincing alternative either, then the rebellions in the (soon to be former) colonial world might point to a way forward.[6]

With the gaze turned outwards, leftist thinking changed

fundamentally. No text exemplifies this more powerfully than Frantz
Fanon's *The Wretched of the Earth*, published in 1961 with a preface by
renowned philosopher Jean-Paul Sartre.[7] Born in 1925 on the Caribbean island of Martinique, a long-time French colony and a French
département since 1946, Fanon had enlisted in the Free French Army
during the Second World War to fight Nazism. This was to prove a
deeply disappointing experience. Not only did he come to realize
that French farmers cared little for the struggle against fascism, but
he also witnessed the racism of the French troops. After the war,
Fanon trained as a psychiatrist and went on to work first in Blida-
Joinville (Algeria), where he treated the traumatized fighters of the
Algerian National Liberation Front (FNL), then in Tunis. In 1961, as
the French government was starting to negotiate with the FNL,
Fanon dictated *The Wretched of the Earth* after he had learned that
his leukaemia was terminal and his death imminent.[8]

Fanon depicted the colonial world in deeply antagonistic terms. In
many ways, his analysis mirrored how Marxists had written about
the capitalist world: the book's title (*Les Damnés de la terre*, in the
French original) was, after all, a quote from the Internationale, the
great song of the international working-class movement of the late
nineteenth century. But whereas the old working-class movement
had called upon the industrial working class to rise against capitalism, Fanon called upon colonized peoples around the globe as the
new 'wretched of the earth' to fight imperialism. In the colonial
world, it was racism that structured society on its most fundamental level and effectively produced the capitalist class antagonism. In
Fanon's reading, violence and dehumanization characterized the
relation between colonizers and colonized, and hence violence
was necessary to overcome and destroy the colonial system and to
create an absolute 'free subject'. Fanon's justification of violence
has, unsurprisingly, received most attention and sparked sharp
critiques – though we need to keep in mind the very real violence
and torture committed by French troops during the Algerian
War that was a backdrop for his book.[9] But what matters more
for our understanding of leftists' fascination with revolutionary

movements in the so-called Third World is that Fanon introduced a new, revolutionary subject: the colonized peoples struggling for liberation. Armed peasants engaged in violent uprisings came to replace industrial workers on strike as heroes of the revolutionary left. In Fanon's thinking, the West thus ceased to function as the central stage for the revolutionary drama it had hitherto been.[10]

While Fanon wrote his book for an audience in the (post-)colonial world, Jean-Paul Sartre's preface explained its relevance for metropolitan readers. According to Sartre, Fanon provided the West with a mirror in which it could see the naked truth about itself, stripped of its humanist rhetoric. For Sartre, such a perspective offered an opportunity for Europe itself to change: 'We, too, peoples of Europe, are being decolonized.'[11] With the liberation of colonized nations, a 'new beginning of humanity' loomed on the horizon. The struggles of the 'Third World', and the voices in them, mattered deeply for the 'First World'.

Fanon's book was only the most famous text about anti-colonial struggles. In the 1960s, leftists discovered these struggles around the globe in numerous books and the pages of magazines such as *Partisans* in France and *Kursbuch* in West Germany that offered authors from the Third World chances to publish their work.[12] At the same time, militants from Asia, Africa and Latin America forged solidarity in the streets, thereby shaping Western European protest cultures. How much of a leading role these activists could take became clear in 1964, when Congolese prime minister Moishe Tshombé came to Western Europe, facing protests wherever he went.[13]

Congo had been a Belgian colony until it gained independence in June 1960.[14] The first prime minister of the Democratic Republic of Congo, as the new state was officially called, Patrice Lumumba, promised to pursue a nationalist, independent economic policy that would keep the country politically neutral by aligning neither with the Soviet Union nor with the United States. Western leaders found such ideas deeply concerning. They worried about maintaining access to the country's rich natural resources, in particular its copper, uranium and manganese deposits in the province of Katanga.

Not surprisingly, then, a secessionist movement in Katanga became the grateful recipient of Western support, particularly from Belgium, which, by 1960, sent military aid to the rebels. Lumumba appealed first to the United Nations for support against the rebels and their European mercenaries, then, when the UN did not respond, to the Soviet Union. This, of course, only alienated Western powers further. Relying on their support, Joseph-Désiré Mobutu staged a military coup in September 1960; four months later, in January 1961, Lumumba was shot by an execution squad.[15] Another three years later, Moishe Tshombé, the exiled Katangan leader, returned to the country with American and Belgian help to become prime minister and to suppress a leftist uprising. Once again supported by white mercenaries and Belgian paratroopers, the Congolese military put a bloody end to the rebellion.

Around the globe, the murder of Lumumba brought outraged protestors to the streets in their hundreds of thousands in cities such as Cairo, London, New Delhi, Colombo, Dakar, Tel Aviv, Accra, Tehran and many others.[16] African (and not just Congolese) students studying abroad in the US and Europe played a prominent role in organizing these protests alongside native – and usually white – students. When Moishe Tshombé visited Western Europe in the autumn of 1964, the protests resumed. In Paris, about a thousand French and African students took to the streets, and in Naples, the protests led to clashes with the police. In West Berlin, members of the Socialist Student Union and other German left-wing groups coordinated their demonstrations against the prime minister's visit, scheduled for 18 December 1964.

The protest against Tshombé was a remarkable and radicalizing event for the West German extra-parliamentary left.[17] African students in West Germany, and even in the GDR – they were allowed to move more freely in the divided city because of the need to receive money transfers from families via Western banks – flocked to West Berlin, where they took direct action, something that was unfamiliar to most German militants. They had not shown their posters and slogans to the police for prior approval, as was required in the 1960s, and were loudly chanting, ignoring the fact that authorities had permitted only a silent protest. When Tshombé did not appear as expected at the main entrance of Tempelhof airport and protestors realized that he had been escorted out through a side door, they broke through a disorganized police line to reach the nearby Rathaus Schöneberg, the city hall where the Social Democratic mayor and later chancellor Willy Brandt would receive Tshombé. There the protestors encountered a second line of police officers. Pretending to be local shoppers, they crossed over into the market in front of the building. Once inside the cordon, they reassembled to resume their chanting. When Brandt became aware of the protest, he not only received a delegation of the demonstrators that included both representatives of African student organizations and the SDS, but also cut his meeting with Tshombé short to the 'minimum required by protocol'.[18] This was a great success for the protestors, emboldening West German activists to pursue more confrontational protest tactics.

The protest against Tshombé's visit to Germany was not the only one in which foreign students played a major role. Three years later, in June 1967, Persian Shah Reza Pahlavi and his glamorous wife Farah Diba visited West Berlin.[19] Again, it was foreign students, this time from Iran, who initiated the protest against the hated monarch, who had come to power after a coup in 1953, staged by the CIA, and deposed the democratically elected prime minister, Mohammed Mossadeq. Iranian students found eager support in West Berlin's radical leftist scene. The protest on the evening of 2 June 1967 turned out to be extremely violent. While the Shah and his wife were watching a performance of *The Magic Flute*, around 6,000 protestors gathered in front of the German Opera, where both the police and Iranians loyal to the regime attacked them. As the battle between police and protestors raged, plain-clothes police officer Karl-Heinz Kurras shot twenty-six-year-old student Benno Ohnesorg, who had not been actively involved in the fighting, in the head. The student died that same night. Ohnesorg's violent death became a formative moment for the West German student movement. Over the next days, thousands went to the streets across cities in West Germany, while droves of students joined the SDS, as we've seen in Chapter 2.

The intellectual interest in the 'Third World' and the rousing street protests of the 1960s grew into movements for international solidarity in the 1970s. Of course, the American war in Vietnam was at the heart of many protests, with students organizing demonstrations and international congresses that expressed solidarity with the Vietcong and accused American forces of war crimes.[20] But militants also looked beyond this conflict, to other revolutionary uprisings and socialist movements around the globe. In 1973, they campaigned for Chile and its socialist leader Salvador Allende, who had been toppled by a military coup, again with American help, that led to the dictatorship under General Pinochet; later in the decade, attention turned to socialist movements in Nicaragua and El Salvador. Likewise, the anti-colonial movement in Mozambique against the last European colonial power, Portugal – which ultimately ended with a revolution in Portugal itself – and the anti-apartheid movement in South Africa received wide support.[21]

Local support committees disseminated information about political developments in these countries. They collected donations to support revolutionary movements or sold commodities such as coffee from Nicaragua (branded as 'solidarity coffee': drinking the right brand of coffee turned into a political act). Often, these committees involved only a small number of militants, but nevertheless, international solidarity was an essential aspect of leftist protest cultures in the 1970s and 1980s. Even left-leaning high-school magazines frequently published articles about revolutionary movements across the world. More adventurous activists travelled to the hotspots of revolutionary activism, most often to Latin America, to give practical support to their comrades and to gain first-hand insights into building a better world from their revolutionary heroes.[22] At times, this revolutionary tourism turned into a moment of disillusionment as radicals were confronted with the harsh realities of those revolutions. Having spent several months in Cuba doing 'political education work', German left-wing author Hans Magnus Enzensberger, for example, came to realize that the country was deeply authoritarian rather than socialist.[23]

By and large, such grassroots campaigns for the Third World

were a Western phenomenon. In communist Eastern Europe, solidarity with anti-imperialist movements was part of the official political ideology.[24] To take just one example, the GDR developed a highly ritualized calendar of solidarity weeks. Every year in May, the regime organized a 'week of solidarity with the anti-imperialist struggle of African peoples'; a similar week dedicated to the struggles of Arab peoples followed in June, and finally a week for the struggles in Latin America in September.[25] The GDR also devoted significant resources to supporting campaigns for African-American activist Angela Davis, a symbol of the struggle against racism in the United States, and sent development aid workers known as 'friendship brigades' to socialist 'brother countries'.[26] Beyond these state-sponsored activities, however, small independent groups did exist, usually under the umbrella of the Protestant church, that sought to support movements in the Third World. The Sandinista revolution of 1979 in Nicaragua and the attempts to build a socialist society, for example, sparked interest and fascination across the Iron Curtain. It provided a vision for a different future beyond both capitalist and Soviet systems that had the potential to encourage critical attitudes towards communist regimes 'at home'.[27]

What are we to make of this international solidarity? Scholars, some of them former activists, have provided rather damning assessments. In their mind, solidarity was nothing more than a 'phantasmagoria', lacking any relation to reality; the Third World and its revolutionary movements merely provided 'projection screens' for Western militants looking for revolutions elsewhere to distract from their own distinctly non-revolutionary situation in the metropole.[28] From today's perspective, middle-class students, after all a small elite group, chanting 'Ho-Ho-Ho Chi Minh', or identifying with Fidel Castro and Ernesto Che Guevara, might look absurd.[29] Building on critiques already being formulated in the late 1960s, some historians have also drawn a direct line from solidarity with armed uprisings in the Third World to terrorism in the 1970s.[30] It is true that Brazilian Carlos Marighella's *Minimanual of the Urban Guerrilla* was a foundational text for groups such as the Red Army Faction

in West Germany. Even more troubling, its terrorists received training in Palestinian camps.[31] If solidarity with the Third World
movements had any real effect, in short, it was not positive.

These critiques have some credibility given that many came from
the militants themselves. They cautioned that Third World activism
might be nothing but an escape from the political realities at home;
that the objects of solidarity were easily interchangeable, which spoke
to the lack of genuine interest in any particular case; that Western
militants often acted with a paternalist attitude; and that activists were
more interested in pure theory than in complex realities.[32] From the
perspective of Western (wannabe) revolutionaries, all the different
struggles in the Third World, whether by guerrillas in Latin America
or by Fedayeen in Palestine, were the same: 'our' struggle. The specific context of a conflict no longer mattered.[33] No doubt, there is
much truth to these arguments. Often enough, it was the revolutionary (and deeply masculine) heroism, the seeming authenticity of
Third World peoples not yet corrupted by Western thought and
consumer culture, that leftist in Europe students found appealing.[34]

And yet, we miss something important about these internationalist movements if we focus only on the ways in which they fell
short. Solidarity meant something in activists' everyday lives. It
encouraged both critical analysis and naive idolization. Most importantly, calls for solidarity created a common political horizon. They
implied that people across the world, in the Third World and in the
West, joined together in a common cause, that they were part of
the same political fight. This is precisely what some commentators
such as Jürgen Habermas considered dangerous: it created a deep
and emotional link between the Third World and the First World,
and made forms of fighting – violence – that might be appropriate
in one context (say, Vietnam) acceptable in another, in fact very different context (say, West Germany).[35]

It's hard to deny that Habermas had a point. But it's a one-sided
view. Invoking solidarity calls for a particular way of seeing people
from the Third World, a gaze that recognizes them as political
actors and interlocutors whose voices deserve to be listened to in

'the West'. And while this was perhaps more of an ideal in many cases, it was *also* a reality, as the impact of texts by authors such as Frantz Fanon or joint demonstrations in the streets of West Berlin have shown. This genuine interest in what we now call the Global South, in its political conflicts and revolutionary projects, and in people coming from these countries as actors with their own political voice, is worth keeping in mind today – not to engage in violent politics, but to carefully listen to what those voices are saying.

Humanitarianism and Human Rights

'"Two, three . . . many Vietnams," Che Guevara said. No, none of that has happened!' So wrote an anonymous author in 1972 in the last article dedicated to the Third World in *Partisans*, referring to leftist dreams of creating a domino effect that would make the entire colonial world rise in an anti-imperialist struggle (dreams that, of course, never materialized).[36] As the war in Vietnam drew near to its end, radical leftists in Western Europe who had once celebrated the Vietcong for their fight against American imperialism looked at the horrors of the war and came to realize, as the 1972 *Partisans* author argued, that 'repeating them could not be the goal of leftist politics'. For those on the left who had looked for an alternative in the Third World, it was a moment of utter disillusionment. They could no longer hope that revolutionary movements in the colonial world would also usher in a new revolutionary era in the West to shatter imperialism and capitalism.[37] Of course, international solidarity movements did not simply disappear overnight. They continued to draw attention to socialist revolutionary movements, particularly in Latin America, and their oppression by imperialist powers, throughout the 1970s and 1980s. Yet, by the mid-1970s, the fundamental hopes tied to the uprisings in the Third World had diminished. As the politics of solidarity receded, it gave way to a new discourse with its own distinctly international dimension: that of humanitarianism and human rights.[38]

This discourse has a long and complicated history that reaches back, at least, to abolitionist movements fighting slavery in the eighteenth century.[39] But the real breakthrough of modern human rights approaches that continue to shape politics and activism today happened in the mid-1970s, as dissidents in the Soviet bloc embraced a rhetoric of human rights in their critiques of the state.[40] In the West, the collapse of Third Worldism allowed these ideas and debates to flourish. They fundamentally changed the form that internationalist activism took.

A decisive moment in this transformation was the Biafran War (1967–70).[41] Biafra was part of Nigeria, which had gained independence from the British Empire in 1960. Africa's most populous country was considered by many in the West to be one of the most promising Third World states, not least because of newly discovered oil.[42] The country's population was composed of three major ethnic groups: in the east, the Igbo dominated, in the north the Hausa-Fulani and in the west the Yoruba. In early 1966, a combination of military coups and massacres of Igbos in northern Nigeria resulted in a mass migration that brought two million Igbos to the eastern region. There, military governor-general Chukwuemeka Odumegwu Ojukwu declared Biafra an independent state on 30 May 1967. The federal government in Lagos refused to accept its independence, and a bloody civil war ensued. Realizing that they had no chance to win the war on the battlefield, the Biafran leadership appealed to an international audience. But their pleas for help fell, at least initially, on deaf ears. This only changed when the humanitarian dimension of the conflict gained attention.[43]

Nigeria's federal army had blocked the rebels' access to the sea, causing a massive famine that threatened to cost hundreds of thousands of lives. Christian (and Western) missionaries who had refused to leave the country when other foreigners were evacuated were the first to call for support. By 1968, at the height of the student movement and alongside campaigns for solidarity with Vietnam, a diverse alliance of non-state actors in the West campaigned for relief measures to save lives. These groups included conservative

Christians who emphasized the religious dimension of the conflict (the Igbo were Christian, their opponents Muslim) as well as moderate leftists.[44] Radical militants who otherwise showed a keen interest in the Third World remained, however, mostly silent. In contrast to the struggles in Vietnam, Algeria and Cuba, the Biafran War lacked a revolutionary dimension. This was not a war fought for building a better society as an alternative to Western capitalism and imperialism. Indeed, the activists campaigning for an independent Biafra did not seek to challenge Western values and domination, but to find a place within a Western world order.[45] Politics was not absent in the pro-Biafra campaigns, but it was a very different politics to the Third Worldism that had dominated left-wing discourse. Yet, the political cause of the Biafrans, namely national independence, receded into the background as campaigners focused on the human suffering the war caused.

Ultimately, the rebellion failed. By January 1970, the Biafran secessionists surrendered. Yet, in the process, a new rhetoric and iconography emerged: that of suffering human beings, most notably children. 'Biafran babies' became a 'new icon of Third World misery'.[46] The contrast to the heroes of revolutionary Third Worldism is remarkable. Leftist magazines – *Partisans* in France and *Kursbuch* in West Germany are only the most famous examples; there were myriad small magazines employing a similar rhetoric – had celebrated peasants engaged in armed struggle against imperialism, they had looked at them as exemplars of a 'new man' to be emulated in the metropole, and they had eagerly listened to intellectuals from the Third World and their politics. A starving infant, by contrast, was not to be admired, celebrated or even emulated. They were not a hero, but a victim, with no name, no voice and certainly no political agenda. This new iconography symbolized a transformation whereby, as Kristin Ross aptly summarized, 'Fanon's "wretched of the earth" as the name for an emergent political agency has been essentially reinvented: the new third world is still wretched, but its agency has disappeared, leaving only the misery of a collective victim of famine, flood, or authoritarian state apparatuses.'[47]

For the most part, the Biafra action committees in Western countries collapsed with the end of the war, with the notable exception of France. There, the experience of Biafra became a founding myth for humanitarian activists such as Bernard Kouchner.[48] Trained as a doctor, Kouchner had participated in the May 1968 movement as leader of the Communist Student Union. After the hot days of May had ended, he wanted to put his studies to practical use and enlisted with the International Red Cross to work in Biafra, together with some other veterans of the student movement. What the young doctors experienced in Biafra was to change the course of their lives. One day, some wounded Biafrans came to their clinic with the Nigerian army still in pursuit. Against the advice of the Red Cross, which was to leave the village and their patients because of the looming threat, the doctors stayed to witness the army 'massacre unarmed and wounded men, women and children'. Disobeying the Red Cross's policy of silence and non-intervention, Kouchner and his comrades chose to speak up about the atrocities and to call for international assistance. Upon Kouchner's return to France, the group continued to organize medical aid for victims of war and natural disaster. Four years later, on 3 January 1972, they announced the foundation of Médecins Sans Frontières (MSF), or Doctors Without Borders. In line with the Red Cross, MSF pledged to honour the Hippocratic oath 'as well as the principles of collegiality, material disinterest, and an apolitical stance' – the last a telling move for a former 'Gueverist'.[49]

Yet MSF did have a political goal – that of humanitarianism and human rights. It was (and is) an ideology claiming, in marked contrast to the revolutionary Third Worldism of an earlier decade, to be 'above and beyond politics'. Human rights advocates and humanitarian activists did not just fill a void left by the disappointed hopes of Third World politics of the 1960s. Rather, Kouchner and other so-called new philosophers vociferously turned against romanticizing Third World socialism.[50] Jacques Julliard, a one-time advocate of Algerian independence turned 'anti-Third-Worldist', for example, claimed: 'In Africa' – and, by extension, anywhere else in the Third World – 'there will be no socialism except a totalitarian socialism.'[51]

For the left, it was the time to give up 'old dogmas' and 'return' to explicitly Western (or French) ideas: democracy, ethics or, in the case of Julliard, human rights.[52] The political map changed decisively. The opposing sides in the Third World were no longer 'American' and 'Soviet' or, we might add, imperialist and anti-imperialist, but 'those of the torturing State and the martyred people'.[53] From this perspective, the entire project of solidarity with Third World revolutionaries and their critique of Western claims of superiority had from the very beginning been misguided. As Pascal Bruckner, another anti-Third-Worldist, wrote, 'If the peoples of the third world are to become themselves, they must become more Western.'[54]

With this renunciation of the politics of the 1960s came a remarkable lack of interest in historical and political contexts. This is perhaps most pronounced in what Michael Barnett has called 'emergency humanitarianism', that is, a form of humanitarian aid that is concerned with saving lives and nothing else, a point made explicitly by MSF president Christophe Fournier in 2009.[55] A good example is the Live Aid concert event of 1985, organized by Irish musician Bob Geldof. Shocked by images of the famine in Ethiopia, Geldof had convinced international rock and pop stars including David Bowie, Dire Straits, Bob Dylan and Madonna, to perform simultaneously in London and in Philadelphia to raise funds for humanitarian aid. The concerts attracted hundreds of thousands of people, while an estimated audience of 1.5 billion viewers watched the event live on TV. Financially, it was a huge success, raising donations of around £150 million.[56]

But while it may be tempting to celebrate the event as a testimony to Westerners' concern for starving Africans, a careful look at how the event was framed and sold is revealing. In his autobiography published in 1986, Geldof describes what had motivated him to organize the concerts. He had come home and seen a TV documentary about the famine in Ethiopia. What he saw shocked him: 'The pictures were of people who were so shrunken by starvation that they looked like beings from another planet. Their arms and legs were as thin as sticks, their bodies spindly. Swollen veins and huge, blankly staring eyes protruded from their shrivelled heads.'[57] Something, he felt, had to be done to ease their suffering. The political situation in Ethiopia, the ongoing civil war, and problems of global inequality, all issues that anti-imperialist militants would have been alive to twenty years earlier, were of no concern to Geldof. It was the very visceral experience of bodily suffering, no matter what had caused it, that evoked his response.

A 'star-book' *Live Aid*, published just six weeks after the concert, painted a similar picture. Only nine pages were devoted to the situation in Africa under the headline 'They Are the Children' – another example of how suffering children had replaced fighting adults as representations of the Third World. As the text explained, the concert had not been 'about the pulsing, energetic music of rock and roll played by the world's greatest musicians, not about the wonders of technology that spanned the globe and united the continents – but about hunger. About hunger, about drought, about famine. About despair.' However, most of the booklet was devoted to the 'greatest musicians' and the 'wonders of technology'. In this vision, the Western world appeared to be 'active and dynamic', whereas only 'hunger, passivity and despair' reigned in Africa.[58]

We can see a similar turning away from revolutionary ambitions in the case of Amnesty International.[59] Founded in July 1961 in London, the organization came to play a crucial role in what historian Samuel Moyn has described as the human rights revolution of the 1970s, even receiving the Nobel Peace Prize in 1977.[60] Whereas the revolutionaries of the 1960s had dreamed of radically changing the entire world, Amnesty International's aims were more modest: 'saving the world one individual at a time'.[61] It was a Campaign Against Torture, initiated in 1972, that helped the organization raise its international profile and become the most influential NGO working on human rights.[62] At the centre of attention stood the 'martyred' individual, tortured by the state – and usually, these were either Third World states or states in the Soviet bloc, though Latin American cases were most prominent in the 1970s. Just as humanitarian activists had relied on images of starving bodies, typically those of children, human rights activists in Amnesty International depicted suffering bodies, ideally in combination with individual stories including names.[63]

'I began with a detailed description of a horrible form of torture,' Jeri Laber, an activist in the New York chapter of Amnesty International, described this rhetorical strategy. Then, she explained 'where it was happening and the political context in which it occurred; I ended with a plea to show the offending government that the world was watching.'[64] While Laber did call attention to the political context, it was not the political cause of those who were tortured that called for solidarity or even inspiration, but the infringement on their rights, independent of their cause, that motivated action. In a campaign for victims of torture in Chile in the 1970s, for example, Amnesty International did not mention that all those tortured were students belonging to a revolutionary Marxist organization fighting the Pinochet regime.[65] Moral standpoints, focusing on individual rights and their violation, came to substitute for 'political utopianism', as Moyn has noted. Human rights partisans 'abjured the maximalism that had once lent utopias glamour – especially utopias that required profound transformation, or even revolution and violence'. But, as Moyn adds, 'their substitution of plausible morality for failed politics may have come at a price'.[66]

The price was political recognition. On the surface, it might look like humanitarian and human rights activists simply gave up on utopian politics once their hopes for radical transformation both in the Third World and at home came to nothing. This, of course, is true, and perhaps it is right that armed revolutionary fighters have ceased to inspire Western militants (with the possible exception of Kurdish fighters). Yet, something else has been lost in the process: the recognition of actors from the Third World as political subjects with a voice, with complex political causes that require understanding and reflection and not merely an emotional reaction, causes that connect different parts of the world. Perhaps like nothing else, it is the prominence of suffering or dead children in humanitarian iconography that exemplifies this price. These children do not speak, except through their bodies.[67] They call for emergency landings by 'commandos in white coats' (Claude Liauzu), the doctors who 'parachute' into crisis situations in a way that, as Kristin Ross noted, resembles 'their colonial *parachutiste* predecessors' in the Algerian War of Independence.[68] Even military interventions like those in Afghanistan that result in massive death tolls are now justified with reference to human and particularly women's rights.[69]

Of course, it might be argued that by recognizing suffering bodies, we recognize the humanity of those who suffer. The victims of war and violence, of famine and epidemics, become 'a little more human for us. And this is no small thing, given the dehumanization of which they are frequently the object,' writes anthropologist Didier Fassin, himself a former vice-president of Doctors Without Borders and author of one of the most insightful critical analyses of 'humanitarian reason'. Yet, Fassin continues,

> the very gesture that appears to grant them recognition reduces them to what they are not – and often refuse to be – by reifying their condition of victimhood while ignoring their history and muting their words. Humanitarian reason pays more attention to the biological life of the destitute and unfortunate, the life in the name of which they are given aid, than to their biographical life, the life through which they could, independently, give a meaning to their own existence.[70]

We can observe the effects of this humanitarian logic in the movement that emerged in response to the 'refugee crisis' of 2015, a movement I myself have been involved in.[71] When close to a million refugees, mostly from war-torn Syria and Afghanistan, but also from Iraq, Iran and Eritrea, arrived in Germany in the autumn and winter of 2015/2016, they were met with a spontaneous 'welcoming culture'. Ordinary citizens went to train stations to distribute food, water and teddy bears for children, they offered language classes, supported refugees in their struggles with bureaucracy, provided shelter for those in need or donated clothes and money. While Germany received the most international media attention, similar movements emerged in Sweden and Austria; and volunteers from all over Europe flocked to Greece to rescue refugees from drowning and support them in the chaotic and miserable conditions of Greek refugee camps. The movement has come to represent Europe 'with a human face'.[72]

It is a deeply humanitarian and necessary movement, but it also faces the very same problems that Fassin and Ross critically analysed. In the iconography and rhetoric of the movement, refugees appear above all as people who suffer: they are traumatized by the loss of their homes, they have survived a perilous journey to Europe, and in the country of destination, they have to endure months in overcrowded refugee camps. There is no doubt these refugees need rescuers and help. But in the figure of the refugee, 'biographical' lives, that is, political lives, disappear. When the revolutionaries from Syria who challenged the authority of the Assad regime flee abroad they are turned into refugees who, like children, must be taught about democratic politics and liberal values. It is the price of the humanitarian gaze: political recognition.

Global Solidarity Today?

In the autumn of 2019, the Global South was on fire: in Colombia, Ecuador, Chile and Bolivia, thousands took to the streets demanding social justice, better laws to protect the environment, and an end to endemic corruption. Across cities in South America, protestors clashed with the police, resulting in the death of several dozens of people. Meanwhile, the Arab Spring that had started in Tunisia in 2010 and then rapidly spread across the Arab world, to Egypt, Libya, Yemen and Syria, where it led to a bloody war, seemed to resume. Earlier that year, a massive protest movement in Sudan ended the dictatorship of Omar al-Bashir, bringing the country on a hopeful path to democracy. In Algeria, street demonstrations toppled the long-term president Abdelaziz Bouteflika. In Iraq, hundreds of thousands flocked to the streets to protest against corruption, unemployment, sectarianism and the influence of foreign powers such as Iran and the United

States. In Iran, fuel price fluctuations and increased levels of poverty, caused in large part by American sanctions, led to violent protests against the regime. Perhaps most impressively, Lebanese citizens rose up against corrupt elites and occupied public spaces, overcame sectarian divisions and called for political accountability. In both Iraq and Lebanon, women played a prominent role in these protests, as countless videos on social media show. Further east, protests in Hong Kong that started with demonstrations against police reforms turned into a full-scale challenge against the political system. With the notable exception of Sudan, few of the protests resulted in tangible change – for now. But the uprisings showed how fragile the situation in many countries was and still is.

There was something inspiring about these revolutions. A report in the German newspaper *Frankfurter Allgemeine Zeitung*, not known for its revolutionary fervour, said of the events in Lebanon:

> Protestors sit on the roof of a former movie theatre, wielding their flags. Street vendors sell grilled corn cobs and pita bread. NGOs offer first aid, legal support, story time for children, and quick introductions into garbage separation. For a while, this really resulted in parents with their children gathering rubbish in the area, separating and reusing it – cigarettes for an NGO that is producing surfing boards with them, bottle caps for another NGO using them to build wheelchairs. In the evenings, there are debates in open rounds. It is as if, in downtown Beirut, a model society *en miniature* has developed that gives an idea of what could be, and also of what once was.[73]

As I write these lines in the autumn of 2022, women in Iran have started another revolution whose outcome remains to be seen. It's not hard to imagine how these revolutions might have found support in the West. After all, they stood for women's rights, free speech, and even the protection of the environment, all issues of great concern in Western societies nowadays. Unlike the Third Worldism of the 1960s, these movements did not provide a revolutionary vision for the West. If anything, they appeared to take the liberal democracies of the West as a source of inspiration. This too might have created a common cause: not revolution, but democracy, something that, numerous books and articles claim, is under threat in the West. These common causes might have provided a good foundation for solidarity.

But there wasn't much of a solidarity movement to speak of. In 2019, there have been protests in Berlin in support of both the Lebanese and the Iraqi uprisings. I've attended some of these gatherings, where I've met friends from Lebanon and Syria who chanted for freedom and unity; but only a few Germans took an active interest. This is despite the broad refugee support movement that, one might have imagined, could have stirred an interest in the revolutionary movements of the Middle East.

What I've witnessed in Berlin is, of course, nothing but anecdotal evidence; whether there is more support for the uprising in Iran remains to be seen. Nevertheless, it is indicative of a general trend. Despite the spread of post-colonial studies in academe and the constant demands for Europe to acknowledge the crimes of its colonial past, Western leftists don't show much of an interest in the contemporary revolutionary movements of the Global South.[74] It is hard to imagine that any intellectual, leftist or not, would today claim that their 'growing political awareness' is linked to the Arab Spring. Contrary to Robin Yassin-Kassab and Leila Al-Shami's claim that the Syrian revolution has inspired movements such as Occupy and the Indignados in Spain, these revolutions have not left much of a visible trace in Western political activism.[75] No text coming out of the Arab Spring has become canonical in the way that Fanon's *The Wretched of the Earth* did in the 1960s, and there have been no protests in support of the Syrian Revolution in European cities akin to the demonstrations for the Vietcong's struggle against the United States. Arguably, this is an effect of the rise of a humanitarian discourse that is focused on rescuing and helping people in need, but not engaging with their political struggles. The history of Third World solidarity in the 1960s and 1970s might remind us of the potential of such solidarity today and the value of recognizing the relevance of political voices of those outside the West.

8.

Solidarity in the Backyard and the Struggle for Citizenship: Anti-Racism and Migrant Activism

The radical students of 1968 not only inhabited a shared political and discursive space that connected their struggles with those of Third World revolutionaries. They also inhabited a very real shared space with foreign workers. The University of Nanterre on the outskirts of Paris, the hotbed of student activism seen in Chapter 2, was located just across some railway tracks from one of many shanty towns in France where migrants, mostly from North Africa, lived.[1] In West Berlin, too, the number of migrant workers was increasing. Considering them a potentially revolutionary force, radicals like Rudi Dutschke hoped to agitate among these workers.[2] In France, Maoist students went to the shanty towns, distributed pamphlets and, on one occasion, handed out foie gras, champagne and cakes they had stolen from a luxury food store. And at Nanterre, leftist activists established a 'wild crèche' for the children of both students and immigrant residents of the local neighbourhood. 'French and immigrant babies – same bottle', their slogan read.[3] It encapsulates the vision of a better world in which national differences ceased to matter.

Making this vision a reality was difficult. Student radicals and other activists, who entered shanty towns like 'commandos', as historian Daniel Gordon writes, were often not welcome. Fazia Ben Ali, the sister of an Algerian teenager murdered in October 1971 in northern Paris, recalled her experience of working with intellectuals such as Jean-Paul Sartre and Michel Foucault in a solidarity committee formed in the wake of her brother's murder: 'It was all very well to denounce racist crimes, but when you started to denounce the housing and the filth of the neighbourhood, I asked myself "Why have they only noticed this now" . . . I felt that you had only come when there was something important and spectacular, like my brother's death.' What shocked the outside intellectuals was entirely normal for local residents like Fazia: 'I remember that as soon as one of them came to our home, he immediately said "Good God, it's not possible to live like that, ten to a room!" Ok, for *you*, it wasn't possible, but we had always lived like that.'[4]

More often than not, migrants (and their descendants) themselves engaged most powerfully and most successfully in struggles for equality and liberty. They fought against racist attitudes and violence, they demanded social inclusion, and, as non-citizens, political rights. This chapter traces these 'forgotten struggles' – forgotten, because most accounts of protest in Western Europe tend to be rather 'white', neglecting the activism of people of colour.[5] It first explores how so-called guest workers in the Federal Republic during the early 1970s challenged both the authority of employers and established German trade unions. The chapter then turns to France and the *sans papiers*, 'illegal' migrants fighting for a secure legal status. Finally, the chapter investigates struggles against overt and often violent forms of racism and attempts to build inclusive communities in the United Kingdom.

Migrant Workers in the Federal Republic

Neuss in North Rhine-Westphalia is not a town of international, or even national, fame. Located on the west bank of the Rhine in West Germany's industrial heartland, it's a pretty average German town with a population of about 140,000 in the early 1970s. Yet, in those years, it was the site of a series of remarkable strikes. Neuss was home to A. Pierburg AG, a company producing carburettors that supplied the entire car industry in the Federal Republic. Like many other West German companies in the 1960s, Pierburg had hired numerous so-called guest workers – *Gastarbeiter*, in German – coming mostly from Greece, Yugoslavia and Turkey.[6] By 1973, more than 2,300 of its 3,500 employees were migrant workers, including 1,700 women, or 70 per cent of the total migrant workforce. Even though most women worked at fast-paced conveyor belts, they were paid lower wages than male workers. Male foremen, by contrast, were usually German. Most of the migrant women had come to Germany via family unification programmes and had received work permits because of their contracts with Pierburg. Nevertheless, 300 female workers from Yugoslavia had to live in company-owned barracks – which were effectively rundown shacks in miserable conditions – where they were not allowed to receive any male visitors, including their husbands. In May 1970, these women had had enough. They took action and went on strike, protesting at first against their housing situation, and then also demanding better wages. With the support of German female colleagues, the strike succeeded: the management agreed to raise wages for all female employees, and in the following years, the number of women living in shacks declined.[7]

The women who had walked away from their jobs at Pierburg were among hundreds of thousands of foreign workers who migrated to the Federal Republic from the late 1950s to the early 1970s to compensate for labour shortages in Germany. Coming from Southern European countries such as Italy, Greece, Spain and Yugoslavia, and, by the early 1960s, increasingly from Turkey, these workers faced dire living conditions. Like the Yugoslav women at Pierburg, many were housed in simple and overcrowded shacks, deemed inappropriate for German workers. Assuming that these 'guest workers' would return to their home countries after working in Germany for a few years – which, in fact, the majority did – German authorities made little effort to integrate them into society. And neither did trade unions, who looked at foreign workers with suspicion, fearing that they might take jobs from Germans and keep wages low.

Far from being the docile labourers they were supposed to be, these migrant workers fought to improve their lot. In the early 1960s, miners from Italy, Greece and Turkey staged walkouts on several occasions to demand better wages and working conditions, and in general to be paid and treated like their German colleagues. In other sectors, from car manufacturing (e.g. at Volkswagen) to mechanical engineering and the textile industry, foreign workers protested against housing conditions, the quality of the food in canteens or the unreasonable pace of work. All in all, wildcat strikes involving migrant workers affected about 335 companies in West Germany during the summer of 1973. Most of these strikes, however, failed. Management frequently fired striking workers, called the police and had strike leaders arrested, who then faced deportation to their home countries. German trade unions for their part had no interest in supporting the strikes, though they carefully registered the complaints by foreign workers and urged them to join the unions.[8]

The successful strike at Pierburg in May 1970 was in this sense an exception. Yet it wasn't the last time female migrant workers went on strike at Pierburg. In June 1973, they downed tools again. They wanted Pierburg to abolish the low-wage bracket II, in which mostly female workers were grouped despite them doing the same work as better-paid male workers. They also demanded extra payment for working at particularly unsanitary workplaces; a pay rise of one mark per hour for all workers, male or female; one paid day off per month as a 'housewives' day'; and the firing of two particularly unpopular employees, a foreman and the head of the human resources department. After two days of striking, the union representatives negotiated with the company to set up a commission charged with reviewing female workers' wage classification, which would report back by early September. Wage bracket II, however, was not to be dissolved, as the women on strike demanded.

For a while, the strike came to an end. But the agitation on the shop floor continued. Militants distributed pamphlets in multiple languages, urging their colleagues to join the next strike movement. The factory council, the *Betriebsrat*, warned the management in no uncertain terms that another strike was to be expected. On 25 August 1973, workers took action. They had reduced their list of demands, focusing now on abolishing wage group II, and the pay-rise of one mark per hour. Some 300 foreign workers, male and female, gathered in front of the factory gates, despite German foremen and technicians imploring them to return to work. The management refused to even negotiate. Soon enough, police arrived to clear the entrance. The German foreman named Freiberg, whose dismissal workers had demanded in June, pointed out a female Greek worker by the name of Elefteria Marmela, accusing her of being a ringleader. When police tried to arrest her, a melee ensued. Her colleagues succeeded in protecting Marmela, at least for now. 'Dirty foreigners, I'll kill you,' a police officer allegedly yelled.[9] When reinforcements arrived three hours later, they arrested three women, Marmela among them. At first, strikers were frightened, and many left the scene. But the violent police intervention encouraged others to act in solidarity and join the strike. By breakfast break, production came to a halt.

The following day, striking workers gathered before the morning shift. Once again, the police arrived. Without even trying to talk to the strikers, they assaulted them with truncheons, injuring some of them so badly that they had to be hospitalized. Only when a TV camera team showed up did the police stop. Nevertheless, scenes of violence made it to the news and caught the attention of various leftist groups. Members of a Committee of Foreign Workers, representatives of the Protestant church in nearby Düsseldorf and Young Socialists affiliated with the Social Democratic Party expressed their solidarity with the striking workers, while radical militants flocked to the factory to support workers on site. The powerful metal workers union IG Metall condemned the police brutality, but refrained from supporting the strike movement. Still, the management was not willing to engage in negotiations.

On the evening of the strike's third day, something important happened outside the factory. Foreign workers, both male and female, headed to bars usually frequented by German workers and engaged in heated debates with them. At first, they faced hostile reactions: as foreigners, they should keep quiet and work, not go on strike. 'We foreigners', one woman responded, have been working for eight years for Pierburg, but for less money, even though the cost of bread isn't any lower for foreigners. She demanded equal wages, but also solidarity among workers. Apparently, her argument was convincing, and German workers expressed support. 'They can't deport us, and after all, they [the migrants] also fight for us,' one of them said. Someone else suggested buying red roses and distributing them the next day at the factory gate.[10]

The next morning, German workers at the tool production department joined the movement. They issued an ultimatum to force the management to negotiate with the factory council. After all, it was also their factory council, and the refusal to negotiate affected them as well. The threat worked; the management finally agreed to talk. Meanwhile, the strike took on an increasingly festive character: kids came and played football in the factory's courtyard, people danced, ate, drank beer and flirted. 'It's the best day of my life,' an elderly German worker remarked. 'Today, we all stand together. I've never seen that. Pierburg can't take it out on us.'[11] And indeed, after five days of striking, the management gave in. Some 1,200 workers were immediately moved into wage bracket III, the rest by the end of the year, which effectively meant the end of the detested wage bracket II. In addition, all workers received a pay rise ranging between 53 and 65 pfennigs to compensate for inflation. After another protest the following Monday, the management also agreed to pay the workers for four out of five days of strike action. The workers celebrated their victory.

At first glance, the strikes at Pierburg might look like a rather unremarkable affair: they were limited to one company, addressed wage questions, as strike movements typically do, and they only lasted a few days. But the strikes went deeper than this. They went to the heart of issues in West German society, in particular unequal pay between men and women and the situation of foreign workers: their living conditions, their relationships with German colleagues, their political and social rights. By going on strike, the workers from Greece, Turkey, Yugoslavia and other countries combated racist attitudes and structures in the Federal Republic.

At the same time as the strike at Pierburg, the most famous

migrant workers' strike, the so-called 'Turks Strike', was taking place at the Ford factory in Cologne.[12] The American car manufac- turer also relied heavily on foreign labour. In total, Ford employed some 12,000 Turkish workers, constituting about half the workforce of its production facilities in Cologne (excluding office employees). Nowhere else in the Federal Republic did a company employ that many Turkish workers. By 1971, some 59 per cent of those were housed in company-owned residencies, which usually meant over- crowded shacks like those at Pierburg; by 1973, the number had gone down to 40 per cent, as compared to 32 per cent for the entire Federal Republic (in 1972). Though they did not pay as much as other car manufacturers in Germany, wages at Ford were relatively high in comparison with other industrial jobs in the area. Yet Turk- ish labourers typically worked in low-paid positions. As late as 1979, about 80 per cent of them were employed as unskilled or semi- skilled workers, compared to 10 per cent of Ford's German workforce. The result was that Turkish workers earned about one mark less per hour than their German colleagues.[13]

Work was monotonous and fast-paced, the workplace loud and dirty. An average worker had to repeat a single production process 550 times per day. Any interruptions to the production process meant an increase in the work pace. The noise in the factory made communication with colleagues on the job virtually impossible, and after work, Turkish workers remained isolated from their Ger- man colleagues due to their housing situation. Few of them learned German under these conditions and therefore had to rely on unpopular interpreters, who failed, or so workers claimed, to ade- quately convey demands and complaints to line managers. A sense of discrimination and division, historian Simon Goeke notes, was widespread among Turkish workers at Ford.[14]

Given these working conditions and the sense of isolation from their German colleagues, Turkish workers were, unsurprisingly, not keen to play by the usual rules of German labour conflicts. In September 1970, the powerful IG Metall had called for a brief warn- ing strike. It was only supposed to last for a few hours, but when it ended, Turkish and Italian workers refused to return to work. Instead, they organized a protest march through the factory hall, demanding control over the pace of the production line. Militants forcefully prevented other workers from resuming work; some even damaged the factory equipment. Management did not give in to their demands, but also refrained from firing anyone. Union officials, however, were furious about what they considered a lack of discipline among foreign workers. In the future, employees at Ford would not participate in any warning strikes, they decided.[15]

In fact, union membership among foreign workers at Ford was strikingly high: around 90 per cent. Yet the union had made little effort to actively integrate those workers into its organization. Only a tiny minority of union delegates and shop stewards (*Betriebsräte*) were foreigners, and those usually faced discrimination. Turkish worker Mehmed Özbagci discovered this at first hand in 1972, just after a reform of the Labour Relations Act (*Betriebsverfassungsgesetz*) had allowed workers from countries outside of the European Economic Community to be elected as shop stewards. Özbagci decided to stand for election. Workers voted for lists of candidates, nominated by the union, rather than individuals (a common voting practice in Germany). The more votes a list received, the more of its candidates would be elected. Özbagci, however, ran on his own, with no other names on his list; he won 31 per cent of the vote. With more names on his list, this would have been enough to elect ten candidates. But the other factory council members argued that Özbagci wasn't sufficiently competent and lacked the necessary language skills. For that reason, they refused to grant him the exemption from work common for elected council members. The incident was further proof of the German unionists' lack of interest in working alongside their Turkish colleagues.[16]

By August 1973, tensions at Ford reached a boiling point. After the annual summer vacation, lasting from 2 to 27 July, about 1,000 foreign workers had not returned to work in time. This was not an uncommon issue. For several years, Turkish workers who often travelled to their home country by car had extended their vacation without authorization, and management had tolerated the practice. In the summer of 1973, this changed. For one thing, the number of workers who returned late had reached a stunning 28 per cent, twice as many as the year before. In addition, managers planned to reduce the workforce anyway given the early signs of a recession. Workers who had returned late now faced, somewhat unexpectedly, dismissal or disciplinary measures. German workers had little understanding for what they considered a lack of punctuality in their Turkish colleagues and approved their dismissal. Among Turkish workers, though, there was a great deal of solidarity. After all, it was mostly foreign workers who would have to compensate for the labour of their dismissed colleagues, which only added to their fury.[17]

On Friday, 24 August 1973, the situation exploded. When a Turkish worker loudly complained about the increased work pressure, a protest march formed. Somewhat surprisingly, many German colleagues joined the march as it moved through the factory. As at Pierburg, the entirety of the tool-making department left their workstations. The protestors raised three demands: first, revoking the dismissals; second, a pay rise of one mark per hour; and finally, better working conditions at the conveyor belt. Initial negotiations between the factory council and management led nowhere, and the workers went home for the weekend. They returned for work on Saturday – weekend shifts were better paid and did not involve work on the production line, which made them popular with Turkish workers – but on Monday, the strike continued. With little trust in the mostly German factory council, strikers elected their own representatives, who reflected the international composition of the workforce at Ford: nine Turkish workers, two Germans, two Italians and one worker from Yugoslavia. Now, workers also demanded two more weeks of annual holidays, financial compensation for the strike, and for management to abstain from disciplinary measures.

As the management refused to negotiate with the elected strike leaders and did not offer meaningful concessions to the official factory council, the strike became radicalized. In the evening, striking workers occupied the entrance to the factory. Fights broke out, in which Turkish workers often faced their German colleagues on the other side. But strikers managed to stay in the factory, with some 400 of them spending the night on the shop floor. The strike was now firmly in Turkish hands, and, like the strike at Pierburg, it took an increasingly festive character: workers played music, danced and joked. A Turkish hodja even came to lead a communal prayer. This further alienated German workers. Both the factory council and union delegates turned against the strike, and when the company issued an order to return to work on Wednesday, 29 August, the factory council wanted to accept the management's offer: a cost-of-living bonus of 280 marks, and compensation for the strike days. The specific demands by Turkish workers, such as additional holidays or better working conditions, were not addressed at all, except for the promise to rehire workers who could demonstrate that their late return to work after the holidays in July had not been their own fault. Understandably, Turkish workers were not satisfied by this outcome. On the evening of the 29th, some 2,000 workers decided to spend the night at the factory and continue the strike.

The next morning, confusion reigned: some workers joined the strike, while others willing to return to work, almost all German, formed a protest march through the factory. Confronting their Turkish colleagues, German workers broke the strike, while the police made thirty arrests. The strike ended in defeat, and many Turkish workers lost their jobs.

In the minds of the trade union bosses, the 'guest workers' had fallen prey to radical leftist agitators who had exploited the workers' inexperience with labour struggles. Such remarks were not entirely unfounded. In the wake of 1968, numerous radical students had taken to heart calls to literally join the working class and agitate among marginalized foreign workers. Giving up on academic careers, they found work at companies like Ford in Cologne, which in fact became a hub for various leftist groups that tried to build alliances with foreign workers.[18] For example, Baha Targün, the Turkish spokesperson of the strike leadership, was a communist student.[19] Yet, the influence of German leftist students should not be exaggerated either. When the strike broke out, they were rather surprised. And while many leftist groups came to the factory gates to distribute pamphlets and food, they did not lead the strike. German media and trade unions presented the strike as a form of illegitimate terror by foreign workers, who, incited by German extremists, disrupted the 'industrial peace'. It was hardly imaginable for them that foreign workers might have their own legitimate demands.

Far from being the result of extremist agitation, the strike at Ford shows the autonomy of migrant struggles. Foreign workers fought to improve their situation as migrants; they organized independently, developed their own forms of protest and tried to build alliances with their German colleagues. Sometimes they succeeded, as at Pierburg, where German workers seem to have enjoyed the festive character of the strike; sometimes they failed, as at Ford, where cultural and institutional barriers were too high. But, successfully or not, migrant workers made themselves heard in West German society.

The Sans Papiers, *or: No One Is Illegal in France (or Anywhere)*

The Federal Republic of Germany was not the only country in Western Europe that saw a massive influx of immigrants in the years following the Second World War. After the collapse of colonial empires, migrants from former colonies – often those who had worked and fought for colonial powers – arrived in Portugal, the Netherlands, the United Kingdom and France. In some ways, the situation of these migrants resembled that of guest workers in West Germany: they, too, were often housed in shacks or lived under miserable conditions in shanty towns on the outskirts of large cities, and they contributed to the economic boom of the post-war years by taking up unpopular, badly paid and dangerous jobs. And they, too, had to deal with blatant racism. After all, French president Charles de Gaulle, in a conversation with his friend Alain Peyrefitte, had famously declared France to be a nation 'of the white race, of Greek and

Latin culture and the Christian religion. The Muslims, have you seen them, with their turbans and their *djellabas*. You can see clearly that they are not French!' Immigration had to be restricted, he argued, otherwise 'my village would no longer be Colombey-les-Deux-Eglises [i.e. Colombey of the Two Churches], but Colombey-les-Deux-Mosquées [Colombey of the Two Mosques]'.[20]

What was specific to France was the political context of the immigrants' arrival. These migrants had not come in the context of an officially encouraged labour migration, but in the wake of the dissolution of an empire that was, particularly in the case of the Algerian War of Independence (1954–62) extremely violent. The war had not remained limited to Algeria, but had reached mainland France, where supporters of the Algerian National Liberation Front both engaged in acts of violence and organized peaceful protests. The French state responded with brutality, most notoriously on 17 October 1961 in Paris, when the French police attacked a peaceful protest by Algerians and killed nearly 200 people by throwing them into the Seine, where they drowned. For the French authorities, Algerians living in France were potential enemies of the state.[21]

When the war came to an end in 1962, another group of Algerians fled to France: those who had fought for the French and their families, who now had to fear revenge by Algeria's new government. In the eyes of the French, these were refugees, but, partly given their Muslim faith, they were not considered French citizens.[22] While the struggles of guest workers in the Federal Republic mostly addressed their social situation (at the workplace or regarding housing), the migrant protests in France were about the political rights and voices of those not considered legal residents in a nation state.

The story begins on 26 October 1972 in Goutte d'Or, a Parisian neighbourhood known as the 'unofficial capital of North African France'. That day, two residents of the neighbourhood, Faouzia and Saïd Bouziri, Tunisian nationals, wanted to renew their residence permit. The couple had legally come to Paris in 1966, where Saïd was to train as a bookkeeper. He had participated in the May 1968 protests, and since then in various other political campaigns, including a solidarity committee for Palestine. By the autumn of 1972, both he and his wife had become prominent militants. Normally, renewing a residency was a straightforward piece of bureaucracy, but that day, the couple faced a problem. They were late, the authorities told them, and would face expulsion from France. The Bouziris, however, suspected that something else was behind the French authorities' desire to expel them: their political activism. Given that numerous political militants had been deported in the preceding years, this was not far-fetched.

The couple had been given ten days to leave France voluntarily, but they decided to fight. On 6 November, Saïd Bouziri went on hunger strike (because she was pregnant, his wife did not join him). Bouziri himself went into hiding, fearing arrest, while a group of fellow French and Tunisian militants joined the hunger strike to publicize it. Intellectuals including Michel Foucault and Jean-Paul Sartre, who had supported the campaign surrounding the murder of Djellali Ben Ali in the same neighbourhood during the previous year, rallied to the cause. To justify their decision to expel the Bouziris, the Interior Ministry cited a number of protests in which they had participated, thereby confirming suspicions that the deportation was politically motivated. Ultimately, however, the campaign worked, and the police offered the Bouziris a two-week permit to stay in France (astonishingly, they had to renew the permit first every week, then every month for a decade). The Bouziris had won; they could legally remain in France.[23]

Bouziri's hunger strike initiated a long-lasting movement for the legalization of foreigners living in France without papers, who came to be known as *sans papiers*. Two ministerial decrees at the beginning of 1972 had made it a particularly pressing issue. The decrees had tied the residence permits of foreign workers to their employment, meaning that a loss of employment invalidated a residence permit so that workers could no longer claim unemployment benefits. Furthermore, the decrees put an end to the common practice of retrospectively granting legal status to immigrants who had entered the country without proper papers. Effectively, the decrees created 'illegal immigrants'.

Leftist militants had already campaigned against the decrees throughout the summer of 1972, but it was Bouziri's hunger strike that inspired a broader movement. Shortly after Bouziri had won his case, one of his supporters, Tunisian Rabah Saïdani, organized a similar hunger strike with eighteen other Tunisians in Valence in southern France. Remarkably, the Tunisians could rely on the support of Catholic clerics, who allowed them to gather in a local church. On Christmas Eve, priests staged their own 'mass strike' in support of the Tunisians, and a chaplain even joined the hunger strike. Like the Bouziris, the Tunisians in Valence received residence permits as a result. In the following months, Tunisian but also Moroccan and Portuguese workers organized more hunger strikes in twenty cities across France to claim their rights as foreign workers. As a group of workers on hunger strike in the Mediterranean town of La Ciotat wrote:

> You know, brother worker, that our life was not secure; we have no rights. If something happened to us, an accident at work, for example, the boss sacks us and doesn't want to know. He says, 'Get lost or I'm calling the police.' Naturally, the worker is scared, he leaves and abandons his rights. Why? Because he hasn't got his papers in order . . . Brother Arab worker, think carefully! You work without papers, your life is in danger, you do the most dangerous and difficult work for the lowest wages. Don't forget that. Wake up and claim your rights.[24]

It was a stunningly successful movement: by October 1973, about 50,000 immigrants received their residency papers. In the following years, immigrants in France time and again campaigned for residency status by going on hunger strikes. In February 1980, for example, seventeen Turkish workers went on hunger strike demanding residency papers, proper labour contracts, and better working conditions. Supported by French unionists, their strike, too, succeeded, resulting in some 3,000 'illegal' foreigners receiving proper papers. In the wake of the campaign, the left-wing government under Prime Minister Pierre Mauroy reformed immigration procedures, which allowed about 130,000 *sans papiers* to obtain legal status in France. Another major campaign happened in between April 1991 and September 1992, when roughly 1,500 rejected asylum seekers, many of them from Turkey and Zaire, organized hunger strikes throughout France to demand if not recognition as political refugees, then at least a regularization of their residency. Once again, the government granted legal status to most of the strikers and regularized another 17,000 individuals. These non-violent and personal protests – after all, the hunger strikers suffered themselves – were highly effective. They presented immigrants as human beings who had to risk and potentially sacrifice their bodily well-being to claim their political rights. Hunger strikes succeeded in drawing public attention and sympathy to the immigrants' cause, and forced governments to make concessions.[25]

But these campaigns were only a prelude for the *sans papiers* movement of spring 1996 that gained media attention around the world. On 16 March 1996, a couple of men sat together in a residence for foreign workers from Africa in Montreuil, part of the greater Paris region. Their lives had become a 'black hole', they felt. They were pushed to the margins of society. The local administration at the prefecture constantly handed them rejections, no matter what job they had applied for. Something had to be done, the men agreed. They reached out to other Africans in a similar situation, and decided to take action: on 18 March, about 300 men, women and children, the majority of them from Mali, the rest from Senegal, Mauretania, Guinea, Zaire, as well as Northern Africa and one couple from Haiti, occupied the Saint-Ambroise church in the 11th arrondissement of Paris. Like their predecessors, they demanded their own legal status, and *papiers pour tous*, papers for everyone; if the government wouldn't accept, they would rather be deported.

The following days, countless people came to the church, both supporters and other *sans papiers* who joined the struggle. Some of them knew each other from protests back in Senegal. Leaders of the church expressed sympathy for their cause, but also signalled that they wouldn't tolerate the occupation. By the end of the week, police evicted the *sans papiers*. For a few weeks, the group moved around to different venues across Paris, until they occupied another church on 28 June 1996, just two days after France's interior minister, Jean-Louis Debré, had announced that only twenty-two members of the group would be eligible for legalization. This time, the local priest welcomed the group and allowed them to stay.[26]

Significantly, most members of the group came from former French colonies such as Mali and Senegal. For the *sans papiers* (or at least the more politically outspoken among them – they weren't a homogeneous group), this colonial past mattered. Their current struggle for papers in France was connected to past and current relations between France and Africa, as Madjiguène Cissé, one of the group's spokespersons who came originally from Senegal, argued. France had invaded and colonized these territories, it had enslaved and exploited the local population, and even in the 1990s, Europeans who remained there lived a privileged life. Africans had fought for the French in both World Wars, and after 1945 they had helped rebuild the French economy. But despite all of this, France did not accept them as citizens, but treated them as 'illegal' migrants. The *sans papiers'* struggle then was about more than just getting the right papers. It was a challenge to the post-colonial order. 'The rebellion of 18 March [1996] resembled an attempt to put this never settled historical debt back on the agenda,' writes Cissé in her account of the struggle. It was a way of saying: 'We no longer accept that France continues to treat us the way it treats our countries of origin: with exploitation, contempt and paternalism.'[27]

Stepping out of the proverbial shadows in which the *sans papiers* lived, they not only demanded citizenship in the legal sense of the term, but began to act as citizens, even without papers. This made their struggle profoundly political, Cissé emphasizes: 'When we left our apartments, the social housing projects' – that is, the infamous *banlieues* outside of cities such as Paris, Lyon and Marseille where many impoverished migrants lived and still do – 'when we escaped from the residence halls and *foyers*, out of the ghettos, we've erased the ethnic boundary that kept us there.' Their struggle made them citizens, not in a legal sense, but because they crossed the boundaries that kept them out of the public and hence political sphere.[28]

While they appreciated the support of French organizations, the *sans papiers* were always keen to emphasize their autonomy. At the same time, they fostered relationships with French citizens who helped in often mundane ways: they took children to the playground, kept the occupied spaces clean or signed up for night watches in case of trouble. In these ordinary moments of support and collaboration, ethnic origin and legal status ceased to matter, and a new vision of citizenship emerged. 'After all, is citizenship anything else than the content of these relations between human beings, who share the same space and who take care of others' well-being within the social fabric?' asks Cissé.[29] In the churches and other spaces the *sans papiers* occupied, an alternative to a society that divided people into legal and illegal migrants became a brief reality.

But this alternative did not last. On the morning of Friday, 23 August 1996, after nearly two months of peaceful occupation, over 1,000 regular and riot police stormed Saint Bernard church, where the *sans papiers* had found refuge. Soon, the smell of tear gas filled the church, even though the activists remain by and large peaceful. 'A baby of seven days is tear-gassed, thanks for democracy,' one of the occupants commented bitterly.[30] In the midst of the chaos, the parish priest wanted to celebrate a mass, as the group had planned. He began reading Martin Luther King's famous 'I Have a Dream' speech, but a police officer wrested the microphone from him. As if to confirm allegations of racism, the police separated the occupants into blacks and whites. The latter could just leave, while the former were all arrested. That way, some white *sans papiers* went free, while many of the black men and women detained in the church were supporters of the group with legal papers, or French citizens. Apparently to the police, black people couldn't be properly French.[31]

The movement wasn't over after the eviction from the church:

more demonstrations followed, and across the country, a network of *sans papiers* collectives emerged. Yet, it had reached its apogee. By the early 2000s, the cycle of mobilization that had begun with the occupation of the church Saint-Ambroise was effectively over. In terms of the law, little had changed. Yet, the *sans papiers* had staked a place for themselves as political actors in France which they still hold, even if their voice is not as loud as it was.

Fighting Racism: Rock Against Racism in the UK

Just like France, the United Kingdom saw massive immigration from former colonies in the years after the Second World War. From 1948 until 1962, anyone from the Commonwealth could freely enter the United Kingdom and permanently settle. Immigrants arrived particularly from the West Indies and the Indian subcontinent. According to the 1951 census, 15,300 West Indians lived in Britain; by 1971, their number had risen to 446,200, half of them born in the UK. The number of immigrants (and their descendants) from South Asia also went up, though less dramatically: from 106,000 in 1961 to more than a million by 1981. In the 1950s, the official attitude towards these migrants was fairly positive. 'In a world in which restrictions on personal movement and immigration have increased, we still take pride in the fact that a man can say *civis Britannicus sum* whatever his colour may be, and we can take pride in the fact that he wants and can come to the Mother country', the minister of colonial affairs, Henry Hopkinson, declared in 1954.[32]

This changed dramatically in the early 1960s, when Conservative politicians called to limit immigration from the Commonwealth. Under Harold Macmillan's Conservative government, the 1962 Commonwealth Immigrants Act introduced new restrictions, limiting entry into the UK to those born in the UK or with a passport issued in the UK, and Commonwealth citizens with a skills-based employment permit. Another Immigration Act of 1968 made these initially temporary measures permanent, but also allowed those

Commonwealth citizens with a British (i.e. usually white) parent or grandparent entry into the UK. The effect was a significant drop in immigration into the UK. For example, 260,000 West Indians had migrated to the UK between 1955 and 1962; between 1962 and 1968, the number went down to 64,000. Even more dramatic was the decline in public support for unrestricted migration of 'new Commonwealth' workers into the UK. In 1956, 37 per cent of Britons had supported such immigration; by 1964, the number dropped to 10 per cent, and by 1968 to a mere 1 per cent. These numbers, comments historian Peter Gatrell, indicate 'that intolerant opinion was less the cause than the consequence of restrictionist legislation'.[33]

Even in the 1950s, when official rhetoric was more welcoming, immigrants often faced hostility and racism in the streets and in the workplace. In 1955, for example, British workers in the West Midlands went on a union-organized strike to protest against the employment of an Indian bus driver.[34] Then in 1958, white youth assaulted the black residents of North Kensington, London, using iron bars, leather belts and butchers' knives in what came to be known as the Notting Hill riot.[35] A year later, Kelso Cochrane, a thirty-two-year-old man born in Antigua, was stabbed to death in the same area.[36] In addition, far-right groups formed, most notably the National Front (founded in 1967). While leaders of the National Front initially eschewed street demonstrations, this changed in the early 1970s. Flags, marches and a beating drum, chairman John Tyndall argued, would appeal to the masses more than speeches and articles – a distinctly fascist argument.[37]

Leftists rallied in response to fight the National Front. Across the UK, they set up anti-fascist committees. More than once, clashes in the streets resulted in violent confrontations between anti-racist militants and their right-wing opponents or the police. Kevin Gately, a twenty-year-old student at the University of Warwick, was killed on 15 June 1974 during clashes with the police at London's Red Lion Square while protesting against a National Front meeting at Conway Hall.[38] It wasn't the only violent altercation. In spring 1975, about 2,000 people protested against the National Front in Oxford.

Equipped with bicycle chains and iron bars, some fifty National Front members, including Tyndall himself, tried to push through the hostile crowd, beating seven protestors so badly that they had to be hospitalized.[39] For the left, these were frightening years. They witnessed a resurgent far right, with nothing that seemed to stand in their way. Activists felt that mainstream leftist organizations such as the unions did little to combat racism. Thus, it fell to far-left groups such as the International Marxist Group or the International Socialists to organize the struggle.[40]

Immigrants and even more often their children, for whom Great Britain had become the only home they knew, too, took up the fight. After all, they were the ones who the National Front wanted to see deported, and who felt the brunt of racist violence in the streets. Sometimes, small confrontations could turn into personal moments of empowerment that paved the way to more organized forms of struggle. Saeed Hussain, who joined the United Black Youth League, for example, recalled a kid at school who had been bullying him and his mates. One day, Hussain and three friends encountered the bully on their way to a local shop. 'Get out of my way, you fucking Pakis,' the boy said. But that day, Hussain and his friends confronted him. 'And we looked at each other and said, "We're not going anywhere. If you want you can walk either through us or you can walk round us. It's your choice today." And then after about a minute's stare, he did walk around us . . . head down and just walked off. That was the most liberating experience.'[41]

In other instances, young members of local communities mobilized in response to deadly violence, as happened in Southall, London, in June 1976. Two white men, Jody Hill and Robert Hackman, stabbed and killed sixteen-year-old Gurdip Singh Chaggar. When the day after the murder twenty-two-year-old Suresh Grover and his friend Denis Almeida walked past the scene and saw the blood on the ground, Grover asked the police officer whose blood it was. 'It was just an Asian,' the officer replied. In response, they covered the blood with red clothes and wrote on the pavement, with a dozen people watching: 'This racist murder will be avenged.' On the same evening a crowd of some 500 people gathered in front of the theatre where Chaggar had been murdered. As it happened, the Indian Workers' Association had already scheduled a meeting for the following Sunday on fascism. Local residents, old and young, flocked to the meeting to discuss how to respond to the murder. Frustrated by the older generation's reluctance to engage in activism, youngsters left the meeting and went on to form the Southall Youth Movement to struggle 'against racial and police harassment'.[42]

The United Black Youth League and the Southall Youth Movement were two of many groups and organizations led by British people of colour that emerged in these years fighting racism. Jamaican writer Winston James, a resident of Leeds and London, recalled the moment of collective uprising: 'Most of my generation of Afro-Caribbeans in Britain was in one way or another profoundly affected by the Rastafarian movement that swept across the Atlantic to Britain. Besieged as we and our parents were by British racism, we welcomed its attack upon white supremacy and its attempts to decolonize our minds. From the United States, Black Power also came to Britain, and we became familiar with the writings and struggles of George Jackson, Huey Newton, Bobby Seale, Angela Davis and Stokely Carmichael.'[43] Some activists, such as Leila Hassan, who wrote for *Race Today*, a magazine founded by Trinidadian Marxist C. L. R. James, 'believed in working-class power' and supported white workers when they went on strike. Yet she also stressed that 'our major thrust was to get a black independent movement going with a black magazine'.[44] As elsewhere in Europe, alliances formed between migrant militants and white anti-racists were not always easy. For example, when 600 supporters of the National Front marched through the predominantly black neighbourhood of Manningham in Bradford in April 1976, they faced roughly 3,000 opponents. Tellingly, however, these anti-racist opponents of the National Front were divided into two blocks. Whereas most white protestors marched through the city centre, black residents of Manningham preferred to protect their neighbourhood.[45]

In the midst of these tense months of confrontation, rock

guitarist Eric Clapton gave a short political speech during a concert at Birmingham's Odeon in August 1976.

> I used to be into dope, now I'm into racism . . . Fucking Saudis tak-
> ing over London. Bastard wogs. Britain is becoming overcrowded
> and Enoch will stop it a[nd] send them all back . . . This is England,
> this is a white country and we don't want any black wogs and coons
> living here. We need to make clear to them they are not welcome.

Clapton's racist slurs and his reference to Enoch Powell's infamous 'Rivers of Blood' speech from 1968, in which he had warned that whites might become a 'persecuted minority' in England, outraged many other artists. Members of the radical theatre group Kartoon Klowns, including photograpgher David 'Red' Saunders, Peter Bruno, Jo Wreford, and Angela Follett (who were just rehearsing a play called *Yes, But: Socialism or Barbarism*, the name of a famous new leftist French magazine from the 1950s – a fascinating detail showing how connected movements were across national bounda- ries), wrote a reply to Clapton. They reminded him that 'Half your music is black, where would you be without the blues and R&B?' To take action, they proposed organizing a 'rank and file movement against the racist poison in rock music'. It was the birth of Rock Against Racism, known as RAR, an alliance between reggae and punk musicians and activists to combat growing racism in the United Kingdom.[46]

The response to Saunders' call for action was massive. Hundreds of people from across Great Britain wrote to Saunders, and soon local committees were set up, organizing concerts under the banner of Rock Against Racism. Usually, organizers tried to have white (punk) and black (reggae) bands together on stage, thereby attract- ing and mixing two different kinds of audiences. Saunders recalled 'one of the most wondrous gigs' in Hackney Town Hall in August 1977: 'We had the reggae band The Cimarons on with the punk act Generation X. Everyone jammed together at the end. It became the blueprint.'[47] Rock Against Racism concerts also at times attracted racist thugs, some of them in fact fans of the bands on stage, like Sham 69, whose following harassed and assaulted anti-racist concertgoers. After one scuffle at Middlesex Poly, the band ended up on stage performing in a show of solidarity with the Rasta group Misty in Roots. 'This is Rock Against Racism,' Saunders proclaimed. 'The white working class and a reggae band and we've brought them all together.'[48]

Meanwhile, confrontations between National Front supporters and opponents continued, most famously during a march by the Front through the London neighbourhood of Lewisham on 13 August 1977. It was an area with an ethnically mixed working-class population including Irish as well as African and Caribbean families. That day, many protestors were not content with a peaceful march far away from the National Front meeting. 'They shall not pass,' they announced, with a reference to the Spanish Civil War. Saunders was present, too. 'All these Christians and Communists', he remembered, told the anti-racist protestors to go home. But they didn't. Then 'this old black lady, too old to march, came out on her balcony. She put out her speakers, as loud as they could, playing "Get up, stand up". That did it for me.'[49] Protestors charged the National Front demonstration, stopping it from marching through Lewisham. In the ensuing clashes, some fifty policemen were injured, and hundreds of protestors arrested.[50]

The following year, Rock Against Racism continued to organize as many as 300 concerts and five larger carnivals throughout Great Britain. By far the largest was a street carnival in London's Victoria Park on 30 April 1978, just before the May local elections. It started as a political march at Trafalgar Square and ended at the park. The organizers, who included not only Rock Against Racism but also the newly found Anti-Nazi League, had hoped for 10,000 attendees. But tens of thousands came, according to some estimates up to 100,000. Seeing the 'hundreds and hundreds of people marching, side by side in a display of exuberance, defiance and most important victory . . . marching, chanting to help me and my family find our place in our adopted homeland', eighteen-year-old Kenyan Asian

Gurinder Chadha remembered, made her feel that she had 'found my tribe, my kindred clan'.[51] And the example of Victoria Park shone beyond London. Carnivals in cities such as Cardiff, Edinburgh, Southampton and Manchester followed, the latter attracting some 35,000 attendees.

Outside of Great Britain, leftist militants in West Germany founded Rock Against the Right initiatives in Hamburg and Frankfurt, where a concert in protest against the far-right National Democratic Party of Germany drew a crowd of up to 50,000, making it one of the largest anti-Nazi demonstrations in the history of the Federal Republic.[52]

Yet, migrants played no major role in the German Antifa movement that emerged out of these initiatives. When Turkish immigrant and poet Semra Ertan set herself aflame in Hamburg on 26 May 1982 in protest against growing racism, having informed a local radio station of her plans, some 5,000 people joined an anti-racist demonstration. But soon, Ertan was forgotten.[53] Unlike in the UK, where the struggle against racist violence and the far right had brought different communities together, the distinctly white and radical leftist Antifa movement rarely provided the ground for an equivalent coming together.

The Victoria Park carnival and Rock Against Racism more generally embodied a vision of a world in which people could be 'citizens of the world' beyond racial divides. As Dave Widgery put it in an article for the Carnival special edition of *Temporary Hoarding*:

> Jamaicans like Guinness, Greeks listen to reggae, the Irish go to tandoor restaurants, we all eat doner kebabs and smoke as much dope as we can get our alien hands on . . . We've stopped waiting for the Good Samaritan and crossed the road ourselves. In fact, it's pathetic that it's taken the Front to bring us together. Tens of thousands of unknown unfamous people have worn a badge or won an argument or moved a resolution or put on a gig. Roots, radicals, rockers, reggae: We came together today. Let's stay together.[54]

Unfinished Struggles for Citizenship

By the very act of protesting, those on the margins of society, those without formal rights and without a political voice – as 'guest workers', 'illegals' and 'refugees', immigrants are usually denied the right to vote – made a claim for citizenship, as Madjiguène Cissé so powerfully argued. During these protests, a vision of a better world came to the fore: a world in which people could work, live and dance together, no matter their ethnicity or nationality. It was the vision of a world without borders put into practice.

And the vision has not gone away. The strikes by 'guest workers' at Pierburg and Ford, the church occupations by *sans papiers* in Paris, the carnivals in London and other cities – these struggles laid the foundation for the decades of protest that followed, continuing until today. In 1996, around the time the *sans papiers* in Paris demanded their papers, refugees in the East German state of Thuringia found *The VOICE: Refugee Forum Germany* to campaign for better living conditions. Many of them were housed in former army barracks, isolated from the rest of the population, often lacking basic amenities such as sufficient toilet paper or access to showers. Another twelve years later, Iranian asylum seeker Mohammed Rahsepar committed suicide in Würzburg, fearing deportation. In response, other Iranian refugees set up a protest camp in the city and went on hunger strike in a protest against their living conditions; in June, they escalated their strike by sewing their lips together making it next to impossible to drink anything except with a straw.[55] And most recently, tens of thousands of people of colour and their allies took to the streets in countless European cities during Black Lives Matter campaigns in the spring and summer of 2020, speaking up against racist violence and demanding that Europe come to terms with its colonial past. In new forms, the struggle against racism lives on in the twenty-first century.

9.

Camps: The Better World of Peace and Environmental Movements

Robert Karsch was a frustrated young man. He had just finished high school in the Hessian town of Fulda; now, he felt a huge emptiness inside him. His parents wanted him to join his father's painting and decorating business, which would have provided Robert with a materially secure future. But Robert wasn't interested. He didn't want to 'suffocate amid paint, varnish, and wallpaper . . . Balance sheets, gains, and losses. No, not such a life.' Waiting for the bus on a hot summer day, Robert ran into a young peace activist on his way to a peace camp in a nearby village. The activist tried to convince Robert to join him. But Robert wasn't interested. 'That's all dream-dancing and wishful thinking,' he told the activist. If Robert were to hit him, wouldn't he fight back? 'I would try not to,' the activist said. The response made Robert angry. What if he'd insult him, what if he'd spit at him? He'd remain calm, the activist claimed. Robert became only more furious. He started hitting the young activist, first with his hands, then spat at him, and when the young man did not fight back, as Robert had assumed he would, he jumped at him, hit him in the face, kicked him in the testicles. Only when passers-by threatened to call the police did Robert stop and run away, leaving the bloody activist behind.

At home, Robert realized what he had done. He was shocked and plagued by a guilty conscience. Suddenly, he decided to join the peace activist at the camp. The next morning, he packed his ruck-sack, leaving his worried parents behind, and went to the bus stop, silently hoping to meet the young activist again. But he didn't show, so Robert took the bus to the next village. Maybe he would find the activist at the peace camp. But the young man wasn't there either.

Still, Robert decided to stay and help the activists to prepare for pro-tests by painting banners and getting to know them. The camp provided a radical alternative to the emptiness he felt. 'Here, you may show your feelings,' Robert told his father when his parents came to visit. 'You lacked nothing at home,' his father replied, add-ing that his son should feel lucky as he did not have to suffer like his parents in the wake of the Second World War. 'But you created a different kind of misery,' Robert retorted, a world in which only 'utility, security, and appearances' mattered.[1]

Robert Karsch is a fictional character. He is the main protagonist of Gudrun Pausewang's *Something Can Be Changed: A Novel from the Peace Movement*, published in 1984. The novel, while of course fictional, gives a sense of how West German peace activists of the 1980s viewed the world: as a cold place, where people strove for material wealth, thought in terms of national security and deterrence and adhered to a technocratic rationality that exploited nature. In this world, values such as friendship, solidarity and peace counted little. The peace camp, by contrast, was a place where these values could be nurtured. Here, people talked to each other, their feelings mattered, they could connect with the natural and physical world by producing objects (wooden demons, in Robert's case) that they enjoyed making.

Pausewang's novel draws our attention to the peace and environ-mental movements of the 1970s and 1980s, two deeply intertwined movements in terms of actors, styles of protest and ideas – and movements in which Pausewang's works were immensely popular. Contrary to what some scholars have claimed, these weren't single-issue movements focused on one specific concern, such as pacifism or the environment, at the expense of the bigger picture.[2] As much as these activists campaigned against the militarization of society, against nuclear armament and against technologies that, they believed, put the future of the entire planet at risk, they equally sought to develop alternatives: a life in peace and harmony with nature, that valued friendship rather than competition and conflict, that did not exploit natural resources but respected the environ-ment. Across Western Europe, activists set up camps that provided them with an opportunity to practically build such a better world *en miniature*.

This chapter explores the better world that peace and environmental activists tried to create. It takes off in Larzac, France, where local farmers and shepherds joined leftist militants to struggle against the expansion of a military camp. The chapter then turns to the campaign against the construction of a nuclear power plant in Wyhl, southwest Germany. The third part brings us the Greenham Common Women's Peace Camp in Great Britain, where women not only protested against nuclear missiles, but also experimented with life beyond the patriarchy in an exclusively female space. Finally, the chapter moves across the Iron Curtain to study peace activism in the GDR. Setting up protest camps was, of course, impossible under the communist regime. But East German activists shared the same values of friendship and harmony that their Western counterparts cherished.

Gardarem lo Larzac: *Protecting the Land and Fighting the Military in Rural France*

On 28 October 1971, plans by the French Defence Ministry to expand a military camp on the Larzac plateau in the southern Massif Central became public. The area had been home to a military base since the beginning of the century; by and large, local farmers and the military got along. With the new plans, the base would be massively enlarged, from 3,000 to 17,000 hectares. Defence Minister Michel Debré didn't foresee any problems. The vast, rocky area in the middle of the mountains in the Occitan region was more or less deserted, he argued, and the few peasants who would have to be expropriated (in fact, more than a hundred families), were living much the same life as they had since the Middle Ages. There was no reason to expect resistance from a 'backward peasantry' fighting against the necessity of progress and the objective needs of the state and its military.[3] Debré was mistaken. Over the next ten years, local farmers allied with leftist militants from all over France and Western Europe in a struggle against the military base, and would not be moved.[4]

Rumours about the plans to enlarge the base had been circulating for a while already before the official announcement. Those were enough for leftist militants to organize a demonstration in May 1971 to 'protect Larzac'. Yet the protest attracted mostly leftists from nearby towns and cities, while local farmers remained suspicious and did not join the rally.[5] Debré seemed to be right in his assumption that no major protests would impede the enlargement of the base.

It was an unlikely figure who changed this by convincing the local peasants to join the campaign: Lanza del Vasto, a Sicilian nobleman by origin, who considered himself a disciple of Mahatma Gandhi. In 1962, he had moved to the neighbouring department of Hérault, where he found an abandoned farmhouse that he used as the headquarters for his spiritualist Community of the Ark. Where the urban leftists had failed, the biblical figure with his long beard, homespun cotton robes and philosophy of non-violence succeeded. Around Easter 1972, del Vasto brought the local shepherds together and convinced them to leave their quarrels behind and join the struggle against the military base. 'Lanza del Vasto was the cement of our union,' recalled local farmer Guy Tarlier, 'because at the start we were very different in our upbringings and ways of seeing agriculture. There were quarrels about hedges and sheep that went missing on the neighbour's meadow. All that was swept away by Lanza. He was the catalyst.'[6] Among the profoundly Christian peasants, del Vasto's spirituality fell on fertile ground.[7] On 28 March 1972, 103 out of the 109 farmers who were to lose their property swore an oath to defend the land and to give in to neither intimidation nor money, until the military abandoned the project.[8]

Leftist militants were thrilled to see peasants pick up the fight.[9] A mere four years after the upheavals of May 1968, many on the radical left felt that there was no use waiting for another catalytic event that might overthrow capitalism. Society, they came to believe, would have to change more gradually, in a number of independent struggles that might yield local autonomy. Under the influence of

Mao's Cultural Revolution in China and its celebration of the countryside, leftists in France, too, became interested in rural struggles.
Just like the countries on the post-colonial periphery, marginal
regions within Europe, such as Brittany in France, faced colon-
ization by the industrial and bureaucratic metropoles, militants
argued. These spaces and their autonomy had to be defended
against intruders from the outside, whether they were technocrats
planning large-scale infrastructure projects or the military building
bases.[10] Some radicals even moved to the countryside, where they
hoped to escape consumer society.[11] So when news about the farmers' determination to resist the military spread, young activists,
'Maoists, Catholics, scouts, schoolteachers and workers' felt elec-
trified and flocked to the Larzac to join the fight. Where radical
students in 1968 had tried to forge alliances with workers, they now
turned to farmers. It was another moment of social boundaries
temporarily dissolving.

Encounters between *gauchistes* (left-wing militants) and peasants
were not always easy. Profoundly Catholic and conservative, the
farmers and shepherds of the Larzac had typically cheered for the
re-establishment of order in 1968. The students' alleged sexual
promiscuity and their reputation for causing nothing but trouble
disgusted the peasants.[12] 'They are layabouts. They only think about
having sex,' farmer Jean-Marie Burguière said, recalling his father's
thoughts in a later interview with historians in 2008. 'We said, "It's
disgusting", because we were very modest.' But actual interactions
with leftist activists changed these perceptions. Burguière remembered his father later declaring that 'I don't look at the colour of the
hand that is held out to me.'[13] And when Defence Minister Debré
claimed that the Larzac was barren and deserted like a 'French Sibe-
ria', locals felt disillusioned by a government that continually
overlooked them. Practically, the construction of an illegal sheep-
fold in June 1973 brought locals and young militants together. Robert
Pirault, a Franciscan worker-priest overseeing the project, made
sure to turn away any youngsters simply looking for adventures and
partying. But if they were serious, militants could join the social life

of the community at the construction site and engage in animated political discussions with locals.[14]

The protests in Larzac soon grew beyond defending a small group of peasants against the might of the French state. They came to symbolize a struggle for local autonomy, for the sanctity of the land and of nature, and for peace that reached beyond the borders of France. Two large rallies in August 1973 and 1974 at the Rajal de Gourp ('Crow Rock' in Occitan) showed how the Larzac connected different struggles. Among the many thousands of protestors who flocked to the plateau in 1973 – estimates vary between 60,000 and 100,000 – were 200 workers from the LIP watch factory in Besançon, famous for their attempt to take over the factory (see Chapter 12), who celebrated a 'marriage of LIP and Larzac'.[15] From outside France, Irish republicans came to exchange flags with the Occitan rebels. A year later, peasants rebranded the traditional celebration of the harvest a 'Festival for the Third World'. 'No to French arms sales abroad, No to nuclear tests, No to the extension of military bases, No to the pillage of the Third World,' the invitation poster for the event announced, adding: 'Yes to real solidarity with the people of the Third World, and Yes to a real policy for peace.' Third Worldists and local peasants had united in the 'same struggle' – *le même combat*, the slogan read in French – against the authority of the central state.[16]

With the government making no concessions, the peasants and their allies realized they were in for a long fight. For those living on the plateau, activism became a part of everyday life.[17] When they saw military vehicles, they let the air out of their tyres; when shepherds encountered a military convoy while herding their sheep, they used the animals to block the road. Sheep, which provided the milk for the Roquefort cheese the region was famous for, indeed became activists themselves. In October 1974, farmers drove some sixty sheep to Paris, where they happily grazed under the Eiffel Tower, while policemen unsuccessfully tried to round them up, as the amused shepherds looked on.[18]

On the plateau, outside militants turned to increasingly radical though still non-violent methods. From all over France, conscientious objectors unwilling or unable to complete military service or its civil equivalent sought refuge at Larzac. These militants were willing to break the law and challenge military authorities more openly: they illegally occupied land and farms that had already been sold to the army. Most spectacularly, on 28 June 1976, a group of conscientious objectors and local farmers broke into the military base where they photographed documents proving that the army had secretly bought land on the plateau. Police arrested twenty-two protestors, seventeen of whom were put on trial. Tellingly, local farmers were released soon so that they could participate in the harvest, whereas the outsiders, including future peasant leader José Bové, had to spend between one and three months in jail.[19] Ultimately, however, the struggle was successful. When socialist François Mitterrand became president in 1981, the new government abandoned the plans, and the plateau was preserved.

The struggle at Larzac had a profoundly utopian and romantic dimension.[20] As one militant put it: 'For the generation of 1968 Larzac was our promised land. It was a place where we could put our ideas into practice.'[21] Larzac was a chance to try out direct democracy, building diverse alliances, and developing autonomous protest independent of large and dogmatic organizations. Such ideals were common across Europe during and after the events of 1968. But the struggle at Larzac had a specific dimension, perhaps best captured by the name of the journal the movement produced: *Gardarem lo Larzac*, founded in 1975. The Provençal – not French! – word *gardarem* can roughly be translated as 'to defend' or 'to protect', similar to how a shepherd looks after his herd.[22] It implies a particular relation to the soil, *la terre* in French, that gains a near-mythic quality. It's the territory with its local traditions, languages and landscape that needs to be defended against the encroachment of a modern, industrial and militarized society.[23] Larzac was a land apart, with its sheep and birds, the hills that seemed to touch the sky, 'its roads lined with trees, its rare plants and animals, its houses built like Romanesque chapels'.[24] The better future that militants hoped to find on the Larzac was intimately tied to this vision of an authentic land.

Better Active than Radioactive: Protesting
Nuclear Power in Wyhl

The protestors at Larzac inspired similar movements across the country and the continent. One of those places was the Alsatian village of Fessenheim, located in the Upper Rhine valley right at the border between France and the Federal Republic of Germany. The area fascinated nuclear engineers and government agencies in France, the Federal Republic and Switzerland alike. With the Rhine providing cooling water, the region seemed ideally suited for nuclear power plants. Nobody expected serious resistance from locals. Nuclear power as a technology enjoyed broad public support. It promised to provide cheap, safe energy and symbolized progress and the scientific mastery of nature. In Kaiseraugst on the Swiss side of the border, such arguments were well received, and the local population broadly supported building a new nuclear power plant. Opposition in Fessenheim was larger. In April 1971, about 1,000 people joined a march; their numbers included three members of Lanza del Vasto's Community of the Ark as well as some 150 militants from nearby Freiburg across the border in Germany. It was the largest anti-nuclear power protest to that point in Europe. But in Fessenheim, just like Kaiseraugst, opponents failed to stop the power plant because most villagers ultimately supported it.[25]

Across the Rhine in Germany, the regional government of Baden-Württemberg planned to build a nuclear power station near the village of Wyhl, located on the right bank of the Rhine some thirty kilometres north of Freiburg. Here, too, initial attempts to mobilize opposition did not get far. When country doctor Engelhard Bühler and Freiburg-based nuclear physicist Walther Herbst organized an event in May 1971 to inform other physicians about the dangers of nuclear energy, few people bothered to show up. Nuclear power didn't seem to threaten their lives and health. This changed when the focus turned away from the health risks for human beings to the consequences for the local rural economy, notably fishery and wine production. The cooling towers, critics argued, would produce more fog, leading to less sunshine and inferior grapes. Such prospects profoundly worried local winegrowers, who saw their livelihood endangered. Now, they took an interest, and meetings and rallies began to attract larger audiences. Dismissive responses by state representatives and experts who did not take such concerns seriously only fuelled the rage. The authorities had a hard time making sense of the unexpected opposition. They suspected radicals with sympathies for the Red Army Faction were behind the protests; they could not imagine that conservative farmers would ally with left-wing, non-violent students from Freiburg to oppose a nuclear power plant.[26]

In February 1975, the protests escalated, and the movement gained decisive momentum. On Monday, 17 February, construction workers had begun quietly sealing off the planned construction site without any of the conventional ceremonial groundbreaking. Authorities feared that activists might try to occupy the site, following the lead of French militants who had occupied the construction site of a lead plant just six months earlier; they had even levied pre-emptive fines against eight suspected ringleaders. They could hardly have expected what happened on the next day.

On 18 February, some 300 opponents of the power plant, many of them women from local villages, gathered to hear Siegfried Göpper and Hans-Helmuth Wüstenhagen speak. The two men, who were leading voices in the opposition, emphasized the need to fight the power plant by going to the courts and stressed that no occupation was planned.[27] Then a woman suggested walking over to the construction site. Whether or not they had planned to occupy the site doesn't ultimately matter: once the protestors 'saw how the forest was being destroyed', they 'broke down the fence and surged into the site'. Some militants 'jumped onto the shovels of diggers, positioned themselves in front of the treads of the bulldozers and entered into conversations with the construction workers'.[28] The scene that greeted them, Erasmus Schöfer remarked, looked like a 'dance between man and machine, a dead-serious, threatening war dance'.[29] It didn't take long before the crowd was in control of the area, forcing construction workers to stop.

And the protestors would not leave. Using construction trailers, a covered wagon and beat-up tents, they prepared to stay. Politicians were outraged. This could not be the local citizenry, Minister President Hans Filbinger claimed, but 'nationally organized manipulators'.[30] The police would quickly put an end to their illegal occupation. In the early hours of 20 February, a police force of 600 officers, a helicopter and two water cannons cleared the construction site, dragging passively resisting protestors through the mud. Police tried to particularly target young people they considered outsiders, but also arrested twenty local villagers.[31] The occupation seemed to be over. But it was just beginning.

For the following Sunday, 23 February, citizen initiatives had called for a rally to be held near the construction site. It turned out to be one of the largest protests against the power plant so far, with some 28,000 people attending. The atmosphere was festive, with 'information booths and sausage stands'.[32] As the rally came to an end, the last speaker, Meinrad Schwörer, invited the crowd to walk along the Wyhl forest nature trail, which led close to the construction site. Meanwhile, a group of roughly 100 activists gathered in the forest nearby. Unbeknown to the organizers of the rally, they were eager to make another attempt to occupy the site. Making their way through the woods, shoving away the police officers who tried to stop them, they reached the construction site. In a confusion of pushing, shoving, police batons and rocks, the militants succeeded in entering the site.

When those who had attended the nearby rally became aware of what was going on, they too poured into the site. They had to cross the Mühlbach, a small stream leading to the Rhine. Police tried to stop them, pushing some into the icy water. In the midst of the chaos, a protestor managed to grab a police megaphone. 'Do you have no hearts in your bodies? How can you be so awful? Don't you have families?' he yelled. His pleas seem to have worked, as a police commander who had just arrived at the scene ordered his men to fall back; they jumped into the vans and drove away. Protestors were in control of the construction site, and they would remain so for the next nine months.[33]

The events of February 1975 transformed the protests at Wyhl. Activists quickly built an improvised camp on the occupied construction site that attracted militants from all over the Federal Republic. Like Larzac, the small town in southwestern Germany became a sort of mecca for West German militants. A 'Friendship House' that activists built shortly after the occupation symbolized their vision of a better world like nothing else. The 'large round construction, with space for several hundred people' offered more than just protection from the cold and rain. It was a place where the community came together, where people exchanged ideas, debated and sang.[34] Women, recalls Eva Quistorp, spent long nights discussing the history of their home region and the dangers of plutonium.[35]

The Friendship House also housed the Wyhl Forest Community College, a project reminiscent of the Critical University, but more practical and less radical in its outlook. Scientists informed activists and locals about their research into nuclear power, helping them to become experts able to speak about 'all topics related to nuclear energy, from the workings of reactors to their dangers, and even their economic and political components', according to a sympathetic observer.[36] Lectures at the Community College did more than just educate. They also tried to foster a sense of community and connection to the region by addressing local customs and traditions like folk songs, or the fauna and flora of the Black Forest. And finally, they connected the protests at Wyhl to other struggles, such as those at Larzac.[37]

'Friendship House' as a name was a statement of intent: whereas the technocratic authorities in favour of nuclear power stood for capitalist competition and attempted to divide protestors into good local citizens and bad outside agitators, the Friendship House symbolized an attempt to overcome such divisions and foster friendships between people who would usually not have spoken to each other: radical, city-based students and conservative local vintners. As in Larzac, there were points when the gaps between the two groups seemed too large to bridge. Some locals suspected the students were effectively squatters, just coming for cheap food and a place to sleep.[38] But witnessing police violence as well as students' courage, local peasants came to see them in a more positive light. 'I'm quite a dare-devil,' a young father from the nearby village of Endingen noted in heavy dialect, 'but jumping on a driving excavator and just pulling the ignition key, like one of the students did, that's something I wouldn't have dared.' And a local woman whose son was studying in Heidelberg remarked that she had previously reacted rather dismiss-ively when he talked about political issues. But after the police had forcefully evicted the first occupiers, 'we see this [i.e. political mat-ters] with different eyes'.[39] Perhaps, as one long-term squatter argued, such unlikely friendships between the old and young, between students and vintners, between people speaking High German and those speaking local dialects were the true success of the struggle.[40]

The protests in Wyhl did achieve their stated aim, too. In 1983, Baden-Württemberg's new minister president, Lothar Späth, an-nounced that the power plant would not be built for another ten years; eleven years later, the project was abandoned altogether. The struggle against nuclear power continued elsewhere. In Brokdorf, Schleswig-Holstein and Wackersdorf, Bavaria, protests at construc-tion sites turned extremely violent during the late 1970s and 1980s.[41] Above all, Gorleben in the Wendland region of Lower Saxony became a symbol of resistance to nuclear power. In the 1980s and 1990s, a broad coalition of local peasants, non-violent activists and violent militants from all over Germany flocked to the area to campaign against a nuclear depository. Already in early May 1980, protestors occupied land at a drilling site and proclaimed the foun-dation of the Free Republic of Wendland. A decade later, Gorleben became the site of protests that attracted tens of thousands of peo-ple trying to prevent the arrival of transports carrying spent nuclear fuel by blocking roads and railways.[42]

Ultimately, with the rise of the Green Party, which in part emerged out of the anti-nuclear power movement, the movement saw their arguments become mainstream. Responding to the Fukushima catastrophe of March 2011, the German government decided to phase out the use of nuclear power. By April 2023, the last German nuclear power plant was shut down.

Fighting Nuclear Armament and Patriarchy: The Greenham Common Women's Peace Camp

As the anti-nuclear power movement in Germany gained momentum during the late 1970s, another development caused even greater fear among Europeans: the arms race between the United States and the Soviet Union, with the threat of mutually assured destruction in a nuclear war.[43] In December 1979, NATO had announced its so-called Dual-Track Decision. The Soviet Union's modernization of its nuclear arms arsenal, and in particular the new SS-20 mid-range missiles that targeted Western Europe, had disturbed the nuclear power balance in Europe, NATO argued. Hence, the Western alliance planned to deploy new missiles, known as Pershing IIs and ground-launched Tomahawks, throughout Europe. At the same time, NATO offered to negotiate with the Soviet Union about a mutual and complete ban on all mid-range nuclear missiles.[44]

Horrified by the prospect of a nuclear confrontation that would effectively eradicate human life in Europe if not globally, peace activists took to the streets. On 10 October 1981, up to 250,000 protestors gathered in the West German capital of Bonn to call for an end to nuclear armament. About 200,000 people joined a demonstration in Brussels two weeks later, and as many as 400,000 people rallied in Amsterdam on 21 November that year.[45] Beyond these immense rallies, there were countless small, local protests against nuclear armament. Having learned from the anti-nuclear protests in Wyhl and elsewhere, peace activists, many of whom had previously participated in environmental protests, too, tried to give their campaigns a local dimension by informing the population about military bases in their direct vicinity.[46] Equally, they organized countless demonstrations and peace marches that connected protestors across countries. In

June 1981, for example, a group of women from Scandinavia organized a peace march that started in Copenhagen and reached Paris in early August; a year later, another march brought women from Stockholm to Minsk via Leningrad and Moscow.[47]

News about the women's march also reached Wales. Fascinated by the idea, some women from Cardiff wanted to do something similar: a march across the country, from town to town, primarily led by women, with men only playing a supportive role. Agreeing on the destination of the march was easy: Greenham Common in Berkshire, England, where the first Cruise Missiles were to be stationed at an American-run military base.[48] On 27 August 1981, the Women for Life on Earth, as the group called itself, left Cardiff: thirty-six women, joined by four men as well as a couple of children. Nine days and 100 miles later, they arrived. A few hours before the march reached the base, four women who had gone ahead chained themselves to the fence at the main gate. They expected trouble, or immediate arrest. But not much happened. After the other women had joined them and started taking photographs, a lone police officer showed up and advised the women that they had better leave. It was Saturday evening, American soldiers were probably getting drunk on Jack Daniel's, and the women were putting themselves at risk of being raped, he added.[49] Not surprisingly, the women did not follow his advice. The marchers had prepared a letter calling for an end to the arms race, which they wanted to hand to the base commander. And the commander came to meet them. He was furious, recalled Helen John, a midwife of forty-four years who was among the women chained to the fence. He would have liked 'to machine-gun the lot of us', John remembered. But then he added: 'As far as I'm concerned, you can stay there as long as you like.'[50] He might have been sarcastic. But the women took him by his word and stayed. It was the birth of what became known as the Greenham Common Women's Peace Camp.[51]

From the very beginning, women took the lead at Greenham, though a few men had joined the march and initially lived at the camp. This changed in February 1982, when women at the camp took the decision to make it exclusively female. Men would be allowed to visit, but were not to participate in any action, nor to sleep in the camp. With men present, confrontations with the police would more easily turn violent, the women reasoned. Facing a bunch of joyful, laughing and singing women was something the police weren't trained for. The decision put women thoroughly and visibly in charge of both running the camp and the protests against the base. Men might take a supportive role by looking after children and taking care of the household back at home – that is, by taking over tasks traditionally performed by women.

It was an immensely controversial decision. The men who were living at the camp reacted angrily. One even took an axe and smashed the tarpaulin he had just built. Some women, too, felt they would betray male partners and comrades who had done so much to support them. Wouldn't it be necessary, they argued, for men and women to learn how to live together in peace? Outside the camp, many in the Campaign for Nuclear Disarmament (CND), the main organization of the peace movement, considered the step to be profoundly divisive and called for unity in the urgent struggle against the Cruise Missiles. But despite all the criticism, the decision stood.[52]

Over the next months, the camp grew. Women set up additional camps in front of the various gates leading into the military base, which would allow them to closely monitor the progress of the base and eventually the stationing of the missiles. Each camp was named after the different colours of the rainbow, and each gained a particular character. Yellow Gate, at the main entrance, was the site of the first camp, where many of the women who had participated in the initial campaigns lived. It drew most attention from the media and was perceived as the centre of power.[53] The women at Green Gate shared a sense of spirituality, with 'witches jumping over the fires and wishing out the evil',[54] while Violet Gate gained a reputation for the quality of their food. Blue Gate stood out. It was known as the 'tough gate' right 'on the front line', but also as the 'Frivolous Gate' that attracted young, lesbian, working-class women, a place of booze, dope and just 'a hell of a lot of fun'.[55]

The Greenham Common Women's Peace Camp became the site of multiple protests against nuclear armament. In December 1981, women sat down in front of excavators to prevent the construction of a canalization system necessary to house an additional 1,200 US military personnel.[56] Then on 22 March 1982, after thousands of women rallied to celebrate the Spring Equinox Festival, up to 150 women attempted to block the entrance to the camp by chaining themselves together across the gates; thirty-four women were arrested and faced charges for obstructing the highway. More non-violent blockades followed throughout the spring of 1982 as women tried to prevent construction machinery from arriving at the site by sitting and sleeping in front of the gates.[57]

Amid court trials and attempts to evict them, the activists prepared for what was to become the most famous protest at Greenham Common: the Embrace the Base rally. It was scheduled for Sunday, 12 December 1982, the anniversary of the NATO Dual-Track Decision. 'The Peace Camp has been a women's initiative. Reversing traditional roles, women have been leaving the house for peace, rather than men leaving home for war,' the circular letter calling on women from across the country to join the protest read. 'EMBRACE THE BASE ON SUNDAY . . . CLOSE THE BASE ON MONDAY.' Women should 'bring personal things that represent the threat of nuclear war to us and that express *our* lives, our anger, our joy . . . We want to decorate the entire fence with personal things.'[58]

The plan was to bring enough women (men were not welcomed at the protest) to encircle the entire base with a human chain. At least 16,000 women would have to come, the organizers calculated. Throughout the UK, local peace and women's groups organized coaches that would bring women to the rally. At the camp, women worried that it might still not be enough. But when twenty-seven-year-old activist Rebecca Johnson looked out of her tent on the morning of the 12th to see that 300 women who had arrived overnight were already standing in front of the gate, 'with candles in the sleet, totally silent', she realized that 'it was just going to be the most incredible day of my life'.[59] Some 35,000 women came to Greenham that day, joining hands around the entire base. As planned, they decorated the fence with children's toys, balloons, tampons and even an entire China tea set. 'You knew that the base was completely surrounded by joyous, strong, determined women,' one participant remembered.[60] The day was a success for the peace movement.[61]

The action was not over. Many women stayed overnight, and the next Monday morning, some 2,000 of them tried to block access to various gates in what became known as the Close the Base blockade. It was the largest non-violent collective action at the base to date. Unlike the day before, the police acted much more brutally. One woman present later described how 'a lot of women got boots in their ribs . . . And yet, when they kept going back again and again and again . . . you'd get flung to one side, and a woman would help pick you up, and you'd hug each other, and then you'd both go back.' The police made no arrests, and ultimately the work at the base continued, but the protesters could also claim it as a victory because construction had been significantly disrupted and delayed.[62]

As important as the actual blockade was the preparation. Women organized in 'informal affinity groups', where they go to know each other. Lynne Jones recalled: 'We all [were] really excited; and we sat up in these soaking wet marquees *all* night, getting into groups.' They shared tips on arrest and its legal consequences. And it was a moment for women to share feelings. 'Women were getting to know each other . . . We went through "This is what I'm frightened of. This is what I'm really scared [of]. This is my name. This is where I'm coming from. Who are you."' As Jill Liddington remarks, the Close the Base blockade marked a 'significant transformation of the culture of nonviolence in Britain', precisely because it 'revealed small informal affinity groups as an ideal *feminist* way of working'.[63]

Gradually, the actions became more daring. Embracing or blocking the base was no longer enough. In the early morning hours of 1 January 1983, women equipped with ladders and carpets climbed over the barbed wire fence. Two police officers tried to stop them and push the ladders away, but more than forty women made their way to one of the unfinished missile silos. Filmed by the watching press, who had been informed in advance, they sang and danced on the silo's roof, and used stones they found to make women's peace symbols before they were arrested after an hour. Women were 'crossing the boundaries of destruction', and in doing so, they had also overcome their fears of the authorities.[64]

They acquired a taste for overcoming boundaries, both physical and emotional. For 29 October 1983, the Greenham activists had organized a Halloween party. Women from all over Great Britain were invited to bring along 'black cardigans', a code for bolt cutters. Dressed up as witches, about 1,000 women approached the fence in the early morning hours. Standing on each other's shoulders, activists cut down more than a mile of the fence. By the end of the day, police had arrested 187 women, who were charged with criminal damages.[65] It was impressive, but also the last large act of protest at the peace camp. The camp existed until the base finally closed in 2000, but its attraction declined. Sustaining such a high level of activism over several years was just too much.

The camp at Greenham Common was not only a famous site of protesting against nuclear missiles. It was also a place to experiment with queer ways of living: queer in the sense that the women living in the camp subverted patriarchal norms and transgressed heteronormative boundaries. For example, women continued to clean up and cook – the 'feminine' household chores. Yet, ideals of cleanliness and order lost their meaning in the mud and dirt of the camp. Helen John, who had been a housewife before joining the camp, remarked that upon realizing that younger women didn't bother to wash used dishes, she didn't want to 'mother people'. If 'they wanted to get up and have dirty cups and saucers, that was great, that was their decision. It wasn't my responsibility. So it freed me from a lot of that. And you know, it's like cutting a big knot around your neck.'[66] While household tasks became less important, women put lots of energy into work traditionally considered masculine, such as building benders and mobile kitchens, chopping wood, or repairing the cars and vans necessary to keep the camp going.[67] It was an empowering experience: 'And I think that was a really good thing about Greenham, which made it a positive experience for me to stay, was just the fact that you were with a group of other women who were all doing everything for themselves, often for the first time in their lives,' remembered Katrina Allen.[68]

The British media often portrayed Greenham as a space of sexual deviance and lesbianism. Indeed, many of the women were lesbians; yet, it would be misleading to characterize Greenham as a lesbian community. Above all, it was a space in which sexual categories became fluid. The boundaries between heterosexuality and lesbianism, between friendly affection and sexual activity collapsed. 'We touched each other all the time. You couldn't go anywhere without kissing everyone,' recalled Jinny List.[69] Whether all the hugging, touching and kissing was an expression of friendship or sexual desire was hard to tell – and did not matter.

While Greenham destabilized a sexual order, it also challenged an emotional order. All too often, politics was and is considered a deadly serious business; and certainly, the threat of nuclear Armageddon was nothing to joke about. Particularly in West Germany, the peace movement used a rhetoric of apocalyptic fear: if people weren't afraid of a 'nuclear Holocaust', then clearly something was wrong with them, activists believed.[70] Greenham was different. Dancing on missile silos was fun. Despite all the hardships, women thoroughly enjoyed life in the camp, the caring, the laughing, the cuddling and the booze; or at least, this is how they recall it. As such, Greenham became a queer space where, as Sasha Roseneil puts it, women could try out practical alternatives to the Cold War world characterized by rationality and bureaucracy.[71]

Swords to Ploughshares: Peace and Environmental Activism in the GDR

East Berlin, sometime in the late 1980s. Well-trained men, neatly dressed, shaved and with their hair cut short, walked around the streets of Prenzlauer Berg and Friedrichshain, always in pairs. They carried small bags around their wrists, in which, rumour had it, radio phones were hidden. Inconspicuously standing in entrance halls, they looked out for passers-by. The men formed an 'invisible ring' around the churches in the area: Zion's church in Prenzlauer Berg, Gethsemane church close to Schönhauser Allee or Samariter church in Friedrichshain, known to house so-called information services (*Informationsandachten*, church services used to inform attendants about political developments) or blues masses, church services that allowed anti-government youth bands to perform. In the regime's eyes, these events were, in its typically clumsy language, 'public-relations actions' by 'hostile-negative forces'. For anyone able to read the signs, the presence of the plain-clothes officers functioned like a code: something would happen in one of the churches. In fact, the implicit code helped attract anyone who had not yet heard about the event.

Then the 'hostile forces' approached. They looked different. The men had long hair and beards, they were dressed in washed-out jeans, green coats, with colourful scarfs and jute bags; the women in long, flittering dresses in black. They didn't shake hands but hugged each other. The majority of them were in their thirties. When their peers in Western Europe and Czechoslovakia had rebelled around 1968, they had been sitting at school. They had seen images of barricades in Paris and tanks in Prague; they might have listened to the rebellious music of the Rolling Stones, and perhaps even had a poster of Che Guevara above their beds. But those exciting things were happening elsewhere. Their lives had remained dull. Many had grown up in religious families somewhere in the East German provinces, in Thuringia, Saxony or Mecklenburg, before moving to the capital of the GDR. When approached and aggressively interrogated by the police officers (and sometimes even arrested for a few hours), they tried to remain friendly; after all, they wanted to overcome enmity and hatred. Some even tried to hand a flower to the officers, though the latter rarely found this funny.

The scene never happened in quite this way. It is an 'ideal-typical portrait', as historian Stefan Wolle puts it, a sort of condensed description of multiple similar events that really did happen. Yet, it captures something about the East German peace and environmental movements. Organizing mass demonstrations or peace camps as in Western Europe was impossible under the conditions of a communist dictatorship. In the GDR, most oppositional activities happened under the roof of the Protestant Church, the only institution that kept its legally enshrined independence from the state. Though Church officials were expected to refrain from openly criticizing the regime, and faced persecution if they overstepped boundaries, the Protestant Church nevertheless offered independent-minded teenagers and young adults, whether they were devout Christians or not, the space to voice critical opinions.[72] For most ordinary GDR citizens, this non-conformist scene must have looked as shocking as the leftist students coming to Wyhl did for local peasants. Had they found their way into one of the churches, little would have reminded them of an ordinary service. The air stank of cigarette fumes, and loud music blared from speakers. It was a small scene, in East Berlin counting perhaps an inner core of 350 individuals, and ten times as many sympathizers: at most, a couple of thousand people, that is, a tiny minority of the capital's population.[73]

Peace activists in the GDR faced a socialist regime that presented itself as committed to the cause of bringing peace to the world.[74] Official media reported approvingly about the peace movements in Western Europe. Given this socialist commitment to peace, however, the regime argued, a similar independent peace movement in GDR was simply unnecessary. After all, it was the very military strength of the communist bloc that protected peace. 'I know that I don't have to be afraid of Soviet missiles: there is no one in the Soviet Union who would benefit from a war. But I also know that I don't have to be afraid of American missiles, because there are Soviet missiles,' wrote East German author and regime loyalist Wolfgang Tilgner in 1981 in the *German Teachers' Magazine*.[75] Peace, the official slogan went, had to be 'armed'.[76]

As such, society and everyday life in East Germany were much more thoroughly militarized than in the West.[77] In early 1978, amid debates about the modernization of nuclear arsenals on both sides of the Iron Curtain, news began to circulate of government plans to introduce military education (*Wehrkunde*) for ninth and tenth graders (roughly age fifteen to sixteen) throughout the GDR. Parents, teenagers and young adults, particularly those with ties to the Protestant Church, were horrified. A letter signed by the Protestant Student Parish (Evangelische Studentengemeinde) of Naumburg, for example, worried that an 'entire generation's thinking and acting' might be militarized. Being a 'state of peace', schools in the GDR should instead teach 'peace education'. Reacting to pressure from their enraged parishioners, the Church leadership appealed to the state to reconsider the plans, but to no avail. In September 1978, the first students had to take the new course.[78]

On the surface, the campaign against military education had been a failure. Yet, it sparked further activism in Protestant communities. In November 1980, peace activists affiliated with the Church organized 'Ten Days for Peace' (*Friedensdekade*) under the motto 'making peace without weapons', a direct challenge to the official claim that peace had to be armed.[79] In parishes throughout the GDR, events addressing different aspects of pacifism attracted small but dedicated audiences.[80]

A second *Friedensdekade* a year later saw the invention of one of the most powerful slogans of the peace movement in the GDR: 'swords to ploughshares', visualized by a drawing showing a strong, heroic smith beating a sword to turn it into a ploughshare. Based on a sculpture by Evgeniy Vuchetich, which the Soviet Union had donated to the United Nations in 1959, the slogan was an astute choice that subversively appropriated the socialist rhetoric of peace. It became immensely popular among young peace activists in the GDR, who sewed patches of the drawing onto their jackets, backpacks and caps. Under a communist dictatorship, such small acts of dissent could put young people at serious risk. The police frequently harassed them and forcefully removed the patches, while headteachers banned the symbol on school premises. Anyone displaying such a patch risked not being admitted to higher education or being denied apprenticeships. Initially, the Church had tried to defend the symbol and supported youngsters victimized by the police. But by March 1982, Church leaders declared they would be unable to protect anyone wearing it, and urged people to avoid displaying it in public.[81]

One of the central demands in the campaign against military education at schools had been the call for 'peace education'. And while the state did not introduce such a subject in schools, discussions about what an 'education for peace' might look like continued among pastors and other Church officials.[82] Among them was Christoph Wonneberger, then pastor of the Weinberg's church in Dresden, who developed the idea of a 'social peace service', akin to the social service (*Zivildienst*) conscientious objectors to military service could opt for in West Germany. After discussions within the Church, he published a proposal for such a service in May 1981. To make it unattractive to mere 'shirkers', the service should last for twenty-four months, that is, six months longer than usual military service. While not an overtly political critique, the text was nevertheless a challenge to the regime by equating armament on both sides of the Iron Curtain and worrying about the 'increasing weight of military matters in our society'. The text quickly circulated within peace groups and even reached youths with no links to the Church. Close to 5,000 individuals sent letters in support of it to the Church. The popularity of the proposal alarmed the regime, whose officials ultimately pressured the Church to give up on the project. But it was impossible to stem the tide. When the Church leadership refused to support the idea, a grassroots movement continued to propagate it.[83]

In the meanwhile, Berlin pastor Rainer Eppelmann and chemist Robert Havemann worked on a text that became known as 'Berlin Appeal', published in January 1982. The text, which had been debated in private and not within Church-based peace groups, was more radical than the call for a social peace service. Havemann, after all, was a dissident Marxist and former member of the communist resistance to Nazi Germany who was expelled from the Socialist Unity Party (SED) in 1964. It not only demanded the removal of nuclear weapons from all of Europe, but also a general demilitarization of society and free debate about questions of peace. The regime reacted immediately. Even before the plea was published, the GDR's secret police – known as the Stasi – arrested Eppelmann, but released him only two days later, with no charges filed, as the authorities did not want to create a martyr. But even though Church officials publicly criticized the text and the Stasi tried to find and destroy any copies of it, more than 2,000 GDR citizens had signed the Berlin Appeal by April 1982.[84]

It was still not a large peace movement, but it was becoming increasingly visible. Texts were circulating, and young people were courageously displaying the swords-to-ploughshares symbol. Amid all of this, a group of teenagers in Dresden around a girl named Johanna Kalex had called (anonymously, of course) for a silent protest in front of the ruins of Dresden's Church of Our Lady (*Frauenkirche*) on the evening of 13 February 1982, the anniversary of the city's bombing during the Second World War. Worrying that a public demonstration might result in confrontations with the police, Dresden's bishop Johannes Hempel negotiated with local authorities to hold a peace forum in the nearby Kreuzkirche.[85]

More than 5,000 mostly young people from all over the GDR made it to Dresden that day; even more were stopped by the police on their way. A few hundred of them ignored the request to move to the Kreuzkirche and remained at the ruins of the Frauenkirche, where they lit candles and put up posters. After the peace forum was over, another couple of hundred teenagers joined them for a silent protest. At the forum itself, Church officials addressed the young peace activists. But while Bishop Hempel appreciated their desire to 'raise alarm' regarding the dangers of nuclear Armageddon, he also asked them to appreciate the 'difficulties of peace politics in our era' and to realize the limitations of the Church that could not engage in politics. The audience did not react favourably to such calls for moderation. When another Church official outlined the Church's critical reaction to the Berlin Appeal, he was met with boos and whistles. 'I'm nineteen years old, and nevertheless,

I've nothing to lose. You talk and talk behind closed doors. Do you want to put us off until the final downfall,' one member of the audience commented.[86]

By the end of 1983, the peace movement in Germany on both sides of the Iron Curtain was losing steam. In November, the West German parliament had voted in favour of stationing Cruise Missiles, a move the Western peace movement had tried to prevent. Now, the battle seemed to be lost, for Western activists as well as for their Eastern counterparts. By 1984, many groups had dissolved, and former members now turned to human rights and environmental issues.[87] The nuclear catastrophe at Chernobyl in April 1986 made environmental politics all the more urgent.[88] Official media in the GDR tried to hide the real extent of the catastrophe, but with easy access to West German media, citizens quickly understood the danger. Playgrounds remained empty, and lettuce, usually a rare item in the GDR, was left untouched for fear of contamination. Environmentalist groups reacted quickly. Writing petitions to authorities and organizing events and seminars about nuclear power, they criticized both the regime's failure to properly inform its citizens and its over-reliance on dangerous nuclear power.[89]

Like its counterpart in Western Europe, the peace and environmental movements in the GDR developed a more fundamental critique of industrial society on both sides of the Iron Curtain. The problem wasn't merely the arms race between the superpowers, the militarization of society and the 'organized irresponsibility' with regard to the environment, but the ideals of permanent economic progress and increased efficiency which lay behind them. A 1980 statement by the Church-run research institute at Wittenberg, a pioneer of environmental activism in the GDR, for example, rejected the constant accumulation and consumption of an ever-increasing amount of material goods, and instead called for devoting more attention to 'intellectual and cultural activity, social engagement, and a way of life characterized by solidarity'.[90] For these critics, Western capitalism was hardly going to be the remedy for the malaise of consumer society on either side of the Iron Curtain.

The most famous environmentalist group that emerged in the wake of Chernobyl was the Environmental Library (*Umweltbibliothek*) in East Berlin. Founded in September 1986 at Zion's Church in Prenzlauer Berg, the library quickly became an important venue for opposition groups of all kinds. Its newsletter, the *Umweltblätter*, circulated throughout the GDR and connected different groups by addressing a variety of topics beyond environmental issues.[91] Responding to the regime's abysmal communications policy, which considered reports about environmental problems a state secret, activists of the Umweltbibliothek tried to gather and publish such material. And with the help of fellow activists from West Berlin, they campaigned against the hypocritical trade across the Iron Curtain, whereby West Germany and other Western countries dumped their waste in the GDR in exchange for foreign currency, which the regime desperately needed.[92]

With such activities, the Umweltbibliothek quickly became the target of an investigation by the Stasi. In November 1987, security forces raided the library and arrested several of its members, though they were released a few days later after public protests. The network of 'alternative' groups to which the Umweltbibliothek belonged had become a political threat for the regime. It fed into the growing opposition of the late 1980s that would ultimately lead to the regime's downfall (see Chapter 15).[93]

Legacies of Peace and Environmental Movements

The peace and environmental movements changed European politics. They facilitated the emergence of Green parties, the Federal Republic being a forerunner in this regard. The critiques of consumer society they had formulated inspired future generations of protestors such as the anti-globalization movement of the 1990s. While the peace movement broadly came to an end with the Cold War, with the exception of protests against the 2003 US-led invasion of Iraq, the environmental movement continued to thrive. If anything, its calls seem increasingly prescient. Most recently, Fridays for Future has mobilized millions of teenagers around the globe, demanding policymakers take urgent action against climate change and allow today's youth a future. And where economic and political elites in the 1970s often treated environmental protestors condescendingly, depicting them as enemies of progress, today's militants find support among scientists and politicians, who at least claim to offer a listening ear (with some notable exceptions). Their radical demands might remain unfulfilled, but they are taken seriously. Globally and locally, environmental protection has become part of official politics, with American president Joe Biden proposing a Green New Deal, and Paris Mayor Anna Hildago trying to ban cars from the city centre. However much remains to be done, in putting the protection of the environment high up the political agenda, climate activists have accomplished something. Arguably, the movements of the 1970s and 1980s have sown the seeds for this success story.

In some ways, today's activism resembles that of a generation ago. Just like their predecessors, environmental protestors today think globally and act locally, as a famous slogan put it, by campaigning against environmentally damaging projects in their vicinity. They, too, profess a sense of profound concern if not anxiety about the future of the planet. But rather than pessimistically resigning themselves to it, activists have shown a remarkable determination to continue to fight for a liveable planet. At stake is more than preventing a climate catastrophe. It is a struggle, as philosopher Eva von Redecker writes, against a capitalist logic that prioritizes profit over everything, including the planet; it's a struggle for 'saving life'. In that sense, today's climate activists continue a fight that started in the 1970s.[94]

The legacies of the peace and environmental movements of the 1970s and 1980s reach further than present-day climate activists. In the context of these movements, a practice developed that spread well beyond them: setting up protest camps as spaces for practically trying out alternatives, for experimenting with forms of direct democracy and queer sexuality and for bringing together local residents and dedicated militants. Such camps became a common feature of different protest movements across Europe: the NoBorder camps at various European borders since 2002; the 2005 HoriZone eco-village near Gleneagles, Scotland, to protest against the G8 summit; or the Occupy movement, which spread in the autumn of 2011 from New York's Wall Street around the globe.[95]

Like the camps of an earlier period, these camps are more than protest sites. They constitute, as an organizer of the HoriZone camp remarked, a 'demonstration of the world we want': an 'eco-village to demonstrate sustainable alternatives to life under capitalism', with energy produced by 'little windmills, solar panels and bio-diesel generators', meat and dairy products banned and buildings made of scrap wood.[96] Those camps form a sense of community. For occupants of the construction site for a high-speed train line in Val di Susa, Italy, in 2005, living in the camp produced a sense of a 'shared intimacy'. These were 'unforgettable nights', as one activist remembered, with a 'wonderful encampment under the falling snow, fires burning, children and dogs playing. There were pots full of food, young people from all over Italy – because at this point, we became the focus and hope for a series of struggles.' Occupied construction sites were places, as another militant from Val di Susa claimed, 'inhabited by a different kind of life', where money played no role and problems were solved by dialogue and with mutual trust.[97] But as so often, the police put an end to these utopian spaces of building a better world here and now.

Taking the City: Urban Activism

Environmental and pacifist protestors took their struggles to remote bases buried deep in the countryside. Generally, however, protests in post-war Europe were a profoundly urban phenomenon. Cities such as Paris, West Berlin, Bologna, Wrocław, Amsterdam or Zurich attracted rebellious teenagers and students. Here, radicals took to the streets, engaged in violent battles with the police, but also found spaces to develop countercultural milieus in bars, clubs and communes. And if cities facilitated protest, they were also the object of it, with activists demanding affordable housing and public spaces they could enjoy.

In 1968, French Marxist philosopher Henri Lefebvre famously proclaimed a 'Right to the City', a slogan that has become a rallying cry for urban activists in recent years.[1] Today's activists demand that local residents rather than international investors should determine how urban space is used. Cities, they argue, are not for profit, but for living. Across the continent, residents campaign against what has become known as gentrification: artists, bars and clubs benefiting from cheap rents give a neighbourhood an authentic feel, thereby attracting wealthier residents and businesses, who in turn drive up prices and displace not only the artists that made the neighbourhood attractive in the first place, but also other long-term, more precarious residents.[2] These protests bring people to the streets who might not participate in traditional leftist activism, like the sex workers in Madrid who campaigned in 2007 and 2008 against investors buying up property in the streets where they used to work.[3]

On the surface, such urban activism seems to be concerned with economic questions: who should own the city, its buildings and infrastructure – the local government and thus the public, or private investors? Should rent and property prices be left to market forces, or should the state put a cap on rents? Activists campaign against investor landlords who buy up property and sell it at a higher price at the cost of poorer tenants who have to move out; they protest against big commercial chains replacing small local businesses, and in general against an economic logic that seeks to wring maximum value out of urban space. Yet, understanding urban struggles merely in terms of poor local residents pitted against rich (often international) investors (and equally rich new residents who then move into gentrified areas) would be misleading. These are fundamentally political questions about the character of urban life and the *right to the city*: who has the authority to determine a city's future?

This urban activism has a rich history. In the years following the upheavals of 1968, activists did much more than protest against the price of rent. Critics in the 1970s bemoaned the architecture of cities, which they saw as monotonous, dull and grey. They fought against high-rise apartment blocks that all looked the same replacing older buildings with an individual character. Such modern cities left no space for informal conversation, for children to play outside, for neighbours to get to know each other. Cities, one German critic remarked in March 1981, resembled prisons. While people might move around freely, the concrete and the neatly cut lawns caused the same 'sensory deprivation' that a 'cell tiled in white' would have.[4] Trying to combat this urban monotony, activists sought to change the urban landscape by painting murals onto walls or by building adventure playgrounds for children. While not as dramatic as large anti-gentrification protests or even the illegal squatting of empty buildings, these interventions into urban space were important practical attempts to start building better cities.

The Struggle for Housing: Rome in the 1970s

In the wake of the Second World War, Italy – like much of Europe – faced severe shortages of affordable housing. The taxation regime of the 1950s favoured private investors, who were responsible for much of the construction boom that followed the war. However, they built primarily for middle-class residents who had access to mortgages or who could afford rents that were increasing faster than wages.[5] Working-class families, by contrast, had great trouble finding adequate housing. Urban planners proved incapable of dealing with this development, resulting in the chaotic and often illegal construction of cheap apartment buildings and shanty towns in the outskirts of cities such as Rome. Not surprisingly, such areas also lacked an adequate infrastructure of hospitals, schools and kindergartens, all necessary to build sustainable communities.

A particularly drastic example of the corruption and wilful ignorance of building regulations that characterized the development of new neighbourhoods was Magliana, located to the south of Rome on the west bank of the Tiber. The area was frequently flooded by the Tiber, which had previously made it an unattractive prospect for construction projects. Following the war, however, the municipal authorities included it in their urban extension plans, stipulating that it should be raised by seven metres to prevent future flooding. Despite development plans being finalized in 1954, not a single building was completed by 1962. Only in 1965 did a construction boom set in, stimulated by ambiguous changes in building regulations that allowed for more densely populated areas: by 1969, roughly 2.3 million square metres of residential space had been constructed, and by 1975, the neighbourhood was complete, with 7,800 apartments.[6] But official stipulations were apparently entirely irrelevant. Not only did builders ignore the requirement to raise the ground level by seven metres, but they had the audacity to calculate the maximum height of buildings, limited to twenty-two metres, not based on the actual ground level, but the hypothetical seven metres above that. After all, the lower floors would eventually disappear once the landfilling process was completed, which of course never happened. Predictably, the overcrowded area was frequently flooded.[7]

Private construction firms did not bother to invest in infrastructure either, expecting the municipality to take care of it. There were no asphalted streets, and the neighbourhood's wastewater system was not connected to the public waterways. Public services were equally lacking: by 1974, there was only one elementary and one middle school, but no parks or hospitals, and a single market had to serve 40,000 residents.[8] A photo dramatically depicts the situation: a long line of children is waiting in front of a single slide in the middle of a street.[9] For investors, it was an opportunity to quickly maximize profits. While their expenditure remained low, the municipality of Rome had to rent or purchase apartments at a high price to be able to provide social housing. It was a classic example of private enrichment at the cost of the community.

But in 1971, the neat plans of private investors were disturbed. In the spring, a group of women marched into the office of the real estate firm Lisbona to demand a rent reduction. They were enraged that council flats were being allocated to former residents of a shanty town who paid much lower (and subsidized) rents than the tenants of privately owned apartments; now, they demanded similarly low rents. Immediately afterwards, some 300 women, renters of Lisbona and another company named Prato, attended a meeting and proposed reducing the rent themselves. This was not an uncommon practice for renters of publicly owned apartments. Throughout Rome, some 10,000 families did this, including some in Magliana, without getting into much trouble with the state. Yet, such a self-reduction (*auto-riduzione*) of rent in privately owned apartments was a novelty. Even the secretary of the tenants' union argued against the move, fearing that it would result in evictions. Ignoring his pleas for caution, the women unanimously decided to go ahead and reduce rents by 50 per cent, starting in June 1971. The call for action was enthusiastically responded to: some 500 families participated in the rent strike, which amounted to 90 per cent of the tenants of these two companies. Tenants of seven other companies quickly joined the movement. Some families not only reduced their monthly rent payments, but stopped paying them altogether, out of sheer need. By the end of the summer, about 1,000 families were reducing their rents.[10]

The rebellious residents soon organized from the ground up in 'fighting committees' based on the stairways of individual apartment buildings. The first chance to prove the effectiveness of this local organization came in September 1971, when landlords sent out eviction notices to fifty families participating in the rent reduction. The day before the scheduled evictions, more than 1,000 residents marched through the neighbourhood; the following day, some 300 people blocked the entry to the apartments, preventing the officer of the court from delivering the official eviction note. It was the beginning of a militant struggle that would last for years.[11]

Such *autoriduzione* was not a new tool in the arsenal of protestors. As we've seen in Chapter 2, Italian workers in 1968 had taken measures into their own hands and reduced the pace of work. In the mid-1970s, workers in Turin refused to pay their electricity and telephone bills.[12] Most spectacularly, leftist activists in Italian cities organized 'self-reductions' of grocery bills: they filled their trollies, mostly with staple foods, then left 5,000 lire and a pamphlet with the cashiers, and encouraged other shoppers to do the same via megaphone while fellow militants kept the security guards in check.[13] In Magliana, too, neighbourhood committees coordinated with other activists in Rome to reduce electricity bills – the more moderate by 50 per cent, the more radical from 45 to 8 lire per kilowatt-hour, the amount industrial companies had to pay. Residents hardly had to fear severe consequences for doing this. They could count on sympathetic employees of electricity providers who were not keen to cut their power supply. In fact, it was leftist workers of the energy provider ENEL who had first suggested the self-reduction of electricity bills![14]

Taking direct action by refusing to pay the full price, for rent, bills or grocery shopping, residents and activists fought the impact of the escalating inflation that ate up any gains workers had won in previous labour struggles. But *autoriduzione* was not the only way to address the problem. Neighbourhood committees in Magliana and elsewhere organized illegal 'red markets', where vendors sold their produce, usually staple foods, directly to consumers, without paying for middlemen or taxes. Aside from offering cheaper food, they helped to pressure local merchants to reduce their prices. And it worked: when the neighbourhood committee called a meeting to discuss proper prices, half the merchants of Magliana attended. Red markets were thus part and parcel of an attempt to construct an 'organic neighbourhood' for which moral values mattered more than profit-making.[15]

Other activists were keen to take more radical steps, and moved on from reducing rents to occupying vacant buildings. In November 1973, 220 families, some with small children, squatted an empty apartment block in Magliana. It was a well-planned operation. Families came from all over Rome, including Magliana itself. The group anticipated a swift crackdown by the authorities and had prepared to defend the building by placing materials for barricades in nearby streets. Yet, to their surprise, the police didn't show. Thus, occupants started organizing everyday life in their new home: they cleaned the hitherto uninhabited building, brought furniture and household items – after much discussion about the décor – and negotiated their own water and electricity supply (for which, this time, they paid). Contrary to the squatters' initial expectations, the occupation turned into a success that quickly inspired other families to occupy more vacant buildings nearby. In the meantime, the committee reached out to the local community. Given the neighbourhood's history of rent reduction, they hoped for solidarity among local residents. Activists distributed leaflets and held a meeting with Magliana's neighbourhood committee, which had organized the rent reductions. The groups agreed that, even if their tactics differed, they both fought for the same goal: a 'political price' of rent, meaning that not just the market, but residents' needs and their willingness to fight should determine the price.[16]

While not paying electricity bills rarely caused trouble, reducing rents could lead to eviction notices. To make sure those weren't even delivered, residents organized blockades. Initially, such blockades remained peaceful and effective, because the single officer of the court who was to deliver the notice was usually unwilling and incapable of breaking through it. Eventually, however, police began to protect court officers. Confrontations between residents and the forces of order escalated. When 200 officers tried to break through a blockade in November 1972, they left one woman with severe head injuries. Activists reacted by extending the protest to the entire neighbourhood and blocking major roads. Most spectacularly, on 5 July 1973, hundreds of residents stopped the dense traffic on the Via della Magliana – the main road leading to Rome's airport – and erected barricades out of burning tyres. Within minutes, a cloud of smoke signalled to the police that activists were ready to defend their neighbourhood. The tactic worked: police forces got stuck in the traffic jam, and by the time firefighters finally extinguished the barricades, the landlord's lawyer was willing to negotiate.[17]

Outside of Magliana, confrontations turned even more violent. In September 1974, several hundred policemen tried to evict squatters in the neighbourhood of San Basilio, using excessive force, including tear gas. Squatters in turn set fire to barricades and fought back with rocks, Molotov cocktails and slingshots. Clashes lasted for several days before reaching their peak on 8 September 1974. Militants stopped garbage trucks and buses to use them as barricades, pulled out telephone poles to block streets, and even attacked a police station with Molotov cocktails. By the afternoon, the police started shooting with live ammunition. Around 7.15 p.m., Fabrizio Ceruso, a nineteen-year-old member of the far-left organization Autonomia Operaia, was shot in the chest. He succumbed to his wounds on the way to the hospital.[18]

Urban activism in Rome was about more than economic benefits. Activists tried to make their neighbourhood more liveable and communal. In the newly built, sterile neighbourhood that lacked public spaces, residents felt isolated, especially women who took care of the household and did not leave Magliana for work. As resident Aurora Atzeri said: 'I recall that I started feeling very lonely when I moved to Magliana. I was lost, I felt like in prison, so many tears.'[19] Such feelings of isolation were one factor that made participating in blockades against evictions attractive,

particularly for women: here, they could get to know their neighbours and develop a sense of community.[20] Activists did their best
to fight this isolation, for example by occupying an empty plot of
land to create a communal garden. Any remaining undeveloped
space should be reserved, they demanded, for communal facilities
such as schools and kindergartens.[21] Magliana's neighbourhood
committee engaged in a variety of community-related activities.
It set up a 'popular school' that enabled residents to complete
their middle-school degree and offered leisure-time activities for
younger children like doing crafts and making pottery.[22] Activists
also organized numerous festivities, plays and film screenings in
the streets of Magliana, where neighbours could connect with
each other. Such activities did nothing to support financially struggling families, but they provided residents with an opportunity to
'have some fun together beyond all the problems', as former militant Franco Moretti put it. They proved that a good life was still
possible in the middle of a 'monstrous city'.[23]

Ultimately, the struggles for affordable housing in Magliana
and elsewhere in Rome were surprisingly successful. Though the
police violently evicted many squatting families, the confrontations in San Basilio compelled the authorities to accept
neighbourhood committees as legitimate representatives and to
provide subsidized housing at least for those squatters who could
prove financial need. In Magliana, too, tenants who had reduced
their rent were able to stay. Due to the pressure their protests had
caused, private investors who had illegally built 670,000 square
metres of living space had to pay a penalty of 60 billion lire,
money that was to be spent for neighbourhood improvements.
After private investors defaulted on credits, the publicly owned
Banca Nazionale del Lavoro (BNL) took over numerous apartments. In the early 1980s, the tenants of the BNL negotiated the
option to purchase the apartments at about a third of their market value, an opportunity around 90 per cent of the tenants made
use of. For the residents in Magliana, it was a victory in their
struggle for affordable housing.[24]

The Struggle against Deserts of Concrete:
Making Liveable Cities

'In the end, we don't have any neighbours. Even in the hallway where you live cheek by jowl with four other families, you don't get together . . . Man, it's like being in jail. All those long corridors, that really isolates you,' said Irene Rakowitz, a working-class mother of four, in 1972.[25] Rakowitz lived in Märkisches Viertel, an infamous neighbourhood, finished in 1975, which consisted mostly of high-rise buildings in the north of West Berlin. Her words echoed those of Aurora Atzeri in Magliana, who had felt she was in prison.

Many urban critics, from left to right, thought about the social housing estates built after the Second World War on the outskirts of European cities in such ways. From the 1960s, French observers had complained about the monotony of the *grands ensembles* and the sense of isolation and depression among their inhabitants. A journalist on the communist daily *L'Humanité* surmised in 1960 that any new resident of such a neighbourhood would be 'exposed to his own loneliness among 999 other lonely people'.[26] And West German psychoanalyst Alexander Mitscherlich wrote about the 'half a dozen eight- to ten-storey buildings, barely separated from the highway with its roaring noise' that characterized modern cities. The problem began with the very physical shape of cities, as these large highways cut neighbourhoods into pieces. 'Nobody knows each other. The place is unfriendly, it does not encourage openness.'[27] The new lower-class suburbs, these critics charged, lacked the dense social interaction that had characterized old working-class neighbourhoods like Wedding or Kreuzberg in West Berlin. Even on the other side of the Iron Curtain, in East Berlin, residents bemoaned the 'cityscape's hectic and stressful lifestyle', whose 'monotony and lack of communication' fostered a 'sense of alienation'.[28]

For critics on the left, these urban monstrosities were the effect of a capitalist logic of functionality and profitability that left no space for community or joy. The spatial organization of modern cities, West

German Detlef Hartmann wrote in 1981 in the leftist magazine *Große Freiheit*, precisely defined how space should be used: for shopping, for traffic, for working, and so on – an echo of the Situationist critique of modern cities we encountered in Chapter 1. Yet, there wasn't any place where people could just do whatever they wanted. Everything had a purpose, and spontaneity became impossible.[29] Buildings looked all the same with their grey concrete and the clean glass fronts of office buildings. 'The dull death-grey of concrete devours living green,' wrote anonymous authors from Nuremberg in 1976.[30] And a women's collective from Frankfurt added that life amid the 'concrete, noise, exhausts, smog, canteen-food, phosphorous sausages, rubber bread' was 'crippling' senses like 'tasting, smelling, listening, seeing, feeling'. Urban life caused 'stabbing headaches', it made people depressed and drove them to suicide.[31] No matter their economic situation, it was an emotionally deprived life.[32]

In reaction to this, activists sought to find, as a group from Stuttgart wrote in 1976, 'our happiness in the city'.[33] But how to go about it? Reclaiming urban life in this understanding did not call for dramatic actions like occupying vacant buildings or large demonstrations, but for small acts of insubordination and disruption, like playing the violin in a shopping arcade even though it was forbidden: 'just doing something that might be fun'.[34] By making use of streets and squares for purposes beyond consumption and traffic, these protests tried to bring people together and turn the 'monstrous city' into an enjoyable place.

This understanding of urban activism gave seemingly trivial activities a profoundly political meaning. Any improvised concert in the streets, argued a West German group who called themselves the 'asphalt activists', was a form of 'street occupation' that claimed the street as a public space until the forces of order, or local businesses, intervened. Playing music made passers-by who usually wouldn't look at each other stop, smile and clap their hands; it enabled residents to overcome their isolation and brought an unexpected moment of joy into otherwise dull and perfectly ordered days.[35]

Other urban activists, like those in Italy, tried to beautify grey walls with colourful murals. Reviewing a book about these murals, West German Klaus Bernd Vollmar enthusiastically described them as 'trees and sun on concrete, colour against grey, dragons on brick walls in bleak neighbourhoods and children playing under the sun of a lawn, where no sun gets through, where no grass grows'.[36] Just like street music, painting walls in the city would facilitate communication between residents, urban activists believed. In Berlin-Kreuzberg, according to the book Vollmar was reviewing, painting the walls of their house allowed tenants to 'break out of the isolation and anonymity of our one-to-two-bedroom apartments'. Other residents in the same area also organized a street festival, providing free beer, which understandably helped to build a sense of community among neighbours.[37]

Of particular interest to urban critics, academics and activists alike, was the situation of children who suffered, they claimed, the most from life in high-rise buildings. Studies by social psychologists found that children living on the upper floors were less likely to play outside, which kept them isolated from other children and resulted in psychological problems.[38] Even reaching the buttons of the lift could be a challenge for small children. And if they needed to use the toilet, they'd rather pee in the hallway than risk wetting their pants on the long way up to the twelfth floor, where their angry parents would beat them up: or at least, that is how the 1981 movie *Christiane F.* depicted West Berlin's Gropiusstadt.[39] But there wasn't much to do outside anyway. Urban planners had reserved space for parking lots, but not for parks and playgrounds. The playgrounds that did exist looked all the same, with equipment that encouraged repetitive movements, like swings and slides, but left no space for creativity and fantasy. Some parents, Detlef Hartmann noted, even worried that their children would turn into 'conveyor-belt workers for slides', while a woman living in a densely populated neighbourhood of Hamburg feared that the lack of any parks and playgrounds besides sandboxes would turn children into 'sandbox idiots'.[40]

Creating spaces for children that would allow for more spontaneous and wild play therefore became a central goal for urban activists during the 1970s. They campaigned for adventure playgrounds, particularly in social housing projects with high-rise buildings. The idea of such playgrounds goes back to 1943, when a 'junk playground' designed by Danish landscape architect Carl Theodor Sørensen opened in Emdrup near Copenhagen. Here, children could use debris and rubbish to construct their own play spaces. They could dig caves in the ground or build huts with old wooden slats.[41] In the 1950s, similar playgrounds were established in various European cities. Only after 1968, however, did a genuine movement for adventure playgrounds develop. Significantly, it was in Märkisches Viertel that the first adventure playground in West Germany opened in 1967. In an area measuring over 2,000 square metres, children could use wood and a variety of tools to construct their own playground – and tear down whatever they had built if they wanted to, always under the watchful eyes of (usually left-leaning) social workers. It was an attempt to stimulate autonomy and creativity but also socially responsible behaviour among children in an urban context that limited their capacity to freely explore.[42]

Performing music in the streets, colourfully painting walls or establishing adventure playgrounds in suburban housing estates: these were all attempts by grassroots activists to facilitate a better life in dull modern cities. Whether they worked is difficult to assess. For one thing, it remains open to debate how emotionally miserable life in neighbourhoods like Märkisches Viertel really was. While residents like Irene Rakowitz complained that they felt imprisoned, others were happy about their housing situation and glad they could leave the shanty towns behind them. A spontaneous street concert might bring a moment of fun, but long-term projects like adventure playgrounds ran up against numerous challenges, ranging from angry neighbours to restrictions imposed by local authorities, and children not behaving as creatively and socially responsibly as enthusiastic activists might have hoped for. At the playground in Märkisches Viertel, they wouldn't do anything without clear instructions, they lost, destroyed or stole tools and they were unwilling to share anything. And yet, the playground has survived, albeit in a different form, until today. Arguably, it is a tangible improvement in a poorer part of the city.

And to this day, beautifying grey cities can be a small act of rebellion. In the aftermath of the Gezi Park protests in Istanbul in the summer of 2013, activists established common gardens on vacant plots of land. 'We thought why is this land not used as a green area, instead of being full of debris? We need green areas, in a city which is full of concrete,' they argued.[43] Another resident named Hüseyin Çetinel painted the grey stairs connecting two neighbourhoods in the vicinity of Gezi Park with the colours of the rainbow. On social media, commentators assumed that the rainbow colours were meant to symbolize support for the queer movement, but Çetinel gave a different reason: 'I didn't do it for a group or a form of activism. I did it to make people smile.' Only two days later, the district mayor had them repainted in grey during the darkness of the night. But he had not anticipated the outrage of local residents, who had come to love the colourful stairs. They quickly organized via social media to repaint the stairs, and not only that: throughout Istanbul and other Turkish cities, residents started painting other stairs as well.[44] It might not have been outright political activism, but it was a defiant act by citizens who claimed the city and its physical appearance as their own.

Taking the City: Squatting Movements

In 1965, a group of sixty students occupied an entire apartment block in the Christianshavn district of Copenhagen, where they opened a self-organized student dormitory known as Sofiegaarden. The squat lasted for four years, until police forcefully evicted the occupants. Copenhagen's squatters movement, though, lived on, and brought a variety of leftist activists together who pursued an alternative life in the derelict houses of Christianshavn. In September 1971, some of these activists took down a fence around the neighbouring former military barracks to turn the area into a neighbourhood playground. It was a fairly quiet, unremarkable action that resulted in one of the most famous squats of Europe: Freetown Christiania in the middle of Copenhagen. Responding to a call to occupy the entire area of 34 hectares, several hundred people moved into the barracks. They transformed the military buildings into 'homes, music venues, work-shops, kindergartens, a communal bathhouse, a post office and a number of collectively owned businesses'. By 1973, Social Democratic authorities in Denmark officially acknowledged Christiania as a tem-porary 'social experiment'. And despite a 2004 Christiania Act revoking the rights of cooperative land ownership that had laid the foundation for its status, Christiania in its different forms continues to exist.[45]

Christiania wasn't Europe's first squat. In the aftermath of the Second World War, homeless families in cities such as Marseille, Paris, London, Birmingham, Bristol and Glasgow sought shelter in aban-doned buildings. Many of these squatters were impoverished and disenfranchised families, above all needing a place to sleep. With the support of communist organizations, they also formulated demands for a right to housing.[46] Christiania activists, however, wanted more: they took parts of the city to create a space for communal living.

West German activists, too, were thrilled by the idea of commu-nal living. They looked for large vacant buildings they might squat to put such ideas into practice. In December 1971, leftist apprentices and high-school students in West Berlin occupied the former nurses' dormitory of the Bethanien Hospital in Kreuzberg, naming it Georg-von-Rauch-Haus after a member of the Movement 2nd June who had recently been shot.[47] The first larger 'housing struggle', as such squatting activism came to be called, took place in Frankfurt, where local activists formed alliances with migrant workers, par-ticularly from Italy, who brought militant traditions of rent strikes to the Federal Republic. In the early 1970s, they squatted several buildings in the relatively wealthy neighbourhood of Westend, where investors planned to replace nineteenth-century villas – beautiful historical buildings in disrepair – with modern office buildings. Pushed by property owners who were eager to clear the space for developers, police evicted the squatters house by house, frequently leading to heavy riots.[48]

Yet, it was only in the early 1980s that a genuine squatting movement emerged across cities in Northern Europe.[49] First came Amsterdam. Squatting was relatively easy in the Dutch metropolis. Not only were there numerous vacant buildings (somewhat ironically, the popularity of squatting caused its own housing shortage), but squatters also enjoyed unusual rights. As early as 1914, a Dutch court had ruled that anyone who spent a night with a chair, a table and a bed in a building that had been vacant for more than a year would have established residency, effectively legalizing squatting, at least until an official eviction notice came.[50] Occasionally, there had been violent confrontations between squatters and the police, as in 1975, when the city wanted to demolish a huge squatted housing block in the district of Nieuwmarkt to build a new metro line and faced massive – though ultimately unsuccessful – resistance by squatters. But most squatters did not resist eviction, not least because squatting other buildings was so easy.[51]

Things changed in 1978, when *krakers*, as squatters were known in Dutch, in a house in the Kinkerbuurt neighbourhood decided to fight back. A group of politically motivated squatters barricaded the house and threw oil and soapstone powder on the floor to make it slippery, hoping to make the police look ridiculous when they entered the building. In front of the house, squatters and local supporters gathered for a peaceful blockade. The police, they expected, would simply drag them away. Yet, to their surprise, the police came in full riot gear and immediately assaulted the peaceful squatters. A film-maker documented the violence. In the following weeks, the footage was shown over and over in squatter circles. For the squatters, the beatings were a shock. It changed attitudes towards violence and resistance.[52] They would no longer allow the police to beat them up without responding in kind. In 1979, militant squatters began fortifying a group of occupied buildings known as the Groote Keyser and prepared for battle. Everyone expected an eviction to result in massive violence. But fearing fatalities, Amsterdam's mayor called off the eviction and hence the battle.[53]

This only delayed the confrontation. In February 1980, the police evicted squatters in Vondelstraat, falsely claiming that a regular tenant was still living in the building. The squatters refused to give up. They organized a protest march to the mayor's residence, the police always on their heels. Yet, this was only a decoy. With the police distracted elsewhere, squatters retook the building, and when the police tried to evict them again, they forced the police to retreat with clubs and a barrage of stones. Using material from a nearby roadwork site, they erected barricades on the square in front of the house and held the site for three days, until the police brought tanks that broke through the barricades. But while the police could clear the streets, squatters negotiated their right to stay in the house. Victory was theirs.[54]

The tumultuous events in Amsterdam were the beginning of a wider wave of urban youth protests. Over the course of 1980, protestors violently clashed with the police over demands for autonomous spaces, whether these were independent youth centres in Zurich or squatted houses as in West Berlin (see Chapter 3).[55] The neighbourhood of Kreuzberg became particularly well known as a squatters' stronghold. The numbers alone are impressive: at the end of 1979, there were less than a dozen squatted houses in West Berlin; by June 1981, at the apex of the squatters' movement, there were 165.[56] The authorities initially did little to stop the movement, partly because the West Berlin government had collapsed amid a banking scandal and new elections were held in May 1981. After a conservative government took over and hardliner Heinrich Lummer became the city's senator of interior affairs, the police began cracking down on squatters.

West Berlin's abysmal housing market certainly played a major role in the emergence of the squatting movement. Early in the morning, students and other young people looking for a place to live would rush to buy a newspaper with housing advertisements and then hurry to the nearest public telephone booth to snatch one of the treasured viewing appointments, only to be rejected if the landlord didn't like the look of them. At the same time, numerous apartment blocks built around the turn of the century in neighbourhoods adjacent to the Wall stood empty, as developers planned to tear them down to turn the area around Mariannen-platz, nowadays one of the most popular spots in the city, into a giant highway intersection. In this context, squatting one of these decaying buildings seemed like an obvious solution.[57]

Yet, squatting in West Berlin was about more than just having a place to sleep. The squatted houses offered an intense and collective life that was an escape from the dull and isolating life in modern cities that activists despised. 'We wanted to live and work together,' squatters from Schöneberg declared after they had been evicted. 'We wanted to put an end to isolation and the destruction of collective living. Who in this city doesn't know the agonizing loneliness and emptiness of everyday life . . . ?'[58]

Life in the derelict houses certainly wasn't easy. They lacked amenities such as central heating and inside toilets, and often there was neither electricity nor running water, at least until squatters illegally connected their houses to the grid. Even then, lots of dirt and debris had to be removed before actual renovations could begin. Many squatters were eager to get to work, setting up networks that allowed them to pool expertise and building material.[59] Despite these hardships, squatters recalled the exuberant atmosphere in the houses during the summer of 1981. In an effort to live truly collectively, many houses had abolished private rooms, meaning that everyone slept in one large room, if they didn't spend the warm summer nights on the roofs. Disrupting the normal routines of everyday life, they put up long tables in the street and had breakfast all day. At times, squatters even managed to establish relations with their legal neighbours, inviting nearby Turkish families or 'grannies' to visit and share cake with them. Evidently, not all squats worked that way, but for some activists, the squatted houses became a 'true home' where they could overcome the isolation of living alone.[60]

West Berlin's squatting movement was intense, but short-lived. By the autumn of 1981, amid mounting police pressure and the death of a protestor who was run over by a bus, the movement was visibly in decline. While some squatters managed to become legal tenants of their houses, others were forcibly evicted; by 1984, the movement was definitively over.[61] Yet, the squatters had a lasting impact. For one thing, West Berlin's senate gave up on plans to build huge highways through Kreuzberg and instead pursued a more careful policy of urban renovation that kept old buildings intact and that allowed local residents to participate in the planning. Squatters who managed to legalize their projects set up institutions like bars and bookshops in their houses and heavily contributed to the neighbourhood's rebellious and alternative character. Without the squatters' movement, Kreuzberg would look very different today.[62]

And the idea of squatting did not go away. In the late 1980s, the Hafenstraße in Hamburg became another squatting hotspot, leading to more violent confrontations between militant activists and the police.[63] Then, to everyone's surprise, the Berlin Wall fell in November 1989, and quickly thereafter the East German state, its municipal administration and police forces, lost any authority. This power vacuum in East Berlin created ideal conditions for a second wave of squatting during the early months of 1990, which saw some 130 buildings occupied, most of them in Prenzlauer Berg and Friedrichshain.[64] In fact, illegally moving into vacant buildings was nothing new in East Germany either. Facing long waiting lists for accommodation (access to housing was centrally administered in the GDR), especially young people moved into rundown buildings, started renovating them, and, after a few months, simply registered there and thereby legalized their situation. According to one estimate, there were at least 1,000 cases of such occupations per year during the 1980s. Yet, even though many opposition activists lived in squatted apartments, squatting itself rarely had a political dimension.[65]

When the Wall came down, things changed. East Berlin squatters began to publicize their occupations and put them into the context of the collapsing GDR that allowed West German investors to buy up property in the East at a cheap price. 'As of Christmas 1989 the GDR is open for plundering. Therefore, we find it necessary to protect the assets that are accessible to us from abandonment,' one group announced. They had survived the Stalinist dictatorship, now they were prepared to survive the dictatorship of 'world capital-ism'.[66] In April 1990, East Berlin squatters learned about confidential plans to hand over parts of Friedrichshain to West German prop-erty developers. To fight those plans, they called on squatters from West Berlin for support. West Berlin activists happily responded. Within a few weeks, they had squatted several buildings, most fam-ously in Mainzer Straße. It was another intense summer of activism: fighting against neo-Nazis who had themselves occupied a house in the adjacent neighbourhood of Lichtenberg, but also organizing street festivals, exhibitions and art performances in the squatted buildings. Once again, it was short-lived, at least for the squatters at Mainzer Straße. Shortly after reunification on 3 October 1990 made the squats part of the Federal Republic's jurisdiction, a force of 3,000 police officers, ten water cannons and a unit of helicopters moved into the area to clear the squats. Their defenders had prepared by building barricades and fought back with rocks and Molotov cock-tails, but after hours of fighting, the police had won the battle. Though many other occupied houses managed to negotiate a legal right to remain, the fall of Mainzer Straße marked a clear end to Berlin's second squatting movement.[67]

The Right to the City Today

The 'Right to the City' was (and still is) a complex issue. It had an economic dimension when residents fought for affordable housing and sought to undermine the capitalist logic of property value. But urban activism was also an attempt to create the conditions for a better life in dull and monotonous cities. It was about changing the colour of walls, the sound in the streets, the places where children play; about the architecture of buildings, and whether they facili-tated or prevented communication among residents. In multiple ways, activists and residents alike claimed the right to *their* city.

Today, in light of exploding property prices and international real-estate companies buying up property in search of investment opportunities, urban activism has regained momentum across the globe.[68] Activists campaign against urban development projects that, they argue, turn cities into a place for rich elites, while pushing those on the margins of society – migrants, precariously employed service workers, the homeless, sex workers – to the margins of the city. They call for public ownership of communal services such as water supply that have been privatized, and more radically demand the expropriation of large property owners. In Berlin, a referendum calling for such an expropriation succeeded in 2021, though it remains to be seen how it is implemented. But activists also try to establish places where neighbours can come together, such as social centres or community gardens, that defy the logic of profit-driven urban development. These are all renewed struggles for a right to the city: a city whose cultural and economic riches, whose material infrastructures and communal spaces, whose houses, streets, parks, libraries and theatres are accessible to everyone, not only those privileged by income, nationality or education.

In many ways, today's protests build on earlier forms of urban activism. The central demands are still about affordable housing and communal spaces and most fundamentally about challenging the valorization of urban space. Yet, today's housing activism is also markedly different. The massive rent strikes and squatting movements that led to violent riots are a thing of the past. Nowadays, urban activists call for the state to intervene in the market, for example by imposing rent caps or buying up property for council housing, and they tend to operate within the law. In other words, urban activism has become less confrontational. There are certainly many reasons that explain this transformation, perhaps most importantly that leftist activism in general has become less militant, but one has to do with how the urban landscape itself has changed. The derelict buildings that offered the space for the improvised lifestyle of squatters are gone, and cities are no longer the wild space for anarchic experimentation that their inhabitants once found in Copenhagen, Amsterdam and Berlin.

The Personal Is Political: Women and Gay Movements

Consider a 'Who's Who' of the student movements of 1968. In France, there's Alain Geismar, Alain Krivine, Jacques Sauvageot and most prominently Daniel Cohn-Bendit; in West Germany, there's Karl Dietrich Wolff, Hans-Jürgen Krahl, Bahman Nirumand, Reimut Reiche and of course Rudi Dutschke; in Italy, where individual students gained less prominence than in France or West Germany, there's Marco Boato and Mauro Rostagno. You could keep going. They have one thing in common: they are all male. This is not to suggest that women did not participate in the protests, riots and strikes.[1] But the formal and informal leaders, those who attracted media attention and who dominated discussions, were almost always men. Certainly, in parts of the 1968 countercultural scenes, gender roles and ideals of strong masculinity were questioned. In her famous essay 'Let's Spit on Hegel', Italian feminist Carla Lonzi, for example, praised the hippies as 'a mixture of the masculine and the feminine'.[2] Yet, as protests turned increasingly violent and radicals sought to mobilize the (male) working class, such positions were soon pushed to the margins. It's hard to deny that there was something profoundly sexist about the student movement, and indeed about many of the movements discussed in this book, from intellectual to countercultural scenes.[3]

Female activists were quick to notice and challenge their male comrades' behaviour. The annual convention of the Sozialistischer Deutscher Studentenbund (SDS) in Frankfurt in September 1968 became famous in this regard. Helke Sander, co-founder of West Berlin's Action Committee for the Liberation of Women, was one of very few women to give a speech. She delivered a harsh critique of gender relations in the SDS. The revolutionary student organization, she charged, simply ignored the exploitation of women, in the world and within its own ranks, by relegating the issue to the private sphere and thereby depoliticizing it. Those women who succeeded within the organization did so only because they had adapted to the male 'performance principle' (a reference to Herbert Marcuse). Sander therefore demanded that her male comrades finally discuss the situation of women. 'Why are you all buying [books about the sexual revolution by Wilhelm] Reich? Why are you talking about class struggle here, but about orgasm issues only at home?' Women in the SDS, Sander noted, were tired of this psychic repression (*Verdrängung*). Therefore, they had decided to focus their political work on women with children, who were the worst off. As politically minded women, they no longer wanted to raise their children according to the 'performance principle', preparing them for the permanent competition in capitalist society. They hoped to develop 'models of a utopian counter-society within existing society', which would give space to their own needs as women. To put these ideas into practice, they founded several kindergartens (called *Kinderläden*) in West Berlin. With this focus on education, their work differed from that of the male-dominated SDS, Sander explained. They genuinely wanted to 'politicize private life'.[4]

When Sander sat down after her speech, chairman Hans-Jürgen Krahl thanked her and moved on with the agenda. At this moment, Sigrid Rüger, another member of the Action Committee, stood up and confronted Krahl: 'Comrade Krahl! You are objectively a counter-revolutionary and an agent of the class enemy as well.' Then she took a ripe tomato from her bag and threw it at Krahl, hitting him. The tomato had the desired effect. Simply returning to the agenda became impossible: clearly, the SDS had to discuss the situation of women.[5]

The tumultuous SDS convention galvanized the women's movement in West Germany. The West Berlin Action Committee had already existed before September 1968, and it was not the first time that demands for discussing the oppression and exploitation of women were made.[6] But only after Frankfurt did action committees and women's councils flourish across the country. As the events in

Frankfurt show, the women's movement emerged out of the student movement; in fact, it always remained part of the leftist scene. But at the same time, it also emerged in opposition to this movement, turning into a lasting critical thorn in its side. Elsewhere in Western Europe, the situation was similar, even though women's movements had their own trajectories in distinct national contexts.[7]

This chapter explores how these women's movements throughout mostly Western Europe challenged male-dominated politics that sought to relegate the exclusion, exploitation and repression of women to the private realm: *the personal is political*, women famously responded. In their view, personal relations, among women but also between men and women, were profoundly political, as were their feelings and bodies. Women thus set out to understand and improve their position in consciousness-raising groups and campaigned for autonomy over their own bodies, most notably by demanding the right to free and legal abortions; they questioned the authority of medical experts and tried to develop forms of sexuality that would please women. In doing so, the women's movement set the stage for another movement that initially developed in the context of feminist activism: the gay liberation movement, which the chapter's final part explores. Like women, gay activists argued that the most intimate issues – their very desires – were profoundly political. They, too, challenged a radical politics that privileged class struggles and the fight against imperialism, but had nothing to say about desires and their oppression.

Coming Together for Solidarity and Autonomy: Women's Movements in the Wake of 1968

When women like Helke Sander began fighting the sexism of their male comrades on the radical left in the late 1960s, they found theoretical and practical inspiration in the United States, where an independent Women's Liberation Movement had already emerged in the mid-1960s.[8] Across Europe, protagonists of the emerging women's movement read texts by American authors such as Betty Friedan's *The Feminine Mystique* (1963), Anne Koedt's 'The Myth of the Vaginal Orgasm' (1968), Shulamith Firestone's *The Dialectic of Sex* (1970), Kate Millet's *Sexual Politics* (1970) and Pamela Allen's *Free Space* (1970); they looked at groups such as New York Radical Women, Berkeley's Women's Liberation and most famously the Boston collective Bread and Roses, who led the way by refusing to collaborate with men, as the reformist National Organization for Women (founded in 1966) had done.[9] The writings by American feminists provided a radical critique of patriarchal society and called for revolutionary change that would put an end to women's economic dependency on men and to institutions that oppressed women, such as the nuclear family. To overcome patriarchal society, intimate and personal relations had to change. Women's sexuality had to be liberated. The personal, that is, became political.

American feminists did more than provide theoretical critiques of patriarchal society. They also offered practical guidelines for how to organize a struggle against this society. Most influential in this regard was the practice of consciousness-raising, which Pamela Allen described in her booklet *Free Space*, though without using the term. Allen had been active in New York's radical women's movement before moving to San Francisco, where she joined the women's group Sudsofloppen.[10] Drawing on her experience in this group, Allen proposed a path for women 'to become more autonomous in thought and behaviour'. In small groups, which she deemed particularly well-suited for liberating women from 'male-supremacist values', women should pursue this goal in four steps: opening up, sharing, analysing and abstracting.[11]

In the first instance, women should talk about themselves, their experiences and feelings. Society, she argued, usually alienated women from their feelings (and men even more so). Most women, Allen wrote, 'have been isolated and alone and the group experience is the first time they have found others who like themselves are frustrated with their lot as women in this society'. Talking about such feelings without being ridiculed, with other women listening and acknowledging the emotions, helped foster a sense of 'intimacy and trust', a 'feeling of unity with others, of not being alone'. Based on these individual experiences, participants would develop a shared understanding of their oppression as women in seemingly private contexts. 'We know that our most secret, our most private problems are grounded in the way women are treated, in the way women are allowed to live.' In isolation, these experiences would result only in frustrations, but coming together could 'lead to action'. Action, however, required analysis that went beyond 'the realm of subjectivity' and, ultimately, abstracting to develop a 'vision of our human potential'.[12]

While Allen proposed a model for how women might come together and overcome their isolation, Anne Koedt turned attention to women's sexuality. In her famous essay 'The Myth of the Vaginal Orgasm', Koedt argued that it was not the stimulation of the vagina, whose function she considered primarily reproductive, but of the clitoris that allowed women to climax. Men, however, she claimed, 'have orgasms essentially by friction with the vagina, not the clitoral area, which is external and not able to cause friction the way penetration does'. For a long time, women's sexuality had therefore been defined by 'what pleases men; our own biology has not been properly analysed'. This situation called for a radical and practical rethinking of sexuality as well as 'new techniques' that would 'transform this particular aspect of our current sexual exploitation'. For patriarchal society, such a transformation would pose a danger, because recognizing 'clitoral orgasm as a fact would threaten the heterosexual institution. For it would indicate that sexual pleasure was obtainable from either men or women, thereby making heterosexuality not an absolute, but an option.'[13]

These ideas radically redefined the field of politics, as Foucault would theorize about a decade later. They made the body, sexual desire and pleasure as well as questions of reproduction a central political issue; they made personal feelings and experiences the starting point for radical activism, rather than the seemingly objective conditions of class society, or even an abstract analysis of patriarchy.

Across Europe, activists of the women's movement emerging in the wake of 1968 eagerly took up these ideas. They challenged men's predominance in leftist circles, not least because women often insisted on organizing autonomously, that is, without the participation of men. With their focus on subjective experiences, women also rejected an understanding of politics, common on the radical left, that considered anything unrelated to revolutionary class struggle to be ultimately apolitical.[14] More than once, male leftists neatly proved women's point by reacting furiously to their claims for independence. When female students at Vincennes, Paris, called a women-only meeting in June 1970 to discuss the 'women's problem', men tried to disrupt the meeting 'in the name of revolution', telling women that there was no 'women's problem' and that they were just 'under-fucked' (*mal baisées*).[15] Such resistance notwithstanding, ideas and practices that first developed within the women's movement also changed broader leftist scenes in the course of the 1970s.[16]

Sexual liberation had been one of the famous rallying cries of students in 1968. Recall how students at Nanterre had demanded the right to visit dormitories of the opposite sex. 'When will our liberation happen? You are not allowed to go out at night, have sex, and choose certain professions,' an undated leaflet by a women's liberation group at a Parisian high school read. Girls, it argued, were only raised to do their homework, clean their rooms, help their mothers, and when they got married, they were nothing but their husband's maid 'in the kitchen as in the bed'.[17] Women, however, were quick to note that the sexual liberation their male comrades demanded all too often meant an expectation that they should always be available for sex; and when they refused, they were accused of being 'frustrated'.[18] Facing what they called the 'socialist screw-pressure' and charges of being 'penis-envying, frustrated, hysterical, uptight, asexual, lesbian, frigid, short-sighted, irrational', Frankfurt-based feminist group Weiberrat (literally 'women's council') responded: 'Liberate the socialist eminences from their bourgeois dicks.'[19] For women, sexual liberation had to mean something other than permanent sexual availability: a different kind of sexuality (an issue Chapter 13 explores in more depth), the right to sexual pleasure and, in principle, bodily self-determination.

This fundamental right was also at stake in the issue that galvanized women's movements across much of Western Europe in the 1970s: the right to have an abortion. When readers of the French weekly magazine *Le Nouvel Observateur* opened its pages on 5 April 1971, they were confronted with a shocking, full-page advertisement. 'One million women undergo abortions each year in France,' the text read.

> They have them in dangerous conditions because they are condemned to secrecy, whereas this is one of the simplest operations when performed under medical supervision. Silence reigns over all these millions of women. I claim I am one of them. I claim I have aborted. Just as we demand free access to contraception, we demand the freedom to have an abortion.

It became known as the 'Manifesto of the 343', after the number of signatories, which included celebrities such as actress Catherine Deneuve, writer Marguerite Duras and philosopher Simone de Beauvoir, author of the famous *Second Sex*. The manifesto had 'the effect of a bomb', French feminist Françoise Picq remarked. 'Abortion, as taboo as it was, suddenly was on everyone's lips.'[20]

Though the manifesto was, of course, not the first time that feminists had demanded the right to abortion, in France or elsewhere in Europe, it initiated a long and ultimately successful campaign for legal abortion in various European countries. In France, activists of the women's movement and their supporters – notably male doctors who publicly confessed to having performed abortions despite the ban – pressured for legal reforms. It was a matter of social equality, they argued. While wealthy women might be able to go to Switzerland or the Netherlands, where it was easier to have a legal abortion in a clinic, those without financial means had to have illegal and dangerous back-street procedures, and risked prosecution.[21]

The struggle for reproductive rights quickly spread across

Western Europe. Two months after the publication of the 'Manifesto of the 343', the West German magazine *Stern* published a similar 'Manifesto of the 374'. Inspired by French feminists, prominent journalist Alice Schwarzer, at that time based in Paris, had organized German women to equally confess to having had an abortion. As in France, the manifesto's publication had a tremendous impact. Though some of the radical socialist women's groups that had formed in the wake of 1968 remained sceptical of what they considered the manifesto's reformist, bourgeois character, the campaign against Article 218 (the article in the German penal code banning abortion) ultimately led to the formation of an independent women's movement in the Federal Republic.[22] A few years later, the struggle for legal abortions also spurred on the Italian women's movement. In January and December 1975, women-only marches in Rome demanding free and assisted abortions attracted 20,000 protestors; a subsequent protest in April 1976 reached 50,000.[23] Ultimately, campaigns in all three countries at least partially succeeded, with abortions becoming legal under specific circumstances, usually within the first trimester of the pregnancy (the exact timing varied) and only after a mandatory consultation process.[24]

At the heart of these campaigns were women's demands to be in charge of their own bodies. In Italy, the slogan *Io sono mia* (I am mine) expressed this principle; in West Germany, the slogan *Mein Bauch gehört mir* (My belly belongs to me) did the same. Neither (usually male) lawmakers nor medical experts should take crucial decisions about women's bodies. Reclaiming authority, women believed they needed to know their bodies; they had to become experts themselves, as the West Berlin group Brot & Rosen wrote in the first *Frauenhandbuch* (Women's Handbook, 1972), which provided readers with information about contraception.[25]

Demanding reproductive rights and becoming experts in these matters was not the only way in which women claimed authority over their bodies. The same applied to giving birth. West German feminists, for example, urged women to remain suspicious of male medical experts and technologies. In a hospital with harsh lighting and medical apparatuses, the experience of childbirth would turn into a lonely and traumatic event. A 'soft childbirth', ideally at home, where the woman would remain in charge, by contrast, could be 'fantastic, splendid, great'. Women should have faith in their own bodies and not give in to the authority of male doctors or midwives, one (interestingly male) author from Munich claimed. Then, giving birth might become an 'ecstatic event only women can have'.[26] In West Germany, but also in Italy, activists of the women's movement translated theory into practice by establishing local self-help clinics that offered advice on contraception, sexual health, childcare and abortion.[27]

Women equally reclaimed authority over their bodies when campaigning against the beauty norms dictated by the male gaze. Taking their cue once again from American feminists, militants of the women's movement disrupted beauty contests that turned female bodies into an object for men to evaluate and measure. In November 1970, women in London protested against a Miss World beauty pageant by throwing flour, stink bombs and tomatoes into the audience. A pamphlet they distributed charged: 'Women's bodies used by businessmen to sell their garbage – legs selling stockings, waists selling corsets, cunts selling deodorants, Mary Quant selling sex . . . our sexuality has been taken away from us, turned into money for someone else, then returned deadened by anxiety. Women watching . . . why are you here?'[28] Three years later, women in Frankfurt disrupted a similar though much smaller contest in a local club, throwing pig tails and pork knuckles at the horrified jury. If the men on the jury wanted to measure women's legs, then women, too, should be able to check if the men's 'dicks [were] too gristly, too mingy, too slack, too buckled, too wizen, or lacking at all', as their pamphlet stated.[29]

Bodily autonomy was also at stake in campaigns against the sexual harassment and violence women had to face both in public spaces and domestically. At the end of an international conference dealing with crimes against women held in Brussels in March 1976, participants organized a night-time protest against the many ways that men made streets unsafe for women after dark: the first Reclaim the Night demonstration. From Brussels, the idea travelled to Italy, West Germany and the UK.[30] On the night of 30 April 1977, known as Walpurgis Night – traditionally an exuberant and sexually transgressive feast of witches – women across West Germany took to the streets to reclaim the streets as their own, often armed with torches and dressed up as witches. They marched in front of sex shops and brothels, inviting women to join them and hurling insults at pimps and punters.[31] A few months later, in November, British women organized similar protests at night, after the police had told them to avoid public spaces in the dark in response to a series of murders of women. 'No Curfew on Women – Curfew on Men', their signs read.[32] These were moments of emotional empowerment for women: they had taken back the streets without feeling afraid.

Women activists also took practical steps to support other women in need of protection from male violence, for example by opening shelters for women fleeing abusive partners. In the UK, a first shelter, the Chiswick Women's Aid, opened in 1971, paving the way for similar refuges throughout the country and across Europe.[33] In these women-only spaces, called *Frauenhaus* (women's house) in German, women would have the possibility to organize their own lives and gain a sense of self-worth, but also learn how to overcome self-destructive habits by sharing their experiences.[34] In Yugoslavia, feminists established shelters, and, by the late 1980s, SOS telephone helplines for women and children facing domestic abuse. In the first months alone, Zagreb's helpline, the first of its kind, received 500 calls from women, and thirty-two from children.[35]

By campaigning for reproductive rights and freedom from violence, women's movements fought to make the world a better place. But women also tried to change themselves: how they felt about their bodies, how they expressed their feelings and desires, and how they interacted with other women: all issues dealt with in the small groups that came to characterize the women's movement: consciousness-raising. Originating in the American women's movement, as we have seen, the practice spread to the United Kingdom, to Italy, where it was called *autocoscienza*, to France (though here, it seems, consciousness-raising was less common), to West Germany, where it was called *Selbsterfahrung*, and from there even across the Iron Curtain to the GDR.[36]

Guidelines circulating within the transnational women's movement provided instructions for how to do consciousness-raising, and what it might accomplish. Groups should be small, usually no more than ten participants; membership should not fluctuate; there should be no one leader; and women should meet on a weekly basis. Participants should avoid making generalizing statements, but instead speak in the first person about their own experiences. Every meeting should be dedicated to a specific topic related to their situation as women, such as their upbringing as girls, experiences at school and work, how they thought about their bodies and their sexual experiences, about contraception and abortions. At the outset of each meeting, all the attendees should talk about their personal experiences. At first, women should just listen and not interrupt the initial statements; only then should they ask questions in order to understand, but without being judgemental or offering advice (unless the speaker explicitly asked for it). Discussing seemingly personal problems and understanding how they were grounded in patriarchal power structures would allow women to formulate a politics that started with their own oppression and needs.[37] But talking to each other about feelings and personal experiences would also help women to overcome their isolation, to foster relations built on personal trust, and to avoid male forms of competitiveness.

In these small groups, women hoped to learn how to relate differently to their bodies. And this required more than just talking. Famously, women collectively examined their genitalia using speculums to familiarize themselves with their own bodies, seeking to overcome feelings of shame and inferiority by realizing that their vagina did not look 'ugly and unappetizing, but beautiful and aesthetic', in the words of Alice Schwarzer.[38] 'Our desire was to acquire a completely new understanding of our bodies. And to base our search for new ways of being a woman on this. We felt that what hindered us in our *libertà* [liberty] was in a first instance located in our relationship with our bodies,' an Italian feminist told historian Maud Bracke.[39] For centuries, a feminist group from Frankfurt argued, women had been oppressed by men, which had resulted in women having a 'disturbed relation to their bodies', for example feeling afraid or insecure when looking at or touching them. To overcome these feelings, they produced nude paintings of each other, hoping to 'achieve a better relationship with our female bodies and a better understanding among us'.[40]

For many women, both those writing at the time and those looking back in oral history interviews, participating in consciousness-raising groups was a transformative and liberating experience. It helped them to confidently articulate their feelings and political standpoints. Writing for the British feminist magazine *Spare Rib* in 1978, Mica Nava described the year of her participation in a consciousness-raising group as 'probably the most explosive and passionate in my life'.[41] In West Berlin, a seventeen-year-old participant of a girls' group initiated by her female teacher reported: 'We talked about our sexual problems, masturbating, sleeping together, and it was a really great experience for me to say things in that area that I was thinking about. It was all very much free of fear.'[42] And a former member of the East German group Lesben in der Kirche (Lesbians in the Church) recalled her experience in a consciousness-raising group: 'We also spoke about our sexuality. This was an even bigger taboo than lesbianism. It was very difficult to speak about it, but it was a very positive experience.'[43]

Yet, such enthusiastic accounts should not detract from the fact that, for many women, participating in consciousness-raising groups was anything but liberating. In women's groups, it was not only possible to talk about feelings, but often required. For some participants at least, this was an immense pressure, especially if they were less eloquent. One of the members in the West Berlin girls' group, for example, noted: 'I've felt a group pressure, that is, everyone has to talk about herself, and that means that everyone has to have had certain experiences to be able to keep up in these conversations.'[44]

Sharing personal feelings could be empowering, but it could also be troubling. Looking back, Turin-based feminist Angela Miglietti described consciousness-raising as a 'devastating' practice, which 'tore us up as individuals and broke the bonds between us'.[45] Other women noted the 'exhaustion of consciousness-raising'.[46] When women began to closely monitor their bodies and feelings, not only writing down their temperature to determine their menstrual cycle but also keeping track of their emotions and dreams, such self-observation could turn into a massive burden. 'Every day hectic, depressive, sad, disrupted, relationship troubles. That's something we can only suppress,' was how apparently exhausted members of a West German women's group summarized their experiences. But their example also shows how a women's group could be a space for learning. After giving up on the detailed self-observation, they did succeed in developing a more positive relationship with their bodies. While they had previously felt disgusted by their periods, they now enjoyed the experience, despite the pain.[47]

Fragmentation and Diversification

Around the late 1970s and early 1980s, the women's movement that had emerged in the wake of 1968 reached its apex. After the campaigns to legalize abortion had resulted in reforms in West Germany, France and Italy, women's movements across Western Europe began to fracture. Sometimes bitter debates about the movement's direction led to splits and the dissolution of groups. In France, the second half of the 1970s came to be known as the women's movement's 'black years'. With the abortion campaign over and political parties at least rhetorically embracing women's demands, the movement lacked a common rallying cause and was divided over where to go next.[48] In the UK, the national conference of the Women's Liberation Movement of 1978 resulted in a split between socialist feminists and radical feminists.[49] And in Italy, the general decline of leftist activism in the aftermath of terror campaigns and state repression in the late 1970s also affected the women's movement, with numerous major collectives disbanding. 'We consider a phase of the movement's life to have ended,' feminist magazine *Effe* proclaimed in March 1980.[50]

Yet, such narratives of decline only capture part of the picture. While the time of huge single-issue campaigns was over, the women's movement lived on, in myriad ways. Major political parties took up some of its demands, such as equal pay for equal work and bans on discrimination against women in the workplace; this integrated aspects of the movement into mainstream politics, but also deradicalized it. And while some of the major groups disbanded and more radical publications such as West Germany's *Courage* ceased publication, other grassroots institutions, such as the refuge shelters, survived and expanded. Equally, cultural initiatives such as women's libraries, bookshops and publishing houses flourished: Virago and the Women's Press in the UK, Frauenoffensive and Frauenselbstverlag (now Orlanda) in West Germany, French Éditions des Femmes and Éditions Tierce, and Scritti di Rivolta Femminile in Italy.[51] And women found new avenues of activism. The Greenham Common Peace Camp was only a particularly prominent example of distinctly female campaigns in the context of the peace and environmental movements. Employing less radical tactics, women in East Germany organized as Frauen für den Frieden (Women for Peace), while the Mütter gegen Atomkraft (Mothers against Nuclear Power) took part in the West German environmental movement.[52]

As the women's movement fractured in the late 1970s, it also saw one of its foundational beliefs challenged: the vision of something like a universal sisterhood connecting all women, regardless of class, race or sexual identity, against a common enemy, patriarchal society. Already in the late 1970s, a potentially divisive issue appeared, when some women had made a case for lesbianism as a radical alternative to male-dominated sexuality.[53] 'All our "affectivity" is directed towards women, for women, with women: nothing for the oppressor,' a group by the name of Lesbiennes de Jussieu (a university in Paris) wrote in June 1980. 'We refuse femininity ... All women should become lesbian, that is: stand together, resistant and not collaborators.'[54]

This political lesbianism raised practical and potentially divisive questions: would it be possible for radical lesbian feminists to collaborate with heterosexual feminists? An article in the West Berlin *Lesbenpresse* from March 1976, for example, reported about conflicts between female flatmates: would the sole heterosexual woman living in the commune with three lesbians and an 'autosexual woman' (a previously heterosexual woman who had become a lesbian out of conviction and dedication to the movement, a 'head- and movement lesbian', as the text put it) be allowed to have her boyfriend stay over? While the heterosexual woman wanted to live 'free of fear' with her boyfriend at home, others wondered about the point of an 'autonomous women's movement' that radically broke with male society, if it still let men hang around.[55] And how should the lesbian women's movement deal with transgender people? Should people born and categorized as men but self-identifying as women have access to exclusively female spaces and lesbian groups, or should they be considered men, as a group of lesbian women in Hamburg argued in 1976 – a position that would today be criticized as transphobic?[56] Such questions caused bitter debates within the women's movement.

At least as troubling were questions of race and class. The women's movement of the 1960s and 1970s had been predominantly middle-class, well-educated and white. Of course, women of colour and working-class women had fought their own struggles; they had gone on strike and had campaigned against racism, as we've seen in Chapter 8. Yet, within the women's movement strictly defined, their voices, experiences and perspectives were overlooked. Her 'sisters', recalled black feminist Ika Hügel-Marshall, a former member of a Frankfurt women's group, did not 'want to see that our society is racist as well as sexist'.[57] For black feminists, such ignorance amounted to racism. 'The WLM is racist because it does not take seriously the experiences of non-white women,' wrote the black British feminist newsletter *We Are Here* in 1985.[58] And black American feminist Audre Lorde told a white audience in Berlin: 'Racism in Germany, in Switzerland, in Europe must become an issue for white feminism, because it is part of your lives, it affects your lives in every way, and the fact that you are not people of colour does not make you safe from the effects of it.'[59] For white feminists who considered themselves as self-evidently anti-racist, such criticism was a shock.

From a black perspective, many of the issues white feminists struggled for looked radically different. While the white women's movement, for example, criticized the nuclear family as an oppressive, patriarchal institution, black women argued that the family could also be a source of support in the face of a racist society.[60] When white women in British cities called for better policing in response to sexual violence, such demands rang hollow for black women familiar with police harassment and violence, including the killing of innocent black women.[61] And if for white women freedom of choice meant the right to a free abortion, black women, who were often 'encouraged' to use contraceptives or even have an abortion, had to struggle for 'a woman's right to choose to have a child', recalled Stella Dadzie.[62]

Across Europe, then, the women's movement became more diverse during the 1980s. The assumption of a universal female perspective gave way to a multiplicity of feminist voices that included women with different identities and experiences. This is not a story of decline and failure, but of broadening perspectives and increasing inclusivity. In that sense, the story of the women's movement, though far from over, is a story of success. They won significant legal battles, most notably concerning reproductive rights and equal pay, while also changing the field of protest itself: intimate relations, feelings, desires, sexualities could no longer be relegated to the private sphere, but had to be understood as inherently political.

Politics of Desire: Gay Liberation Movements

Paris, 10 March 1971. Ménie Grégoire was hosting a radio show, in front of a live audience, about the 'painful problem' of homosexuality. André Baudry, head of the homophile association Arcadie, a psychoanalyst, a Catholic priest and a journalist, all presented as experts, were supposed to discuss the suffering of homosexuals. When the priest Guichat said that many homosexuals came to see him to talk about their misery, a commotion emerged within the audience. 'Don't talk to us any more about *your* suffering,' a militant woman yelled. Other women joined in: 'We demand freedom for ourselves and for you! Fight! Fight!' and 'Down with the heterocops!' they chanted. The protestors were lesbian women, including leading members of the French women's movement such as Christine Delphy and Monique Wittig, some of whom had organized as a splinter lesbian group in the preceding months. That evening, the group gave itself a name: Front homosexuel d'action révolutionnaire (FHAR, Homosexual Front for Revolutionary Action). A press release announced: 'Homosexuals are fed up with being a painful problem. They want to smash the patriarchal family, the basis of the foundation of this society preoccupied with therapy. Doctor, treat yourself.'[63]

In the weeks that followed the spectacular protest, the group's membership surged. Men began to attend the meetings that had hitherto been dominated by lesbian women. Soon the gathering at the Beaux-Arts de Paris attracted hundreds of people, mostly, though not exclusively, homosexual. They discussed sexual liberation, but they also wanted to put their ideas into practice. Talking about liberating the body, speakers such as author and founding member of the FHAR Françoise d'Eaubonne and old anarchist writer Daniel Guérin simply undressed in front of everyone. Others searched for sexual liberation behind sculptures or in the institute's attic. 'The regulars went right upstairs and crouched and clustered together in corners,' one participant recalled.[64]

While there was no formal leadership, Guy Hocquenghem soon emerged as the group's informal leader. A Maoist militant in 1968, he had witnessed the homophobia within radical leftist circles, which forced him to keep his homosexuality a secret. With the emergence of the FHAR, this changed. Hocquenghem, formerly a Maoist militant who happened to be gay, became a 'gay activist', his biographer Antoine Idier writes. Inspired by the American gay liberation movement and its slogan *say it aloud, we are gay and proud*, Hocquenghem called for radical (homo)sexual liberation.[65]

The Front homosexuel d'action révolutionnaire was part of a transnational gay liberation movement that formed in the early 1970s, stretching from the United States to Western Europe and even reaching, albeit in a less visible form, across the Iron Curtain into the GDR.[66] Throughout post-war Western Europe, gay men faced not only social prejudices but also legal discrimination, though, by the early 1970s, at least the legal situation was gradually improving. In England and Wales (though not in Scotland and Northern Ireland), the 1957 Wolfenden Report had recommended decriminalizing sexual activity between men as long as this was consensual, kept in private, and all involved were over the age of twenty-one – though it took another decade before the report's recommendations were put into law. West Germany, which had seen thousands of homosexual men charged and convicted during the 1950s, followed two years later. Yet restrictions remained, even in countries where homosexuality had been legal for a long time such as France, the Netherlands and Italy. Often, the age of consent for homosexual acts was higher (usually twenty-one, as opposed to between fourteen and sixteen for heterosexual acts in most European countries; Italy was a notable exception with sexual acts being legal above the age of fourteen, whatever the sexual orientation), and laws against indecent exposure particularly targeted homosexual men. Legal changes, though they certainly were an improvement, did not end discrimination. For the gay movements, there were still battles to be fought.

Organizations such as Arcadie that described themselves as homophile, campaigning against the social exclusion and legal persecution of (usually male) homosexuals, had existed for a long time, not only in France.[67] But the homosexual groups of the 1970s such as the FHAR, the London-based Gay Liberation Front (GLF), the Homosexuelle Aktion Westberlin (HAW) or the Italian Fronte Unitario Omosessuale Rivoluzionario Italiano (its acronym 'Fuori!' also meant 'Out!' in Italian) marked a rupture in gay militancy. Their activism was more provocative, more visible and often more explicitly left-wing. The FHAR, wrote the group, was 'only homosexuality on the march . . . Yes, we are a nebula of feelings and action.'[68] Like the women's movement, the gay liberation movements were a product of the upheavals of the 1960s, albeit more of the transatlantic countercultural scenes with their disruptive and exuberant lifestyle than of the sober student movement, which was as homophobic as it was sexist.[69] Indeed, the gay movement was in many ways inspired by the women's movement. Women, Hocquenghem noted, had created a breach for gay liberation.[70] In France, but also in West Germany, lesbian women played an important part in founding homosexual groups, before leaving them and turning to the women's movement around the mid-1970s.[71] Just like feminists, gay activists questioned the conventional distinction between seemingly trivial personal questions and profound political questions; like women, many gay men practised consciousness-raising, with equally ambivalent results.

The 1970s were the heyday of radical gay activism. Gay men took to the streets with colourful demonstrations, sometimes provocatively taking over mainstream leftist demonstrations (as in Paris on 1 May 1971); they staged exuberant festivals and international meetings such as Homolulu in Frankfurt in July 1979; and they published countless small magazines about gay lives and politics, such as *HAW-Info* and *Schwuchtel* (meaning roughly 'fag'), coming out of Heidelberg and West Berlin, or *Le Fléau social* and *L'Antinorm* in France.[72] But despite all the activism, those years were not some kind of exuberant utopia for gay liberation. There is no neat line to be drawn between the 1950s and 1960s, allegedly characterized by shame and fear, and the 1970s suddenly marked by feelings of pride and hope. To start with, there was hardly consensus among gay activists on the goals and methods of the movement. Some activists sought legal and social recognition by showing that homosexuals were normal, that they could be ordinary colleagues and neighbours like anyone else. Others, by contrast, celebrated difference, urging their colleagues and neighbours to accept that difference. For some, gay liberation was inherently revolutionary, as it challenged the sexual and gender order altogether; for others, it meant finding a place for men-desiring men and women-desiring women within the societal order. And if the personal was political, if sexual practices did have a political dimension, what did this mean for the gay scene? Was BDSM an inherently oppressive and perhaps even fascist form of sexuality, or was there something subversive and liberating about it? What about cruising and anonymous sex in toilets or in darkrooms? Was this a form of impersonal and alienating sexuality that gay men should overcome, or was it a radical way of acting out desires? Such questions divided gay movements.[73]

Among those arguing for the radically subversive potential of (homo)sexual desires was Guy Hocquenghem. In his 1972 book *Homosexual Desire*, Hocquenghem provided a radical theory of desire – and not just homosexual desire.[74] Indeed, he considered the very notion of homosexual desire to be problematic. In his view, there is just desire, 'unbroken and polyvocal flux', appearing in multiple forms; only *a posteriori* would it be possible to designate elements of that desire as heterosexual or homosexual.[75] Hocquenghem thus questioned the assumption of gendered desire itself. Encountering desire, he wrote, meant 'to forget the difference in the sexes'.[76]

By calling stable gender and sexual identities into question, Hocquenghem foreshadowed what later came to be known as queer theory.[77] But his argument wasn't about identities and their performance, it was about desire, its fluid and non-exclusive nature, which he saw expressed in the homosexual practice of cruising. This gave homosexuality a profoundly subversive dimension, undermining the stability of heterosexual love relations. For Hocquenghem, 'homosexual love is immensely superior, precisely because everything is possible at any moment'. The 'homosexual pick-up machine', he wrote in somewhat obscure language, 'is infinitely more direct and less guilt-ridden than the complex system of "civilized loves"' meaning that 'its mechanical scattering corresponds to the mode of existence of desire itself'.[78] Seen from this perspective, the goal of the gay movement was not the social integration of homosexual men (Hocquenghem had little to say about lesbian women); it was not about making homosexuality normal and accepted. The point was to undermine and change the social organization of desire, to make the difference between the sexes disappear.

Hocquenghem's work is a dense, theoretical text, difficult to understand with its obscure language. It was hardly representative of the gay movement. How much of an influence it had, especially outside of France, remains difficult to say. Yet, the book raised questions about gay activism that were debated on the ground among activists. Whether they had read the book or not, those were immensely divisive questions.

Those questions also lay behind the famous *Tuntenstreit* (Queens' Dispute) in West Germany. The occasion for the dispute was a demonstration at the end of a six-day-long international gathering of gay activists in West Berlin in June 1973. During the demonstration, French and Italian activists in drag stepped out of the march, danced in the streets and engaged with passers-by. Their behaviour was a shock, not only to the tabloid press, but also to many in West Germany's gay activist scene who wanted the demonstration to look serious and respectable. Running around in drag, they charged, turned a political protest into a carnivalesque spectacle. Even gay activists sympathetic to drag worried that men wearing women's clothes would be too much for the general public to digest. Ultimately, the public display of drag would only confirm prejudices about effeminate gay men, and would not help further the cause of normalization. The *Tunten*, however, disagreed. Wearing drag, they argued, was a way to contest the social norms that so clearly distinguished between male and female, between the private and the public realm, and that were the very root of homosexual oppression. Like Hocquenghem, their goal was not to make homosexuals look normal and acceptable, but to undermine standards of normality and thereby to create space for queer difference.[79]

All too often, gay groups fractured along these dividing lines, and individual activists were left feeling isolated, frustrated and lonely. As one former activist, Gerhard from Frankfurt, argued in an oral history interview: 'You cannot say that this gay movement made people happier.'[80] Yet, regarding the decade as a catastrophe, as Gerhard did, wouldn't do justice to its complexity. The gay movement did accomplish something, by making gay life more visible, by normalizing sexual diversity, and even more importantly by creating spaces for gay men in which it was possible, in the words of historian Benno Gammerl, to 'feel differently'. Those could be temporary spaces such as demonstrations that fostered a sense of shared hope and enthusiasm, but also more stable settings such as gay coffee shops, bars, saunas and discos.[81] Gay communes provided a sense of family and home. 'We are twelve men. We are gay. We are a family,' declared a group from Notting Hill facing eviction from the building they had squatted.[82] In those venues, though they were by no means free of conflict, activists started building their own alternatives.

Like the women's movement and the post-1968 extra-parliamentary left more generally, radical gay liberation groups changed by the early 1980s. The gay movement, however, also had to face a much more profound challenge: the new, mysterious disease that came to be known as AIDS, which initially seemed to particularly affect gay men. For gay activists, it was a terrible shock. With people 'dying like flies',[83] including Guy Hocquenghem, who died of the disease in 1988, they were years of anxiety and constant mourning.[84] It wasn't only the disease itself that was a threat, but also, and even more importantly, how society dealt with it, which reinforced stigmas activists had spent years trying to overcome. Conservative politicians toyed with plans to require gay men (as well as sex workers and drug users) to take HIV tests, and to set up internment camps for those infected. [85] Even gay activists such as Rosa von Praunheim blamed the sexual promiscuity of the gay scene during the 1970s for the crisis.[86] Fearing social stigmatization, many individuals kept their infection a secret.

Even so, the crisis also spurred new activism. Once again taking up practices first developed in the United States, militants organized public 'die-ins' to raise awareness of people dying of HIV. And building on traditions of self-help groups within the women's movement, gay activists acquired expert knowledge about medical research, treatment and prevention strategies. The virus, activists argued, did not distinguish between homosexual and heterosexual men and women, but was a problem for society as a whole, an argument that was ultimately accepted.[87] Though the AIDS crisis caused intense suffering for a whole generation of gay men, it did not reverse the gains gay men and lesbians had already made. The crisis did, however, necessitate more pragmatic, deradicalized forms of activism – in line with the larger activist trends of the 1980s – and complicated the celebration of unrestricted desires. Gay activism was not over, though it had lost some of its radical edge.

Equality, Diversity and Queer Desires

Much has changed with regard to the causes both the women's and the gay movement fought for. Abortions are, with certain restrictions, legal in many European countries; homosexual couples can marry; promoting gender equality has become part of official government policy; and discrimination on grounds of sexual identity is now illegal in many places. In much of Europe, sexual diversity is visible and increasingly normalized. Queer activists question gender binaries, while more and more states officially recognize a third gender that is neither male nor female. These are, unquestionably, significant improvements. And yet, none of the struggles has ended, and these accomplishments are under attack. There remains a significant gender pay gap; the recent Covid-19 crisis resulted all too often in women being, once again, charged with most of the care work at home; and people who do not conform to hetero-normative expectations still face discrimination and often violence. The world is no paradise of gender equality and sexual diversity. But the visions and ideals of the women's and gay movements live on. Some have even seen a recent revival, such as the undermining of rigid, binary gender and sexual identities, and the emphasis on fluidity and transgression in the context of queer politics.

And bitter conflicts within those movements, around very similar issues, continue. Should feminists campaign to make prostitution illegal, following the 'Nordic Model', which prosecutes clients rather than sex workers, or should they campaign to improve the legal and social situation of sex workers, freeing sex work from stigma? Should people born and categorized as men but identifying as women be accepted within the women's movement? And should feminists fight religious practices such as wearing the hijab as a symbol of patriarchal oppression, or is covering oneself part of women's self-determination over their own bodies?[88] These remain deeply divisive questions, sometimes even leading to violent confrontations at LGBTQIA pride marches: in 2018, members of the anti-trans lesbian group Get The L Out took over the front of the London Pride March with banners claiming that 'trans activists erase lesbians'.[89] On the other side, a group by the name of Résistance Lesbienne from Bordeaux claimed in September 2021 that 'anti-TERF' (trans-exclusionary radical feminists) trans activists had assaulted women during a demonstration with a burning flare (and video footage about the incident supports the accusations).[90]

But perhaps the most important accomplishment of these movements is something more subtle though no less fundamental, something that cannot be measured in terms of specific improvements. Both movements challenged an understanding of the political, shared within the traditional radical left, that focused on large-scale social structures. With the women's and gay movements, politics moved into the seemingly private space of the bedroom (or wherever people might have sex), and it rendered feelings, bodies and child-rearing political. Politics had to start with personal, subjective experiences. This conception of politics is still with us in what has become known as identity politics: a politics for which the recognition of subjective experiences, in particular personal suffering and vulnerability, has become central – experiences that are, as feminists so powerfully argued, never individual, but embedded in and produced by power structures: they are profoundly political.

PART IV

A Better Life: The Here and Now

Living Differently: Dwelling, Working, Travelling

Militants in the 1970s and 1980s didn't want to wait for a grand revolution to come and change everything. They wanted a better life, here and now; they wanted to start building the better society they were dreaming about. A cartoon published in West Berlin's *radikal* in January 1978 captures this spirit. It depicts three potential ways of reaching the realm of 'the sun, freedom' rising on the horizon: first, there is the capitalist way, in which a fat capitalist tells a worker to jump, only to kick him in the butt and send him falling into the abyss; second, the 'orthodox-communist way', with a leader, Stalin, who announces that 'the infallible party has decided the great jump', leaving workers confused as no preparations for actually overcoming the abyss had been made. The third, 'alternative' way, by contrast, shows a group of people debating different approaches – building a suspension bridge, using a hot-air balloon, or 'smoking some weed and floating over to the other side' (*einen durchziehen und rüberschweben*), while others mock them as 'theoreticians' and get to work building a rather shaky bridge.[1] Reaching the realm of freedom, the cartoon suggested, required imaginative discussions; it called for activists to do something, even if it wasn't quite perfect. It was an experiment, a process of constant learning by doing, with an uncertain outcome.

Activists set out to work on this better future in many small ways. Being profoundly critical of conventional family life, but also the lonesome life of singles in modern cities, they tried to develop communal forms of dwelling, both in urban and rural settings. They began to forge an 'alternative economy', with bookshops, ecological farms and collectively owned, self-managed enterprises. And, for those who wanted to leave everyday life behind altogether, an alternative travelling culture emerged, with backpackers hitch-hiking across Europe, on both sides of the Iron Curtain – though not across it – and some going as far as Afghanistan and India via the Hippie Trail. All of this was part of an alternative lifestyle. Often, though by no means always, the same people who lived in left-leaning communes also found work in collectively owned shops and liked to travel as backpackers, visiting communes and protest sites like the Larzac on their way. Some conceived of such practices as a form of political activism, while others simply wanted a more exciting, more fulfilling personal life. There was no grand theory behind these attempts to live differently. However, two general ideas characterized activists' efforts: a desire for autonomy and collectivity. Activists wanted to make their own decisions in work and in life, without being subject to bosses, foremen or any restrictive norms. And they didn't want to do so individually, but communally, hoping to find a sense of intimacy and belonging based on shared ideals.

Dwelling: Living Together in Communes

'We live together, not alone.' This was how a 1984 book from West Germany summarized the aspirations of what it called the 'commune movement'.[2] In the 1970s, hundreds of thousands of mostly younger people were moving into shared apartments (*Wohngemein-schaften*, or WGs, in German) or communes across Northern and Western Europe (communes existed in Southern and Eastern Europe as well, but they were far less common).[3] During the 1968 rebellions, individual communes such as West Berlin's Kommune 1 had gained fame, but living collectively was not yet a mass phenomenon. This changed in the years that followed. Denmark counted 15,000 communes in 1974, with some 100,000 inhabitants (out of a total population of 5 million).[4] In West Germany, numbers swelled from perhaps 1,000 (according to an estimate by communard Rudi Damme) in 1970 to 100,000 in 1976, meaning that up to half a million people lived in communes.[5] In Denmark and West Germany, most of these communes were urban, though by the late 1970s, an increasing number of people moved to the countryside.[6] In the UK, by contrast, the commune movement was a predominantly rural phenomenon. Rapidly increasing property prices pushed prospective communards out of urban centres, but some actively wanted to get out: 'We need space to work, space to be alone, space to run screaming through the woods,' Jan Wysocki wrote in 1969.[7]

Today, collective living might just seem normal, at least in the form of having flatmates in shared, usually urban apartments. For activists in the 1970s, however, living in communes had a profoundly political, if not utopian, dimension. Communes were 'islands', said a German communard named Ulrike, where it was possible to 'develop and realize desires "not tomorrow, but now", a piece of paradise, of communism, of socialism, of anarchism, of anything that we can anticipate'.[8] Here, activists could put ideals of a collective and self-determined life into practice. Living communally presented a radical alternative to conventional family life. 'Why wall yourself in with a little nuclear family when you could live together and enjoy one another's differences,' recalled Danish Ulla Gravesen.[9] It was a dream of overcoming family constraints and isolation by finding a new way of living together, and 'dealing with all problems collectively'.[10] Social scientists interviewing people about their motivations for moving into communes similarly noted a 'desire for communication' and 'overcoming individual isolation'.[11] A French group moving to the countryside hoped to live with others in 'authentic relations' and with 'the fewest possible constraints'. Their children should be raised collectively, and 'complete sexual liberty' would reign. Such a rural community would help them 'flee the alienations, hypocrisy, isolation, misery and boredom' of ordinary society they so much despised.[12]

'Equality was, of course, a must,' Danish ex-communard Morten Thing said in an oral history interview.[13] In one way or another, the vast majority of communes shared that ideal. Many pooled financial resources. In some communes, members paid rent according to their financial means, meaning that those with well-paying, stable jobs supported younger students and apprentices. More often, communes purchased major household items and occasionally a car together, and had a common kitty for necessities such as toilet paper and groceries.[14] Beyond economic equality, most communes sought to establish egalitarian structures. Decisions were to be made collectively, and chores were to be shared. Of course, there were informal hierarchies which could lead to bitter conflicts, but sometimes also frank discussions. Morten Thing's intellectual and emotional skills, for example, made him a de facto leader of his commune. 'This resulted in a good deal of self-reflection,' said one of his former housemates. 'We discussed it and kind of reached an agreement that this was how it was going to be. So Morten was the dad.'[15] This was less fortunate for the women who ended up being 'mum': the ideal of shared chores came up against different ideas of cleanliness, but also with deeply ingrained gender roles, meaning that all too often women did most of the cleaning and cooking.[16]

The most far-reaching, but also most difficult aspect of the challenge to traditional family life concerned children. Ideally, the entire commune and not only the biological parents should be responsible for raising children. Such an upbringing would help them, left-leaning educational scientists believed, to develop a sense of autonomy vis-à-vis adults. Growing up in an egalitarian environment where gender roles had been overcome, children, too, would adopt such values. Some even argued that children should be able to choose to stay in the commune if their parents moved out. Communes, in short, might prevent the psychological damage that growing up in nuclear families usually entailed.[17] That, at least, was the theory.

In practice, communes frequently failed spectacularly to live up to their aspirations. Not surprisingly, biological parents ended up looking after their children, while other communards only did so if they didn't have anything more important (or more fun) to do. Communards without children preferred spending time in bars, going on dates, and generally enjoying their single life, but had little concerns for the needs of children, parents complained.[18] And the small children themselves were not happy about adults taking turns to sleep in their room (again, not surprisingly), but cried for their mothers, much to the dismay of some communards.[19] In general, the frequency with which communards moved in and out – a West German study from 1978 found that on average, communards only stayed for eighteen months before moving on – prevented children from building stable relations with anyone else besides their parents.[20] Arguably, not all experiences were that bad, and for some children, growing up in a commune was exciting. Yet, as a utopian project presenting an alternative to nuclear family life, communes did not catch on.[21]

If communes did not overthrow the nuclear family, many communards nevertheless felt that they succeeded in escaping the isolation and loneliness of life in modern cities. Communes provided 'emotional support' and became a veritable 'ersatz family', in particular where relations with the biological family were difficult.[22] They became genuine spaces of intimacy. Seemingly small things mattered. 'It starts with when it's your turn to do the shopping,' a German communard remarked, 'you think, what does someone like to eat, that Abu likes sausages, and so on. You do feel and think about other people here. Or something nice happened to you, and you come home and can talk about it with everyone.'[23] One communard interviewed in the 1970s noted in passing that commune members often sat together in the bathtub, which helped them talk through their problems.[24] Nudity ceased to be an issue as roommates frequently saw each other without clothes on.[25] Some communes even arranged therapy sessions with the hope to solve individual problems in a collective manner.[26] And in some cases, this seems to have worked. Living in a commune, a West German man named Knut claimed, had facilitated 'lots of emotionality and openness'. It helped him develop new 'feelings and values', though he did not say anything more specific.[27]

Typically, urban communes were located in old, sometimes even decaying houses that required extensive renovation work. This not only had financial reasons – such old apartments often had cheaper rent – but also reflected different ideals of living. Modern apartment buildings, argued the Hamburg-based group Humanes Wohnen, were constructed 'rigorously according to inhuman square-metre norms'.[28] Old buildings, the now extremely popular *Altbauten* in German, by contrast, accommodated their inhabitants' needs, which made them suitable for experimenting with collective living.[29] Elaborating on this line of thought, architects and communards Richard Meng and Wolfgang Thiel argued in the jargon-heavy language typical of the time that under the conditions of capitalism, 'living areas' had become a mere 'area of retreat' in which individuals hoped for protection against the 'effects of the dissected reality based on a division of labour'. The spatial arrangements of such apartments, they claimed, failed to foster social relations among residents. Objects determined social relations.[30] In the words of another critic of urban living, philosopher Hans-Dieter Bahr: 'The tedium of the cubical room manifests itself in the shape of furniture that is nothing but plastic or wooden boxes.'[31]

Communes were a protest against this 'monotonous stagnancy of everyday life, the fetishization of things, the sterile depression and the tightness of the home'. Yet, initially, they offered hardly a better alternative, if we follow Meng and Thiel's pointed critique. Early communards, busy with their radical political activism, invested little in making their place a new home. An 'aesthetic nihilism' reigned, with the thick, heavy blue volumes of the Marx-Engels collected edition serving as tea tables in otherwise sparsely furnished rooms. Full of contempt for bourgeois norms of cleanliness, those communards turned the floor into a 'giant ashtray', which was of course very convenient for parties. But eventually, in long-term communes, things changed. Communards came to value qualities like 'sensibility, empathy, self-presentation'. Trying to stimulate feelings, they decorated walls with 'blankets, clothes, photos of themselves and dear friends or self-painted pictures', Meng and Thiel wrote about the commune movement of the late 1970s. Bookshelves, once a status symbol for theoretically minded leftist students, were replaced by spice racks: physical appetites had become more important than theoretical knowledge. And the floor no longer just served as an ashtray, but became 'an additional space for self-expression'. Sitting down on the floor, Meng and Thiel remarked, was 'anti-hierarchical', and hence allowed for overcoming isolation.[32]

No doubt, the transformation of everyday life communards aspired to was difficult to achieve, however much they changed their living space. Residents retreated to their rooms, kept doors shut and therefore remained alone. Studies of communes are full of reports about internal conflicts resulting in people frequently moving in and out.[33] Solving problems with roommates required time and energy, and if they then left, remaining communards felt exploited. People accepted themselves as 'incredibly damaged individuals', one woman noted, but had given up on actually changing this.[34] By the late 1970s, the demand for total communication common in the early commune movement had waned, though 'open and honest' communication was still valued.[35] Frequent discussions about gender roles, with regard to household work as well as emotional behaviour, pushed men to change – though how much they actually did change is, of course, impossible to say. And many communards realized and accepted that living in a commune would be a temporary rather than a long-term alternative to family life.

Over the years, then, communal living became normalized. It ceased to be considered the prelude to utopia. It's simply what young people in particular do before having children. There's nothing rebellious about it any more.[36] Yet, collective living does still present an alternative to isolating urban life. Many communes are still places of sociability where people with similar ideals and lifestyles (like veganism or queerness) can share their everyday lives. And an increasing number of intergenerational housing projects in cities throughout Europe allow young people, families with children and the elderly to live together. From this author's perspective at least, as someone who spent several years living in different communes, including a large housing project, it did make life better: I have fond memories of long breakfasts, of communal dinners, of coming home and chatting to friends in the garden – but also of sometimes quite difficult conflicts. While hardly revolutionizing everyday life in Europe, the commune movement had a lasting impact.

Workplace Democracy: Collective Self-Management and Autonomous Work

Just as alienating as life in modern cities was, according to leftist critics, work under capitalism. Workers, they charged, had no say with regard to the organization of the labour process and the pace of production. When they entered the shop floor or the office, they gave up their autonomy. In the mind of these critics, capitalism turned human beings into mere robots working according to the demands of machinery and bureaucracy.[37] The alternative they envisioned was collective self-management. Employees themselves should be in charge, not only to organize work, but also in all other matters. The origins of these ideas go back to Yugoslavia, which sought to develop a system of self-management after the break with the Soviet Union under Stalin in 1948.[38] In the 1960s, the idea became popular in Western Europe, particularly among leftist trade unionists in France, where entire journals were dedicated to questions of self-management. For leftist intellectuals such as Henri Lefebvre, collective self-management became a 'concrete utopia', that is, a practical way of radically changing everyday life at the workplace, much as the communards thought about collective living. In both cases, it was about working and living together, but autonomously, without the authority of bosses or families.[39]

During the upheavals of 1968, self-management was mostly an idea, popular among leftist trade unionists and radical students alike. Only rarely were such ideas put into practice. This changed in the 1970s and 1980s. In the Federal Republic, self-managed projects mushroomed in those years. They included leftist bars and cafés, bookshops, kindergartens, but also car and bicycle workshops, carpentries, printing houses and ecological grocery stores.[40] Many of these projects were founded with great enthusiasm, as an alternative to hierarchically structured companies. Decision-making processes were supposed to happen in a democratic fashion, and work should be fulfilling rather than alienating. Yet in reality working in self-managed projects could be extremely frustrating. Some claimed that they worked far more than in normal jobs (the refusal to use timesheets to monitor work made it difficult to verify such claims, though social scientists studying self-managed projects found that, on average, the working hours were not much longer than in regular companies), while, for others, the decision-making process with its endless discussions and the demand for consensus was extremely tiring. And the financially precarious situation of many projects did not make life easier.[41]

Among many small projects and collectively managed cooperatives, one case, and the conflict surrounding it, stands out: the 'Affaire LIP' (1973–87).[42] Founded in 1867, the LIP watchmaking company located in Besançon, southern France, had seen difficult and tumultuous years. During the upheavals of May '68, workers had gone on strike and occupied the factory. They pushed the owner of the factory, Fred Lip, to make concessions that went beyond the national agreements, but also learned to organize independently of trade unions and to speak up against their superiors. After May, one woman told a reporter from *Elle*, she 'no longer trembled' talking to her supervisor.[43] More troubling from a management perspective, business did not go well. By 1973, LIP had been running a deficit for several years. Vacant positions were not filled. When president-director general Jacques Saintesprit stepped down in April that year and was replaced by two provisional administrators, appointed to oversee the company's liquidation, workers knew that something was up, though what exactly was still unclear. To pressure management for information, workers began to slow down production, but to no avail.[44]

In June, the conflict escalated. First, on 12 June, a crowd of workers sequestered the provisional directors in their offices and went through their papers. What they discovered was a shock: detailed plans for restructuring the company, plus a list of 480 workers (out of a total workforce of about 1,300) who would lose their jobs.[45] Six days later, on 18 June, workers voted with an overwhelming majority to occupy the factory and to continue producing and selling watches, including some 25,000 watches that workers removed from the premises to sell illegally. In front of the factory gates, a banner declared: 'It's possible, we produce, we sell', later complemented by 'we pay ourselves'.[46] It wasn't merely a fight to defend their jobs. 'This struggle demonstrates that another society is possible, an egalitarian society in which all workers will take charge of their affairs', as a tract of the workers' Action Committee from 6 July 1973 declared.[47] Such announcements quickly made the struggle at LIP a cause célèbre of self-management for leftist activists from across Europe. While workers on strike toured France and neighbouring countries publicizing their struggles, supporters flocked to Besançon to witness the factory occupation at first hand.

A new society was being born on the shop floor, or so it seemed to enthusiastic participants and observers alike. Monique Piton, a thirty-nine-year-old worker at LIP, who published a chronicle of the conflict, gives a sense of the autonomy and the egalitarian spirit in the occupied factory. In the absence of supervisors, watchmakers determined the pace of their own work. The quality of the product, not the speed of production, mattered. Over the entire period of the occupation, Piton claimed, not a single work accident happened. Hierarchies between different workers and employees disappeared: technicians worked on the production line or supported groups charged with tasks such as informing media about the occupation or giving tours to visitors, and men and women alike cleaned, scrubbed or watered the plants. According to Piton,

> The LIPs are happy to take part in collective work, in the workshops, offices, at reception and sales . . . The tasks are no longer monotonous or meaningless . . . Everyone becomes an individual

again in this big beehive, in this freedom that has moved in here, and everyone can develop spiritually in exchanges with others and physically by changing their activity.[48]

Whatever the reality behind this account, Piton's words convey a sense of the euphoria that reigned in LIP's occupied factory in the summer of 1973.

The LIPs, as the company's employees came to be called, transformed the factory. They opened the gates to family, friends and neighbours from Besançon, and received sympathetic visitors from all over France and other European countries. They showed them around, sold watches, informed them about the production process and distributed posters. It was a festive atmosphere, reminiscent of the summer of 1936 during the Popular Front, when hundreds of thousands of workers went on strike and occupied factories after the electoral victory of the left.[49] Photos show people dancing, playing music, singing and chatting on the grass in front of the factory. The workplace was no longer a site of alienating labour, but of producing something meaningful, of communication and collective joy.[50]

However, such euphoric accounts should not conceal the difficulties the militant workers at LIP encountered. Internal divisions came to the fore, which activists like Monique Piton attributed to patronizing trade unionists who were more interested in advancing the position of their union (in France, there were several competing unions) than in workers' independence and unity. By July, fewer workers attended general assemblies, and intense debates gave way to merely approving decisions already made in small circles.[51] At the same time, external pressures mounted. By 1 August, all employees had received letters of termination, and on 8 August, the local commercial court ruled that the factory had to be sealed, though workers quickly removed the seals. Then, on 14 August, on the orders of the national government, the police cleared the occupied factory. The authorities had even brought in police units from a different region, fearing that the local police might show solidarity with the workers. In response, some 4,500 protestors gathered in the streets of Besançon, and throughout France workers went briefly on strike to express their solidarity.[52]

The expulsion of the workers from the factory did not end the struggle. To the contrary, it made negotiations between the government, business representatives and trade unions possible. But they seemed to lead nowhere. In October, a vast majority of LIP employees rejected a government-sponsored plan for restructuring and splitting up the company, because it would have resulted in 400 to 500 workers being laid off, despite the trade unions urging workers to accept it. With French prime minister Pierre Messmer declaring that 'LIP, that's over, it doesn't concern me any more', the situation looked bleak for the LIPs.[53] Yet, just at this moment, a group of self-declared progressive business leaders formed in the wake of May 1968 stepped forward.[54] They developed a novel plan that would allow all workers to return to their jobs, though most would go through several months of additional, state-sponsored training. And the new director, Claude Neuschwander, promised a different management style, based on 'engagement with unions and communication and dialogue with workers'.[55] When the LIPs saw the plan in January 1974, their room for manoeuvre had shrunk. The business leaders had received support from the Ministry of Industry before presenting their plan to national trade unions, who also agreed. Only then were the employees at LIP informed. Without much discussion, they voted in favour of the plan. The first phase of the struggle was over.

But it was only a short respite. In the midst of a generally deteriorating economic situation in France, LIP's successor companies quickly ran into difficulties again. In April 1976, they filed for bankruptcy. Workers decided to reoccupy the factory and to continue production on their own terms. Yet, it would be a very different struggle. With unemployment mounting, the LIPs could hardly count on the same national support. Once again, the workers refused to be considered as individually unemployed and instead presented themselves as a community in need of an employer.[56]

This time, however, their hopes for a new investor and for support by the state were in vain. Thus, by November 1977, workers resolved to form a cooperative and to manage their own company, Les Industries de Palente, L.I.P. (Palente being the name of the neighbourhood where the factory was based). It was a decision made out of necessity, not out of enthusiasm for self-management.

The second factory occupation also attempted to democratize the workplace. Once again, workers held general assemblies, even though they had more of an informative character with fewer debates. Workers also resumed their travels to organize support across France and Europe.[57] But compared to the first factory occupation, the second movement lost momentum. The chances of winning the struggle looked much bleaker. Other factory occupations in France had yielded little in the way of results, and union leaders now argued against occupations as a tactic. Increasingly, only a small circle of militants, known as the 'limited committee', made decisions.[58] More tensions emerged after the establishment of the cooperative. Discipline returned to the workplace. Union leaders acted as 'little bosses', assigned jobs to individuals and monitored punctuality at meetings as well as at work.[59] For those workers who had hoped for a radically different life at the workplace, these developments were a bitter disappointment. When Christiane André, a militant involved in the struggle from the very beginning, was told to return to her old position in watch production, she went on a personal strike lasting two months. 'What task rotation? What decision-making powers? The question that arises is also: will we work again as before? With the same hierarchy? After the same capitalist scheme?' she asked in an interview.[60] Ultimately, she left L.I.P, as did other militants, including Monique Piton. L.I.P. ceased to be a role model of self-management.[61]

L.I.P. survived as a cooperative until 1987. Elsewhere in Europe, there were and still are companies and projects organized as cooperatives. Yet, the ideal of workers' self-management was fading away by the early 1980s. Did these ideas and practices of self-management then have any lasting impact on European societies, like the commune movement did?[62] Some scholars have argued that alternative, self-managed projects functioned as laboratories in which participants could acquire 'entrepreneurial virtues', learning about the importance of flat hierarchies, communication and self-motivation. One example for such a learning process would be Matthias Horx: having played an important role in Frankfurt's alternative scene during the 1970s, he went on to establish a consulting firm in 1993. Management, he urged his clients, which included major companies such as Unilever and Beiersdorf, had to allow for more independence, as employees' autonomy and flat structures of decision-making would be the most efficient way of leading a business.[63] Horx was exceptionally successful. Many of these self-managed projects and cooperatives failed due to internal conflicts and financial problems. Yet, the ideals they promoted – creativity, self-determined working hours, working in a flat network rather than a hierarchy, the need for intrinsic motivation and so on – live on in today's equally profitable and exploitive start-ups, places where what French sociologists Luc Boltanski and Eve Chiapello have labelled the 'new spirit of capitalism' reigns.[64]

On the Road: Alternative Tourism

In 1977, West German left-wing publishing house März Verlag posthumously published an autobiographical novel by Bernward Vesper called *Die Reise* (The Journey). Vesper had been part of the West Berlin student movement in 1968; only three years later, in 1971, he committed suicide in a psychiatric ward. The novel described childhood memories, arguments with his nationalist father, drug experiences with hashish and acid, and, last but not least, trips in the literal sense, hitch-hiking through the Federal Republic of Germany and Western Europe.[65] Vesper's novel was one of several widely read books celebrating a nomadic life, beyond the restrictions of modern industrial society. The best-known example is Jack Kerouac's *On the Road*, a cult novel of the American as well as the European counterculture, in which the protagonist trades a sterile, sedentary existence for a life on the road, full of adventure, drugs and sex.[66] Other books had a decidedly more political tone, such as Christiane Rochefort's *Encore heureux qu'on va vers l'été*, which recounts the attempt by schoolchildren, especially two teenage girls, to escape the oppressive world of adults by setting out to reach an undetermined place, somewhere in the south.[67]

These immensely popular works throw a spotlight on an aspect of alternative countercultures on both sides of the Iron Curtain that is often overlooked: travelling. Many members of countercultural scenes were regularly out and about. Rejecting organized mass tourism, they hitch-hiked across Europe and Asia, they went to alternative music festivals and protest camps and they travelled to post-revolutionary Portugal in the 1970s. Not only was hitch-hiking low cost, it also promised personal encounters, adventures and a 'vastly educational and personally rewarding way to discover Europe, Europeans, and yourself', as Ed Buryn, an American 'professional vagabond', wrote in 1969.[68] It allowed for spontaneity, quickly changing plans and more or less fleeting personal relations with other self-declared vagabonds. Such alternative tourism was an opportunity to break out of the monotony of well-organized everyday life. Even more so than living in communes and working in self-managed companies, hitting the road promised radical freedom and independence, but also a sense of community while exploring the world with fellow travellers.

Though part of the appeal of hitch-hiking and other forms of unorganized travelling was that it took travellers to destinations beyond the usual hotspots of mass tourism, alternative vagabonds from Europe (and the United States) tended to flock to specific places where they could meet like-minded young people. Not surprisingly, the sunny south of Europe, particularly Greece with its wild islands, but also Spain after the end of Franco's dictatorship, was popular among backpackers.[69] But if there was a capital of alternative tourism in Europe, it was Amsterdam. 'Every type of young vagabond traveler crosses through here. The crush is terrific, but so is the level of excitement', wrote Ed Buryn.[70] In the summer, hundreds of youngsters slept outside, first at Dam Square close to the central train station, then at Vondelpark, until the city council prohibited rough camping in the park in 1974. Of course, liberal Dutch drug policies that tolerated the consumption of cannabis were part of the city's attraction. Groups of young tourists sitting in the grass and circulating joints became a common sight. It was a bonding ritual that formed a transnational community. 'We were part of a new nation, as big as the planet earth,' two young Italians wrote about their 1970 trip to Amsterdam, 'without borders, without written laws, inhabiting an invisible state, all equal, all different, all colors, all beautiful, with a thousand foreign tongues but speaking the same language. There was a strong solidarity among those who dressed, lived, traveled and dreamed the same way, we all belonged to Hippie Nation.'[71]

The 'modern tourist nomads', as a Belgrade newspaper called the long-haired (and, according to the paper, alarming) travellers, sought to explore the world beyond Western Europe. Countercultural scenes were fascinated with anything 'oriental' – spirituality, music, drugs. 'People were listening to Ravi Shankar, sitting on cushions, and burning incense,' Eva Douglas, a young Swede, wrote about the scene in London during the late 1960s. 'The music, the Indian ambience, Timothy Leary, the Beatles meeting the Maharishi Mahesh Yogi: all this said to us that India was where the magic, the mystic, that *something else*, might be found.' From London, she travelled to Greece, a 'first step to the East', and then to Morocco, the 'real' East, no matter that it's geographically located west of Greece. 'This going from Sweden to London to Greece to Morocco and finally to India was a gradual undoing of my upbringing. India was to finish off this undoing process and then introduce a whole new way of life, a whole new set of perceptions.'[72]

The journey Douglas took became known as the Hippie Trail. Exploring the shores of the Mediterranean beyond Europe came first: Turkey, Israel, Tunisia, Algeria, and Morocco. For those who wanted to go further, Istanbul became the hub for a journey that would lead via Tabriz in Northern Iran and Kabul in Afghanistan, to Kathmandu, Nepal and Goa in India. By the late 1960s, bus tour operators offered trips (and a functioning sound system) along that route starting in London or Amsterdam. At their destinations, the travellers gathered in 'drifter enclaves', like Gülhane Park in Istanbul, Chicken Street in Kabul and Freak Street in Kathmandu, with bars and guesthouses where they could chat in their native tongue, or English, and listen to Western countercultural music. At times, young locals took an interest in the Westerners, their music, books and looks, though authorities often regarded them as a moral menace. By and large, however, the 'alternative vagabonds' remained in their enclaves, merely observing and touring local cultures.[73]

Such long-distance international travel was, of course, the privilege of Westerners. Reaching India was near impossible for countercultural youths in the Eastern bloc. But there were alternatives. Soviet hippies, too, could travel east, to Soviet Asia, to places like Uzbekistan or Tashkent, hoping to find spirituality there just like their Western peers hoped to do in India. And here, too, hitch-hiking 'became the soul of the movement'.[74] 'In hitch-hiking, there is something truly incomparable. First and foremost, it is probably its unpredictability,' wrote Garik Meitin, a hippie from Riga, in his memoir about the late 1970s and early 1980s. 'It is not clear where you will be this evening . . . And the main thing is not to define any kind of goals for the day – for example reach one particular town . . . Better from the very beginning to accept that it will be how it will be.'[75] On the road, it was possible to evade the Soviet state control system and form an underground network, not least to procure drugs. This turned the road into Soviet hippies' 'playground, where they lived out their vision of freedom, love, and community'.[76]

The road was the centre of another young subculture as well: the New Age Travellers. They first emerged in the United Kingdom during the 1970s, when young people spent their summers touring the countryside with their caravans to attend alternative music festivals at places such as Stonehenge, Windsor and Glastonbury. By the 1980s, life on the road had become a year-round pursuit for a community of Travellers. In the words of one young Traveller, it was 'a spontaneous experiment in human trust and co-operation . . . to live an alternative without the state'.[77] While musical preferences changed, the subculture lived on: from the hippie style of the 1970s, to punk during the 1980s, and finally to techno music in the 1990s, when Traveller collectives like the Space Tribe and Circus Warp organized improvised raves in forest clearings and vacant warehouses.[78] By the late 1980s, an increasing number of Travellers left Great Britain to evade police harassment and continued their itinerant life throughout Europe, where they became part of a fluid, transnational community. 'There is no personal space in our camp; everyone is lumped together in a jumbled, fluid community,' wrote a British woman in her twenties named Em who spent several summers touring Southern Europe, adding that 'there are no rules, we are free. There are no boundaries, no perimeter fences.'[79] Travellers became, as another woman put it, a 'worldwide tribe', a community beyond nationalism and borders, united by a common itinerant lifestyle.

Even when it wasn't overtly political, the vagabond lifestyles of hippies, New Age Travellers and other countercultures evoked hostile reactions from the authorities. For some activists, though, travelling did have an explicitly political dimension. They travelled to learn from comrades elsewhere, but also to practically support alternative projects like rural communes. At times, activists welcomed these international guests. For instance, the Danish reform school Tvind, founded in 1973 and famous in leftist circles for its attempt to combine learning, living and working, had a special guest school for the numerous visitors. Others, though, were less happy about such political tourists. A group of West Germans who travelled to Sardinia in the 1970s, hoping to learn about the rural commune movement there, found it difficult to find a commune that would welcome them, or could find a use for the skills they had to offer. Similarly, activists who had renovated abandoned villages in the French Pyrenees and had initially invited comrades to come and support them declared a year later that in light of past experiences they had changed their mind: they no longer wanted to be a 'holiday camp for polit-tramp-tourists'.[80] Political tourism was thus a highly ambivalent phenomenon, all too often reproducing 'imperialist' power relations, as the activists would have put it, that made alternative tourism look rather similar to conventional mass tourism.[81]

Critics have remarked, and not without justification, that alternative tourism was merely a hedonistic search for individual freedoms and fun, perhaps more exciting than conventional travelling, but certainly no attempt to create a better world. Hitch-hiking throughout Europe was not likely to change political or social structures. Even so, the itinerant lifestyle of hippies and New Age Travellers was an attempt to live a radically different life, a life beyond the constraints of regular working hours, the necessity to pay rent, and the attachment to a specific locality or nation. It was an attempt to create a fluid community that reached across national identities. It may not have profoundly changed mainstream society, or even tried to do so, but it did represent an alternative.

Living Utopias, Here and Now

Living in communes, whether they were urban or rural, working in self-managed projects, independently travelling throughout Europe and beyond: these were all experiments of collectively living an egalitarian life, without hierarchies. People tried to carve out spaces for intimacy beyond the family, for communities beyond national belonging; they longed for personal freedoms and a fluid, unrestrictive life. It was an attempt to anticipate utopia in the here and now, without transforming society as a whole. All too often, activists began such projects with immensely high hopes, but quickly faced practical, mundane problems. Communards fought about doing the dishes or looking after children. Collectively owned and supposedly egalitarian enterprises found it impossible to escape from market dynamics and ended up reintroducing hierarchies that they had hoped to overcome. Dreams of different dwelling, working and travelling were hard to put into practice.

Yet, activists continued to try. As they learned, they became more modest with their ambitions. Many people simply gave up on their radical hopes. Some started families, moved into their own homes and found regular jobs. Others continued to live in communes and to work in cooperatives, though no longer viewing them as ways to change the world. As so often, the process of deradicalization went hand in hand with a process of normalization. This is arguably the most lasting legacy of the attempts to anticipate utopias in the present. While there is no longer a commune movement as it existed in the 1970s, and self-management has lost its appeal as a revolutionary slogan, living in shared spaces and working in companies with flat hierarchies has become the new normal for many people – or at least the ideal that companies claim to promote: employees working happily together without a boss yelling at them promise to generate more profits. It wasn't a grand revolution, it might sound trivial and insignificant, but, for better or worse, everyday life did change.

Emotional Politics: Changing the Self, Changing the World

Feminists and gay activists powerfully argued for understanding seemingly private issues as profoundly political, as we saw in Chapter 11. They were not alone in doing so. Many in the post-1968 Western left believed intimate, personal relations to be shaped by capitalist society, and that their individual suffering should be the starting point for political activism. They promoted what was called a 'politics of the first person'.[1] In a capitalist society, these activists claimed, there was no space for genuine feelings, or at least expressing them, as only rational calculation mattered for making money; and if consumer society appealed to feelings, then it was only to manipulate them for the sake of profit. Yet, while repressing good feelings, capitalism also produced bad feelings: fear, loneliness and frustration. According to these critiques of capitalism's emotional regime, people were left incapable of connecting with others, living in isolation and always afraid of showing what they truly felt. People, the claim went, related to their bodies in a fragmented and functionalist way, using only those parts needed for the task at hand, whether at work or when having sex. In short, leftist critics argued that capitalism damaged the self and the body as much as personal relations.[2]

Such an emotional predicament called for a new kind of activism: a struggle for better feelings, and for a world that would allow for such feelings. In practical terms, this meant creating spaces that might allow people to build meaningful, authentic relations with lovers, friends and comrades. But even more importantly, people tried to repair, as it were, their broken selves and personal relations. They envisioned new ideals of masculinity and femininity that valued emotionality; they looked for experiences that would involve the entire body, notably when having sex. And above all, they talked and wrote about feelings, in numerous consciousness-raising and therapy groups, in fictional literature like children's books to educate a new generation on emotional ideals or in autobiographical accounts about personal experiences. These were attempts to *feel better*, in all senses, to overcome fear, to enjoy bodies without shame, and to simply 'be together' (*stare insieme*, as Italian youth activists of the late 1970s put it).[3]

This chapter explores these emotional politics. It firstly reconstructs the problem: what was it about capitalist society, according to leftist critics, that made it so emotionally damaging? What kind of feelings did this society produce, and what did it suppress? But leftists did more than criticize; they looked for remedies. The chapter thus explores how activists engaged in a variety of practices that would help them 'fix' their 'damaged' selves and repair broken relations, in particular by talking about feelings in groups. Equally important were bodies: leftists longed for bodily and sexual practices that would yield more pleasure. These practices, and debates about them, are the subject of the chapter's final part. Empirically, it draws mostly on examples from West Germany, the place that has been studied most intensively. How these activists talked about their feelings, and what they did to change them, provides us with fascinating glimpses into the world of emotional politics.[4]

Broken Selves, Broken Relations: Emotional Suffering

In the summer of 1973, *Hundert Blumen*, an anarchist-leaning magazine based in West Berlin, published an entire special issue on 'schizophrenia, politics and psychiatry'. A central tenet of its analysis was the 'necessary unity of individual and social emancipation'. Capitalism, the anonymous authors argued, not only produced 'material misery', such as 'bad working and living conditions', but also 'psychic misery'. The self under capitalism was 'weakened,

broken, depressed, fearful, neurotic, fixated on authorities, dependent, intolerant, dogmatic, aggressive against those who are
themselves oppressed, consumption-oriented, dominated by constant frustration and existential fears.' Its symptoms? 'Difficulties at
work, depression, competitive behaviour . . . communication and
contact difficulties, psychoses, functional diseases (circulatory,
digestive and nervous system), lack of imagination, addiction, drug
abuse . . . (please fill in the gaps yourself).' On the one hand, such
psychic misery should be the source of political action, but on the
other, it also hindered activism because it caused fear and prevented
solidarity. Class struggle therefore required these psychological
problems to be addressed, the authors posited. This alone would
enable members of political groups to treat each other humanely
and not like 'cattle'. They had to learn to 'reveal our feelings, tenderness, sympathy and aggression'.[5]

The article encapsulates how many on the left in the 1970s
thought about the emotionally damaging effects of capitalism. In
their view, most ordinary people in capitalist societies (leaving aside,
of course, capitalist elites living in financial safety) lived in a permanent state of fear, loneliness and alienation. They were subject to
market forces beyond their comprehension and control. Forced to
sell their labour, they were always at risk of losing out and ending
up unemployed. The constant pressure to perform at school, at university, at work, but also at home and even when having sex, caused
equally constant fears of not doing well enough. There was nothing
existential about fear, leftist author Dieter Duhm claimed in his
widely read book *Fear in Capitalism* (1972); it was a profoundly social
feeling. Yet expressing such feelings was not possible in capitalist
society, leftists held, because it would be considered a sign of weakness in the permanent competition of all against all.[6]

Ultimately, it was the belief in an 'efficient, anonymously calcu-
lating logic', as an author of the Frankfurt *Pflasterstrand* wrote in
1977, that made modern society so hostile to feelings.[7] Emancipatory politics thus had fight against the 'brutality of the dominant
rationality'.[8] In that struggle, anything opposed to rationality was a

potential ally: dreams, fantasies, feelings, and those still capable of having them, notably children. On the horizon was, Herbert Röttgen predicted in the same year, a revolt of the 'party of feelings and senses against the party of rationality and alienation . . . of the party of playing [children] against the party of work [adults]'. Children, he held, were still able to 'launch fantasies, desires and feelings against the adult world of work'.[9] Indeed, leftists of the 1970s frequently idolized children as embodiments of a struggle against oppressive rationality. The December 1977 cover of *Pflasterstrand*, for example, showed a young, naked child from the back (leaving their gender undetermined) confronting a large, presumably male robot. In the face of the robot emitting smoke, the child seems to be dreaming of a small house, surrounded by flowers and trees.[10]

Part of what made rationality so destructive according to many on the radical left was its tendency to order and categorize everything, notably bodies. Young girls, Christiane Matties wrote in a publication tellingly subtitled *Zeitschrift für Vernunftkritik* (Magazine for Criticizing Reason), enjoyed becoming or playing at being boys, albeit only for a brief moment. But by putting on a bra and suspenders for the first time, they became unambiguously women. As women, they had to show bodily restraint, and if their bodies 'laughed, snorted, giggled, cried' in public, then they were no longer seen as women, but as 'foolish chicks' or 'stupid cows'.[11] Along similar lines, another author named Lucy Körner argued that children were capable of feeling with their entire bodies. When they felt joyous, they bounced and jumped around, they laughed. Yet, growing up, they had to learn to restrain their feelings, which made them 'cramp'.[12] Ultimately, people felt alienated from their bodies because 'factory society' was 'destroying human beings into parts of the machinery, into head, belly, and sex'.[13] The young persons' novel *Der Job* by Gerd-Gustl Müller, for example, depicted factory labour as profoundly dissatisfying. 'Ass, stomach, noggin, cock, and feet – none of that was necessary. Ready to be amputated. All you needed was your thumb and two fingers.'[14]

Above all, this functionalist fragmentation of bodies resulted in an impoverished sexuality that remained limited to genitalia, leftists argued.[15] Teenage boys, a men's group from Frankfurt claimed, learned to masturbate, but not to 'caress their entire body', which would 'by necessity result in a fixation on genitals. The rest of the body remains dead.' Male masturbation was 'entirely goal-oriented'. Only the final ejaculation (and whether that was actually an orgasm was not always clear, the men's group argued) was important. What mattered for men was how they performed in bed, a fundamentally capitalist principle. And if men actually cared about their (female) partner's sexuality, then their masculinity would be measured by their ability to 'make women climax as often and as intensely as possible'.[16] In the lesbian women's scene, at least some authors claimed, a similar 'performance pressure' reigned: the fixation on (male) penetrative sex had simply been replaced by a fixation on clitoral orgasms, but the rest of the body still remained neglected.[17] 'By adopting this orgasm insanity', a lesbian woman from Hamburg wrote, 'we accept the sexuality of men, which is performance-oriented but devoid of feelings. Being lesbian is then not much more than a reformed version of heterosexuality.'[18]

Such texts, often written from a first-person perspective and appearing in various small DIY magazines, depicted an emotional and bodily misery caused by modern consumer capitalism. Students complained that academic competition destroyed any meaningful relationship between them.[19] In the overcrowded lecture halls, fellow students remained 'strange anonymous beings one doesn't know and one will never get to know', a student from Heidelberg bemoaned.[20] To escape from such loneliness, people went to discos or bars. But the loud music made conversation impossible, and in the end, everyone returned home alone, as a high-school magazine from West Berlin commented.[21] Getting drunk in bars or taking drugs wasn't a viable alternative either, for intoxication prevented genuine communication and an honest show of feelings. Tellingly, this was a problem for commercial discos and leftist bars alike.[22]

Some of these critiques might sound rather strange nowadays

(like linking genital sex with the capitalist performance principle), but in the 1970s, many in the leftist scene found such ideas appealing. Importantly, such critiques also pointed to remedies: if boys had been taught not to express their feelings, and above all their fears, then men had to relearn how to talk about their emotions; if conventional discos prevented teenagers from communicating, then setting up independent youth centres might provide an alternative; if genital sex was so limited and goal-oriented, then maybe it was time to have a different kind of sex which would involve the entire body.

Repairing the Self, Fixing Relations

How could a better, more emotional self be formed? The most important places where activists worked on transforming their selves were countless groups, modelled on the consciousness-raising groups of the women's movement and variously called self-experience, therapy or (for male activists) men's groups. Outside of West Germany and, to a lesser degree, the UK, such groups have received relatively little scholarly attention, but evidence suggests that they existed in the Nordic countries as well as in France and Italy.[23] These groups may not seem to fit the idea of a typical 'protest'. However, for participants, they were a way to practically do something against their emotional deformation; as such, they were a form of combating a capitalist emotional regime. Not least, groups were immensely popular, in particular within leftist circles: according to one estimate from 1983, up to half a million West Germans participated in some kind of group therapy (not all, of course, in a leftist context).[24]

Participants often came with high expectations. A men's group from West Berlin, for example, noted that they had been 'dissatisfied with their role as men', which meant that they had to be tough, could not show any feelings, had to compete with other men and had a 'sexuality of the hard dick'.[25] In the group, they hoped to learn how to open up to both women and other men. Meanwhile, British men's magazine *Achilles Heel* asked men to 'delve deeply into our inner lives and to consciously explore and develop our sense of ourselves as emotional, sensual and spiritual beings capable of a whole range of experiences which our society on the whole denies to men'.[26] Sometimes, this search for feelings took an explicitly political, anti-capitalist bent. In the view of leftist magazine *Carlo Sponti* from Heidelberg, capitalism was reducing 'the senses, characteristics, drives and desires' to a focus on 'property, power, labour power, character masks' – note the Marxist jargon! – 'surplus-value production, and so on.' The Heidelberg activists hoped for therapeutic practices to have an emancipatory effect by 'supporting us in our struggle against abstractions and the reductions of our five senses, for the multiplicity of our characteristics and capabilities'.[27]

Accomplishing those emotional goals was a complicated matter. To make it work, some groups turned to advice literature and various therapeutic techniques, sometimes even with the help of professional experts. But results tended to be mixed. Sometimes, talking honestly about one's feelings was liberating and exciting. But other groups, who often wrote in detail about their experiences, also reported 'performance and competition pressure', noting that 'verbal power does not create emotionality, verbal orgasms don't yield emotional climaxes'.[28] Men yelled at each other, and conflicts even resulted in violent altercations between group members. A men's group in Heidelberg disbanded over the most traditional issue: competing over a woman.[29] Another group in Liverpool broke apart over debates about how to react to one of its members assaulting a woman: should the man be excluded, or should he receive anti-violence counselling?[30] Rather than liberating buried feelings, these groups (and the leftist scene more generally) created new emotional norms, as participants clearly recognized: showing aggression was forbidden, while everyone had to talk about their fears. At times, group members who did not conform to such norms, for example because they did not speak openly enough about their feelings, even had to face a mock trial where other members would deliver judgements. What was meant to 'liberate' repressed feelings could become a traumatizing experience that left some participants with suicidal thoughts.[31]

This pressure to talk about feelings extended beyond formal groups. It existed in the entire scene, in communes small and large that effectively functioned like a group. Clearly, those who had some psychological training were in a privileged position. Knowing how to talk about feelings was a source of power. In a remarkably reflective account, one man from West Berlin wrote about how he and his four male flatmates, all pedagogy students, had constantly talked about their personal relations, which made one of his flat-mates' girlfriend, a 'spontaneous, relaxed' sports student, feel rather uncomfortable. Her boyfriend was 'a superb example of the sensible man', who knew how to listen and understand. But in a subtle way, enlisting his fellow flatmates, he pushed his girlfriend in what the man writing the account retrospectively called 'psycho terror' to address her alleged 'sexual problems', only to have sex with him more often.[32] Given such frustrating experiences, scholars have tended to be somewhat dismissive about the quest for personal transformation in groups. It was hardly the emotional emancipation activists looked for.[33]

Yet, while there are good reasons to remain sceptical about any one-sided narrative of emotional liberation, these more or less formal groups did offer spaces to experiment with different emotional norms and practices. Such experiments could fail, but they could also result in significant change. Some men reported that talking about feelings in a group had a positive impact on their romantic relationships, one effect being that girlfriends no longer had to push them to address personal issues. Manfred from Berlin, for example, noted how he had become 'more sensitive', that he paid attention to 'human feelings and problems', and made an effort not to 'drag a conflict [with his girlfriend] to a rational level'. Another man, named Leo, found that the group experience had resulted in him paying more attention to his girlfriend's sexual desires.[34] No doubt, this is individual, scattered evidence, which doesn't allow for any larger conclusions regarding the scale or duration of change. But clearly, groups allowed their members to express feelings in novel ways. Sometimes, this could be a liberating experience; sometimes, it was just another way to exert power (not least by men over women).

By talking about their feelings in groups, participants worked on themselves. They refused who they were supposed to be, and at the same time reimagined who they could be.[35] What might it mean to be a man or a woman, to be gay or lesbian, or something else? Activists questioned old identities and developed new ones. Men challenged ideals of virility, of toughness, of physical strength, but also of intellectual superiority, and instead promoted a 'softer' and 'more feminine' vision of masculinity.[36] This new 'softie type', commented Claudia Rößler in the feminist *Frauenoffensive* with more than a hint of irony, was a tall man with an athletic body, but so afraid of his own strength that he did not dare touch his girlfriend.[37] The new ideal of masculinity demanded men to admit to their emotional problems, their inability to communicate, and their fixation on genital orgasms, under which they of course suffered. Other authors challenged the very distinction between masculinity and femininity. Both men and women, an author from Munich wrote, were simply human beings who were losing 'their fears of tenderness'. Those 'new guys and gals' would 'integrate body, soul and spirit', and the line between masculine and feminine would become meaningless.[38] Those, at least, were the new gender ideals.

A particularly interesting source for such contested questions of identity are personal dating ads. How did those seeking intimate partners choose to present themselves? Studying such advertisements of women loving women in the West German feminist magazine *Courage* between 1976 and 1984, historian Benno Gammerl notes a variety of self-descriptions. Not surprisingly for a feminist magazine, most writers simply referred to themselves as women (and added their age), indicating a strong sense of identity rooted in womanhood. Some, however, used terms like 'human being' (with a female-sounding suffix in German: *Menschin* rather than *Mensch*) or 'individualist', indicating a rejection of a strong gender identity. And one advertiser wrote: 'Personal data – don't know – always consider them rather generalizing and restrictive – despite all information'; another noted a 'permanent identity crisis'. By the early 1980s, then, an increasing number of advertisers began using characteristics coded as masculine or feminine, though by no means always in a binary way: 'mascul. type, very sensible', one wrote, and another said directly: 'feminine to masculine (adaptable)'.[39] Such personal advertisements suggest that already in the 1970s and then increasingly in the 1980s lesbian feminists began simultaneously confirming and subverting gender identities, a process we can observe in countercultural and leftist circles more widely.

Such questioning, subverting and dissolving of gendered and sexual identities did not, of course, end in the 1980s. Since the early 1990s – a definite timing is impossible to give here – the umbrella term *queer*, or the acronym LGBTQIA (meaning lesbian, gay, bisexual, transgender/transsexual, queer/questioning, intersexual, asexual/aromantic/agender; the acronym has expanded over the years from the original LGBT) has come to signify a variety of gender and sexual identities that differ from heterosexual masculinity or femininity. It indicates an ever-increasing diversity of identities, or a refusal of fixed identities altogether and instead a celebration of subversive fluidity. There's a plethora of alternatives that allow us to constantly reimagine who we want to be, if we choose to do so.

There is much to appreciate about this development. Being able to choose an identity can be a liberating moment. Yet, there are also reasons to remain cautious about celebratory narratives of liberalization or even emancipation. All too often, the new freedoms came with new constraints and new norms, something activists were well aware of. Disrupting old emotional norms that prohibited men from showing their feelings might be liberating; but it could easily turn into a new stricture, demanding the display of feelings. Working on the self, choosing and shaping an identity did not necessarily become easier with the variety of new options, and pressures to succeed in that endeavour did not necessarily decrease. Rather than

telling a one-sided success story of increasing diversity and freedom, we should see an expanding field of options, all coming with
their own complications and constraints. Once we *can* imagine who
we want to be, we *have* to do so; this can enable people to live the
life they want, but it can also create immense social pressures.

Feeling the Body: Sexuality and More

For those longing for better feelings, just talking openly about emotions was not enough: they wanted to feel and appreciate their
bodies, and every inch of them. Men and women, gay and straight
alike joined groups in an effort to overcome feelings of shame and
anxiety related to their bodies, and to show affection in a physical
manner – something we've already seen in the context of women's
and gay movements. They undressed, hugged and cuddled. For
some, this could be an exciting and liberating experience. Hans, a
member of a Munich men's group, for example, reported how during a weekend trip to the Alps members of his group had got naked
and massaged each other. At first, he was afraid of getting an erec-
tion, but when this did not happen, it turned into a pleasurable,
even erotic experience. After that weekend, hugging turned from a
formality between friends into an act of 'real tenderness'.[40] Unsurprisingly, however, such experiments could also be fraught, with
men worrying about the length of their penis and women about
their breasts being too saggy.[41] And rather than caressing each other,
members of another group remained afraid of bodily contact.[42]

But important as it was for men to cuddle, the really crucial issue
with regard to emotional development was – of course! – sex. Calls
for more sexual liberty, meaning the decriminalization of non-
heterosexual practices (and sometimes, in a rather troubling way,
also of paedophilia) and a challenge to conservative sexual mores
were frequent in leftist circles.[43] Yet, there were also worried
voices, especially in parts of the women's movement during the
1980s. More sexual liberty, some women argued, resulted in the

commercialization of sexuality and hence the objectification of female bodies. 'Pornography is the theory, rape the practice,' as American legal scholar Catharine MacKinnon famously wrote.[44] These debates then went beyond liberation. They addressed the right kind of sexuality. What sexual practices would yield genuine pleasure? What parts of the body should be involved? How might it be possible to achieve a sense of profound physical intimacy? Or were intimacy and even love a completely separate matter? Were there forms of sexuality that (re)produced oppression and violence and so needed to be overcome?

As we've seen, many on the left during the 1970s – lesbians and gay men, as well as straight men and women – complained that typical sex, or what they felt was typical, was too focused on genitalia and achieving orgasms. The rest of the body, however, remained inactive. Better sex needed to be more wholesome; it had to involve the entire body. A cartoon published in the gay magazine *HAW-Info* from West Berlin made that case: it showed a drawing of a man and a woman, their bodies divided into parts, which were all designated as 'erogenous zones', to be 'kissed, sucked, fondled', and so on.[45] Challenging the primacy of genitalia and orgasms, many different bodily and non-bodily practices should count as sex. Truly 'free sexuality', an author for the *Hamburger Frauenzeitung* argued, would 'only be possible once we stop categorizing everything', distinguishing between '"harmless" fondness, [different] erogenous zones . . .'. In her view, 'an orgasm should have no more meaning than holding hands, massaging the back, or dancing closely'.[46] Such arguments challenged the very distinction not only between sexual and non-sexual forms of interaction (or 'communication', as some authors called it), but also between homo-, hetero- and bisexuality. These categories, argued one man, would only oppress (his) sexuality and 'the potentialities of my tenderness'.[47] There was no 'need to define', French women activists felt, when they could refuse to have any specific sexuality and instead become simply 'desiring machines', in Gilles Deleuze's words.[48]

It is, of course, difficult to assess whether such sexual ideals actually changed sexual practices, and whether sex was, in the end, better and more fulfilling, as people hoped for.[49] Some reports suggest that people tried to put these ideas into practice. 'We have very few sexual problems. We cuddle quite a lot, but rarely fuck,' one man from West Berlin wrote about his relationship with his girlfriend.[50] And one of the seventeen-year-old girls from Berlin who had participated in a girls' group (see Chapter 11) commented that she had stopped taking the pill and therefore no longer had sexual intercourse with her boyfriend. This enabled them, she claimed, to get to know each other much more 'intensely'. 'Since tenderness can no longer be focused on genitalia, we experience every piece of skin, we have much more time and I'm no longer under this awful pressure to sleep with him even though I don't want to, which was something I could never say.'[51] At times, the effort to move beyond genital sexuality could take drastic turns: men voluntarily undergoing sterilization. 'A common experience [after the sterilization] is that cuddling, fondling and similar caresses are, for us, no longer degraded to "foreplay", because the dick has mostly lost its dominance,' members of a Berlin 'sterilization group' (there really were groups for everything!) wrote.[52]

Whether this version of sexuality was indeed better, less restrictive and more diverse might be open to debate. One woman in the late 1970s noted that she liked 'dick fucking' and enjoyed the 'horniness in my vagina' and ultimately the orgasm that 'whirls me into the universe with countless sparks'. Yet, taking pleasure in penetrative sex also made her feel guilty because she was not acting in solidarity with the women's movement. 'But who represents the horniness of women?' she wondered.[53] Gay men, too, mocked the 'softie' types for remaining 'fixated on their dicks', albeit in a negative way. Genitalia had become a taboo, but a taboo everyone constantly talked about. 'Whatever you do, the dick can't be part of it,' commented one anonymous author in West Berlin's leftist magazine *Info BUG* in June 1976. Heterosexual men, he argued, denied that 'sexuality is lively, animalistic, something that in the first instance has nothing to do with domination. All your affectionate behaviour is making you asexual.'[54] By the end of the 1970s, the rejection of genital sexuality within leftist, alternative circles was waning. All the talk about affectionate sexuality, worried influential leftist sexologist Günter Amendt in 1980, kept teens from actually having sex.[55]

In the 1980s, ideals of soft, non-genital sexuality also came under attack in the women's movement. Once again, the debates originated in the United States: the famous 'sex wars'.[56] Fighting pornography as a sexist industry which reduced women's bodies to objects for male desire, rejecting a phallocratic sexuality and promoting ideals of equality, tenderness and affection had been more or less commonsense stances among political lesbians and feminists. In this context, the publication of a 1981 'Sex Issue' by the American magazine *Heresies: A Feminist Publication on Art and Politics* was a provocation. Not only did it contain texts on subjects like 'Pornography and Pleasure', but also reproduced porn cartoons and images of nearly naked women wrestlers. In its pages, author Paula Webster charged that anti-porn feminists had embraced, if unwittingly, a morality that denied women's sexual desires. 'Television, film, and our mothers all reinforce the notion that only bad girls like sex . . . Our . . . desires threatened Mom and Dad, and they told us how dangerous sex was, especially curiosity or experimentation.' Women should engage in experimentation, and they should enjoy sex without judgement, the argument went.[57]

Such claims were a shock for feminists, who had cherished ideals of equality and tenderness, in the US but also in Europe. Even more shocking than articles in magazines like *Heresies* were lesbians openly displaying their preferences for sadomasochistic sexual practices. Whipping, bondage and playing with submission and domination seemed to be a challenge to feminist ideals of sexual equality. 'Sado-masochistic sex is the eroticisation of power, pain and humiliation in a relationship based on domination and submission. It glorifies the very oppressions many people are trying to struggle against,' a 1986 leaflet by the British group Lesbians Against Sado-Masochism (LASM) claimed.[58] Like some gay activists in the

1970s, lesbian opponents of S&M considered it a precursor to fascism. It had been part, LASM wrote, of Berlin's 'decadent' scene in the 1930s. 'People acclimatized to S[&]M brutality would have failed to notice the threat of the "real Nazis" approaching.' For their opponents, a group of sexual radicals called Sexual Fringe, which included S&M lesbians, men, bisexuals and transsexuals but also celibates, condemning S&M as fascist only trivialized 'the real fight against fascism'. Facing a women's movement that had become, they felt, 'more concerned with constructing and policing its own categories of sexual identity than with attempting to understand the complex and often contradictory construction of women's sexuality in a male-dominated, capitalist society', they called for 'self-determination of our bodies'.[59]

In the end, the 'pro-sex' side won the debate.[60] Consensual BDSM (the acronym that replaced S&M, standing for bondage, discipline/ dominance, submission/sadism, and masochism) has become a widely accepted sexual practice in queer scenes. Few people nowadays would condemn it as a glorification of oppression. Rather, BDSM sex is often considered a way to test and potentially transgress boundaries in a safe space; BDSM is, many argue, not about violence and humiliation, but about living out 'deviant' desires in a relationship of profound intimacy and trust. Queer porn festivals celebrate diverse sexual desires and practices, and feminist sex shops sell all kinds of sex toys, including dildos:[61] once criticized as symbols of male, penetrative sexuality, they are now seen to signify the 'lack of fixity of gender'.[62] S&M literature in the UK, to quote feminist activists Susan Ardill and Sue O'Sullivan, 'has brought into the open naked desires'. Yet, amid this celebration, something has been lost, as Ardill and O'Sullivan note: that 'vanilla sex', too, can be exciting, and that some forms of sex can be problematic. Groups such as Sexual Fringe 'romanticized categories of "deviant" sexual practice – if you can't claim one of their identities, well, frankly, you're boring.'[63]

On the face of it, these practices – BDSM, feminist and queer porn, penetrative sex toys – might look like a radical departure from the soft, non-genital sexuality leftists of the 1970s called for.

Yet, their differences notwithstanding, the fundamental question remained the same: how might the body be turned into a source of sexual pleasure? What parts of the body should be involved, what kinds of objects might be used, and what might contribute to arousal? Whether activists questioned genital sex or celebrated S&M, they always sought to challenge social norms, capitalist society or the women's movement itself, and to demolish the restrictions imposed on sexual pleasure. Yet, this always went hand in hand with the constructions of new ideals that made other forms of bodily intimacy seem less legitimate: oppressive, boring, uncool, violent, masculine. The search for better sex, then, hasn't ended.

Something else, however, did change – something that is easily overlooked with all the attention paid to sexuality. When leftists in the 1970s worried about what they felt was a hostility towards bodies in modern, industrial societies, they had more than sex in mind. They criticized the way labour processes fragmented the body, the idealization of clean, strong (and hence unnatural) bodies in consumer society, and the feelings of shame associated with nudity. To facilitate a happier relationship with the body, they did much more than envisioning better sex: some practised karate, hoping to develop a 'body feeling', some experienced their bodies in therapeutic contexts while yelling, dancing and screaming; others meditated, massaged each other, danced around campfires, or engaged in mutual body painting during alternative camping trips.[64] All of this might sound trivial, but for activists it was part and parcel of an attempt to feel their bodies in a better, fuller way. So when a group of some fifty leftists in Stuttgart went nude swimming in a public pool in the late summer of 1977, just before the wave of terrorism of the German Autumn, much to the amusement of other visitors, they didn't just 'mock workers' or 'waste their energies', as their more traditional comrades charged, but they tried to 'anticipate a concrete social utopia, and had fun'.[65] Amid all the focus on gender and sexuality, this bodily and not just sexual utopia seems to have been lost.

A World for Better Feelings?

Did activists trying to repair their 'broken' selves succeed? Did this emotional work have any impact on intimate relations and sexual practices? And was this a way to change the world, or were these, at best, personal transformations without any consequences on a societal level? Obviously, there isn't a single answer to these questions. At times, such emotional work did yield the feelings that people longed for; personal relations changed, and people did experience their bodies in more wholesome ways. But all too often, it was also immensely frustrating and exhausting. The project of personal self-transformation required people to engage in emotional labour, to constantly reflect on their feelings and to talk about them. Instead of liberating sexual desires, activists effectively imposed new norms and restrictions, only for those to be challenged in turn.

The effects of these emotional politics reached beyond individuals. Working on the self became a new imperative, not only in leftist scenes. Ideas and practices that initially had a deviant and subversive dimension became mainstream, losing their rebellious potential. Nowadays, we all have to be happy, and if we aren't, we need to seek professional advice; we need to express our true feelings and find our authentic selves. This at least is what a barrage of advertisements and promotional emails about personal well-being and emotional health suggest, like a recent advertisement on my Facebook feed that invited me to practise yoga and 'write the book of your own life' in order to find happiness and my true self (for only a couple of hundred Euros). All of this gives us reason to remain hesitant about uncritically celebrating attempts to liberate feelings and desires. Yet, it shouldn't keep us from seeing real changes either. It has become possible to experiment with bodily pleasures, to talk about feelings, and to imagine different forms of intimate relationships – the current fascination with polyamory being only the latest example. The new emotional politics isn't always easy, but arguably it can mean more freedom, at least for some.

In Search of a Different Reality:
Alternative Spirituality

In April 1978, Michel Foucault made a trip to Japan. He was going to meet Omori Sogen, a Zen Master leading the International Zen Meditation Centre at the Seionji Temple in Uenohara, where Foucault hoped to learn about the philosophy of Buddhism, but even more so about the 'practice of Zen, its rules and regulations'. The spiritualist practices of Zen intrigued Foucault because they sought 'the dissolution of the individual', his biographer Didier Eribon notes. This contrasted markedly with Christian spirituality, which, in Foucault's view, was all about grasping 'the foundation of an individual's soul'. He even tried to meditate himself, to sit and breathe correctly, according to the instructions given by Master Sogen, but found it quite difficult. For a thinker like Foucault, who questioned 'Western rationality and its limits', Zen Buddhism provided a fascinating alternative, even though it was also 'a puzzle extremely difficult to decipher', Eribon writes.[1]

Foucault's brief flirtation with Zen Buddhism was part of a broader phenomenon. Across Europe, members of countercultural scenes shared a profound scepticism about the wisdom of what they identified as Western scientific or technocratic rationality, including scientific Marxism, which – in the words of West German militant and author Dieter Duhm – wasn't able to grasp the 'extrasocial dimension of life', its 'cosmic and natural side'.[2] In their minds, a more holistic understanding of the world was necessary that would allow people to reconnect to both the natural world and to their bodies, something the cold, critical and analytical gaze of rationalism could not provide.

Dissatisfied with endless discussions about Marxist theory in the 1960s and 1970s, (former) activists instead devoured the works of

Carlos Castañeda about his alleged encounters with Navajo healer Don Juan (that his stories were most likely fabricated did not quite matter).[3] They found inspiration in reports about American Indians and their teaching that were critical of technology.[4] And they practised Zen and yoga, which facilitated, or so they hoped, 'experiences of illumination', to quote Duhm again, during which 'the Ego dissolves into an all-embracing foundational ground [*Urgrund*], into a divine self. The boundaries that separate the Ego from its environment no longer exist.'[5]

The fascination with spirituality, with myths and magic, is perhaps one of the strangest, and least studied, facets of protest cultures in post-war Europe. It's impossible to exactly say how widespread a phenomenon this was. Observers in West Germany and in the UK noted how yoga classes, meditation centres, New Age bookstores, and alternative healing practices mushroomed in the 1980s. In the Federal Republic, estimates put the number of people doing yoga in the mid-1980s at about 100,000, with another 20,000 attempting to learn the particularly demanding practice of Zen meditation. Magazines like *esotera* in West Germany or *Mind Body Spirit* and *Kindred Spirit* in the UK reached tens of thousands of readers, and American New Age authors such as Marilyn Ferguson and Fritjof Capra became bestsellers. Even across the Iron Curtain, hippies in the Soviet Union turned to spiritualist ideas and practices – again, notably, yoga.[6]

To make sense of this alternative spirituality and its appeal, we need to turn our gaze away from the leading intellectuals whose works have become canonical. We need to engage with authors outside of academia, who are nowadays mostly forgotten, but who enjoyed tremendous success in the 1970s and 1980s. Some of these bestselling books were published by mainstream presses and found a readership far beyond leftist circles, while others came out with small left-wing publishers and reached a more politically inclined audience. This was particularly the case for West Germany, where spiritualist ideas were more explicitly linked with leftist politics than elsewhere in Europe.

The world of these books is a strange one. In the works of authors like Swiss folklorist Sergius Golowin or West German Hans Peter Duerr, we encounter a dreamscape populated with healers and sorcerers, werewolves, nymphs and other mysterious creatures.[7] Why did such imaginary worlds speak to people who had previously been dedicated Marxists? How would acquiring the secretive knowledge promised by books about Indian American folklore, practising yoga or moving to an Indian ashram offer the liberation they had once sought through class struggle? To answer these questions, this chapter first investigates the different, supposedly more holistic understanding of the world that spiritual knowledge promised. The chapter then explores the 'different politics' leftist believers in New Age ideas called for, a politics for which once again the body played a fundamental role, before turning to real and imagined spiritual escapes. And what, we might wonder, did this fascination with myths and fairy tales, with yoga and meditation, have to do with a struggle for a better world? After all, this search for spiritual enlightenment was far removed from any conventional form of protesting. There was no taking to the streets with banners, organizing strikes or squatting vacant buildings; it wasn't quite a *struggle*. We could describe it more aptly as an attempt to develop a different relationship to the world, or even to escape from the world into a different reality. If this would result in a better world, it would be through a process of self-transformation rather than a confrontation with established authorities.

Beyond the Scientific Mind: Holistic Understandings of the World

The history of global protest movements since the 1960s read as a myth – that's how we might summarize one of these obscure and strange texts that heralded a different, spiritual politics: the introduction to the anthology *The Return of the Imaginary: Fairy Tales, Magic, Mysticism, Myth. The Beginnings of a Different Politics* (1981). Its co-author, Herbert Röttgen, was one of the most prolific writers in Munich's leftist scene during the 1970s. Among other things, he had founded the influential Trikont publishing house, which made West German readers familiar with struggles in the so-called Third World.[8] Yet by the late 1970s, Röttgen's thinking took a mythological turn: in a book called *Volcano Dances* (1978), he made a case for the rebellious power of myths,[9] then he renamed the publishing house Trikont Dianus (and later himself Victor Trimondi). *The Return of the Imaginary* was programmatic in this regard. It assembled contributors (all men – women were promised a separate volume that never materialized) ranging from long-term leftist activists such as Klaus Bernd Vollmar and Peter Mosler to German New Age thinkers such as Arnold Graf Keyserling or Sergius Golowin, who all embarked on an 'expedition' that would lead them, the introduction promised, 'beyond the technical, abstract world [*Diesseits*] into the realm of a sensual afterworld [*Jenseits*]'.[10]

In the introduction to the volume, the story of the global new left becomes a fairy tale. Across the world, rebellious youth had celebrated mythological heroes, the text claimed: Ernesto Che Guevara, the proud and courageous warrior from the West, whose image adorned countless walls, T-shirts and forearms, and Ho Chi Minh, the 'far-Eastern sage'. A third man joined them, Mao Zedong, and together, they formed a triumvirate of the 'party of order within the revolutionary camp of North America and Europe'. But there was also a 'revolutionary party of disorder', born in 'sunny California', whose 'gods were Jack Kerouac, William S. Burroughs, Allen Ginsberg and Timothy Leary', all authors of the American counterculture. And, like the party of order, this revolutionary party of disorder had both ugly and beautiful children, hippies but also drug addicts. When the two parties entered a marriage, they produced 'strange beasts with two heads' (whatever that might mean), like Herbert Marcuse and Rudi Dutschke or Autonomia Operaia and Lotta Continua in Italy, the latter managing to 'carry the vibration fields of chaos into the working class'. But soon enough, the revolutionary body dissolved into a plethora of diverse movements, ranging from spiritual sects to gay and lesbian movements. With this fragmentation of the movement, 'everything seemed to be over'.

'But then came the strangers,' the tale continues. They descended from the past: 'from the lonely refugia of the Rocky Mountains, from the jungles of the Amazonas, from the canyons of the Himalayas, from Australian deserts, the hills of Kashmir, and the shores of the Niger'. Like the shepherds and wise women who saved the fairytale realm from peril, 'Tibetan monks, American Indian tribal leaders, Jamaican bards' appeared in Europe, sometimes in a spectacular fashion, manifested in the concerts of Bob Marley, sometimes in 'utter seclusion', as in Buddhist cloisters in Provence, France. With the help of 'mind-expanding drugs' and 'techniques of meditation', they made the 'white youth of Babylon' appreciative of 'extralogical events'. Their teachings in the form of images and allegories offered a profound insight: they showed that it was possible 'to dance in the heights and depths of the soul – rather than being torn to shatters between them', and that it was necessary to respect 'both demons and gods'. They 'revealed the deepest of all secrets: that oppositions fall together'. Only then, when history and myth, dream and reality, progressive and conservative politics, male and female would all be reconciled, could 'a new world begin'.[11]

Even within leftist circles, such mythical thinking was unusual. Röttgen certainly had a point that figures like Che Guevara and Ho Chi Minh became heroic saints for an entire generation of protestors around the world (see Chapter 7).[12] More importantly, the text provides a sense of what motivated the turn towards spiritualist ideas in some quarters of the radical left. The questions of power, and how to resist it, that had been of such concern to the critical intellectuals discussed in Chapter 5 receded into the background. Instead, these activists raised a question that was even more fundamental: how would it be possible to know anything about this world and humans' place in it?

Echoing Duhm, Röttgen suggested that pure logic and scientific reason failed in this regard. Such critiques were common within countercultural milieus.[13] Rational thinking, with its tendency to measure, categorize and fragment everything, came at a high price, its critics argued. Physicist Fritjof Capra, for example, claimed that 'retreating into our minds, we have forgotten how to "think" with our bodies, how to use them as agents of knowing'.[14] And this disconnect meant that people were equally incapable of relating to the natural world. As Doug Boyd wrote in *Rolling Thunder: Experiences with a Shaman of the New Indian Movement* (1974), 'the people of this society have alienated themselves from the trees, birds, insects, from all the animals and plants and even the weather. That is why they are so alienated from their own self.'[15]

If the issue was that people had alienated themselves from nature, then they needed to reconnect with it. It was necessary to gain an 'intuitive knowledge' of the world, to quote Capra, 'based on direct, nonintellectual experience of reality arising in an expanded state of awareness'.[16] This is what the fairy tales, the teachings of American Indians and a variety of so-called Eastern religions, including Buddhism, Hinduism and Taoism, all promised to provide. They offered insights into a different or extraordinary reality inaccessible to the scientific mind, or so their European admirers thought. 'Mystical states', American New Age author Marilyn Ferguson wrote, quoting late nineteenth-century psychologist William James, 'seem to those who experience them to be states of knowledge. They are insights into the depths of truth unplumbed by the discursive intellect.'[17]

American Indians in particular seemed to be able to communicate with the natural world in a way that remained closed off to Western society. Stan Steiner's *The Vanishing White Man*, for example, contrasted American Indians who were able to 'listen to a foaming steam that is sounding soft in his ears' with 'white men' who would only think about making the 'damned water' work for them with dykes and turbines.[18] Along similar lines, Doug Boyd claimed that the American Indian shaman Rolling Thunder communicated with the herbs he used to heal patients. For Rolling Thunder, Boyd reported, the entire world, with all its animals, plants, rivers and mountains, was a 'gigantic body of a conscious, fighting and living being'.[19] And just like human beings, this natural organism had fallen ill and required curing. While this might sound like a plea for environmental protection, this alone would not be enough. Without a 'spiritual connection' to earth, argued Steiner, saving it would be impossible.[20]

Arguably the most widely read works presenting the (alleged) secret knowledge of American Indians were those by Carlos Castañeda. In a series of books published between 1968 and 1993 (the majority of them came out in the 1970s), Castañeda described how he came to know a Navajo healer named Don Juan and then became his student. With the help of Don Juan, Castañeda undertook a journey that enabled him to overcome the limitations of the rational mind and to enter a 'separate reality', as his second book was titled, that was accessible with the support of 'allies' and 'helpers', namely hallucinogenic drugs like peyote. Critics quickly noted that Don Juan probably never existed and that the stories Castañeda told were most likely utterly fictional. But this didn't make the books any less popular with countercultural readers longing for the seemingly authentic teachings of an American Indian sorcerer. Exactly what he was teaching, though, remained somewhat obscure. After all, this was the very point. It was a secretive knowledge that could not be grasped by constant questioning and critical thinking, as Castañeda tried to, very much to the amusement of (fictional) Don Juan. A 'man of knowledge', Don Juan argued, 'lives by acting, not by thinking about acting, nor by thinking about what he will think when he has finished acting'. Only the active life would enable him to genuinely see the world.[21]

Stories about American Indians, fictional or not, were not the only source of inspiration for those looking for a different understanding of reality. Mythological stories and folk tales from Europe and elsewhere in the world equally found avid readers in countercultural scenes. One of the most wide-ranging books in this regard was Hans Peter Duerr's *Dreamtime: Concerning the Boundary between Wilderness and Civilization* (1978). Like many others, Duerr was critical of scientific thinking that saw the world as 'disenchanted' and 'devoid of colours, of a voice, of ears'. Scientists, he charged, would dissect and categorize everything, cleansing whatever they looked at: 'The things cry, but the researcher does not see any tears.' By discussing various traditions dealing with shamans, werewolves, witches and other mystical creatures, he hoped to recover a way of grasping aspects of the world hidden from the scientific gaze. In particular, Duerr highlighted instances of transgressions, like exuberant Dionysian orgies in ancient Greece, or the 'flaring up of sensuality' in late medieval times, when, Duerr claimed, the social order was unsettled and 'life turned more sensual, passionate, looser and intense'.[22] In Duerr's view, such moments were a return to an original state of being, in which the 'separation of things' collapsed and the 'inner wilderness' buried by civilization might be laid bare. In that sense, Duerr suggested, archaic traditions had a richer view of the world than the modern scientific mind, which was always keen to maintain boundaries and separations.[23]

The celebration of intuitive or even bodily knowledge often had a profoundly gendered dimension. Drawing on the Chinese traditions of *yin* and *yang*, Fritjof Capra, for example, characterized *yang* as 'masculine, demanding, aggressive, competitive, rational, analytical', contrasting it with *yin* as 'feminine, contractive, responsive, cooperative, intuitive, synthesizing'.[24] The domination of rationality and the exploitation of nature, he argued, went hand in hand with the subordination of women in modern society. The coming New Age would therefore herald the final demise of patriarchy and the rise of 'feminist spirituality . . . based on awareness of the oneness of all living forms'.[25] Along similar lines, Marilyn Ferguson praised the growing 'power of women' as the 'powder keg of our time', whose '*yin* perspective will push out the boundaries of the old *yang* paradigm'.[26] And in the women's movement, some feminists came to praise witchcraft as a subversive and anti-patriarchal 'religion of the people'. Witchcraft, argued Anne Kent Rush in her 1976 book *Moon, Moon*, 'was based on the interconnectedness of all things' and respected 'all elements of the life process'. It offered a holistic understanding of the world challenging the 'segmentation' that formed the 'basis of patriarchal socialism or capitalism'.[27]

The search for spiritual enlightenment frequently went hand in hand with a longing for 'roots'. After all, modern society seemed to be fundamentally uprooted, restless and on the move, whereas American Indians and Tibetan monks seemed to still possess an intimate connection to the land. Thus, in their efforts to connect to their own roots, activists became interested in local myths, traditions and dialects, and tried to foster connections to peasants despite their often conservative attitudes, as we've seen in the anti-militaristic and anti-nuclear power struggles in Larzac and Wyhl. Hippies in the Soviet Union were similarly not only fascinated by Eastern spirituality, but also, and increasingly during the 1980s, drawn to conservative Russian Orthodoxy.[28] Hippie Alexander Ogorodnikov, for example, claimed that only Christ, and not Buddha, would be able to form a 'new society', which at the same time would be a 'return to the true roots of the Russian national soul'.[29]

For West German authors Nicola Schulz and Karl Heinz Albers, both veterans of the student movement, rediscovering the 'history of neighbourhoods and villages' was a way to resist 'further uprooting'. In the old days, they believed, peasants felt their 'heavy arms and legs' after working on the 'crumbly, hard, loamy, damp, rough, soft and stony' earth. The physical pain connected them to the soil they worked on. Modern agricultural machinery, however, had severed these connections. Nowadays, a farmer sitting on his '110 PS John Deere tractor' no longer sensed the earth, and would not even notice the 'hare cowering in a furrow' while killing it.[30] Those were decidedly conservative positions. Indeed, Schulz and Albers argued that progressive politics had to preserve positive elements of what existed, a position that many in the environmental and peace movements shared.[31]

For many on the left, this was a dangerous move. All the talk about myths reminded them about fascism, which had, of course, celebrated its own national myths as well. Authors such as Röttgen and Thurn were well aware of such critiques. But, they countered, the essence of fascism wasn't nature and romanticism, but technology; not the folk song, but the *Volkswagen*, not the German forest, but the *Autobahn*.[32]

Changing the Body, Changing the World: A Different Politics

How were these texts, obscure and difficult to understand – tellingly, one reader of Castañeda commented that she was now able to make sense of the texts, but could not convey her insights to others via language – part of a struggle for a better world? They usually didn't challenge political authorities, they didn't call for protests or demonstrations, and they didn't imagine a different social or political organization. In any conventional sense of the word, this alternative spirituality wasn't political, and indeed many on the left made exactly this point. Adherents of spiritualist thinking such as Röttgen, however, believed that myths and magic could pave the way to a 'different politics'.[33]

At the heart of this alternative politics was a belief in the need for a personal self-transformation. 'All revolutions begin within,' wrote Marilyn Ferguson.[34] An 'inner spirituality' and 'harmony in ourselves', many believed, would also yield a more harmonious and peaceful world.[35] The starting point was a profound feeling of alienation from nature, understood as both the inner self and the natural world. Modern human beings, Swami Vishnudevananda claimed in a popular yoga book in 1975, had become 'physical and psychical wrecks', torn apart by the 'demand of performance society'.[36]

Changing the world therefore had to begin with undoing this fragmentation. It required healing both body and soul, which meant for believers in New Age ideas making them whole again, and overcoming any separation between the two. The exploration of the inner self would also lead, Röttgen and Thurn posited, to a 'rediscovery of the inner wildness' and an ability to 'communicate with plants and animals'.[37] To give an example, Austrian futurologist Robert Jungk told the editors of *The Return of the Imaginary* a story about an American soldier who had fought in Vietnam. The GI had got stuck in the jungle, on a giant tree, where he had to learn to survive in the wilderness and to 'listen to the voices' (which voices remains unsaid). It was a transformative experience. For the first time, he said, he felt like a 'real human being'. After that experience, he was no longer able to kill and deserted from the army. For Röttgen and Thurn, the story demonstrated that the 'rediscovery of the senses has a revolutionary force'.[38]

The site for this personal and political transformation was the body. No longer did the revolution happen in assembly halls, one commentator noted, but in people's individual bodies.[39] Jungk, for example, told his interlocutors how he had wandered into the lonely nocturnal woods, listening to animals and, feeling anxious, how he had sensed the wind and the morning thaw on his skin. Such sensual experiences allowed him to return to his 'origins'. Other authors praised a variety of practices that would repair the fragmented body, ranging from meditation to martial arts and acupuncture. And those who were able to heal their own bodies would also be capable of healing the entire planet.[40] This was protest as a sort of (physical and psychic) therapeutic project.

The most prominent practice promising to bring a sense of wholeness and being one with the universe was yoga. New Age believers and hippies across the Iron Curtain all turned to yoga as a way to achieve the 'boundlessness of the self', as Vishnudevananda wrote.[41] In strikingly similar terms, Romanian yogi Gregorian Bivolaru declared in 1972 during an interrogation by the secret police (who had taken an interest in him because he had tried to import illegal material from Western Europe, including literature about yoga but also sex films and magazines): 'I drew myself toward this mysterious science [of yoga, because of] the fact that it has an ultimate goal, a total annihilation of instincts, preaching the idea of universal love which opens the path toward the unknown places of the unconscious.'[42]

Reaching this yogic goal required work on the mind and on the body. With the correct bodily exercises, it would be possible to 'liberate the spirit for higher insights'.[43] An article in *esotera*, for example, promised that sitting correctly led 'to the self'. It instructed readers how to position their legs in order to gain a 'sense of security', how to bend the spine 'as a tree of life raised to the light', how to hold the chin, where to look and what to do with their tongue.[44] Other texts provided guidance on interior design, holistic nutrition and particularly the right way of breathing: deep, calm and abdominal. As a 1970 article about human beings as holistic entities in *esotera* put it: 'Breathing creates the connection between body and soul.'[45] Another author claimed that by focusing on his breathing (*ganz bei meinem Atem*, literally 'being totally with my breathing'), he turned into a circle 'that is constantly opening and closing, that unifies the feminine and the masculine, that unites death and life inside it'.[46]

On the eastern side of the Iron Curtain, Soviet hippies, too, practised yoga and meditated in an attempt to reach a state of *kaif*, an emotional and spiritual experience of leaving the dull, grey world of Soviet socialism behind (listening to music and taking drugs could yield a similar result). As in the West, the spiritual experience was profoundly personal, but in the Soviet Union, it also challenged cultural and emotional norms. In light of hippies' refusal of the socialist ideals of work and discipline, it's perhaps not surprising that authorities looked at yoga and meditation with suspicion. To learn about the traditions and techniques of yoga, Soviet hippies had to rely on anything they happened to find in libraries or that circulated semi-legally in samizdat format. This semi-secrecy gave a particular allure to such texts. A former hippie in Estonia, for example, recalled how a classmate handed her a handwritten notebook, describing it as a 'secret text' she had to return the very next day. She stayed awake all night, full of excitement, copying out the notebook, only to wonder later what about its content – 'regular yoga, breathing techniques, diet recommendations' – would be considered secret.

It is difficult to say what these attempts to connect with the body and reach a higher level of consciousness actually yielded; any results are not exactly quantifiable. Not surprisingly, New Age publications emphasized positive experiences. A participant of a spiritual group experience at the Findhorn community in Scotland reported about an 'ecstatic feeling of freedom' when people were able to 'let go of their long-standing fears of being open to others'. For her, a 'deep and timeless desire for unification with others was fulfilled, even though it was only for an hour or a day'.[47] Another woman explained how the 'meditative dancing workshops' she organized fostered a sense of community. The folkloristic circle dances did not require any training and everyone could simply participate. The dancing became increasingly 'steady, harmonious and calm', and thereby made participants feel equally calm and intense. 'You feel it: these original forms [of dancing] contain a highly intensive meditative element.'[48]

Of course, we should be careful not to take such claims at face value. For one thing, those who might have felt bored or frustrated in their attempts to meditate or practise yoga would have hardly written about it. And focusing on the 'liberating' experience, the sense of bodily wholeness and connectedness with others, would overlook the disciplining element of those practices: their followers had to abide by very detailed instructions about bodily postures, breathing and eating. It was hard and sometimes painful work on the body. With Michel Foucault, we might consider yoga and similar practices part of a peculiar regime of governmentality with a set of informal but strict rules and expectations that produced a specific form of (bodily) subjectivity.[49] That said, experiences of *kaif,* or of being one with one's body and the universe, were no less real or meaningful to those who felt them.

Spiritual Escapes, Real and Imagined

In 1979, popular West German publishing house rororo published a book called *Fully Relaxed in the Here and Now*, written by Swami Satyananda.[50] It promised readers a 'chief witness', speaking on behalf of young people 'searching for salvation through self-transformation'. Satyananda was the name political journalist Jörg Andrees Elten had taken after he had become a disciple of Indian guru Bhagwan Shree Rajneesh; the book is an account of how this happened. He had gone to India planning to interview the Indian prime minister, to write about the Communist Party of Western Bengal, and about Rajneesh's ashram, which was by that time attracting increasing attention in Western media. But then he visited the ashram and participated in an encounter group, a therapeutic technique seeking to lay bare aggressions and fears. In practice, it meant yelling, verbal abuse and brutal physical and sexual violence. For Elten, it was a transformative experience. He decided to become a Sannyasin, that is, a follower of Bhagwan.

Satyananda was not the only Westerner who travelled to India and found spiritual enlightenment. Already in 1968, the Beatles had famously visited India, where they spent time in the ashram of Maharishi Mahesh Yogi, the founder of transcendental meditation – though they left in anger and disappointment after rumours that Maharishi had sexually molested women in the band's entourage.[51] Most influential in Western alternative circles of the 1970s and 1980s, however, was the Rajneesh movement.

Founded by Indian philosopher Chandra Mohan Jain, who had renamed himself Bhagwan Shree Rajneesh after a spiritual awakening, the movement attracted between 200,000 and 300,000 followers worldwide. Rajneesh criticized what he considered the ossification and empty ritualism of existing organized religions, especially Hinduism, as well as the restrictive sexual mores in India. His own teachings were a wild and 'postmodern potpourri' (Hugh B. Urban) of religious and philosophical ideas that incorporated elements of Eastern traditions as well as Western philosophies and psychology. He drew on the writings of Wilhelm Reich and his ideas of a sexual revolution (discussed in Chapter 5), even calling Reich a 'modern tantrika'.[52] In 1974, Rajneesh found an ashram in Pune in Western India that quickly attracted numerous visitors from Western countries. By 1981, he moved his community to a ranch in Oregon, United

States, but was expelled in 1985. In 1987, he returned to India, where he died three years later.[53]

Rajneesh's teaching proved immensely appealing. Already in 1974, West German followers established a Bhagwan commune in the Bavarian town of Margarethenried; by 1981, 126 Rajneesh Meditation Centres existed throughout Europe, with forty-three in West Germany, twenty-two in the United Kingdom and even one in Yugoslavia.[54] Dressed all in orange and red, the Sannyasin quickly attracted public attention (and sometimes concern, or even hostility). But Rajneesh didn't only provide an alternative to industrial society. More significantly, his teachings offered leftist students an opportunity to get away from the 'endless drivel of sterile and pointless debates about strategies and ideology'. One student going by the name Swami G. recalled the first time he had participated in an encounter group: 'I've never experienced that people yelled, cried, laughed, danced in a group . . . I only knew the depressive and fusty political scene at university, where one after the other turned grey.'[55]

Given such remarks, many on the left considered the Sannyasin to be apolitical and merely interested in personal fulfilment. Statements by the increasingly eccentric Rajneesh himself, who praised material wealth (he later owned as many ninety-three Rolls-Royce limousines),[56] nuclear deterrence and, in an interview with German magazine *Der SPIEGEL*, even Adolf Hitler, didn't make the movement look particularly left-leaning either.[57] But supporters of Rajneesh saw this differently. Disempowering the economic elite and transferring power from one class to another wouldn't save the world, Elten argued: 'Real progress can happen only if millions of individuals change their consciousness.' That's what happened in Pune, he claimed, and that was why 'Marx, Lenin, Mao or Che Guevara' were not the Sannyasins' role models, but 'Wilhelm Reich, George Gurdjieff, Carlos Castañeda and Erich Fromm accompany them on their way.'[58] For leftists who felt frustrated about endless, fruitless debates, the Rajneesh movement offered an alternative way to achieve change.

For Westerners trying to drop out of consumer society, India was the most popular destination, but not the only one. Others travelled to remote Greek islands, Ireland and Jamaica to find spiritual guidance and opportunities to reconnect with local mystical traditions.[59] (Interestingly, few people from Western Europe seem to have travelled to the United States to actually meet American Indians, despite their functioning as a role model for a different relationship with nature.) East of the Iron Curtain, it was, of course, much more difficult, if not impossible, to reach faraway destinations like India. But Soviet hippies nevertheless did their best to escape: every year between 1978 and 1987, they gathered for a summer camp at Gauia, near Riga, where they could, among other things, get baptized, meditate and practise yoga.[60]

Countercultural scenes in Eastern Europe also had their own, local gurus. In Bucharest, Gregorian Bivolaru, known as Guru Grig, became the centre of a group of yogis during the 1980s, always under the watchful eyes of the state's security apparatus. Like Western New Agers, his teachings, too, drew on a variety of sources, reaching from Eastern traditions such as the Bhagavad Gita and Vivekananda, to European thinkers such as St Augustine and the anthropologist Mircea Eliade. He taught his followers yoga – naturally – but he also took them to nudist beaches in the remote town of Costineşti on the shores of the Black Sea, believing that with their skin exposed to the sun, their bodies would connect and heal more easily.[61] And in Estonia, Mihkel Tamm, also known as Michael Rama Tamm, an expert on Sanskrit, yoga and meditation, attracted hippies from across the Soviet Union.[62] Just as moving to an ashram in Pune seemed to offer an opportunity to leave the permanent competition of Western capitalism behind,[63] so too did practising yoga and meditating in Eastern Europe open the gates to an 'imaginary elsewhere' beyond the dull daily reality of life under socialism.

A New Age?

It would be easy to point out that the world did not become more harmonious or cooperative, as believers in the New Age had anticipated. Rather than changing the capitalist world, alternative spirituality was quickly appropriated by it, appealing less to drop-outs than to managers and consultants; one organization, called Decision Development, even promised to transform managers into 'spiritual warriors'.[64] If it once had seemed that living a spiritual life would make a career in capitalist society impossible,[65] the reverse seems to have become true: spirituality became another way to make money. Nowadays, every local gym is offering yoga classes, while meditation instructors promise to help with work-related stress and anxiety issues. New Ageism has lost its countercultural dimension.[66]

Perhaps this was a predictable development. Already in the early 1980s leftist critics argued that the search for spirituality was any-thing but subversive, instead effectively stabilizing capitalist society. With the help of the Sannyasins, Joachim Bruhn tartly remarked, capitalism was turning into a giant 'consciousness-raising group, an all-embracing and permanent encounter'. A veritable 'dictatorship of friendliness' had formed, as if merely being nice would change society.[67] Other leftists even considered the submission to gurus such as Rajneesh to be essentially fascist because of the absolute obedience and loyalty he allegedly demanded of his followers.[68] Should we, in light of these developments and critiques, consider the search for alternative spirituality a form of protesting? Did breathing exercises and upright sitting, reading about sorcerers and folk tales in the hope of gaining a more holistic understanding of the universe make the world a better place?[69] Or did it just create a façade of inner happiness while leaving oppressive and exploitive social and political structures untouched?

As tempting as it might be to concur with critics, it is arguably the question itself that is posed in a problematic way. Believers in alter-native spirituality never wanted to contribute to a *struggle* for a better world. After all, they hoped to move beyond such confronta-tional politics. For at least some of those who read Castañeda, who meditated and practised yoga, or who travelled to Pune, to Gauia or Costineşti, these were paths into a different – and better – reality, a world of inner harmony and emotional intensity. What this did to the other, as it were normal, world they left behind was of secondary importance, even if some hoped that a personal self-transformation would ultimately also change the world. For those who found meaning and fulfilment in new spirituality, it was no small thing.

Coda: A Peaceful Revolution

Bringing Down Communism in Eastern Europe: The Revolutions of 1989

East Berlin, 9 November 1989, 6 p.m. The Central Committee of the GDR's ruling party, the Socialist Unity Party (Sozialistische Einheitspartei Deutschlands, SED), was holding a press conference. Günter Schabowski, recently made speaker of the government, took the lead with an announcement. For weeks, there had been protests throughout the GDR, demanding freedom of travel. In the meanwhile, thousands of GDR citizens were leaving the country via Czechoslovakia and Hungary for the West. For an hour, the press conference went on without anything of great interest being said. Then Italian journalist Riccardo Ehrman enquired about travelling regulations. Schabowski looked left and right, appeared to be a bit uncertain, made some general comments about the renewal of society and finally said: 'Anyway, today, as far as I know . . . a decision has been made.' Amid many 'uhs', he explained that the Central Committee had decided to put a rule in place that would allow GDR citizens to leave the country directly to the Federal Republic via GDR border crossings.

Journalists wondered: when would the new legislation apply? Immediately? Schabowski scratched his ear. He started reading a sheet of paper. 'Well, comrade,' he addressed a journalist,

I have been informed that such a message has already been circulated today. It should actually be in your possession. So private trips abroad can be applied for without the existence of prerequisites, reasons for travel or [family] relationships. Approvals are given at short notice . . . Permanent departures can be made via all border crossing points from the GDR to the FRG.

Again, a reporter wanted to know when the new rules would apply. Taking another look at the paper, Schabowski replied: 'As far as I know, this applies right now, immediately.'[1]

From his muddled sentences, Schabowski seemed confused, though it's not quite clear if he was just putting on a show, or if he was genuinely overwhelmed by the developments. Probably, he didn't understand the full implications of what he had just said. But citizens in the GDR, and especially in East Berlin, understood. It would be possible to permanently leave the country, unconditionally and immediately. Effectively, it meant the end of the Iron Curtain.

The press conference was broadcast live by GDR television. Within minutes, a crowd gathered at the checkpoint at Bornholmer Straße in Prenzlauer Berg, East Berlin. Border guards didn't quite know how to handle the situation. They had not been informed about the new regulations that would apply immediately. By 9 p.m., the crowd had swollen to thousands of people who demanded the opening of the borders. Officers on site decided to give in. At first, they asked people to present their ID cards and stamped them with a notice of permanent emigration from the GDR. But most didn't care. An hour and a half later, border guards couldn't control the situation any more and simply allowed anyone to cross. Thousands flooded into West Berlin. At other places in the city, the checkpoints were also opened. Both West and East Berliners flocked to the Wall. At the famous Checkpoint Charlie in central Berlin, West Berliners chanted 'Let us in', while East Berliners responded, 'Let us out!' A festive atmosphere reigned in the streets. People cheered, danced, climbed on the Wall, opened bottles of champagne; friends who hadn't seen each other for years could finally hug one another. After more than twenty-eight years, the Berlin Wall was crumbling.[2]

It was not only the Berlin Wall that fell. Throughout Eastern Europe, communist regimes collapsed in rapid succession amid huge popular protests. These dramatic events were the culmination of a process that had been going on for years. The financial pressures communist economies were facing had become unbearable, not least due to the Soviet Union's military engagement in Afghanistan.

At the same time, economic growth in the West was clearly out-pacing that of the Eastern bloc, in particular with regard to the development of new technologies, namely microelectronics. When Mikhail Gorbachev became general secretary of the Communist Party of the Soviet Union in March 1985, and thus the country's new leader, he understood that, without serious reforms, the commun-ist societies of Eastern Europe, and in particular the Soviet Union itself, would be doomed. Realizing that the immense costs of the arms race put an unsustainable burden on the country, Gorbachev engaged in disarmament negotiations with the United States. He also initiated a reform programme known as *glasnost*, which encour-aged open and honest discussion, and *perestroika* to decentralize the economy. For communist hardliners elsewhere in Europe, such as Erich Honecker, general secretary of the SED's central committee, those reforms were profoundly worrying, especially because Gorbachev indicated that the Soviet Union wouldn't intervene militarily, as it had in Czechoslovakia in 1968, to protect allied gov-ernments. In short, communist regimes were quickly losing their authority.[3]

But the end of communism in Eastern Europe wasn't merely a collapse, an implosion or dissolution of state power. It was a revolu-tion, or more precisely a series of revolutions in different national contexts. They were broad, popular uprisings.[4] Pictures show people celebrating and dancing in the streets. It was a moment full of collective joy and effervescence, when democratically reforming socialism seemed possible.[5] In what follows, I explore these joyful revolutions in Poland, the GDR and Czechoslovakia, the sites of the most seismic protests. The focus on the popular movements is not to suggest that economic or political developments at the top, notably in the Soviet Union, were not important. On the contrary, without the regimes' authority waning, and especially without Gorbachev's reform policies, the revolutions might not have been successful, and they would hardly have remained as peaceful as they were. Yet, my interest here is not in governments and economies, but in the popular uprisings, the sense of joy they created and the visions for a better world that people developed, even if those did not materialize.

Poland: A Negotiated Revolution

Overthrowing communism had taken ten years in Poland, ten months in Hungary and ten weeks in the GDR, British journalist Timothy Garton Ash famously quipped while having drinks with Czech writer Václav Havel on 23 November 1989 in East Berlin. Perhaps Czechoslovakians would need only ten days, he mused.[6]

Garton Ash had a point. To trace the origins of the 1989 revolutions, particularly in Poland, we do need to go back by at least a decade to 1979, when Polish cardinal Karol Wojtyła was elected Pope and became John Paul II.[7] Arguably, we even need to go back further into the 1970s. Throughout these years, workers had repeatedly gone on strike to protest against price hikes of consumer goods, as decreed by the government, which needed to repay the foreign debt it had incurred since the early 1970s, when it had had to borrow money to cover rapidly rising oil prices.[8] Usually, the regime put a quick end to such uprisings, at times using deadly force, while also making concessions. In 1976, for example, the government announced that prices for sugar would go up by 100 per cent, for meat by as much as two-thirds, and for cheese and butter by about a half. In response, workers at the General Walter metallurgy factory in Radom, central Poland, initiated a strike movement that quickly spread throughout the country. And even though the authorities deployed the full force of the state to quell the strike, with at least two workers being killed by security forces, the regime gave in and reversed the price hikes.[9]

Four years later, in July 1980, with no improvement in the economic situation, the government tried again, announcing another – albeit more modest – price increase for meat as well as raising productivity norms for workers in the machine industry, meaning that workers had to work at a faster pace. It didn't take long before workers across the country walked off their jobs to demand compensation through increased wages. Though the regime again gave in and instructed managers to meet the workers' demands, the movement continued to spread.[10] On 14 August 1980, the situation escalated when workers of the Lenin Shipyard in Gdańsk joined the strike movement and a famous unionist stepped onto the stage: electrician Lech Wałęsa. Born in 1943, Wałęsa had worked at the shipyards since 1967, where he played an important role in a strike in 1970 that had ended with several deaths. Above all, he was a gifted speaker, making him popular among workers and a threat to the regime. When he gave a particularly provocative speech in 1976, he lost his job at the shipyards.

That August 1980, his charismatic appearance gave the strike movement a decisive boost. Having learned a lesson from previous years, workers now occupied the premises of the shipyard, where they would be protected against police brutality. 'Factory gates, meant to protect socialist property, now shielded striking workers from the socialist state,' writes historian John Connelly.[11] And their demands went beyond wage increases: they also asked for workers who had lost their jobs for political reasons to be reinstated, and – an issue particularly important to Wałęsa – for a monument to commemorate the four workers killed in the 1970 strike.[12] The strike was taking a political turn.

After only two days, the management of the Lenin shipyards announced that it would meet workers' demands, and Wałęsa declared victory. But as workers were leaving the factory and ending their occupation, a young nurse and editor of an underground newspaper by the name of Alina Pieńkowska intervened. What about the colleagues in smaller factories around Gdańsk, who were still fighting? Had their demands been forgotten, she asked. With the help of three other women, Anna Walentynowicz, Henryka Krzywonos and Ewa Ossowska, Pieńkowska convinced her mostly male colleagues to continue the strike and occupation in support of the larger movement. And as the strike movement grew, moving to nearby Gdynia, the political demands expanded, to include free trade unions, the release of political prisoners, free access to media and better health services.

By late August, some 700,000 workers throughout Poland were on strike. In numerous cities, workers occupied factories, mines and above all shipyards on the Baltic coast. Decorating gates and fences with political slogans and religious as well as nationalist symbols, they transformed worksites into stages where they began to act out an independent, faithful and democratic Poland. In the end, the regime had to negotiate and accept workers' most important demand: an independent trade union, called Solidarność – Solidarity.[13]

But the agreement did not resolve the conflict. The regime did its best to put as many obstacles as possible in the way of the new union: it delayed registering new branches, and occasionally it had its security forces beat up unionists. Solidarność responded with retaliatory warning strikes. Within the government, hardliners prevailed. Shortly after the agreement which had led to the foundation of Solidarność, First Party Secretary Edward Gierek stepped down for 'health reasons'; in July 1981, he was expelled from the party, as hardliners held him responsible for the regime's waning authority. His successor, Stanisław Kania, didn't last long in power. In October, he was forced to resign and make room for the career officer Wojciech Jaruzelski, who was keen to undo the independent trade union. On 13 December 1981, when Solidarność was holding its national congress in Gdańsk, Jaruzelski announced martial law and had the union's leadership detained. Across Poland, the army arrested numerous union cadres. When workers at the Wujek coal mine in Katowice went on strike and clashed with security forces, a special platoon of the riot police opened fire and killed nine workers. After just over a year, the short era of the legal, independent trade union was over.[14]

Despite the government crackdown, Solidarność lived on. The union organized underground, clandestinely producing papers, collecting fees and painting slogans such as 'Solidarity lives!' on walls. Like the Protestant Church in the GDR, the Catholic Church provided a space to express opposition against the regime.[15] People stuck to their Catholic faith and felt fundamentally hostile to the regime's atheism. But how much support the union really enjoyed among workers is difficult to tell, as it avoided a genuine show of strength. When the government announced new price hikes in February 1985, though less severe than in previous years, the union prepared for a brief national strike. Yet, as the government partially stepped back, Wałęsa, by now leading the underground union, called off the strike, the very night before it was supposed to start, thereby leaving the real strength of Solidarność unclear.[16]

At the same time, many unionists, particularly of a younger generation, became increasingly dissatisfied with the limitations of illegal work. They looked for alternative ways to fight the regime. Taking advantage of the government claiming to respect the rule of law, regime critics, for example, started organizing legal support for those facing repression. Official propaganda pretended that there was no organized opposition, only isolated individuals. So when authorities began confiscating cars that were used to distribute illegal papers, lawyers such as Marek Jakubiec representing the spouses of unionists – to whom the cars were officially registered – demanded them back, or at least financial compensation. Spouses, they argued, could not be held responsible for the deeds of their partners. Somewhat stunningly, courts agreed and ruled in favour of such demands; thereafter, confiscations quickly stopped.[17] Others engaged in educating workers, live Father Kazimierz Jancarz in Kraków, founder of the Christian Workers' University. They offered courses, with an official certificate upon completion, on themes ranging from the meaning of solidarity to printing techniques and legal advice.

While Solidarność was the most famous organization, it was not the only force of opposition to the Polish communist regime. In the 1980s, a variety of groups and organizations emerged that engaged in what historian Padraic Kenney has described as a more concrete form of activism, in contrast to the philosophical and ethical debates among intellectual dissidents. Most important among those groups was Freedom and Peace (Wolność i Pokój, or WiP), a campaign group founded in April 1985 in Kraków that provided legal support for protestors facing criminal charges or conscientious objectors to military service.[18] A year later, the nuclear catastrophe at Chernobyl in Ukraine galvanized many people, particularly women, some of them affiliated with WiP, to campaign for more information about the dangers the catastrophe was causing. Alarmed by the risks of nuclear power and concerns for the environment more broadly, WiP and others protested the construction of Poland's first nuclear power plant, at Żarnowiec, a metallurgical plant at Siechnice near Wrocław that threatened the region's clean water supply, and a planned nuclear waste dump at Międzyrzecz.[19] Ultimately, all of these campaigns were successful. Importantly, they brought diverse opponents of the regime together, from conservative Catholics to anarchists of the Alternative Society Movement, providing them with a platform to challenge the regime on specific issues. Along with a variety of underground youth magazines, grassroots campaigns for sobriety and, of course, the cheerful mischief of Orange Alternative encountered in Chapter 4, such protests mobilized Polish society. Their protests, as minor as they might seem, led the way to the wave of 1988 strikes that would initiate the end of communism in Poland.[20]

In February 1988, the government announced another series of price increases for consumer goods. Union leaders on the ground were hesitant about calling for a strike, as they deemed the risk too high. It took courageous individuals to start protests. In the giant steel mills of Nowa Huta in Kraków, it turned out to be a worker with no affiliation to Solidarność who finally pushed the button that automatically stopped all the machinery, thirty-eight-year-old Andrzej Szewczuwianiec. He wasn't even particularly fond of the union, blaming it for 'seven dead years, seven years of people living in dread and fear'.[21] To organize the strike, he did not rely on Solidarność's underground structures, but simply talked to colleagues he trusted. A week later, another worker without union affiliations, thirty-year-old Jan Stanecki, initiated the strike at the shipyards at Gdańsk. On 2 May, he simply stood up in the cafeteria after lunch and asked colleagues not to return to work but instead to discuss the strike at Nowa Huta and more generally the problems the country was facing. He himself did not have much to say, except that the situation was bad, and that Lech Wałęsa would come (who had no idea about this).

The strikes began without any preparation by the union, but Solidarność quickly took control of them. The strike movement, though, did not resemble that of 1980. The strikes remained isolated, as the movement didn't spread to other cities, and the striking workers didn't receive much support from the local population. In 1980, notes Padraic Kenney, 'the factory gates were the hubs of a free society', places where the population gathered and celebrated.[22] Nothing of the sort happened in 1988. At the Gdańsk shipyards, not even a quarter of the workers walked out. Yet, Kenney stresses, this does not mean that the strikes failed. They brought different groups of people opposing the regime together. Student activists from WiP in Gdańsk, for example, who usually inhabited a different social world than the workers, published a flyer – including a drawing of a masturbating elephant – to call for support for the strike: 'If you are not at this moment drunk, stoned on grass or television, or exhausted from love, then listen up: the Gdańsk shipyard and a few other factories are on strike.'[23] Soon, anarchists of the Alternative Society Movement helped with printing leaflets and organizing supplies.

And if the strike wasn't quite the popular neighbourhood festival it had been in 1980, the atmosphere, at least in Gdańsk, turned rather cheerful. At the beginning of the strike, reporter Wojciech Giełżyński noted the 'mournful mewing intonation' of the songs the workers were singing. But then, 'the Mountain Girl' – tellingly, Giełżyński didn't bother to explain who the incarnation of this somewhat mythical figure was – 'appeared, with her own authentic hit song', the Smurf Song. It was a clear allusion to the Orange Alternative in Wrocław, and the blue of the police:

> I'll be here on Saturday, and Sunday too,
> But you Gargamels, you're smurfed, you're through!
> Let them smurf away, let them run
> In hell they're expected, every one!

Boiling water, bubbling tar,
Smurfs will be frying everywhere!
Their blue colour will boil away
Red looks better on them anyway.[24]

Even the riot police in front of the factory gates found the song funny, despite the fact that it was mocking them, and sang along as they memorized the lyrics. This atmosphere does seem to have made a difference. In Kraków, where the mood was much more sober, the police forcefully evicted the striking workers on 5 May. In Gdańsk, the strike ended five days later without violence, when Wałęsa, who had sneaked into the shipyard, gave in and marched out of the shipyard, ahead of his former workmates. Ostensibly, none of the goals had been achieved. Yet, Solidarność now began to organize openly.[25]

It took another series of strikes, first in the coal mines of Silesia, then once again in Gdańsk, in August 1988 for the opposition to accomplish its goals. While the strikes in Silesia were serious, those in Gdańsk turned into another protest-cum-carnival. Workers used Styrofoam to build all kinds of 'weapons' that they aimed at the riot police: an artillery cannon, a tank with a slogan saying, 'Leave your arms at the gate, we want dialogue', a water cannon tied to a hose that could actually shoot a stream of water and a Pershing missile. One day in August, they even staged a riot, with one group of workers acting as 'riot police', fully armed with shields and truncheons made of Styrofoam, the other throwing Styrofoam rocks. It was fun, for them and for the real riot police watching. And it was a way of losing the fear that was so central to the regime's authority.[26]

The protests finally forced the regime into a dialogue with the opposition to restore 'social peace'.[27] In the autumn of 1988, talks began that led to round-table negotiations in February 1989, with the round table symbolizing equality between the different parties. Above all, the discussions revolved around the legalization of Solidarność, with its own press and free, democratic elections. By April, union negotiators had mostly accomplished those goals:

Solidarność was legalized, it could run its newspapers, and on 4 June 1989, there would be semi-free elections, meaning that a third of the seats of the Sejm, the lower house, and all of the seats of a newly created second chamber, the Senate, would be freely elected. For Solidarność, an election at such short notice was a challenge. They had to find candidates and organize a campaign, while the regime could benefit from established structures and probably expected an electoral victory that would bolster its claims to legitimacy. But to everyone's surprise, including the union leaders', Solidarność won all 35 open seats of the Sejm, and 99 of the 100 seats of the Senate.[28]

'It was the first time voters could choose freely. That freedom was used to cross off those who were in power till now,' General Jaruzelski said two days after the election.[29] It was an honest admission of defeat. Communism was coming to an end in Poland. There was still political manoeuvring to be done: negotiations about who would take which post (Solidarność leaders didn't quite feel ready to take responsibilities), and plans to reform the economy. It might sound obvious, and less exciting than the playful strikes with Styrofoam guns – normal politics, after all – but it was a tremendous change in Poland, as normal politics had been absent under communism.

Yet, these negotiations weren't Poland's revolution. That had happened in the streets, in front of and behind factory gates. Young radicals had created the conditions that brought the communist regime down with the protests, happenings and strikes. But they didn't get a seat at the round tables. Those were reserved for the 'constructive opposition', for the serious, respectable older guard of Solidarność leaders.[30]

East Germany: The Fall of the Berlin Wall

In the GDR, there was no opposition comparable with Polish Solidarność, which had millions of members at its apogee. Workers had rebelled once, in June 1953, at first against increased productivity norms and then against the entire leadership of the country. After that, however, the relatively stable economy, effectively subsidized by a West German government that paid for the release of political prisoners with hard currency, kept the working class quiet. Without dramatic price hikes, there were no protests and strikes as we've seen them in the Polish case. Opposition groups typically engaged in peace, environmental and human rights activism, often under the umbrella of the Protestant Church, counting at most a couple of thousand members. Most of them came from the educated middle classes, meaning that the opposition in the GDR lacked a strong working-class element, which was the backbone of its Polish counterpart. And not least, a more significant part of the country's population had bought into the communist ideology. While the Protestant Church could provide the space for voicing critical opinions, there was nothing akin to the deep-seated Catholicism that existed in Poland and that was fundamentally hostile to the regime's atheism.[31]

Nevertheless, by the late 1980s, the critical voices became louder. Many East Germans looked to Gorbachev's reforms in the Soviet Union, hoping that those might initiate change in the GDR as well. But if anything, the reverse was true. Realizing Gorbachev's reforms might undermine its own authority, the regime tried to distance itself from Moscow. When people came to official mass gatherings with unauthorized portraits of the Soviet leader and youths chanted 'Gorbi, Gorbi', security forces intervened violently.[32] In November 1988 the regime also stopped the circulation of the popular Soviet magazine *Sputnik*, which had started publishing articles about the reforms in the Soviet Union and, most disturbingly for the GDR leadership, about problematic aspects of the history of communist parties, such as the role German communists played in the rise of Hitler. For the 190,000 subscribers and purchasers of the magazines, its ban came as a shock. Many submitted petitions in protest to the authorities, and thousands of leaflets demanding a lifting of the ban circulated in secret, passed from hand to hand.[33]

At the same time, street protests became more visible and more daring, particularly in Leipzig, a long-time centre of the opposition. Attendees of peace prayers held each Monday in the St Nicholas Church in the city centre frequently organized small demonstrations. More than once, police arrested protestors, though they were usually released within a few days at the most. For protestors, this was an important lesson: there weren't any serious repercussions. Like the Styrofoam riots in Poland, it helped them lose fear.[34]

Protests continued throughout the spring of 1989. Even the secret police, known as the Stasi, realized that something was changing. 'The population', one internal report stated, 'is showing an increased interest in the development of the overall political situation on the world stage.' Another noted that 'discussions over questions of consumer-goods supply and domestic political events, which arise continually, are increasingly being linked to the events in a series of other socialist countries.' People were 'waiting for perestroika', writer Stefan Heym commented.[35]

Then the regime decided to hold local elections on 7 May 1989 – not free elections, obviously, with candidates of different parties competing against each other, but a charade to create the illusion of public support for socialism. East Germans had been fascinated by elections elsewhere: they followed presidential election campaigns in the US and parliamentary elections in the Federal Republic; voting in the GDR, by contrast, was considered meaningless. All voters could do was approve (or reject) government-sanctioned lists of candidates. In May 1989, things changed. Opposition groups felt energized by the events in Poland and the protests at home. After some debates, they agreed to monitor the counting of the ballots in order to prove election fraud. And they succeeded, particularly in larger cities. According to the regime, 99 per cent of the population had participated in the election, with only 1 per cent rejecting the proposed lists in support of the regime. This made proving the fraud easy. In Dresden, for example, election observers counted 12,379 votes rejecting the lists, out of 104,727 voters in those polling stations they had monitored. According to the official results, however, out of a total of 389,569 votes (opposition groups had not monitored all polling stations), there were only 9,751 opposing votes. This was demonstrably false.[36]

The fraudulent election, argues historian Ilko-Sascha Kowalczuk, had two important consequences. First, it provided the opposition with ammunition to criticize the regime: from then on, every public protest mentioned the fraud. Second, even supporters of the regime were appalled. Why not show the real approval rate, which might be 70 or 80 per cent, they wondered. Why go to such lengths if the results were predetermined? Rather than strengthening the regime's legitimacy, the May 1989 elections undermined it.[37]

Political protest was not the only way of rejecting the communist dictatorship. Many people simply opted to leave the GDR, legally or illegally. In 1989, the number of emigrants swelled. By July, more than 100,000 people had left. Then the summer holidays began, and hundreds of thousands travelled to Hungary. For many, it was the first step to reaching West Germany via Austria. Thousands of GDR citizens flocked to Hungary's western borders, where they hoped to escape the communist bloc into the west. By 11 September 1989, the Hungarian government could no longer resist the pressure and opened its borders for GDR citizens. In the first three days alone, 15,000 East Germans crossed into Austria. Others sought refuge in the West German embassies of Budapest, Prague and, to a lesser extent, Warsaw. (The Federal Republic did not have an embassy in East Berlin, only a 'Permanent Mission', as it did not officially recognize the GDR as a sovereign state.) These were dramatic days. Hygiene conditions in the embassies rapidly deteriorated, particularly in Prague. Hundreds of people were sleeping in improvised tents in the embassy's courtyard, which turned to mud once it started to rain. There were only twenty-two toilets in the entire embassy (and those were clogged), and barely any showers. Doing laundry was entirely impossible. Embassy staff drove daily to the Federal Republic to buy food and toys for the children; eventually, the federal government sent army trucks loaded with provisions and sleeping bags.[38]

In the meantime, West German officials negotiated with the

GDR about releasing the refugees. On 30 September, the West German foreign minister, Hans Dietrich Genscher, announced a solution for Prague: the refugees would be allowed to leave by train, but they had to cross GDR territory. That way, the regime could demonstrate strength, but it could also gather personal documents and keep track of the refugees' identities. Around 4,700 GDR citizens left from Prague, and some 800 from Warsaw that night. But this didn't end the crisis. Quickly, more people took their place in the Prague embassy, resulting in another 8,000 East Germans leaving by train overnight between 4 and 5 October.[39]

For the civic oppositional groups that were forming and gaining strength over the summer, this massive flight was an ambivalent issue. On the one hand, they, too, demanded the freedom to travel. On the other hand, however, they envisioned political reforms within the GDR; simply leaving the country was not an option for those who wanted to change the socialist state. Thus, when some protestors during a demonstration in Leipzig on 11 September chanted 'We want out,' others shouted back, 'We stay here.'[40] Even more troubling were the massive riots in Dresden on the night of 4/5 October, when large crowds tried to reach the train stations, hoping to jump on to the trains carrying refugees from Prague to West Germany.[41] For Neues Forum, a civic group formed in early September that year by veterans of the peace and environmental movements, and soon the most important voice of the opposition, violent rioting was not a means to reform the country. 'We want a level-headed dialogue, serious thinking about our future, not blind action,' one of their leaflets announced.[42]

Dialogue and communication were indeed at the heart of what many opponents of the regime demanded.[43] 'In our country, communication between the state and society is clearly impaired,' stated the first sentence of Neues Forum's founding document, published on 10 September 1989.[44] Without free and open communication, it would be impossible to face the challenges ahead and to rationally balance the divergent demands and wishes for the future.

Where exactly this dialogue would lead remained unclear. Neues

Forum, for example, formulated its vision for a better society in consciously ambivalent terms:

> On the one hand, we wish for an expansion of the range of goods on offer, on the other hand, we see their social and ecological costs and advocate a rejection of unchecked economic growth. We want scope for economic initiative, but not degeneration into a dog-eat-dog society. We want to preserve the tried and tested and yet create space for renewal in order to live more frugally and be less hostile to nature . . . We want to participate in exports and world trade, but we want to become neither the debtor and servant of the leading industrialized nations nor the exploiters and creditors of the economically weaker nations.[45]

Even more explicit was the East Berlin group Demokratie Jetzt (Democracy Now). They, too, called for a 'democratic transformation in the GDR' in order to make the 'socialist revolution' viable for the future. And it wasn't only the GDR that had to change, they argued. To facilitate a 'new unity of the German people', citizens of the Federal Republic would equally have to work to change their society.[46] This wasn't a call for Western-style free-market capitalism, but for democratic reforms within a socialist GDR.

Only two days after the violence in Dresden, on Saturday, 7 October, the regime celebrated the fortieth anniversary of the GDR with a huge military parade in East Berlin. Anticipating protests, the authorities had concentrated massive security forces in the capital and other major cities such as Dresden, Leipzig and Magdeburg. In the late afternoon, the expected protest began. A couple of dozen teenagers began marching from Alexanderplatz to the nearby Palace of the Republic, where the parade was happening, chanting 'Freedom, Freedom.' Passers-by quickly joined the unauthorized demonstration. Soon, thousands of protestors chanted 'Gorbi, Gorbi' – Gorbachev himself was present during the ceremony – 'No violence', 'Democracy, now or never'. Security forces started making individual arrests, then pushed the crowd, counting some 7,000 people, to the adjacent neighbourhood of Prenzlauer Berg, where they beat and arrested both protestors and passers-by. The next day, when most of those arrested had been released, news of the brutal beatings quickly spread. Many believed that the regime was ready to opt for a 'Chinese solution' and crack down on any opposition.[47]

When people gathered to protest in Leipzig on the evening of Monday, 9 October, the tension ran high. Would this finally be the moment for a show of force from the regime? Thousands had attended the usual Monday prayers at St Nicholas Church, and even more people were waiting outside in the surrounding streets. When the prayers ended and attendees left the church, a huge protest march of some 70,000 people formed. Protestors fearfully expected another violent confrontation with the police. But then something happened that took everyone, security forces and protestors alike, by surprise. Using loudspeakers installed in the city's central Ring streets, Kurt Masur, a famous conductor at Leipzig's Gewandhaus concert hall, addressed his fellow Leipzig citizens. He spoke, he emphasized, not only on his own behalf, but also on behalf of two other local dignitaries and, importantly, three named senior party officials. Masur conjured a common responsibility and care for the country, using an unspecified, but powerfully inclusive 'we'. 'We all need a free exchange of views on the continuation of socialism in our country.' He urged everyone to refrain from violence.[48] The plea worked: the protests remained peaceful. Security forces did not intervene, and neither were they attacked. It was a moment of profound relief, not just in Leipzig. The state had withdrawn in the face of a peaceful demonstration.[49]

The peaceful protest in Leipzig gave the opposition movement a boost. The more the regime retreated, the larger the demonstrations grew. It became possible to criticize and mock the authorities without fearing reprisals. A Berlin school student by the name of Olaf Klenke, for example, noted in the autumn of 1989 how someone had graffitied one of the many portraits of General Secretary Honecker hanging at the school with a moustache. 'Yet nothing happened! That would never even have been conceivable before.'[50]

At the protests, a general mood of peacefulness prevailed. Time and again the security forces prepared for violent attacks and riots, only to be surprised by protestors lighting candles in front of places of power such as the Stasi headquarters. In such circumstances, especially the lower ranks of the police and militias were increasingly unwilling to do the failing regime's 'dirty work', not least because many of the protestors were relatives, friends and neighbours.[51]

Those protesting demanded free elections, an investigation into the May election fraud, freedom of movement, assembly and the press, civic service as an alternative to military service and environmental protection.[52] Until the fall of the Wall, however, only a few opposition activists called for German reunification. It was a political awakening of the GDR's population that reached beyond street demonstrations. Authors, songwriters and actors spoke up publicly for democratic change, while theatres and churches provided stages and rooms for political discussions.[53] And in factories, workers started questioning the legitimacy of the state-sponsored trade unions and revealed the incompetence and corruption of party and union officials.[54]

At the same time, the authority of the ruling SED Party began to crumble.[55] Newspapers like the daily *Junge Welt*, which had hitherto unquestioningly supported the regime, published critical articles and letters to the editors.[56] The inner circle of power realized how dangerous the situation had become and sought to ensure their political survival. For that, it seemed to be necessary to replace Erich Honecker as general secretary of the SED. During a meeting of the party's politburo, its highest decision-making body, on 17 October, Willi Stoph, a long-time ally of Honecker, suggested that he step down, much to Honecker's surprise. Change was necessary, argued Erich Mielke, head of the much-hated Ministry for State Security. 'We can't start shooting with tanks,' he commented. In the end, the motion to replace Honecker was unanimously approved, and Egon Krenz, second in command after Honecker, took power. When Honecker officially stepped down a day later, it was a cause to celebrate for the opposition. But when people learned about his successor, they felt deeply disappointed. It was hard to believe that Krenz would initiate genuine democratic reforms. Pressure from the streets had to continue.[57]

Then on 9 November, Schabowski held the famous press conference, and the Berlin Wall fell. Hundreds of thousands of people flocked to the Federal Republic in the following days, collecting the 'welcoming money' offered by the West German government (100 German marks for people over the age of fourteen, 50 marks for children), and all too often twice. They went to explore Western consumer society, which turned out to be an ambivalent experience. One hundred marks didn't get customers very far, and many places did not accept East German marks, or if so, at bad rates. Tellingly, West Berlin department stores reported a rapid increase of theft.[58]

Effectively, Schabowski's announcement to the press had sealed the fate of the GDR. Re-establishing border controls, which the regime briefly attempted, proved impossible. Yet, the abrupt announcement also shut down the possibility for democratic reforms within the socialist state that many oppositional groups still favoured. A stunning number of leading opposition activists were in fact appalled and outraged by the Wall's opening. Rather than struggling for reforms and 'free communication', people would fall prey to the attraction of Western consumerism. 'We worried that the incredible energy and the powerful will for change, to democratize this country, would now be diverted, with people wanting only to travel west,' remembered Marianne Birthler of the Initiative für Menschenrechte (Initiative for Human Rights).[59] Within weeks, any remaining hopes for an independent, democratic and socialist GDR evaporated, as it became clear that reunification was only a matter of time. Protestors now brought black-red-gold West German flags to demonstrations, but showed little interest in themes like the protection of the environment, much to the dismay of opposition groups. The slogan 'We are the people' began giving way to 'We are *one* people'.[60]

Ultimately, unification happened faster than many had expected. Pressured by the West German chancellor, Helmut Kohl, who argued for a rapid unification of the two German states, opposition groups and the SED agreed on 18 March 1990 as the date for national elections. In the election campaign, democratic reforms *within* the GDR were no longer an issue. It was all about unification and currency reforms, that is, the introduction of the West German mark into the GDR.[61] Against all expectations, the Allianz für Deutschland, backed by Kohl and the centre-right CDU, won the election with 48 per cent, while the Social Democrats, who were widely expected to win, received only 22 per cent of the vote. The civic opposition groups such as Neues Forum, Demokratie Jetzt and Initiative Frieden und Menschenrechte, which had formed an alliance under the name Bündnis 90, got a mere 2.9 per cent. These election results paved the way towards unification, which officially happened on 3 October 1990.[62] The civic groups had brought the regime down, but they would not determine the country's future political development. Their somewhat lofty ideals of peace, human rights and ecology did not resonate with the broad majority of East Germans. Only a tiny minority wanted the democratic transformation of socialism within the GDR these groups had called for; the vast majority longed for the wealth that Western consumer capitalism promised.[63] As a toolmaker had argued during a protest in Leipzig in November 1989: 'No more experiments!' There was an alternative to socialism, not some abstract ideals, but something that already existed and functioned: West Germany's liberal market economy.[64]

Much ink has been spilled over the question of how to characterize the end of the GDR. Was it a popular revolution, or the unravelling of a defunct state? And did the protestors get what they wanted – free elections, freedom to travel, a free press? Or was this a moment of disappointed hopes, with Western consumer capitalism taking over and smashing any dreams of reforming socialism?[65] What is often lost in these politically charged debates is how profound a moment of liberation the collapse of the regime was. One sixteen-year-old named girl Linda, who was interviewed by journalist Vera-Maria Baehr in late 1989, gave a sense of this experience of liberation. 'Previously, everything was so tightly boxed in [*fest eingekastelt*]. Now, suddenly, much has become uncertain. Liberated,' Linda said. She didn't like everything about their new freedom. Like many others, she was critical of consumer society. 'I hope I never fall for consumption . . . The illuminated advertising, the oversupply of goods, that's disgusting to me.' People in West Berlin's streets, she felt, looked lonely. But even though it wasn't perfect, the newly won freedoms changed her everyday life. Now, Linda could play music in the streets with her friends, which had been forbidden in the GDR. 'In the old days, they took away the instruments or even arrested the musicians.'[66]

A Revolution of Humanness: Czechoslovakia

In Czechoslovakia, the crushing of the Prague Spring in 1968 had ended hopes for radical political change. There was the small scene of dissident intellectuals such as Václav Havel, trying to live 'in the truth', but most people simply kept quiet and refrained from public criticism. Of course, this doesn't mean that people were happy with the regime, as widely circulating jokes about it show. In one of them, for example, a man on his deathbed asks to finally join the Communist Party. Why would he want to do this, his crying wife wonders. 'I don't want you to cry. You know, you always feel good when a communist dies,' her husband responds.[67] But as in the GDR, Gorbachev's promises of reform gave hope and energized oppositional groups in Czechoslovakia. When the 'glasnost czar', as Václav Havel called the Soviet leader, visited Prague in April 1987, an enthusiastic crowd celebrated him.[68] Change was on the horizon, people felt; as in East Berlin, they sensed that his reform policies promised new freedoms. New groups and initiatives formed that reinvigorated the opposition: the Independent Peace Association, the Initiative for the Demilitarization of Society, the John Lennon

Peace Club, emerging out of Prague's hippie scene, or the Society for a Merrier Present.[69]

Towards the end of the decade, activists started organizing street demonstrations that brought different scenes opposing the regime together: peace and environmental activists, radical students and devoted Catholics. On 25 March 1988, several thousand protestors gathered in Bratislava to demand religious freedom; while they held candles, the police used truncheons and water cannons to disperse the crowd. Though members of a secretly meeting church had organized the event, environmental activists and other dissidents showed up in support of the 'just cause'. It was no longer only about religious freedom, but about civil courage. 'We felt that we are free people, and in that atmosphere we acquired a greater taste for freedom,' participants said. In late May that year, activists of the environmentalist women's group Prague Mothers walked through the streets – some thirty women and fifty children – to demand the protection of the environment. And on 21 August, the twentieth anniversary of the Soviet invasion that had ended the Prague Spring, the Independent Peace Association organized a public protest on Prague's central Wenceslas Square (popularly known as Václav Square) demanding the withdrawal of Soviet troops, free elections and respect for human rights. All these protests helped prepare the ground for what came to be known as the Velvet Revolution.[70]

Of course, Czechoslovaks were keenly aware of the events in neighbouring Poland and East Germany. They watched how young families from the GDR flooded into Prague, sought refuge in the West German embassy and could finally leave for the West.[71] Some opposition activists even travelled to attend the peaceful demonstrations in Leipzig, where they were amazed by the police standing 'on the edge of the road and [making] way for the march'.[72] Czechoslovak peace and human rights activists had already forged ties with their Polish comrades during the 1980s. One outcome of these transnational networks was a Festival of Czech Culture in Wrocław in early November 1989, when the regime in Poland had already fallen. Czechoslovak border police prevented almost all artists and known dissidents from participating, but thousands of students who were not on the government's search lists managed to cross the border. Here, they could freely speak their mind. It was an inspiration for Czechoslovaks to follow the Polish example and stand up for their own freedom.[73]

These protests showed cracks in the regime's authority. But even so, in early November 1989, few people believed that an end of communism in Czechoslovakia was near. This changed dramatically on 17 November. The date marked the anniversary of student protests in 1939 against the country's occupation by the Nazis, which resulted in the closing of the university and the deportation of 1,000 students. Of course, there had to be a state-sponsored student demonstration to commemorate it. But dissident students had something else in mind. 'We don't want just to recall with reverence those tragic events, we want to show our active support for the ideals of freedom and truth, for which those students gave their lives. For even today, those ideals are seriously threatened,' a flyer circulating at Prague's university read.[74]

In the late afternoon of 17 November 1989, up to 15,000 protestors gathered near the medical campus of Charles University. Some carried banners with the 1968 slogan 'Be realists, demand the impossible'. A veteran of the 1939 protest gave a speech, then student Martin Klíma took the stage: 'Subjugation is worse than death,' he said. 'Today we shall not just piously remember; we are concerned about the present.' Following his words, the crowd marched to the National Cemetery. By then, it had swollen to 50,000. So far, the protest march had moved along the permitted route. But now, people wanted to march to Wenceslas Square (according to historian James Krapfl, this was the work of secret police agent provocateurs). In Národní třída, the head of the march was stopped by a cordon of riot police. 'We have empty hands,' the crowd chanted. They handed flowers to police officers and lit candles to create a 'living altar' between themselves and the police's Plexiglas shields. But unlike on 7 October in Leipzig, the police did not back off. Instead, they attacked, leaving 586 protestors wounded. Even though nobody died (despite rumours to the contrary), it felt like a 'massacre', as student pamphlets put it.[75]

If the police succeeded in dispersing the crowd, they also unintentionally helped build a spirit of community. Strangers helped the wounded. Local residents opened their doors to offer refuge to protestors fleeing the violence. Rather than being intimidated, students felt compelled to push further. The next day, they assembled at Prague University and in several theatres – actors and other cultural workers had also been heavily involved in the protests – to debate the next move; they resolved to go on strike and to call for a general strike on 27 November. Lacking access to mass media, students and other activists visited factories to give an account of the violence, helped to organize strike committees and explained their demands: an honest investigation of the police violence, the punishment of those responsible, free reporting, the release of political prisoners and, somewhat vaguely, but most telling with regard to the ideals of the revolution, a 'consequential dialogue with all segments of society without exception'.[76] In the meantime, citizen initiatives formed across the country, most importantly Public Against Violence in Bratislava and the Civic Forum in Prague.

The general strike on 27 November, lasting for two hours, was an impressive success. Half of the country's working population actively participated, and another quarter, including doctors, nurses and elementary school teachers who felt they could not leave their place of work symbolically supported the strike. Workers used the strike time to show amateur videos of the violence of 17 November and take down dogmatic slogans from factory walls, while schoolteachers discussed current events with their students.[77] The strike mobilized people, and pushed them out of apathy.[78] Its political impact was felt almost immediately. The regime understood that its days were over, with the Soviets clearly unwilling to rescue any of the regimes in Eastern Europe. Two days after the strike, the provision in the constitution that guaranteed the Communist Party a leading role in society was removed. A few days later, Prime Minister Ladislav Adamec announced a new government. The cabinet would include five non-communist ministers, and fifteen communists. Though Civic Forum leaders were happy with the proposed changes, radical students and the general public were not. A majority of communist ministers wasn't quite the Communist Party giving up its leading role. Students resumed their strike, and people again took to the streets, forcing Adamec to step down on 7 December. Three days later, President Gustáv Husák also resigned. Civic Forum proposed that writer and dissident Václav Havel should replace him. But somewhat surprisingly to opposition forces, Havel found himself challenged by four other candidates who wanted to become president, among them Alexander Dubček, the famous hero of the 1968 Prague Spring. Even the Communist Party, suddenly subscribing to the principles of democracy, had its own candidate and called for a popular referendum. Ultimately, it took some (not so democratic) behind-the-scenes negotiations and even blackmail until parliament elected Havel on 29 December 1989.[79] Communism had fallen in Czechoslovakia as well.

Was this a movement merely to bring down communism, or did Czechoslovak revolutionaries envision a radically different society taking its place? In a somewhat dismissive tone, German philosopher Jürgen Habermas claimed that the revolutions of 1989 in Czechoslovakia and elsewhere lacked 'ideas that were either innovative or oriented toward the future . . . The recent rectifying revolutions took their methods and standards entirely from a familiar repertoire of the modern age.' In a similar vein, French historian François Furet argued that 'with all the fuss and noise, not a single new idea has come out of Eastern Europe in 1989'.[80] Do we then not need to concern ourselves with the ideas of those revolutions? A plethora of pamphlets and declarations from all over Czechoslovakia suggests otherwise. Though their ideas were not entirely novel, and resonated with concepts already popular in Poland and the GDR, Czechoslovak revolutionaries developed a vision of a society based on values such as non-violence, dialogue, democracy, fairness and, connecting all those ideals, *lidskost*, meaning humanness.[81] The lofty term captures the desire to build a society for human beings rather than party machines and bureaucracies, which in the eyes of the revolutionaries were a form of violence against human beings. The transformation these activists hoped for wasn't restricted to the political system, but also would require people to change their personal behaviour. 'Free people are kinder, more decent and more considerate toward one another,' one poster claimed.[82]

A document entitled 'Ten Commandments of Our Revolution' encapsulated these ideals:

Don't employ violence and never do anyone harm!

Don't settle old scores with anyone!

Deal with your adversaries in such a way that they become your friends!

Apply the principle that ideas are superior to brute force!

Be tolerant, don't offend, don't threaten!

Speak with everyone about everything and listen patiently to every opinion!

Help everyone who needs your help!

Draw attention to those who take recourse to violence and disinformation.

Maintain humanness [*lidskost*] in all situations. Do unto others as you would have them do unto you!

Let us all meet on the basis of universal human values, which are liberty, equality, fraternity, tolerance, democracy and humaneness [*lidskost*]![83]

Along the same lines, another text called 'The Eight Rules of Dialogue' demanded discussants not to treat each other as opponents but as partners 'in search of truth ... Participation in dialogue assumes a triple respect: towards truth, towards the other and towards the self'.[84] Such guidelines became the moral basis for the revolution. And it wasn't merely an abstract vision. In numerous street protests, happenings and so-called human chains – people holding hands to connect different cities or to encircle an area in a town – Czechoslovaks practically forged the kind of community they longed for. Human relations changed, or so it seemed. If money was lost in the crowd, people returned it. It was possible to leave cars unlocked in the streets without fearing that they would be stolen. There was 'a feeling of stupendous wholeness and rightness', student Milan Hanuš said of the atmosphere during an event in Olomouc. 'Around me dozens of unknown and nonetheless intimately familiar faces. And, I believe, even the same feeling within.'[85] This was a vision of a world characterized by honest and authentic humane relations put into practice.

The Velvet Revolution was a moment of potential and hope, across all aspects of life. Students successfully demanded representation in academic senates, and workers organized votes of no confidence in the factory management, though replacing unpopular directors was often difficult.[86] Their revolution would provide a template for the entire world, Prague students believed. In the words of one Miloš Rybáček from January 1990:

> We will offer Europe and mainly ourselves a lifeline, which will evacuate all of us from the depths of the excrement of materialism back to nature, love, clean water, humility, respect for one's fellows, etc. And let us not think it is only we who need this lifeline. That is a mistake! All of Europe needs it; the entire world needs it![87]

Yet, the moment did not last. By the summer of 1990, around the time of the first national elections in June, a sense of disappointment began to spread. The 'gentle revolution' had turned into 'gentle stagnation', people felt, as old apparatchiks remained in power and none of those responsible for the violence of 17 November 1989 had been brought to justice. The effervescence and energy that had characterized the popular uprising gave way to a renewed 'apathy and cynicism that served [people] so well in previous decades', commented Ján Budáj, outgoing chairman of Public Against Violence, in September 1990. People no longer dreamed of a world of dialogue, fairness and humanness, but were concerned with difficult questions of economic reform. On the first anniversary of the

17 November 1989 demonstration that had inaugurated the revolution, students in Prague not only refused to celebrate, claiming that it wasn't a 'gentle' but a 'stolen revolution', but also presented new demands that ranged from the purging of state institutions to a 'rigorous transition to a market economy'.[88] Economist Václav Klaus, serving as finance minister in the government of national unity, transformed the (left-leaning) Civic Forum into a right-wing political party, and pushed for the privatization of state-owned property. For Klaus, this, too, was a revolution, but it had little in common with the ideals of November 1989.[89]

A Revolution to Be Forgotten? What Remains of 1989

The revolutions of 1989 fundamentally changed Eastern Europe and indeed the world. They brought about the end of communism and the Cold War, they turned post-totalitarian communist dictatorships into democratic polities, and state-run planned economies into neo-liberal free markets.[90] The revolutions produced real results, even though the outcomes had little in common with what the civic opposition groups that had initiated them had dreamed of: a democratization of socialism that might even provide a shining example for the West, rather than Western-style consumer capitalism. In comparison with the revolts around 1968, which produced few tangible outcomes, the peaceful revolutions of 1989 were the 'real deal', so to speak: in Eastern Europe, the people really had managed to bring down regimes.

No doubt, the revolutions of 1989 had more tangible effects with regard to political and economic change. In another aspect, however, the revolutions of 1989 remained strangely without consequences, especially in comparison with the revolts around 1968. Unlike them, the revolutions of 1989 did not inspire protests in the years to come; they were consigned to oblivion. 'There was no revolution in Czechoslovakia in November 1989, because a revolution would have brought new institutions and new ideas to power. But if we want to call it a revolution, then we have to add that that revolution, from inexperience, committed suicide,' wrote Jan Urban, a former spokesman of Civic Forum, in September 1992.[91] The ideals of dialogue, non-violence, and humanness hardly informed new struggles. The protest movements of the 1990s and 2000s, campaigns against racism and neo-Nazism, against global summits around the year 2000, environmental movements and most recently queer activism – they all draw, in East and West, on ideas and forms of protest developed in the 1970s and 1980s, as we've seen in previous chapters. In that sense, it was 1968 that profoundly shaped European protest and political cultures, rather than the revolutions of 1989.[92]

Legacies of Protest: An Epilogue

In September 2011, I attended a series of events in Berlin to commemorate the squatting movement of the early 1980s. They offered historical and political analyses and discussed the movement's impact on Berlin's urban development. More interestingly, though, the programme brought former squatters together who reminisced about their past activism. One particular workshop stood out, attended by perhaps two dozen people, most in their mid- to late fifties. Some had settled in life, had become teachers and homeowners, others were still living in communes and couldn't imagine anything else. They had vivid and insightful discussions about the past, and I learned a lot about the sense of excitement, the collective exuberance of those days. But what struck me most when leaving the meeting was something about the present, not the past. The atmosphere at the workshop contrasted starkly with the sense of exhaustion, anxiety and, frankly, unhappiness I was used to from working in academe. The people at the meeting – and I did oral history interviews with a couple of them afterwards – all seemed to be pretty happy. These squatters had, I felt, done something right in their lives.

When studying protests, we tend to focus on tangible results. A protest movement was successful if it accomplished its goals; if not, it failed. All too often, there is the perception that radical movements which aimed to overthrow the entire social and political order were doomed from the start. They were tamed and incorporated into the capitalist mainstream, without accomplishing meaningful change. The rebellious students and workers of 1968 who set out to bring down capitalism and establish a more participatory democracy failed by these metrics: capitalism lives on, and political systems did not change. And while the peaceful revolutions of 1989 did result in the end of communism, protesters' dreams of reforming socialism in a democratic way and rebuilding society based on the principles of fairness, dialogue and humanness did not materialize either. For younger generations of protestors, such shortcomings can mean different things. Some blame their elders for giving up on radical ideals and being corrupted by 'the system', while others believe that their struggles need to continue, in different forms, on different terrains, but ultimately with the same goals.

However, only seeing the radical transformations that *didn't* happen would not do justice to what protests actually accomplished. They did make a difference. Frequently, *sans papiers* in France who went on hunger strikes did gain the right to stay; governments gave up on plans to expand the military base in Larzac or to build a nuclear power plant in Wyhl; the residents of Magliana did get access to affordable housing; with some limitations, women in many European countries now have the right to an abortion. These are notable victories.

Beyond such tangible results, protest movements have helped reshape European politics, society and culture in the last decades. The rise of Green parties, by now part of the political mainstream, is hard to imagine without the peace and environmental movements of the 1970s and 1980s. They put protecting the environment and combating climate change on the agenda so that today virtually all political parties and even large companies claim to be committed to doing so. Similarly, the women's movements have made gender equality a goal – though of course by no means a reality – that most people nowadays would subscribe to. And it's an accomplishment of the gay movement that heterosexuality is no longer an unquestioned norm. More generally, the subcultural richness and diversity of European cities such as Amsterdam, Copenhagen and Berlin is undoubtedly the effect of countercultural urban activism, including that of immigrants. In short, Europe would be a different place today without these movements.

That said, problems, injustices and inequalities persist. Foreigners, that is, people without European citizenship, and people of colour, whether they hold a European passport or not, still face discrimination and are all too often victims of racist violence. While the European Union celebrates multiculturalism, it has virtually sealed off its Mediterranean border to keep out those fleeing from war and poverty elsewhere. The gender pay gap has not been closed, the streets at night are still no safe space for women, and femicides, the killing of women or girls by men because they are female, haven't stopped. And of course, the world is still heading towards climate collapse; whether present attempts to limit global warming will suffice is highly questionable.

It would be easy to go on listing our current problems. The issues that motivated protest movements in post-war Europe have not gone away. And so these struggles continue, in renewed forms. In May 2020, hundreds of thousands of protestors took to the streets under the banner of 'Black Lives Matter' to express outrage about the killing of African American George Floyd by a white police officer in the United States. These protests weren't merely a show of solidarity with an American movement. They drew attention to police violence in Europe as well, as protestors compared the murder of Floyd to the deaths of black men who died in police custody, such as Oury Jalloh in Germany (who died in 2005) and Adama Traoré in France (who died in 2016). It's not like deadly police violence, legitimate or not, hadn't sparked protests and riots before (just think of the frequent riots in the French *banlieues* during the 1990s, depicted in the 1995 movie *La Haine*). But the Black Lives Matter protests have tremendously increased public awareness beyond activist circles. Police violence has come under scrutiny.

The protests against racism and police violence are just one example. Equally impressive are the huge demonstrations of the Fridays for Future movement, which call for politicians to finally take effective measures against global warming. In less well-publicized protests, activists organize often highly localized campaigns against the gentrification of inner cities. They demand affordable living space and a communalization of public services. In Berlin, where I currently live, the initiative Expropriate Deutsche

Wohnen & Co. successfully organized a public referendum on the socialization of nearly 240,000 apartments owned by huge real estate companies such as Deutsche Wohnen (which alone owns nearly 115,000 apartments in Berlin). In September 2021, nearly 60 per cent of Berlin voters approved of the initiative's proposal (though as they only asked the Berlin Senate to take action in somewhat unspecific terms, it remains to be seen what this means in practice).

To many people, then, including the author of these lines, there is still something inspiring about the better world that activists in post-war Europe fought for: a world without racist and sexist discrimination, a world that protects and values nature rather than exploiting it for the sake of profit, a world in which residents have a right to their city, to affordable housing and enjoyable public space. In light of increasing concerns about loneliness in modern cities, the idea of collective living might still be appealing. And who wouldn't want to live in a city where it's unnecessary to lock cars or, given climate change, bikes? Dreams of an alternative live on. They connect protestors of different generations. They inspire new activism.

But studying their history also gives reason to pause and reflect. There is, as it were, a darker side to the story, and not only because of the turn to terrorist violence some radicals took. All too often, attempts to live a different life, based on principles of autonomy and community, freed from the constraints of conservative morality and the necessities of a competitive market economy, were anything but liberating. They produced new and no less powerful social norms and expectations. The informal personal styles of radical students, their way of dressing and speaking, became the new normal, and anyone not acting in accordance with such cultural norms quickly became a social outsider. Similarly, the belief, common among many activists, that all personal and political problems could be solved by talking about them wasn't inherently democratic. To the contrary, it privileged those who had the skills to prevail in endless debates. And all the work in consciousness-raising groups, intended to overcome an internalized morality and to liberate feelings and bodies, could easily become a kind of 'psycho-terror', allowing those versed in psychological jargon to silence those less capable of talking in that way.

We might then wonder whether all the protests in fact made the world (or at least Europe) a better place. After all, some of the values radical activists of the 1970s and 1980s cherished, such as autonomy, creativity and dialogue, but also their critique of hierarchies and authority, have become part of the neo-liberal mainstream, which requires people to constantly work on improving themselves, to be physically and mentally fit for work, to be attractive for potential lovers as much as for potential employers or clients. Rather than overthrowing capitalism, these activists effectively helped with its neo-liberal transformation, critics have argued. It's an ironic, if not cynical story. These observations about the conundrums of protest movements might make us wary about the very ideals of personal emancipation and radical democracy. Don't they merely conceal the fact that it's impossible to escape from the fine nets of power: whatever we do to tear them apart, we also build new ones? Is any glorious struggle for liberation ultimately in vain? Is protesting pointless?

In a word: no. Their accomplishments might be small; they might seem insignificant in view of the persistence of inequality and injustice; and certainly, anyone believing that capitalism itself is the problem will find little reason to rejoice. But these accomplishments, as limited as they often were, mattered. They changed the society in which we live. And as difficult as living a different, better life was – collectively, not alone; in solidarity with strangers; autonomously, without bosses; embracing new feelings and desires – it was possible. The West Berlin summer of 1981, spent on the roofs of squatted houses or over breakfasts in the streets lasting days, must have been beautiful indeed.

Ultimately, what people did is more inspiring than tangible results: that they struggled, that they tried to change the world, that they experimented and learned by trial and error. Perfection wasn't the point; it was enough, as Ludvík Vaculík wrote about his *Dream Book*, to be 60 per cent free. Successes might be fleeting; they might be limited to the burst of laughter in a courtroom, to the brief experience of taking over a company such as LIP, or painting the stairs in Istanbul. In a world in which, as my students once claimed, only career accomplishments seem to matter, where every comment is recorded for eternity on social media, a world in which making and admitting mistakes has become impossible, this is perhaps the lesson to be learned from the protest movements: dare to try something, whether it's by taking to the streets and demanding political change, fighting sexism and racism, or by building a better world, here and now, in your personal relations, living in a commune, or supporting those fleeing from war and violence. Have the courage to try and fail, to reflect, with the help of history – and then try again.

Acknowledgements

This book is the result of many years of thinking about the history of protesting in post-war Europe. While I haven't discussed the project, which came into being during the Covid pandemic, in many academic contexts, numerous conversations with friends and colleagues have, if at times implicitly, shaped how I think about collective struggles for a better world and their role in history.

First and foremost, I'm immensely grateful to my agent Anna Power who helped me shape the project (and encouraged me to write for an audience beyond my usual academic readers) in the first place. Her enthusiasm for the project as much as her meticulous editing of various drafts, from book proposals to chapters, have pushed me in the best way possible. She gave me confidence in moments of self-doubt. I'm equally grateful to the entire team at Penguin Press: to my editors Thomas Penn and Eva Hodgkin, who carefully read drafts of the entire manuscript and provided immensely helpful suggestions for revising it; to the copy-editor David Watson; to Ruth Pietroni and her editorial team, especially the proofreaders Stephen Ryan and Pat Rush, who did an absolutely amazing job meticulously spotting small errors; and to the cover designer Isabelle de Cat.

A couple of colleagues have read individual chapters (or parts of them) and provided me with useful comments, namely Moritz Föllmer, Andrew Port, Marcel Streng, Tilmann Siebeneichner, and Jake Smith. Many thanks to you. My thinking about protesting cultures in broader, transnational terms is not least the result of teaching a final year module on the Politics of Protest in Post-War Europe at the University of Warwick. Working with my students, seeing how protest movements in the past could be meaningful to them in the present, was always a great pleasure and source of inspiration. I'm particularly grateful to them for familiarizing me with British protest cultures, something I was (as a continental European historian) not quite an expert on. So, many thanks to you as well. At Warwick, I also had the pleasure of talking to a number of colleagues about the book's ideas and more generally about the challenges of writing for a trade publisher, namely Ben Smith, Mark Philp, Rebecca Earle, Claudia Stein, Anna Ross and Christoph Mick. I'm indebted to their support and input. And a number of friends on Facebook helped me (as a non-native English speaker) with tricky translations questions; thanks to all of you as well!

Writing the book would not have been possible without the tremendous work by both academic historians and activists, including archivists, on multiple aspects of protesting in those years. While their names appear in the book's endnotes, I would also like to express my explicit thankfulness and appreciation of these works here. This book rests on the shoulders of all their research. In particular, I want to mention Punks at Papiertiger Archiv Berlin, where I have worked for many years, and from whose knowledge of protesting cultures I continue to benefit.

Finally, while working on the book, I often thought of my first academic home, as it were, the University of Chicago, where I received my doctoral training. My way of thinking about history, and in particular my interest in ordinary people trying to build a better world, took shape in the lively intellectual discussions we had there, many years ago. I feel an ongoing sense of gratitude to Leora Auslander, Michael Geyer, William Sewell and Moishe Postone.

Suggested Further Reading

Aust, Stefan. *Baader-Meinhof: The Inside Story of the R.A.F.* Oxford: Oxford University Press, 2009.

Balestrini, Nanni. *We Want Everything: The Novel of Italy's Hot Autumn.* Translated by Matt Holden. London: Verso, 2016.

Bolton, Jonathan. *Worlds of Dissent: Charter 77, the Plastic People of the Universe, and Czech Culture under Communism.* Cambridge, MA: Harvard University Press, 2012.

Bourg, Julian. *From Revolution to Ethics: May 1968 and Contemporary French Thought.* Montreal: McGill-Queen's University Press, 2007.

Bracke, Maud Anne. *Women and the Reinvention of the Political: Feminism in Italy, 1968–1983.* New York: Routledge, 2014.

Brown, Timothy S. *West Germany and the Global Sixties: The Antiauthoritarian Revolt, 1962–1978.* Cambridge: Cambridge University Press, 2013.

Dale, Gareth. *The East German Revolution of 1989.* Manchester: Manchester University Press, 2006.

Debord, Guy. *The Society of the Spectacle.* New York: Zone Books, 1995.

Edwards, Phil. *More Work! Less Pay! Rebellion and Repression in Italy, 1972–7.* Manchester: Manchester University Press, 2009.

Fürst, Juliane. *Flowers through Concrete: Explorations in Soviet Hippieland.* Oxford: Oxford University Press, 2021.

Fydrych, Major Waldemar. *Lives of the Orange Men: A Biographical History of the Polish Orange Alternative Movement.* Translated by David French. Wivenhoe: Minor Compositions, 2014.

Garton Ash, Timothy. *The Magic Lantern: The Revolution of '89, Witnessed in Warsaw, Budapest, Berlin and Prague.* Updated Version. London: Atlantic Books, 2019.

Gordon, Daniel A. *Immigrants & Intellectuals: May '68 & the Rise of Anti-Racism in France.* London: Merlin Press, 2012.

Greenwald, Lisa. *Daughters of 1968: Redefining French Feminism and the Women's Liberation Movement*. Lincoln: University of Nebraska Press, 2018.

Griffiths, Craig. *The Ambivalence of Gay Liberation: Male Homosexual Politics in 1970s West Germany*. Oxford: Oxford University Press, 2021.

Häberlen, Joachim C. *The Emotional Politics of the Alternative Left: West Germany, 1968–1984*. Cambridge: Cambridge University Press, 2018.

Hanshew, Karrin. *Terror and Democracy in West Germany*. Cambridge: Cambridge University Press, 2012.

Havel, Václav. 'The Power of the Powerless.' In *The Power of the Powerless: Citizens against the State in Central-Eastern Europe*, edited by John Keane. London: Routledge, 2015.

Heerten, Lasse. *The Biafran War and Postcolonial Humanitarianism*. Cambridge: Cambridge University Press, 2017.

Hocquenghem, Guy. *Homosexual Desire*. Translated by Daniella Dangoor. Durham: Duke University Press, 1993.

Jobs, Richard Ivan. *Backpack Ambassadors: How Youth Travel Integrated Europe*. Chicago: University of Chicago Press, 2017.

Jolly, Margaretta. *Sisterhood and After: An Oral History of the UK Women's Liberation Movement, 1968–Present*. Oxford: Oxford University Press, 2019.

Kalter, Christoph. *The Discovery of the Third World: Decolonization and the Rise of the New Left in France, c. 1950–1976*. Cambridge: Cambridge University Press, 2016.

Kempton, Richard. *Provo: Amsterdam's Anarchist Revolt*. Brooklyn: Autonomedia, 2007.

Kenney, Padraic. *A Carnival of Revolution: Central Europe 1989*. Princeton: Princeton University Press, 2002.

Krapfl, James. *Revolution with a Human Face: Politics, Culture, and Community in Czechoslovakia, 1989–1992*. Ithaca: Cornell University Press, 2013.

Mercer, Ben. *Student Revolt in 1968: France, Italy and West Germany*. Cambridge: Cambridge University Press, 2020.

Milder, Stephen. *Greening Democracy: The Anti-Nuclear Movement and Political Environmentalism in West Germany and Beyond, 1968–1983*. Cambridge: Cambridge University Press, 2017.

Plant, Sadie. *The Most Radical Gesture: The Situationist International in a Postmodern Age*. London: Routledge, 1992.

Poiger, Uta G. *Jazz, Rock, and Rebels: Cold War Politics and American Culture in a Divided Germany*. Berkeley: University of California Press, 2000.

Reid, Donald. *Opening the Gates: The Lip Affair, 1968–1981*. London: Verso, 2018.

Renton, David. *Never Again: Rock Against Racism and the Anti-Nazi League 1976–1982*. London: Routledge, 2019.

Richardson-Little, Ned. *The Human Rights Dictatorship: Socialism, Global Solidarity and Revolution in East Germany*. Cambridge: Cambridge University Press, 2020.

Roseneil, Sasha. *Common Women, Uncommon Practices: The Queer Feminism of Greenham*. London: Cassell, 2000.

Ross, Kristin. *May '68 and Its Afterlives*. Chicago: University of Chicago Press, 2002.

Slobodian, Quinn. *Foreign Front: Third World Politics in Sixties West Germany*. Durham: Duke University Press, 2012.

Vaneigem, Raoul. *The Revolution of Everyday Life*. London: Rebel Press, 2003.

Vasudevan, Alex. *Metropolitan Preoccupations: The Spatial Politics of Squatting in Berlin*. Chichester: Wiley and Sons, 2016.

Worley, Matthew. *No Future: Punk, Politics and British Youth Culture, 1976–1984*. Cambridge: Cambridge University Press, 2017.

Wright, Steve. *Storming Heaven: Class Composition and Struggle in Italian Autonomist Marxism*. London: Pluto, 2002.

Notes

Introduction

1 For efforts to properly historicize protests, see, for example, Ingrid Gilcher-Holtey, ed., *1968 – Vom Ereignis zum Gegenstand der Geschichtswissenschaft*, Geschichte und Gesellschaft, Sonderheft (Göttingen: Vandenhoeck & Ruprecht, 1998), Philipp Gassert, 'Narratives of Democratization: 1968 in Postwar Europe', in *1968 in Europe: A History of Protest and Activism, 1956–1977*, ed. Martin Klimke and Joachim Scharloth (New York: Palgrave Macmillan, 2008). See also my own historiographical reflections, focusing on West Germany, in Joachim C. Häberlen, '(Not) Narrating the History of the Federal Republic: Reflections on the Place of the New Left in West German History and Historiography', *Central European History* 52, no. 1 (2019).

2 Cited in Julian Bourg, 'The Moral History of 1968', in *May 68: Rethinking France's Last Revolution*, ed. Julian Jackson, Anna-Louise Milne and James Williams (Houndmills, Basingstoke: Palgrave Macmillan, 2011), 17. For a leftist response to Sarkozy, see André Glucksmann and Raphaël Glucksmann, *Mai 68 expliqué à Nicolas Sarkozy* (Paris: Denoël, 2008). For a discussion of different historiographical approaches, see Julian Jackson, 'The Mystery of May 1968', *French Historical Studies* 33 (2010).

3 Alexander Dobrindt, 'Wir brauchen eine bürgerlich-konservative Wende', in *Die Welt*, 4 January 2018. A number of former radical leftists, including Horst Mahler and Frank Böckelmann, turned to the radical right. On connections between 1968 and the New Right, see Thomas Wagner, *Die Angstmacher: 1968 und die Neuen Rechten* (Berlin: Aufbau, 2017). For a historical perspective on 1968 emphasizing nationalist elements, see Götz Aly, *Unser Kampf: 1968 – Ein irritierter Blick zurück* (Frankfurt a.M.: S. Fischer, 2008).

4 Timothy S. Brown, *West Germany and the Global Sixties: The Anti-authoritarian Revolt, 1962–1978* (Cambridge: Cambridge University Press, 2013), 371. See also Brown's book on the 1960s in Europe, written in a similar spirit, *Sixties Europe* (Cambridge: Cambridge University Press, 2020). For a similarly enthusiastic narrative, see Gerd-Rainer Horn, *The Spirit of '68: Rebellion in Western Europe and North America, 1956–1976* (Oxford: Oxford University Press, 2007). More nuanced, but with a similarly positive perspective, are Kristin Ross, *May '68 and Its Afterlives* (Chicago: University of Chicago Press, 2002), Ludivine Bantigny, *1968: De grands soirs en petits matins* (Paris: Éditions du Seuil, 2018).

5 See only Philipp Sarasin, *1977: Eine kurze Geschichte der Gegenwart* (Berlin: Suhrkamp, 2021); Frank Bösch, *Zeitenwende 1979: Als die Welt von heute begann* (Munich: C. H. Beck, 2019), Konrad H. Jarausch, ed., *Das Ende der Zuversicht? Die siebziger Jahre als Geschichte* (Göttingen: Vandenhoeck & Ruprecht, 2008), Anselm Doering-Manteuffel, Lutz Raphael and Thomas Schlemmer, eds., *Vorgeschichte der Gegenwart: Dimensionen des Strukturbruchs nach dem Boom* (Göttingen: Vandenhoeck & Ruprecht, 2016), Naill Niall Ferguson et al., eds., *The Shock of the Global: The 1970s in Perspective* (Cambridge, MA: Harvard University Press, 2010). From a contemporary perspective, see Ronald Inglehart, *The Silent Revolution: Changing Values and Political Styles among Western Publics* (Princeton: Princeton University Press, 1977).

Chapter 1: Rocking the Miracle Years: Rebellious Youth and Critical Intellectuals from the 1950s to the 1960s

1 On post-war communist parties in Western Europe, see Stéphane Courtois and Marc Lazar, *Histoire du Parti communiste français* (Paris: Presses universitaires de France, 1995), Donald Sassoon, *The Strategy of the Italian Communist Party: From the Resistance to the Historic Compromise* (New York: St Martin Press, 1981), Marc Lazar, *Maisons rouges: Les Partis communistes français et italien de la Libération à nos jours* (Paris: Aubier, 1992), Till Kössler, *Abschied von der Revolution: Kommunisten und Gesellschaft in Westdeutschland, 1945–1968* (Düsseldorf: Droste, 2005).

Numbers on election results can be found on Wikipedia, https://
en.wikipedia.org/wiki/1958_Italian_general_election, and https://en.
wikipedia.org/wiki/1951_French_legislative_election.

2   On the KPD in West Germany, see Joseph Foschepoth, *Verfassungswidrig!
Das KPD-Verbot im Kalten Bürgerkrieg* (Göttingen: Vandenhoeck & Ruprecht, 2017), Kössler, *Abschied*. On Social Democrats and their embrace
of Western Democracy, see Terence Renaud, *New Lefts: The Making of a
Radical Tradition* (Princeton: Princeton University Press, 2021), 173–233.

3   The historiography on post-war Europe is, of course, vast. For a gen-
eral account, see only Tony Judt, *Postwar: A History of Europe since 1945*
(New York: Penguin Press, 2005). On the Marshall Plan, see Benn Steil,
The Marshall Plan: Dawn of the Cold War (Oxford: Oxford University
Press, 2018). On West Germany, see, for example, Tamás Vonyó, *The
Economic Consequences of the War: West Germany's Growth Miracle after
1945* (Cambridge: Cambridge University Press, 2018), Hannah Schissler,
ed., *The Miracle Years: A Cultural History of West Germany, 1949–1968*
(Princeton: Princeton University Press, 2001), Axel Schildt and Arnold
Sywottek, eds., *Modernisierung im Wiederaufbau: Die westdeutsche
Gesellschaft der 50er Jahre* (Bonn: Dietz, 1998), Dagmar Herzog, *Sex after
Fascism: Memory and Morality in Twentieth-Century Germany* (Princeton:
Princeton University Press, 2005), Michael Wildt, *Am Beginn der 'Kon-
sumgesellschaft': Mangelerfahrung, Lebenshaltung, Wohlstandshoffnung in
Westdeutschland in den fünfziger Jahren* (Hamburg: Ergebnisse Verlag,
1994), Kaspar Maase, *BRAVO Amerika: Erkunden zur Jugendkultur der
Bundesrepublik in den fünfziger Jahren* (Hamburg: Junius, 1992). On
France and the 'trente glorieuses', see the classical study by Jean
Fourastié, *Les Trente Glorieuses ou la révolution invisible de 1946 à 1975* (Paris:
Fayard, 1979). For a critical perspective, see Céline Pessis, Sezin Topçu
and Christophe Bonneuil, eds., *Une autre histoire des 'Trente Glorieuses':
Modernisation, contestations et pollutions dans la France d'après-guerre*
(Paris: Éditions la Découverte, 2015). For a cultural perspective in a
post-colonial context, see Kristin Ross, *Fast Cars, Clean Bodies: Decolonization and the Reordering of French Culture* (Cambridge, MA: MIT Press,
1995). On Italy, Paul Ginsborg, *A History of Contemporary Italy: Society
and Politics, 1943–1988* (London: Penguin Books, 1990), 141–210.

4 See, with further references, Ben Mercer, *Student Revolt in 1968: France, Italy and West Germany* (Cambridge: Cambridge University Press, 2020), 107–16.

5 Raoul Vaneigem, *The Revolution of Everyday Life* (London: Rebel Press, 2003).

6 I take the title of the section – 'The Wild Ones' – from the excellent study by Uta G. Poiger, *Jazz, Rock, and Rebels: Cold War Politics and American Culture in a Divided Germany* (Berkeley: University of California Press, 2000), 69.

7 László Benedek, *The Wild One* (USA: 1953).

8 Poiger, *Jazz, Rock, and Rebels*, 74.

9 Ibid., 74–5.

10 Sebastian Kurme, *Halbstarke: Jugendprotest in den 1950er Jahren in Deutschland und den USA* (Frankfurt a.M.: Campus Verlag, 2006), 206–24, quote from *Die Welt* p. 217, Thomas Grotum, *Die Halbstarken: Zur Geschichte einer Jugendkultur der 5oer Jahre* (Frankfurt a.M.: Campus Verlag, 1994), 77–144, Poiger, *Jazz, Rock, and Rebels*, 76–7.

11 Curt Bondy and Jan Braden, *Jugendliche stören die Ordnung: Bericht und Stellungnahme zu den Halbstarkenkrawallen* (Munich: Juventa-Verlag, 1957). On the international dimension of these youthful protests, see Horn, *Spirit*, 24–7.

12 Grotum, *Halbstarken*, 201.

13 Kurme, *Halbstarke*, 288.

14 Maase, *BRAVO Amerika*, 120–21, Detlef Siegfried, *Time Is on My Side: Konsum und Politik in der westdeutschen Jugendkultur der 6oer Jahre* (Göttingen: Wallstein, 2006), 108.

15 Kurme, *Halbstarke*, 193.

16 Bondy and Braden, *Jugendliche*, 25. Quoted in Kurme, *Halbstarke*, 193.

17 Kurme, *Halbstarke*, 205, Maase, *BRAVO Amerika*, 134.

18 Grotum, *Halbstarken*, 201.

19 Maase, *BRAVO Amerika*, 120–21, Siegfried, *Time*, 108.

20 Kurme, *Halbstarke*, 334.

21 Poiger, *Jazz, Rock, and Rebels*, 89.

22 Ibid., 89–90. She is referring to Hans Heinrich Muchow, 'Zur Psychologie und Pädagogik der "Halbstarken"', *Unsere Jugend* 8, pt 1

(September 1956), 388– 94; pt 2 (October 1956), 442–9; pt 3 (November 1956), 486– 91.

23 Cited in ibid., 92.

24 Ibid., 12, 145.

25 On West Germany's liberalization and democratization, see Edgar Wolfrum, *Die geglückte Demokratie: Geschichte der Bundesrepublik Deutschland von ihren Anfängen bis zur Gegenwart* (Stuttgart: Klett-Cotta, 2006), Ulrich Herbert, ed., *Wandlungsprozesse in Westdeutschland: Belastung, Integration, Liberalisierung 1945–1980* (Göttingen: Wallstein, 2002). For a critical discussion of such narratives, see Frank Biess and Astrid M. Eckert, 'Introduction: Why Do We Need New Narratives for the History of the Federal Republic?', *Central European History* 52 (2019).

26 On the history of the Situationist International, see Horn, *Spirit*, 5–14, Roberto Ohrt, *Phantom Avantgarde: Eine Geschichte der Situationistischen Internationale und der Modernen Kunst* (Hamburg: Edition Nautilus, 1990), Sadie Plant, *The Most Radical Gesture: The Situationist International in a Postmodern Age* (London: Routledge, 1992), McKenzie Wark, *The Beach beneath the Street: The Everyday Life and Glorious Times of the Situationist International* (London: Verso Books, 2011), Simon Sadler, *The Situationist City* (Cambridge, MA: MIT Press, 1998), Alastair Hemmens and Gabriel Zacarias, eds., *The Situationist International: A Critical Handbook* (London: Pluto Press, 2020).

27 One of these splinter groups was the West German Gruppe SPUR; see Mia Lee, 'Gruppe Spur: Art as a Revolutionary Medium during the Cold War', in *Between the Avant-Garde and the Everyday: Subversive Politics in Europe from 1957 to the Present*, ed. Timothy Brown and Lorena Anton (New York: Berghahn, 2011). For the artistic context, see also Mia Lee, *Utopia and Dissent in West Germany: The Resurgence of the Politics of Everyday Life in the Long 1960s* (London: Routledge, 2019).

28 Guy Debord, *The Society of the Spectacle* (New York: Zone Books, 1995), Vaneigem, *The Revolution of Everyday Life*. For an anthology of Situationist texts translated into English, see Ken Knabb, ed., *Situationist International Anthology* (Berkeley: Bureau of Public Secrets, 1981).

29 Guy Debord, 'Report on the Construction of Situations and on the International Situationist Tendency's Conditions of Organization and

Action', in *Situationist International Anthology*, ed. Ken Knabb (Berkeley: Bureau of Public Secrets, 1981 [1957]), 38, 43. Translation amended.

30 Anon., 'The Sound and the Fury', in *Situationist International Anthology*, ed. Ken Knabb (Berkeley: Bureau of Public Secrets, 1981 [1958]). The text was a polemical critique of the 'angry young men' (like the *Halbstarken*) causing trouble in European and American cities.

31 Guy Debord, 'Perspectives for Conscious Changes in Everyday Life', in *Situationist International Anthology*, ed. Ken Knabb (Berkeley: Bureau of Public Secrets, 1981 [1961]), 95.

32 Ibid., 93. Vaneigem, *The Revolution of Everyday Life*, 39.

33 Vaneigem, *The Revolution of Everyday Life*, 83.

34 Ibid., 54. Emphasis in the original.

35 Ibid., 226.

36 Guy Debord, 'Situationist Theses on Traffic', in *Situationist International Anthology*, ed. Ken Knabb (Berkeley: Bureau of Public Secrets, 1981 [1959]), 69.

37 Constant Nieuwenhuys, 'Another City for Another Life', in *Situationist International Anthology*, ed. Ken Knabb (Berkeley: Bureau of Public Secrets, 1981 [1959]), 71.

38 Vaneigem, *The Revolution of Everyday Life*, 243.

39 Ibid., 188.

40 Guy Debord, 'Theory of the Dérive', in *Situationist International Anthology*, ed. Ken Knabb (Berkeley: Bureau of Public Secrets, 1981 [1958]), 62, Debord, 'Report', 40, translation amended.

41 For an account of this story, see James Trier, *Guy Debord, the Situationist International, and the Revolutionary Spirit* (Leiden: Brill, 2019), 261–72, Horn, *Spirit*, 12–13.

42 Mustapha Khayati, 'On the Poverty of Student Life', in *Situationist International Anthology*, ed. Ken Knabb (Berkeley: Bureau of Public Secrets, 1981 [1966]), 410, 414, 412, 413 (in order of quotes).

43 Ibid., 413, 429 (in order of quotes).

44 The most detailed account of the Dutch Provos available is Richard Kempton, *Provo: Amsterdam's Anarchist Revolt* (Brooklyn: Autonomedia, 2007). See also Horn, *Spirit*, 38–42.

45 Kempton, *Provo*, 23–30.

46 See, with quotes, ibid., 38–42.

47 Quoted in full in ibid., 59–60.

48 Provokatie #5, cited in full in ibid., 47–8.

49 Ibid., 49.

50 Ibid., 50–53. See also Niek Pas, 'Mediatization of Provos: From a Local Movement to a European Phenomenon', in *Between Prague Spring and French May: Opposition and Revolt in Europe, 1960–1980*, ed. Martin Klimke, Jacco Pekelder and Joachim Scharloth (New York: Berghahn, 2011).

51 Kempton, *Provo*, 67.

52 For an account, see ibid., 59–67.

53 On police brutality, see ibid., 69–91, for the incident 81–3.

54 For the programme and a discussion, see ibid., 81.

55 Horn, *Spirit*, 41.

56 Kempton, *Provo*, 107–13.

57 Pas, 'Mediatization', Siegfried, *Time*, 415–28.

58 Quoted in Horn, *Spirit*, 36. *Ragazzi* literally means 'young boys'.

59 On *Mondo Beat*, see ibid., 36–8, Primo Moroni and Nanni Balestrini, *Die goldene Horde: Arbeiterautonomie, Jugendrevolte und bewaffneter Kampf in Italien* (Berlin: Assoziation A, 2002), 56–8. For a detailed chronology of the *Mondo Beat*, including reproductions of the magazine, see the website http://www.melchiorre-mel-gerbino. com/Mondo_Beat_Story/oohomepage.htm, run by Melchiorre Paolo Gerbino, in his own words 'historic leader of the contestation'. While informative, the website is certainly not unbiased.

60 See in general Raj Chandarlapaty, *The Beat Generation and Countercul-ture: Paul Bowles, William S. Burroughs, Jack Kerouac* (New York: Peter Lang, 2009), Sharin N. Elkholy, ed., *The Philosophy of the Beats* (Lexing-ton: University Press of Kentucky, 2012), Nancy M. Grace and Jennie Skerl, eds., *The Transnational Beat Generation* (New York: Palgrave Macmillan, 2012), Kostas Myrsiades, ed., *The Beat Generation. Critical Essays* (New York: Peter Lang, 2002), Steve Watson, *The Birth of the Beat Generation: Visionaries, Rebels, and Hipsters, 1944–1960* (New York: Pantheon Books, 1995). See also Horn, *Spirit*, 16–19.

61 A key example is Jack Kerouac, *On the Road. With an Introduction by Ann Charters* (London: Penguin, 1991). The quote is from Steve Wilson, 'The

Author as Spiritual Pilgrim: The Search for Authenticity in Jack Kerouac's *On the Road* and *The Subterraneans'*, in *The Beat Generation: Critical Essays*, ed. Kostas Myrsiades (New York: Peter Lang, 2001), 81.

62 See Moroni and Balestrini, *Goldene Horde*, 41–6.

63 Cited in ibid., 59–62.

64 Ibid., 69.

65 Ibid., 47.

66 Ibid., 71. For the unofficial history of the movement, see http://www.melchiorre-mel-gerbino.com/Mondo_Beat_Story/oohomepage.htm, Chapters 10 to 14.

67 See Brown, *West Germany*, 62–8, Siegfried, *Time*, 399–411.

68 Siegfried, *Time*, 410.

69 Ibid., 411–13, with quotes. For a documentary, see Peter Fleischmann, *Herbst der Gammler* (Germany: 1967).

70 Siegfried, *Time*, 413.

71 Ibid., 413–28, quote 427.

Chapter 2: All Power to the Imagination: 1968 in East and West

1 K. Christitch, Bernard Girod de L'Ain and Jean Pierre Quélin, 'La Nuit du 10 et 11 mai au quartier latin', *Le Monde 2*, 13 May 1968, online at https://www.lemonde.fr/le-monde-2/article/2008/05/05/la-nuit-du–10-et–11-mai-au-quartierlatin_1037161_1004868.html (accessed 2 August 2021).

2 For an account of the night, see Ingrid Gilcher-Holtey, *'Die Phantasie an die Macht': Der Mai 68 in Frankreich* (Frankfurt a.M.: Suhrkamp, 1995), 232–58, Bantigny, *1968*, 51–4.

3 On workers in 1968 France, see Xavier Vigna, *L'Insubordination ouvrière dans les années 68: Essai d'histoire politique des usines* (Rennes: Presse Universitaires de Rennes, 2007). The literature on May 1968 in France is vast. See, in addition to the works by Bantigny and Gilcher-Holtey and with many more references, Michael Seidman, *The Imaginary Revolution: Parisian Students and Workers in 1968* (New York: Berghahn Books,

2004), Ross, *May '68*, Julian Jackson, Anna-Louise Milne and James S. Williams, eds., *May 68: Rethinking France's Last Revolution* (Houndmills, Basingstoke: Palgrave Macmillan, 2011), Philippe Artières and Michelle Zancarini-Fournel, eds., *68, une histoire collective (1962–1981)* (Paris: La Découverte, 2008), Michelle Zancarini-Fournel, *Le Moment 68: une histoire contestée* (Paris: Seuil, 2008), Xavier Vigna and Jean Vigreux, eds., *Mai–juin 1968: Huit semaines qui ébranlèrent la France* (Dijon: Éditions universitaires de Dijon, 2010), Mercer, *Student Revolt*.

4 For a global perspective on 1968, see the contributions in Jian Chen et al., eds., *The Routledge Handbook of the Global Sixties: Between Protest and Nation-Building* (London: Routledge, 2018).

5 On the transnational and global dimension of 1968, see, for example, Arthur Marwick, *The Sixties: Cultural Revolution in Britain, France, Italy, and the United States, c.1958–c.1974* (Oxford: Oxford University Press, 1998), Carola Fink, Philipp Gassert and Detlef Junker, eds., *1968: The World Transformed* (Cambridge: Cambridge University Press, 1998), Horn, *Spirit*, Gerd-Rainer Horn and Padraic Kenney, eds., *Transnational Moments of Change: Europe 1945, 1968, 1989* (Lanham: Rowman & Littlefield, 2004), Martin Klimke and Joachim Scharloth, eds., *1968 in Europe: A History of Protest and Activism, 1956–1977* (New York: Palgrave Macmillan, 2008), Jeremi Suri, *The Global Revolutions of 1968* (New York; London: W. W. Norton & Company, 2007), Jeremi Suri, 'The Rise and Fall of an International Counterculture', *American Historical Review* 114, no. 1 (2009), Samantha Christiansen and Zachary Scarlett, eds., *The Third World and the Global 1960s* (New York: Berghahn, 2012).

6 Karl-Heinz Janßen, 'Neue Linke – Aufbruch in die Sackgasse', *Die Zeit*, 9 September 1966, quoted in Norbert Frei, *1968: Jugendrevolte und globaler Protest* (Munich: Deutscher Taschenbuchverlag, 2008), 98.

7 On '1968' in West Germany, see in general the recent works by Nick Thomas, *Protest Movements in 1960s West Germany: A Social History of Dissent and Democracy* (New York: Berg, 2003), Brown, *West Germany*, Christina von Hodenberg and Detlef Siegfried, eds., *Wo '1968' liegt: Reform und Revolte in der Geschichte der Bundesrepublik* (Göttingen: Vandenhoeck & Ruprecht, 2016), Detlef Siegfried, *1968: Protest, Revolte, Gegenkultur* (Ditzingen: Reclam, 2018).

8 See Frei, *1968*, 98–101, Ulrich Chaussy, *Rudi Dutschke: Die Biographie* (Munich: Droemer, 2018), 47. On Dutschke's biography, see also Michaela Karl, *Rudi Dutschke: Revolutionär ohne Revolution* (Frankfurt am Main: Verlag Neue Kritik, 2003).

9 On the SDS, see Tilman P. Fichter and Siegward Lönnendonker, *Kleine Geschichte des SDS: Der Sozialistische Deutsche Studentenbund von Helmut Schmidt bis Rudi Dutschke* (Essen: Klartext, 2007). On Subversive Aktion, see Frank Böckelmann and Herbert Nagel, eds., *Subversive Aktion: Der Sinn der Organisation ist ihr Scheitern* (Frankfurt a.M.: Verlag Neue Kritik, 1976). See also Kunzelmann's biography, Aribert Reimann, *Dieter Kunzelmann: Avantgardist, Protestler, Radikaler* (Göttingen: Vandenhoeck & Ruprecht, 2009).

10 For a good summary, see Siegfried, *1968*, 163–8, Brown, *West Germany*, 333–8.

11 See Brown, *West Germany*, 84–103, Boris Spernol, *Notstand der Demokratie: Der Protest gegen die Notstandsgesetze und die Frage der NS-Vergangenheit* (Essen: Klartext, 2008), Martin Diebel, '*Die Stunde der Exekutive': Das Bundesinnenministerium im Konflikt um die Notstandsgesetzgebung 1949–1968* (Göttingen: Wallstein, 2019).

12 See in addition to Brown, Karrin Hanshew, *Terror and Democracy in West Germany* (Cambridge: Cambridge University Press, 2012), 68–109.

13 'Zu Protokoll: Interview von Günter Gaus mit Rudi Dutschke', online at https://www.youtube.com/watch?v=SeIsyuoNfOg&t=414s. The interview is partly reprinted in FU Berlin, *Freie Universität Berlin, 1948–1973: Hochschule im Umbruch. Teil V: 1967–1969, Gewalt und Gegengewalt* (Berlin: Freie Universität Berlin, 1983), 440–43. For a subtle discussion of the interview, see Armin Nassehi, *Gab es 1968? Eine Spurensuche* (Hamburg: kursbuch.edition, 2018), 57–66.

14 On the Free University, see James Tent, *The Free University of Berlin: A Political History* (Bloomington: Indiana University Press, 1988).

15 Mercer, *Student Revolt*, 131–6.

16 Ibid., 178–87.

17 On exchanges between American and West German left-wing students, see Martin Klimke, *The Other Alliance: Student Protest in West*

Germany and the United States in the Global Sixties (Princeton: Princeton University Press, 2010).

18 Quoted in Mercer, *Student Revolt*, 184.

19 Ibid., 177.

20 Quoted in ibid., 189.

21 Quoted in ibid., 190.

22 See Eckard Michels, *Schahbesuch 1967: Fanal für die Studentenbewegung* (Berlin: Ch. Links Verlag, 2017).

23 Wolfgang Nitsch, 'Vorlage für das Hochschulaktionskomitee der Studentenschaft: Argumente für eine von Studenten selbst organisierte "Kritische Universität" in der FU (Freies Studienprogramm der Studentenschaft)', 13 June 1967, reprinted in Fu Berlin, *Freie Universität Berlin, 1948–1973: Hochschule im Umbruch. Teil V: 1967–1969, Gewalt und Gegengewalt*, 201–3.

24 Jürgen Habermas, 'Vorbereitende Bemerkungen zu einer Theorie der kommunikativen Kompetenz', in *Theorie der Gesellschaft oder Sozialtechnologie: Was leistet die Systemforschung?*, ed. Jürgen Habermas and Niklas Luhmann (Frankfurt am Main: Suhrkamp, 1971), 137. On the history of discussing, see Nina Verheyen, *Diskussionslust: Eine Kulturgeschichte des 'besseren Arguments' in Westdeutschland* (Göttingen: Vandenhoeck & Ruprecht, 2010). On changing communicative styles, see also Joachim Scharloth, *1968: Eine Kommunikationsgeschichte* (Paderborn: Wilhelm Fink, 2011).

25 All quotes in Mercer, *Student Revolt*, 265–6.

26 Quotes in ibid., 268.

27 Ibid., 270–84.

28 Anon., 'Bemerkungen zur Putte Veranstaltung', *Info BUG* 5, 31 March 1974, 3–4.

29 On the lack of cooperation between students and workers in West Germany, see Marica Tolomelli, *Repressiv getrennt oder organisch verbündet: Studenten und Arbeiter 1968 in der Bundesrepublik Deutschland und in Italien* (Opladen: Leske + Budrich, 2001). On workers more generally in 1968, see Gerd-Rainer Horn, 'The Working-Class Dimension of 1968', in *Transnational Moments of Change: Europe 1945, 1968, 1989*, ed.

Gerd-Rainer Horn and Padraic Kenney (Lanham: Rowman & Little-field, 2004).

30 See Gilcher-Holtey, *'Phantasie an die Macht'*, 394–419.

31 Ross, *May '68*, 25.

32 Mercer, *Student Revolt*, 231–2. For an extensive discussion of the student rebellion in Paris, see also Seidman, *Imaginary Revolution*, 17–90, Gilcher-Holtey, *'Phantasie an die Macht'*, 115–37, Jean-Pierre Duteuil, *Nanterre, 1965–66–67–68: Vers le mouvement du 22 mars* (Paris: Arcatie, 1988).

33 Mercer, *Student Revolt*, 232.

34 Ibid., 233, Gilcher-Holtey, *'Phantasie an die Macht'*, 119.

35 Cited in Mercer, *Student Revolt*, 233–4.

36 For Cohn-Bendit's biography, see Sebastian Voigt, *Der jüdische Mai '68: Pierre Goldman, Daniel Cohn-Bendit und André Glucksmann im Nachkriegsfrankreich* (Göttingen: Vandenhoeck & Ruprecht, 2015), Sabine Stamer, *Cohn-Bendit: Die Biografie* (Berlin: Europa-Verlag, 2001).

37 Mercer, *Student Revolt*, 238, Gilcher-Holtey, *'Phantasie an die Macht'*, 126–8. On Cohn-Bendit, see also Voigt, *Jüdische Mai '68*.

38 On the congress, see, with further references, Siegfried, *1968*, 191–6, Quinn Slobodian, *Foreign Front: Third World Politics in Sixties West Germany* (Durham: Duke University Press, 2012), 97–9.

39 Avant-garde jeunesse, '21 février, journée du Vietnam héroïque', 14, quoted in Salar Mohandesi, 'Bringing Vietnam Home: The Vietnam War, Internationalism, and May '68', *French Historical Studies* 41 (2018), 236.

40 See the accounts in ibid., Mercer, *Student Revolt*, 243.

41 Mercer, *Student Revolt*, 244–6. On the *enragés*, see also René Viénet, *Enragés and Situationists in the Occupation Movement, France, May '68* (New York. London: Autonomedia, Rebel Press, 1992), Gilcher-Holtey, *'Phantasie an die Macht'*, 143–53.

42 Mercer, *Student Revolt*, 253, Bantigny, *1968*, 46–9.

43 Bantigny, *1968*, 50–51.

44 Gilcher-Holtey, *'Phantasie an die Macht'*, 244.

45 Bantigny, *1968*, 51–4.

46 Ibid., 75f., Michelle Zancarini-Fournel, 'Sud-Aviation, Nantes: La prem-ière occupation de Mai', in *68, une histoire collective (1962–1981)*, ed. Philippe Artières and Michelle Zancarini-Fournel (Paris: La Décou-verte, 2008). See also the documentary by Jacques Willemont, *L'Autre Mai: Nantes, mai 68* (France: 2008).

47 Bantigny, *1968*, 54–5.

48 Xavier Vigna and Michelle Zancarini-Fournel, 'Les Rencontres improbables dans les "années 68"', *Vingtième Siècle: Revue d'histoire* 101 (2009). See, however, Vigna, *L'Insubordination*, 195–9. Here, Vigna argues that workers considered radical students part of a 'decadent and amoral' universe; they weren't part of the 'we' of the working class, but of the hostile 'they'.

49 Bantigny, *1968*, 55–8.

50 Ibid., 241.

51 Ibid., 351, Nicolas Hatzfeld, 'Les Morts de Flins et Sochaux: De la grève à la violence politique', in *68, une histoire collective (1962–1981)*, ed. Philippe Artières and Michelle Zancarini-Fournel (Paris: La Décou-verte, 2008).

52 Bantigny, *1968*, 357–60. See by contrast Seidman, *Imaginary Revolution*, 161–214.

53 Pierre Bonneau and Jacques Willemont, *La Reprise du travail aux usines Wonder* (France: 1968). Quote from Bantigny, *1968*, 270–71. See also Ross, *May '68*, 138f.

54 On '1968' in Poland and Yugoslavia, see Hans-Christian Petersen, 'Der polnische März 1968: Nationales Ereignis und transnationale Bewegung', *Osteuropa* 7 (2008), Daniel Limberger, *Polen und der 'Prager Frühling' 1968: Reaktionen in Gesellschaft, Partei und Kirche* (Frankfurt am Main: Lang, 2012), Madigan Fichter, 'Yugoslav Protest: Student Rebellion in Belgrade, Zagreb, and Sarajevo in 1968', *Slavic Review* 75 (2016), Boris Kanzleiter, *Die 'Rote Universität': Studentenbewegung und Linksopposition in Belgrad 1964–1975* (Hamburg: VSA-Verlag, 2011), Boris Kanzleiter, '1968 in Yugoslavia: Student Revolt between East and West', in *Between Prague Spring and French May: Opposition and Revolt in Europe, 1960–1980*, ed. Martin Klimke, Jacco Pekelder and Joachim Scharloth (New York: Berghahn, 2011), Jerzy Eisler, 'March

1968 in Poland', in *1968: The World Transformed*, ed. Carola Fink, Philipp Gassert and Detlef Junker (Cambridge: Cambridge University Press, 1998), Malgorzata Fidelis, 'Red State, Golden Youth: Student Culture and Political Protest in 1960s Poland', in *Between the Avant-Garde and the Everyday: Subversive Politics in Europe from 1957 to the Present*, ed. Timothy Brown and Lorena Anton (New York: Berghahn, 2011). On 1968 in Eastern Europe more generally, see the contributions in Vladimir Tismaneanu, ed., *Promises of 1968: Crisis, Illusion and Utopia* (Budapest: Central European University Press, 2011).

55 Martin Schulze Wessel, *Der Prager Frühling: Aufbruch in eine neue Welt* (Ditzingen: Reclam, 2018), 138–9.

56 Ibid., 140–43, quote 140f.

57 On the reform discourse, see ibid., 52–137, quote 118. The quote is from Zdeněk Mlynář, *Československý pokus o reformu 1968: Analýza jeho teorie a praxe* (Cologne: Index, 1975).

58 Schulze Wessel, *Prager Frühling*, 144–9, quote 146.

59 The English-speaking literature on the Prague Spring is surprisingly thin, but see H. Gordon Skilling, *Czechoslovakia's Interrupted Revolution* (Princeton: Princeton University Press, 1976), Mary Heiman, *Czechoslovakia: The State that Failed* (Yale: Yale University Press, 2011), 211–42. The following part relies on Schulze Wessel, *Prager Frühling*. See also the contributions in Martin Schulze Wessel, ed., *The Prague Spring as a Laboratory* (Göttingen: Vandenhoeck & Ruprecht, 2019).

60 Schulze Wessel, *Prager Frühling*, 150–53, quote 153. The quote is from Eduard Goldstücker, *Prozesse: Erfahrungen eines Mitteleuropäers* (Munich: Knaus, 1989).

61 Schulze Wessel, *Prager Frühling*, 154–5.

62 Ibid., 156–8.

63 Ibid., 158.

64 Ibid., 173–7, quote 174.

65 Ibid., 163–7, quote 165. He refers to Skilling, *Czechoslovakia's Interrupted Revolution*, 201.

66 The Action Programme of the Communist Party of Czechoslovakia, 5 April 1968. The programme is reprinted in Robin Alison Remington, ed., *Winter in Prague: Documents on Czechoslovak Communism in*

Crisis (Cambridge, MA: MIT Press, 1969), 88–137. For a discussion of the programme, see Schulze Wessel, *Prager Frühling*, 177–81.

67 Remington, ed., *Winter in Prague*, 135.

68 Ibid., 92.

69 Ibid., 88–137.

70 Ibid., 97.

71 Ibid., 95.

72 Schulze Wessel, *Prager Frühling*, 181–3.

73 Ibid., 216–22, quote 220. He refers to Skilling, *Czechoslovakia's Interrupted Revolution*, 235.

74 Schulze Wessel, *Prager Frühling*, 245–51.

75 Ludvík Vaculík, '2,000 Words to Workers, Farmers, Scientists, Artists, and Everyone', in *Literární listy*, 27 June 1968, reprinted in Remington, ed., *Winter in Prague*, 196–202, quotes 200f. For a discussion of the text, see Schulze Wessel, *Prager Frühling*, 254–8. Schulze Wessel gives a different date, 12 June 1968.

76 Schulze Wessel, *Prager Frühling*, 258–60.

77 Ibid., 263–80.

78 Ibid., 280–86.

79 Schulze Wessel, ed., *Prague Spring as a Laboratory*.

80 Ginsborg, *Italy*, 311–16, quote 316, Nanni Balestrini, *We Want Everything: The Novel of Italy's Hot Autumn*, trans. Matt Holden (London: Verso, 2016), Moroni and Balestrini, *Goldene Horde*, 204–7, Robert Lumley, *States of Emergency: Cultures of Revolt in Italy from 1968 to 1978* (London: Verso, 1990), 207–16.

81 On students in Italy, see Mercer, *Student Revolt*, 206–29, 276–84, Lumley, *States of Emergency*, 47–142.

82 Lumley, *States of Emergency*, 111.

83 On autonomy in Italy, see Marcello Tarì, *Autonomie! Italie, les années 1970* (Paris: La Fabrique, 2011).

84 See on this background Moroni and Balestrini, *Goldene Horde*, 79–114. Balestrini's novel *We Want Everything* provides a vivid image of the situation in the South.

85 Quoted in Lumley, *States of Emergency*, 169–70.

86 Quoted in Moroni and Balestrini, *Goldene Horde*, 202.

87 On these struggles, see in general ibid., 185–204, Ginsborg, *Italy*, 311–16, Lumley, *States of Emergency*, 169–80, 217–40.

88 Lumley, *States of Emergency*, 183–5.

89 Ibid., 191–5, quote 192, Moroni and Balestrini, *Goldene Horde*, 188–96.

90 Quotes in Lumley, *States of Emergency*, 192, 193, 194.

91 Quotes from ibid., 189.

92 Quotes from ibid., 190, 228.

93 See ibid., 218–19, 264, 301–2, Moroni and Balestrini, *Goldene Horde*, 234, Ginsborg, *Italy*, 234. See also https://libcom.org/history/porto-marghera-%E2%80%93-last-firebrands, and https://libcom.org/library/working-class-struggle-against-crisis-self-reduction-prices-italy-bruno-ramirez. On rent strikes, see Chapter 8.

94 Quoted in Ginsborg, *Italy*, 316.

95 Lumley, *States of Emergency*, 193.

96 Ibid., 249–53.

97 Ginsborg, *Italy*, 320–22. On the 150-hours scheme, see Lumley, *States of Emergency*, 106, 132, 265.

98 Claus Leggewie, '1968 ist Geschichte', *Aus Politik und Zeitgeschichte* B 22–23 (2001), 16.

99 See for such enthusiastic accounts Horn, *Spirit*, Brown, *West Germany*. With somewhat more sophistication, but equally enthusiastic, see Ross, *May '68*. For a discussion of French debates about 1968, see Zancarini-Fournel, *Le Moment 68*.

100 See Eckart Conze, *Die Suche nach Sicherheit: Eine Geschichte der Bundesrepublik Deutschland von 1949 bis in die Gegenwart* (Munich: Siedler, 2009). For a discussion, see Scharloth, *1968*, 17.

101 For somewhat dismissive accounts of the May 1968 uprising in France, see Seidman, *Imaginary Revolution*, Jean-François Sirinelli, *Mai 68: L'événement Janus* (Paris: Fayard, 2008).

102 Gassert, 'Narratives', 315.

103 See Luc Boltanski and Eve Chiapello, *The New Spirit of Capitalism* (London: Verso, 2005), Paul du Gay and Glenn Morgan, eds., *New Spirits of Capitalism? Crises, Justifications, and Dynamics* (Oxford: Oxford University Press, 2013). See also my discussion, with regard to West Germany, Häberlen, '(Not) Narrating'.

104 Ross, *May '68*.

105 Bantigny, *1968*, 367–72.

Chapter 3: Terror and Violence: Red Army Faction, Red Brigades and Street Violence

1 The pamphlet, part of an entire series, is reproduced in Rainer Langhans and Fritz Teufel, *Klau mich* (Munich: Trikont, 1977).

2 Quoted in Simon Teune, 'Humour as a Guerrilla Tactic: The West German Student Movement's Mockery of the Establishment', *International Review of Social History* 52, Supplement 15: Humour and Social Protest (2007), 123.

3 Stefan Aust, *Der Baader-Meinhof Komplex (aktualisierte Neuauflage)* (Hamburg: Hoffmann und Campe, 2017), 111–13, Petra Terhoeven, *Die Rote Armee Fraktion: Eine Geschichte terroristischer Gewalt* (Munich: C. H. Beck, 2017), 29f.

4 Both terror groups have attracted massive scholarly attention in English, German and Italian (though the RAF more than the BR in English); see, for example, Jeremy Varon, *Bringing the War Home: The Weather Underground, the Red Army Faction, and the Revolutionary Violence in the Sixties and Seventies* (Berkeley: University of California Press, 2004), Leith Passmore, *Ulrike Meinhof and the Red Army Faction: Performing Terrorism* (New York: Palgrave Macmillan, 2011), Hanshew, *Terror*, Stefan Aust, *Baader-Meinhof: The Inside Story of the R.A.F.* (Oxford: Oxford University Press, 2009), Sarah Colvin, *Ulrike Meinhof and West German Terrorism: Language, Violence, and Identity* (Rochester: Camden, 2009), Wolfgang Kraushaar, ed., *Die RAF und der linke Terrorismus*, 2 vols. (Hamburg: Hamburger Edition, 2006), Petra Terhoeven, *Deutscher Herbst in Europa: Der Linksterrorismus der siebziger Jahre als transnationales Phänomen* (Berlin: De Gruyter Oldenbourg, 2016), Petra Terhoeven, *Rote Armee Fraktion*, Raimondo Catanzaro, ed., *The Red Brigades and Left-Wing Terrorism in Italy* (London: Pinter, 1991), Robert C. Meade, *Red Brigades: The Story of Italian Terrorism* (Basingstoke: Macmillan, 1990), David Moss, *The Politics of Left-Wing Violence in Italy, 1969–85*

(Basingstoke: Macmillan, 1989), Tobias Hof, *Staat und Terrorismus in Italien, 1969–1982* (Munich: Oldenbourg, 2011). For the political context in Italy, see also Phil Edwards, *More Work! Less Pay! Rebellion and Repression in Italy, 1972–7* (Manchester: Manchester University Press, 2009), 61–110.

5 On the trial, see Aust, *Baader-Meinhof Komplex*, 127–37, quotes 132. On the trial and how it influenced the founding of the RAF, see also Colvin, *Meinhof*, 42–5, Hanshew, *Terror*, 102–4.

6 Aust, *Baader-Meinhof Komplex*, 160, Terhoeven, *Rote Armee Fraktion*, 30f.

7 Aust, *Baader-Meinhof Komplex*, 160–63.

8 See ibid., 174–99, Terhoeven, *Rote Armee Fraktion*, 31–8.

9 See Aust, *Baader-Meinhof Komplex*, 25–9, 200–205, Terhoeven, *Rote Armee Fraktion*, 38.

10 See Peter Fritzsche, *Die politische Kultur Italiens* (Frankfurt am Main: Campus, 1987), 138–44. On right-wing terror and the 'strategy of tension' in Italy, see also Meade, *Red Brigades*, 34–7. Some accounts give the number of dead as seventeen, see ibid., 36. On the strategy of tension, see more generally Anna Cento Bull, *Italian Neofascism: The Strategy of Tension and the Politics of Nonreconciliation* (New York: Berghahn, 2008).

11 Moroni and Balestrini, *Goldene Horde*, 208–19, Edwards, *More Work!*, 15, Lumley, *States of Emergency*, 123.

12 On the early Red Brigades, see Meade, *Red Brigades*, 1–15, Lumley, *States of Emergency*, 279–83, Edwards, *More Work!*, 64–7.

13 Moroni and Balestrini, *Goldene Horde*, 230–31.

14 Ibid., 254–5, Edwards, *More Work!*, 64.

15 Ginsborg, *Italy*, 362.

16 Cited in Edwards, *More Work!*, 64. See further Meade, *Red Brigades*, 39–45, Henner Hess, *Angriff auf das Herz des Staates*, vol. 2 (Frankfurt a.M.: Suhrkamp, 1988), 72–3.

17 'Die Rote Armee aufbauen', in *agit 883* 62 (5 June 1970), 6, available online at http://www.rafinfo.de/archiv/raf/rafgrund.php. For a discussion see Colvin, *Meinhof*, 80–82.

18 On the internationalist dimension of RAF ideology, see Christian Lütnant, *'Im Kopf der Bestie': Die RAF und ihr internationalistisches Selbstverständnis* (Marburg: Tectum Verlag, 2014).

19 Quoted in Alessandro Orsini, *Anatomy of the Red Brigades: The Religious Mind-Set of Modern Terrorists* (Ithaca: Cornell University Press, 2011), 11.

20 Moroni and Balestrini, *Goldene Horde*, 255. See also Terhoeven, *Deutsche Herbst* 182, and Luigi Manconi, 'The Political Ideology of the Red Brigades', in *The Red Brigades and Left-Wing Terrorism in Italy*, ed. Raimondo Catanzaro (London: Pinter Publishers, 1991), 126–35. It's noteworthy that Moroni and Balestrini write from an explicitly leftist perspective.

21 See Gian Carlo Caselli and Donatella della Porta, 'The History of the Red Brigades: Organizational Structures and Strategies of Action (1970–1982)', in *The Red Brigades and Left-Wing Terrorism in Italy*, ed. Raimondo Catanzaro (London: Pinter Publishers, 1991), 71–9. On terrorist violence in the context of factories, including assaults and killings of managers and sabotage on the shop floor, see Moss, *Politics*, 81–115.

22 Moroni and Balestrini, *Goldene Horde*, 256.

23 Ibid., 256, Hess, *Angriff*, 75.

24 For details, see Aust, *Baader-Meinhof Komplex*, 312–16, 326–31.

25 Ibid., 383–90, Terhoeven, *Rote Armee Fraktion*, 51f.

26 Aust, *Baader-Meinhof Komplex*, 390–412, Terhoeven, *Rote Armee Fraktion*, 52. On internal security, see also Hanshew, *Terror*, 110–51.

27 Colvin, *Meinhof*, 149.

28 Terhoeven, *Rote Armee Fraktion*, 55–7. See also Martin Jander, 'Isolation oder Isolationsfolter: Die Auseinandersetzung um die Haftbedingungen der RAF-Häftlinge', in *Der 'Deutsche Herbst' und die RAF in Politik, Medien und Kunst: Nationale und internationale Perspektiven*, ed. Nicole Colin et al. (Bielefeld: transcript, 2008), Christoph Riederer, *Die RAF und die Folterdebatte der 1970er Jahre* (Wiesbaden: Springer, 2014).

29 See Terhoeven, *Deutscher Herbst*, 339–450, Jacco Pekelder, 'The RAF Solidarity Movement from a European Perspective', in *Between Prague Spring and French May: Opposition and Revolt in Europe, 1960–1980*, ed. Martin Klimke, Jacco Pekelder and Joachim Scharloth (New York: Berghahn, 2011), Karrin Hanshew, '"Sympathy for the Devil"? The West German Left and the Challenge of Terrorism', *Contemporary European History* 21 (2012), Sebastian Gehrig, 'Sympathizing Subcultures? The Milieus of West German Terrorism', in *Between Prague*

Spring and French May: Opposition and Revolt in Europe, 1960–1980, ed. Martin Klimke, Jacco Pekelder and Joachim Scharloth (New York: Berghahn, 2011).

30 Terhoeven, *Deutscher Herbst*, 257–75, Leith Passmore, 'The Art of Hunger: Self-Starvation in the Red Army Faction', *German History* 27 (2009), Marcel Streng, 'Der Körper im Ausnahmezustand: Hungern als politische Praxis im westdeutschen Strafvollzug (1973–1985)', in *Ausnahmezustände: Entgrenzungen und Regulierungen in Europa während des Kalten Krieges*, ed. Dirk Schumann and Cornelia Rau (Göttingen: Wallstein, 2015). For hunger strikes in the 1980s, see Jan-Hendrik Schulz, *Unbeugsam hinter Gittern: Die Hungerstreiks der RAF nach dem deutschen Herbst* (Frankfurt am Main: Campus, 2019).

31 Colvin, *Meinhof*, 166.

32 Terhoeven, *Rote Armee Fraktion*, 59.

33 Ibid., 61–7.

34 Aust, *Baader-Meinhof Komplex*, 503–10.

35 For a detailed account, see ibid., 512–18.

36 Ibid., 588–92.

37 Ibid., 682f.

38 Ibid., 700–704, Terhoeven, *Rote Armee Fraktion*, 76–9.

39 For a detailed account of the Schleyer abduction and its repercussions, see Aust, *Baader-Meinhof Komplex*, 723–954, in particular 725–30, 846–55, 904–16, Terhoeven, *Rote Armee Fraktion*, 79–85.

40 On the situation in Italy, see in general Ginsborg, *Italy*, 379–87.

41 See Meade, *Red Brigades*, 66–8, Hess, *Angriff*, 75.

42 Caselli and della Porta, 'History of the Red Brigades', 82–3.

43 See Meade, *Red Brigades*, 73–77.

44 Caselli and della Porta, 'History of the Red Brigades', 85–6. See also Hof, *Staat und Terrorismus*, 62–3, Hess, *Angriff*, 75–7.

45 Lumley, *States of Emergency*, 282.

46 On the abduction and killing of Moro, see the detailed accounts by Meade, *Red Brigades*, 98–173, Alison Jamieson, *The Heart Attacked: Terrorism and Conflict in the Italian State* (London: Marion Boyars, 1989), 103–71.

47 See Hanshew, *Terror*, 238–53, Hess, *Angriff*, 127–33.

48 Terhoeven, *Rote Armee Fraktion*, 65.

49 Frankfurter Frauen, 'Aufruf an alle Frauen zur Erfindung des Glücks', *Autonomie: Materialien gegen die Fabrikgesellschaft* 10 (January 1978), 10. See also the discussion in Hanshew, *Terror*, 239–40.

50 On Italy, see, for example, Lumley, *States of Emergency*, 286–92. On West Germany, see the discussion in 'Forum: 1977, The German Autumn', *German History* 25 (2007).

51 See for example the depiction of police officers as 'pigs' in publications such as *agit 883*, a leading anarchist 'underground' magazine in West Berlin in the years following 1968. See Massimo Perinelli, 'Longing, Lust, Violence, Liberation: Discourses on Sexuality on the Radical Left in West Germany, 1969–1972', in *After the History of Sexuality: German Interventions*, ed. Dagmar Herzog, Helmut Puff and Spector Scott (New York: Berghahn Books, 2011), Rotaprint 25, ed., *Agit 883: Bewegung, Revolte, Underground in Westberlin 1969–1972* (Berlin: Assoziation A, 2006).

52 See, with regard to the Red Brigades and the radical left in Italy more generally, Angelo Ventrone, 'Der "permanente Bürgerkrieg" und der Staatsbegriff der politischen Linken im Italien der 1970er Jahre', in *Die bleiernen Jahre: Staat und Terrorismus in der Bundesrepublik Deutschland und Italien 1969–1982*, ed. Johannes Hürter and Gian Enrico Rusconi (Munich: R. Oldenbourg Verlag, 2010), 107–9.

53 Balestrini, *We Want Everything*, 185.

54 On the *Autonomen* and the black bloc, see, for example, AG Grauwacke, *Autonome in Bewegung: Aus den ersten 23 Jahren* (Berlin: Assoziation A, 2003), Sebastian Haunss, *Identität in Bewegung: Prozesse kollektiver Identität bei den Autonomen und in der Schwulenbewegung* (Wiesbaden: Verlag für Sozialwissenschaften, 2004), Georgy Katsiaficas, *The Subversion of Politics: European Autonomous Social Movements and the Decolonization of Everyday Life* (Oakland: AK Press, 2006), Freia Anders, 'Wohnraum, Freiraum, Widerstand: Die Formierung der Autonomen in den Konflikten um Hausbesetzungen Anfang der achtziger Jahre', in *Das alternative Milieu: Antibürgerlicher Lebensstil und linke Politik in der Bundesrepublik Deutschland und Europa, 1968–1983*, ed. Sven Reichardt and Detlef Siegfried (Göttingen: Wallstein, 2010).

55 On the history of the Zurich movement, see Hanspeter Kriesi, *Die Zürcher Bewegung: Bilder, Interaktionen, Zusammenhänge* (Frankfurt

a.M.: Campus Verlag, 1984), Heinz Nigg, ed., *Wir wollen alles, und zwar subito! Die Achtziger Jugendunruhen in der Schweiz und ihre Folgen* (Zurich: Limmat Verlag, 2001), Sophie von Vogel and Lars Schultze-Kossack, eds., *Zür(e)ich brennt* (Zurich: Europa Verlag AG, 2010), Andreas Suttner, *'Beton brennt': Hausbesetzer und Selbstverwaltung im Berlin, Wien und Zürich der 80er* (Vienna: Lit-Verlag, 2011).

56 On the movements of 1980/81, see Hanno Balz and Jan-Henrik Friedrichs, eds., *'All we ever wanted . . .': Eine Kulturgeschichte europäischer Protestbewegungen der 1980er Jahre* (Berlin: Dietz, 2012), Bart van der Steen and Knud Andresen, eds., *A European Youth Revolt: European Perspectives on Youth Protest and Social Movements in the 1980s* (Basingstoke: Palgrave Macmillan, 2016).

57 For an elaboration of this argument, see Joachim C. Häberlen, *The Emotional Politics of the Alternative Left: West Germany, 1968–1984* (Cambridge: Cambridge University Press, 2018), 222–64.

58 Anon., 'En heissä Summer, aber subito', *Stilett: Organ der aufgehenden Drachensaat* 56 (June/July 1980), unpaginated.

59 Jürgen, 'Kreuzberg lebt', *taz* 51, 15 December 1980, 5, found in Ordner Häuserkämpfe, Papiertiger Archiv Berlin. See also Benny Härlin, 'Von Haus zu Haus – Berliner Bewegungsstudien', *Kursbuch* 65, October 1981, 1–28, here 1–5.

60 Themrock, 'Die Kunst der Provokation, den Staat der Lächerlichkeit preisgeben, die Ebene der nackten Konfrontation meiden, das Unabsehbare genießen', *radikal: Zeitung für schöne Bescherung*, Extrablatt, December 1980, 4.

61 'Gespräch mit ehemaligen Besetzern eines Hauses in der Mittenwalder 45: "Da gibt's keinen Weg zurück."', *taz*, 3 July 1981, 20. Found in Ordner Häuserkämpfe West-Berlin 7/81, Papiertiger Archiv Berlin.

62 C. M., 'Frieden schaffen, oder: Sie wollen nur unser Bestes – aber das kriegen sie nicht', *radikal: Zeitung für Anarchie und Wohlstand* 98 (October 1981), 10–11.

63 Anon., 'En heissä Summer'.

64 Ibid.

65 Tomas Lecorte, *Wir tanzen bis zum Ende: Die Geschichte eines Autonomen* (Hamburg: Galgenberg, 1992), 81.

66 Die Kämpfer der aufbrechenden sado-marxistischen Internationale, 'Nicht stehenbleiben', pamphlet, June 1982, found in Ordner Anti-Nato Bewegung, Papiertiger Archiv Berlin.

67 For an elaborate version of this argument, see Joachim C. Häberlen, 'Sekunden der Freiheit: Zum Verhältnis von Gefühlen, Macht und Zeit in Ausnahmesituationen am Beispiel der Revolte 1980/81 in Berlin', in *Ausnahmezustände: Entgrenzungen und Regulierungen in Europa während des Kalten Krieges*, ed. Dirk Schumann and Cornelia Rauh (Göttingen: Wallstein, 2015), Joachim C. Häberlen, 'Heterochronias: Reflections on the Temporal Exceptionality of Revolts', *European Review of History* 28 (2021). See also Lukas J. Hezel, '"Was gibt es zu verlieren, wo es kein Morgen gibt?" Chronopolitik und Radikalisierung in der Jugendrevolte 1980/81 und bei den Autonomen', in *Zeitenwandel: Transformationen geschichtlicher Zeitlichkeit nach dem Boom*, ed. Fernando Esposito (Göttingen: Vandenhoeck & Ruprecht, 2017).

68 Anon., 'Anarchie als Minimalforderung', *radikal: Lieber explosives Chaos als kontrollierte Hochspannung* 97 (August 1981), 10.

69 See, for example, 'Interview with "Freizeit 81"', *radikal: Zeitung für Anarchie und Wohlstand* 98 (October 1981), 17; and Anon., 'Die Ereignisse werfen Schatten', *radikal: Zeitung für schöne Bescherung*, Extrablatt, December 1980, 2.

70 For a rather superficial and highly moralizing analysis of violence among the *Autonomen*, see Sebastian Haunss, *Identität in Bewegung: Prozesse kollektiver Identität bei den Autonomen und in der Schwulenbewegung* (Wiesbaden: Verlag für Sozialwissenschaften, 2004), 122. Somewhat more substantial, but still problematic, are Anders, 'Wohnraum', 494–6, Sven Reichardt, *Authentizität und Gemeinschaft: Linksalternatives Leben in den siebziger und frühen Achtziger Jahren* (Berlin: Suhrkamp, 2014), 562–3.

71 See, for example, the documentary Videoladen Zürich, *Züri brännt* (Switzerland: 1980).

72 See Jonathan Neale, *You Are G8, We Are 6 Billion: The Truth behind the Genoa Protests* (London: Vision Paperbacks, 2002), Willi Baer and Karl-Heinz Dellwo, eds., *Die blutigen Tage von Genua 2001: G8-Gipfel, Widerstand und Repression* (Hamburg: Laika, 2012).

Chapter 4: Mocking the Authorities: The Subversive Power of Laughter

1 Personal conversation with G.U., Berlin, October 2011. See also Katsiaficas, *Subversion*, 136.

2 On humour in protest movements, see in general the contributions to Marjolein 't Hart and Dennis Bos, eds., *Humour and Social Protest*, International Review of Social History, Supplement 15 (Cambridge: Cambridge University Press, 2007).

3 See *Spassguerilla* (West Berlin: Selbstverlag, 1984), 64–8, Luther Blissett and Sonja Brünzels, *Handbuch der Kommunikationsguerilla* (Berlin: Verlag Libertäre Assoziation, 1998), 124–30. Both volumes deal with 'fun guerrilla' from an activist perspective, offering fascinating insights and stories.

4 Quoted in Teune, 'Humour', 120. See also Reimann, *Kunzelmann*, 135, Ulrich Enzensberger, *Die Jahre der Kommune I: Berlin, 1967–1969* (Cologne: Kiepenheuer & Witsch, 2004), 93–5.

5 Reimann, *Kunzelmann*, 137–41. On Kommune 1, see also the account by former communard Enzensberger, *Jahre*. For the broader context of Berlin, see Brown, *West Germany*, 51–8, Timothy Brown, 'A Tale of Two Communes: The Private and the Political in Divided Berlin, 1967–1973', in *Between Prague Spring and French May: Opposition and Revolt in Europe, 1960–1980*, ed. Martin Klimke, Jacco Pekelder and Joachim Scharloth (New York: Berghahn, 2011), Belinda Davis, 'The City as Theater of Protest: West Berlin and West Germany, 1962–1983', in *The Spaces of the Modern City: Imaginaries, Politics and Everyday Life*, ed. Gyan Prakash and Kevin M. Kruse (Princeton: Princeton University Press, 2008).

6 Reimann, *Kunzelmann*, 142, Teune, 'Humour', 121f.

7 Reimann, *Kunzelmann*, 143.

8 Ibid., 143–5.

9 Quoted in Enzensberger, *Jahre*, 119.

10 Ibid., 121–3.

11 Ibid., 123–5. See also Reimann, *Kunzelmann*, 144–6, Teune, 'Humour', 122.

12 Reimann, *Kunzelmann*, 149, Enzensberger, *Jahre*, 131.

13 The pamphlets are all reproduced in the unpaginated book Langhans and Teufel, *Klau mich*. See also the discussion of the pamphlets in Reimann, *Kunzelmann*, 149–57, Enzensberger, *Jahre*, 135–45.

14 For an analysis, see Scharloth, *1968*, 142–66, Teune, 'Humour', 124–5.

15 Langhans and Teufel, *Klau mich*.

16 Ibid.

17 Ibid.

18 Ibid.

19 Ibid.

20 Ibid.

21 Reimann, *Kunzelmann*, 185f.

22 Langhans and Teufel, *Klau mich*.

23 Reimann, *Kunzelmann*, 195–210, quote 196.

24 See the accounts of Kommune 1 in *Spassguerilla*, 64–8, Blissett and Brünzels, *Handbuch*, 124–30.

25 Maurizio Torrealta, 'Painted Politics', in *Autonomia: Post-Political Politics*, ed. Sylvère Lotringer and Christian Marazzi (Los Angeles: Semiotext(e), 2007), 104.

26 For a description of the scene, see, for example, Klemens Gruber, *Die zerstreute Avantgarde: Strategische Kommunikation im Italien der 70er Jahre* (Vienna: Böhlau, 1989), 120–21, Edwards, *More Work!*, 89–90, Moroni and Balestrini, *Goldene Horde*, 328–34, Mathias Heigl, *Rom in Aufruhr: Soziale Bewegungen im Italien der 1970er Jahre* (Bielefeld: transcript, 2015), 289–94.

27 On the Movement of 1977, see Heigl, *Rom*, 249–378, Danilo Mariscalco, 'The Italian Movement of 1977 and the Cultural Praxis of the Youthful Proletariat', in *The Politics of Authenticity: Countercultures and Radical Movements across the Iron Curtain, 1968–1989*, ed. Joachim C. Häberlen, Mark Keck-Szajbel and Kate Mahoney (New York: Berghahn Books, 2018), Edwards, *More Work!*, 75–9, 85–92, Lumley, *States of Emergency*, 295–312, Moroni and Balestrini, *Goldene Horde*, 303–54, Sebastian Haumann, '"Stadtindianer" and "Indiani Metropolitani": Recontextualizing an Italian Protest Movement in West Germany', in *Between Prague Spring and French May: Opposition and Revolt in Europe, 1960–1980*, ed. Martin Klimke, Jacco Pekelder and Joachim Scharloth (New York: Berghahn,

2011), Sylvère Lotringer and Christian Marazzi, eds., *Autonomia: Post-Political Politics* (Cambridge: Semiotext(e), 2007), *Indianer und P 38: Italien, ein neues 68 mit anderen Waffen* (Munich: Trikont Verlag, 1978). On humour in the movement, see specifically Patrick Gun Cuninghame, '"A Laughter That Will Bury You All": Irony as Protest and Language as Struggle in the Italian 1977 Movement', *International Review of Social History* 52, Supplement 15: Humour and Social Protest (2007).

28 See Gruber, *Zerstreute Avantgarde*, 110–12, Moroni and Balestrini, *Goldene Horde*, 314–18.

29 Quoted in Edwards, *More Work!*, 77. See also Heigl, *Rom*, 283.

30 Giorgio Mariani, '"Was Anybody More of an Indian than Karl Marx?" The Indiani Metropolitani and the 1977 Movement', in *Indians and Europe: An Interdisciplinary Collection of Essays*, ed. Christian F. Feest (Aachen: Rader Verlag, 1987), 588.

31 See Gruber, *Zerstreute Avantgarde*, 113.

32 Ibid., 114.

33 Pablo Echaurren, in Emanuele De Donno and Amedeo Martegani, eds., *Yes Yes Yes: Revolutionary Press in Italy, 1966–1977 from Mondo Beat to Zut* (Milan: A+Mbookstore, 2019), 429.

34 Quoted, in German, in *Indianer*, 85–6. The text, which circulated widely in West Germany's radical leftist scene, is taken from *Lotta Continua*, 1 March 1977. The Italian version can be found online at https://www.urbanexperience.it/forums/topic/il-movimento-del-77-lultima-avanguardia/.

35 Mariani, 'Was Anybody', 590.

36 The story is summarized and explained in Gruber, *Zerstreute Avantgarde*, 100, Moroni and Balestrini, *Goldene Horde*, 373–6. Original, according to Gruber: Umberto Eco, 'Come parlano i "nuovi barbari". C'è un'altra lingua: l'italo-indiano', *L'Espresso* 14 (10 April 1977), 54.

37 Umberto Eco, 'Für eine semiologische Guerilla', in *Über Gott und die Welt*, ed. Umberto Eco (Munich: Hanser, 1985 [1967]).

38 On Mao-Dadaism, see Jabopo Galimberti, 'Maoism, Dadaism and Mao-Dadaism in 1960s and 1970s Italy', in *Art, Global Maoism and the Chinese Cultural Revolution*, ed. Jacopo Galimberti, Noemi de Haro García and Victoria H. F. Scott (Manchester: Manchester University Press, 2020).

39 Kollektiv A/traverso, *Alice ist der Teufel: Praxis einer subversiven Kommuniktion. Radio Alice (Bologna)* (Berlin: Merve, 1977), 120.

40 Ibid., 37–45. See also the discussion in Marco Briziarelli, 'Tripping Down the (Media) Rabbit Hole: Radio Alice and the Insurgent Socialization of Airwaves', *Journal of Radio & Audio Media* 23 (2016).

41 A/traverso, *Alice*, 50. Also quoted in Gruber, *Zerstreute Avantgarde*, 44. His analysis of Radio Alice and the communication guerrilla in 1970s Italy is unsurpassed.

42 Gruber, *Zerstreute Avantgarde*, 65.

43 A/traverso, *Alice*, 24–5. Also quoted in Gruber, *Zerstreute Avantgarde*, 49.

44 Gruber, *Zerstreute Avantgarde*, 57.

45 Ibid., 67.

46 Ibid., 48.

47 Ibid., 69–70.

48 A/traverso, *Alice*, 50–52.

49 Gruber, *Zerstreute Avantgarde*, 62.

50 Ibid., 58.

51 A/traverso, *Alice*, 122.

52 For the radical left's reaction to Lorusso's death throughout Italy, see also Heigl, *Rom*, 318–27.

53 Briziarelli, 'Tripping Down', 356–7. See also A/traverso, *Alice*, 136–8.

54 On Solidarity and the strikes of 1980, see Michael Szporer, *Solidarity: The Great Workers Strike of 1980* (Lanham: Lexington Books, 2012), Roman Laba, *The Roots of Solidarity: A Political Sociology of Poland's Working Class Democratization* (Princeton: Princeton University Press, 1991), Jack M. Bloom, *Seeing through the Eyes of the Polish Revolution: Solidarity and the Struggle against Communism in Poland* (Leiden: Brill, 2013). Chapter 15 returns to these events.

55 This is based on the autobiographical account by Major Waldemar Fydrych, *Lives of the Orange Men: A Biographical History of the Polish Orange Alternative Movement*, trans. David French (Wivenhoe: Minor Compositions, 2014), 95–101. See also the discussion in Berenika Szymanski, *Theatraler Protest und der Weg Polens zu 1989: Zum Aushandeln von Öffentlichkeit im Jahrzehnt der Solidarność* (Bielefeld: transcript, 2012), 209–58.

56 Fydrych, *Lives*, 10–12.

57 See ibid., 14–62.

58 Cited in Szymanski, *Protest*, 214.

59 Cited in ibid., 217.

60 For an account, see ibid., 217–18.

61 Fydrych, *Lives*, 66–74.

62 Ibid., 91.

63 The best discussion of Orange Alternative is provided by Padraic Kenney, *A Carnival of Revolution: Central Europe 1989* (Princeton: Princeton University Press, 2002). See also Barbara Górska and Benjamin Koschalka, eds., *Happening against Communism by the Orange Alternative* (Kraków: International Cultural Centre, 2011), Lisiunia A. Romanienko, 'Antagonism, Absurdity, and the Avant-Garde: Dismantling Soviet Oppression through the Use of Theatrical Devices by Poland's "Orange" Solidarity Movement', *International Review of Social History* 52, Supplement 15: Humour and Social Protest (2007). There is also an excellent online museum with detailed descriptions of happenings (mostly drawing on Fydrych's account), photos and posters produced by the movement: see http://www.orangealternativemuseum.pl/#homepage. See also the article about Orange Alternative, including video footage of happenings, at https://culture.pl/en/article/the-orange-alternative-there-is-no-freedom-without-dwarfs.

64 Fydrych, *Lives*, 111.

65 Ibid., 113–14.

66 For a lively account of the happening, see ibid., 114–19.

67 Ibid., 124–6.

68 Ibid., 139–48.

69 Quoted in Kenney, *Carnival*, 190.

70 Quoted in ibid.

71 Quoted in ibid., 190–91.

72 On the APPD, see Klaus Farin, ed., *Die Partei hat immer Recht! Die gesammelten Schriften der 'Anarchistischen Pogo-Partei Deutschlands'* (Bad Tölz: Tilsner Verlag, 1998). On the KPD/RZ, see https://www.kpd-rz.de/, and Blissett and Brünzels, *Handbuch*, 162–5.

73 On the Clowns Army, see L. M. Bogad, *Tactical Performance: The The-ory and Practice of Serious Play* (Milton Park: Routledge, 2016).

74 See only the discussion in Blissett and Brünzels, *Handbuch*.

Chapter 5: The Appeal of Theory: Criticizing Power and Imagining Alternatives

1 See, on some of these magazines, De Donno and Martegani, eds., *Yes Yes Yes*, Antonia Lenzi, 'Die Entstehung der italienischen revolutionären Linken: Das Beispiel von "Il Manifesto" und "Lotta Continua"', *Arbeit – Bewegung – Geschichte* 15 (2016), Alain Dugrand, *Libération (1973–1981): Un moment d'ivresse* (Paris: Fayard, 2013), Mischa Suter, 'Ein Stachel in der Seite der Sozialgeschichte: Jacques Rancière und die Zeitschrift "Les Révoltes logiques"', *Sozial.Geschichte Online* (2011), Kristof Niese, 'Vade-mekum' der Protestbewegung? Transnationale Vermittlungen durch das Kursbuch von 1965 bis 1975* (Baden-Baden: Nomos Verlag, 2017), Jörg Magenau, *Die taz: Eine Zeitung als Lebensform* (Munich: Hanser, 2007), Duncan Thompson, *Pessimism of the Intellect? A History of New Left Review* (Monmouth: Merlin Press, 2007), Gerson S. Sher, *Praxis: Marxist Criticism and Dissent in Socialist Yugoslavia* (Bloomington: Indiana Univer-sity Press, 1977), Gisela Notz, ed., *Als die Frauenbewegung noch Courage hatte: Die 'Berliner Frauenzeitung Courage' und die autonomen Frauenbewe-gungen der 1970er und 1980er Jahre* (Bonn: Historisches Forschungszentrum der Friedrich-Ebert-Stiftung, 2007). On leftist publishing cultures in West Germany, see also Uwe Sonnenberg, *Von Marx zum Maulwurf: Linker Buchhandel in Westdeutschland in den 1970er Jahren* (Göttingen: Wallstein, 2016), Sven Reichardt, *Authentizität*, 223–315. On samizdat, see for example Martin Machovec, *Writing Underground: Reflections on Samizdat Literature in Totalitarian Czechoslovakia* (Prague: Karolinum Press, 2019), Friederike Kind-Kovács and Jessie Labov, eds., *Samizdat, Tamizdat, and Beyond: Transnational Media during and after Socialism* (New York: Berghahn, 2013), Wolfgang Eichwede, ed., *Samizdat: Alternative Kultur in Zentral-und Osteuropa: Die 60er bis 80er Jahre* (Bremen: Edition Temmen, 2000).

2 See only, on West Germany, Philipp Felsch, *Der lange Sommer der Theorie: Geschichte einer Revolte* (Munich: Beck, 2015).

3 Lidia Ravera and Marco Lombardo Radice, *Pigs Have Wings*, trans. Jane Sebastian (New York: Pomerica Press Limited, 1977), Svende Merian, *Der Tod des Märchenprinzen: Frauenroman* (Hamburg: Buntbuch-Verlag, 1980). For other, more or less famous, examples from West Germany, see Dieter, *Was wird aus mir werden? Ich hoffe ein Mensch. Ein Männertagebuch* (Berlin (West): Parallel Verlag, 1978), Arne Piewitz, *Ich war der Märchenprinz* (Hamburg: Buntbuch-Verlag, 1983), Verena Stefan, *Häutungen* (Munich: Verlag Frauenoffensive, 1975).

4 Important works of these authors include Carla Lonzi, *Sputiamo su Hegel: La donna clitoridea e la donna vaginale* (Milan: Rivolta Femminile, 1977), Gerburg Treusch-Dieter, *Von der sexuellen Rebellion zur Gen- und Reproduktionstechnologie* (Tübingen: Konkursbuchverlag, 1990), Hélène Cixous, 'The Laugh of the Medusa', *Signs* 1 (1976), Luce Irigaray, *This Sex Which Is Not One*, trans. Catherine Porter and Carolyn Burke (Ithaca: Cornell University Press, 1985). On French feminist theory, see also Gill Allwood, *French Feminisms: Gender and Violence in Contemporary Theory* (London: UCL Press, 1998), Dani Cavallaro, *French Feminist Theory: An Introduction* (London: Continuum, 2003). For an important theoretical feminist magazine in West Germany, see Vojin S. Vukadinović, ed., *Die Schwarze Botin: Ästhetik, Kritik, Polemik, Satire, 1976–1980* (Götingen: Wallstein, 2020).

5 On the appeal of communism among French intellectuals, see Jeannine Verdès-Leroux, *Le Réveil des somnambules: Le Parti communiste, les intellectuels et la culture, 1956–1985* (Paris: Fayard: Éditions de Minuit, 1987), Jeannine Verdès-Leroux, *Au service du parti: Le Parti communiste, les intellectuels et la culture (1944–1956)* (Paris: Fayard: Éditions de Minuit, 1983), Sudhir Hazareesingh, *Intellectuals and the French Communist Party: Disillusion and Decline* (Oxford: Oxford University Press, 1991), Ian H. Birchall, *Sartre against Stalinism* (New York: Berghahn, 2004), Jean-François Sirinelli, 'Les Normaliens de la Rue d'Ulm après 1945: Une génération communiste', *Revue d'histoire du monde moderne* 32 (1986). For the British story, see Dennis Dworkin, *Cultural Marxism in Postwar Britain: History, the New Left, and the*

Origins of Cultural Studies (Durham: Duke University Press, 1997), Harvey J. Kaye, *The British Marxist Historians: An Introductory Analysis* (New York: Polity Press, 1984), Michael Kenny, *The First New Left: British Intellectuals after Stalin* (London: Lawrence & Wishart, 1995).

6 Important works include Wilhelm Reich, *The Sexual Revolution: Toward a Self-Governing Character Structure*, trans. Theodore P. Wolfe (New York: Orgone Institute Press, 1945 (first published 1936)), Karl Korsch, *Die materialistische Geschichtsauffassung und andere Schriften* (Frankfurt a.M.: Europäische Verlagsanstalt, 1971 (first published 1931)), Karl Korsch, *Revolutionärer Klassenkampf: Diktatur des Proletariats und die Staatstheorie bei Marx, Engels, Lenin* (Berlin: Kollektivverlag, 1972 (with texts first published in 1930, 1946, and 1948)), György Lukács, *History and Class Consciousness: Studies in Marxist Dialectics*, trans. Rodney Livingstone (Cambridge, MA: MIT Press, 1971 (first published 1923)), Antonio Gramsci, *Prison Notebooks*, trans. Joseph A. Buttigieg and Antonio Callari (New York: Columbia University Press, 1992 (written 1929–35, first published 1947)). For an intellectual history of some of these thinkers and their influence on the Western left, see Renaud, *New Lefts*.

7 Mario Tronti, *Workers and Capital*, trans. David Broder (London: Verso, 2019), 3. The text was first published in Italian in 1966.

8 On *operaismo*, see Steve Wright, *Storming Heaven: Class Composition and Struggle in Italian Autonomist Marxism* (London: Pluto, 2002).

9 Probably the most famous text depicting history as epic struggles is the *Communist Manifesto* (1848) by Karl Marx and Friedrich Engels.

10 Raniero Panzieri, *La crisi del movimento operaio: Scritti interventi lettere, 1956–1960* (Milan: Lampugnani Nigri, 1973), 113. Cited in Wright, *Storming Heaven*, 19.

11 See Wright, *Storming Heaven*, 23.

12 Ibid., 32–62, quotes 48, 24, 57.

13 Tronti, *Workers*, 30–31.

14 Moishe Postone, *Time, Labor, and Social Domination: A Reinterpretation of Marx's Critical Theory* (Cambridge: Cambridge University Press, 1993).

15 See Sven Gringmuth, *Was war die Proletarische Wende? Ein Beitrag zur Mentalitätsgeschichte der bundesrepublikanischen Linken* (Münster: Westfälisches Dampfboot, 2021), Jan Ole Arps, *Frühschicht: Linke*

Fabrikintervention in den 70er Jahren (Hamburg: Assoziation A, 2011), Ross, *May '68*, 113–37. See also *Arbeit – Bewegung – Geschichte* 15 (1): *Schwerpunkt Linke Betriebsintervention, wilde Streiks und operaistische Politik 1968 bis 1988* (2016).

16 Karl Heinz Roth, *Die 'andere' Arbeiterbewegung und die Entwicklung der kapitalistischen Repression von 1880 bis zur Gegenwart: Ein Beitrag zum Neuverständnis der Klassengeschichte in Deutschland* (Munich: Trikont, 1974).

17 E. P. Thompson, *The Making of the English Working Class* (London: Penguin, 1991), 11. The book was originally published in 1963.

18 Jacques Rancière, *Proletarian Nights: The Workers' Dream in Nineteenth-Century France* (London: Verso, 2012), particularly 3–23. The quote is from the insightful article by Suter, 'Stachel', 29.

19 See Sher, *Praxis*. The international edition of the journal is available at https://www.marxists.org/subject/praxis/praxis-international/index.htm.

20 Mihailo Marković, 'Socialism and Self-Management', *Praxis: Philosophische Zeitschrift* 2/3 (1965), quotes 181, 182, 185.

21 Sher, *Praxis*, 199, 239.

22 Reimut Reiche, *Sexualität und Klassenkampf: Zur Abwehr repressiver Entsublimierung* (Frankfurt a.M.: Verlag Neue Kritik, 1968), Dieter Duhm, *Angst im Kapitalismus: 2. Versuch der gesellschaftlichen Begründung zwischenmenschlicher Angst in der kapitalistischen Warengesellschaft* (Lampertheim: Küber, 1973). On Marcuse and the student movement, see Roland Roth, *Rebellische Subjektivität: Herbert Marcuse und die neuen Protestbewegungen* (Frankfurt a.M.: Campus, 1985), John Abromeit, 'The Limits of Praxis: The Social-Psychological Foundations of Theodor Adorno's and Herbert Marcuse's Interpretations of the 1960s Protest Movements', in *Changing the World, Changing Oneself: Political Protest and Collective Identities in West Germany and the U.S. in the 1960s and 1970s*, ed. Belinda Davis et al. (New York: Berghahn, 2010), Häberlen, *Emotional Politics*, 53–6.

23 Wilhelm Reich, *Der sexuelle Kampf der Jugend* (Berlin: Verlag für Sexualpolitik, 1932), Wilhelm Reich, *Massenpsychologie des Faschismus: Zur Sexualökonomie der politischen Reaktion und zur proletarischen*

Sexualpolitik (Copenhagen: Verlag für Sexualpolitik, 1933), Wilhelm Reich, *Die sexuelle Revolution* (Frankfurt a.M.: Fischer, 1966). On Reich in the West German student movement, see Herzog, *Sex*, 152–62.

24 Herbert Marcuse, *One-Dimensional Man: Studies in the Ideology of Advanced Industrial Society* (Boston: Beacon, 1964), Herbert Marcuse, *Eros and Civilization: A Philosophical Inquiry into Freud* (London: Routledge, 1987 [1955]). On Marcuse and the student movement, see Jean-Michel Palmier, *Herbert Marcuse et la Nouvelle Gauche* (Paris: Éditions Pierre Belfond, 1973), Roth, *Subjektivität*, Abromeit, 'Limits of Praxis', Häberlen, *Emotional Politics*, 53–6. For a general history of the Frankfurt School, see Martin Jay, *The Dialectical Imagination: A History of the Frankfurt School and the Institute of Social Research, 1923–1950* (Berkeley, Los Angeles: University of California Press, 1996).

25 Marcuse, *Eros*, quotes 35, 199–205.

26 The essay, first published in 1978, has been republished many times. I draw on the following edition: Václav Havel, 'The Power of the Powerless', in *The Power of the Powerless: Citizens against the State in Central-Eastern Europe*, ed. John Keane (London: Routledge, 2015). For the greengrocer's story and the following quotes, see ibid., 27–9. On Havel, see his biography by Kieran Williams, *Václav Havel* (London: Reaktion Books, 2016).

27 Havel, 'Power', 31.

28 Ibid., quotes 36–9, 41, 83.

29 Ibid., 62–3.

30 Ibid., 89–92.

31 Ibid., 93.

32 The following draws on the brilliant discussion by Jonathan Bolton, *Worlds of Dissent: Charter 77, the Plastic People of the Universe, and Czech Culture under Communism* (Cambridge, MA: Harvard University Press, 2012). On the broader cultural context, see also Paulina Bren, *The Greengrocer and His TV: The Culture of Communism after the 1968 Prague Spring* (Ithaca: Cornell University Press, 2010). For a source collection, see *Human Rights in Czechoslovakia: The Documents of Charter 77, 1977–1982* (Washington: Commission on Security and Cooperation in

Europe, 1982). On Charter 77 and the Czech underground, see also Machovec, *Writing Underground*, 42–62.

33 Cited in Bolton, *Worlds of Dissent*, 154.

34 Ibid., 192.

35 Havel, 'Power', 48.

36 Cited in Bolton, *Worlds of Dissent*, 155.

37 Cited in ibid., 191.

38 Ibid., 170, 191, 197. See also Havel, 'Power', 78–9.

39 Bolton, *Worlds of Dissent*, 239–43.

40 Ibid., 243.

41 Ibid., 246.

42 Ibid., 265.

43 Foucault wrote in German, *Was heißt Aufklärung?*, though the title of Kant's famous essay is actually *Was ist Aufklärung?*, that is, *What Is Enlightenment?*

44 Michel Foucault, 'The Subject and Power', *Critical Inquiry* 8 (1982), quotes 785, 781. The academic literature on Foucault is vast; see only Graham Burchell, Colin Gordon and Peter Miller, eds., *The Foucault Effect: Studies in Governmentality* (Chicago: University of Chicago Press, 1991), François Ewald and Bernhard Waldenfels, eds., *Spiele der Wahrheit: Michel Foucaults Denken* (Frankfurt a.M.: Suhrkamp, 1991), Thomas Lemke, *Eine Kritik der politischen Vernunft: Foucaults Analyse der modernen Gouvernementalität* (Berlin: Argument, 1997). For a biography, see Didier Eribon, *Michel Foucault* (Paris: Flammarion, 2011).

45 Foucault, 'Subject', 780–81.

46 On Foucault's political activism, see his biography by Eribon, *Foucault*, 315–498. See also Julian Bourg, *From Revolution to Ethics: May 1968 and Contemporary French Thought* (Montreal: McGill-Queen's University Press, 2007), 79–95, Perry Zurn and Andrew Dilts, eds., *Active Intolerance: Michel Foucault, the Prisons Information Group, and the Future of Abolition* (New York: Palgrave Macmillan, 2016).

47 On the perception of Foucault in Germany, see only Felsch, *Lange Sommer*. On Foucault in Italy, see the unpublished Ph.D. thesis by Mark Coté, 'The Italian Foucault: Communication, Networks, and the Dispositif' (Simon Fraser University, 2007).

48 For an intellectual history of French thought after 1968, see Bourg, *Revolution to Ethics*, in particular 105–225. Other influential authors include Jean Baudrillard, Hélène Cixous and Luce Irigaray, whose works were all published in German by the left-wing Merve publishing house. These writers are often described as 'French Theory', a problematic label that obscures differences and disagreements.

49 Michel Foucault, 'Body/Power', in *Power/Knowledge: Selected Interviews and Other Writings, 1972–1977. Michel Foucault*, ed. Colin Gordon (New York: Pantheon Books, 1980), 59, first published as 'Pouvoir et Corps', in *Quel Corps?*, September/October 1975.

50 Michel Foucault, 'Truth and Power', in *Power/Knowledge: Selected Interviews and Other Writings, 1972–1977. Michel Foucault*, ed. Colin Gordon (New York: Pantheon Books, 1980), 116, first published as 'Intervista a Michel Foucault', in Michel Foucault, *Microfisica del Potere* (Turin: Einaudi, 1977).

51 Michel Foucault, 'Subject', 788. For a critique of understanding power as a commodity, see also Michel Foucault, 'Two Lectures', in *Power/Knowledge: Selected Interviews and Other Writings, 1972–1977. Michel Foucault*, ed. Colin Gordon (New York: Pantheon Books, 1980), 89, first published in Michel Foucault, *Microfisica del Potere* (Turin: Einaudi, 1977).

52 Michel Foucault. 'Power and Strategies', in *Power/Knowledge: Selected Interviews and Other Writings, 1972–1977. Michel Foucault*, ed. Colin Gordon (New York: Pantheon Books, 1980), 142, first published as 'Pouvoir et Stratégies', in *Les Révoltes Logiques* 4 (1977).

53 Foucault, 'Subject', 790, Foucault, 'Truth and Power', 142.

54 Foucault, 'Body/Power', 58.

55 Ibid., 56–7.

56 Foucault, 'Subject', 785.

57 For a good summary of these debates, see Lemke, *Kritik der politischen Vernunft*, 15–23.

58 See also Ulrich Bröckling, *Das unternehmerische Selbst: Soziologie einer Subjektivierungsform* (Frankfurt a.M.: Suhrkamp, 2007), 283–97, Ulrich Bröckling, *Gute Hirten führen sanft: Über Menschenriegerungskünste* (Berlin: Suhrkamp, 2017), 365–422.

59 Gilles Deleuze and Félix Guattari, *A Thousand Plateaus*, trans. Brian Massumi (Minneapolis: University of Minnesota Press, 1987), 6, 24–5. Original publications Gilles Deleuze and Félix Guattari, *Rhizome: Introduction* (Paris: Éditions de Minuit, 1976), Gilles Deleuze and Félix Guattari, *Mille plateaux* (Paris: Éditions de Minuit, 1980). The academic literature on Deleuze is vast; for an introduction, see Eugene W. Holland, *Deleuze and Guattari's 'A Thousand Plateaus': A Reader's Guide* (London: Bloomsbury Publishing, 2013), Brent Adkins, *Deleuze and Guattari's A Thousand Plateaus: A Critical Introduction and Guide* (Edinburgh: Edinburgh University Press, 2015), Philip Goodchild, *Deleuze and Guattari: An Introduction to the Politics of Desire* (London: SAGE, 1996).

60 See advertisements for the bar in *radikal* (West Berlin leftist magazine), 92 (May 1981), 30.

61 Herbert Röttgen, 'Sumpf', *Das Blatt* 107 (4–17 November 1977), 14–15.

Chapter 6: Rebellious Sounds: The Music of Protesting

1 See, for example, Manuela Marin, 'The Struggle for the Minds of the Youth: The Securitate and Musical Countercultures in Communist Romania', in *The Politics of Authenticity: Countercultures and Radical Movements across the Iron Curtain, 1968–1989*, ed. Joachim C. Häberlen, Mark Keck-Szajbel and Kate Mahoney (New York: Berghahn, 2018).

2 For a general introduction to the topic, see Jonathan C. Friedman, ed., *The Routledge History of Social Protest in Popular Music* (New York: Routledge, 2013), Timothy Brown and Andrew Lison, eds., *The Global Sixties in Sound and Vision: Media, Counterculture, Revolt* (Basingstoke: Palgrave Macmillan, 2014), Beate Kutschke and Barley Norton, eds., *Music and Protest in 1968* (Cambridge: Cambridge University Press, 2013).

3 For contemporary news footage, see: https://www.youtube.com/watch?v=LXt7OdT5DTk.

4 Ralf Reinders and Ronald Fritzsch, *Die Bewegung 2. Juni: Gespräche über Haschrebellen, Lorenzentführung, Knast* (Berlin, Amsterdam: Edition ID-Archiv, 1995), 14. Cited in Brown, *West Germany*, 158.

5 Brown, *West Germany*, 158.

6 Ibid. For a discussion of rebellious rock music in France, see Jonathyne Briggs, *Sounds French: Globalization, Cultural Communities, and Pop Music in France, 1958–1980* (Oxford: Oxford University Press, 2015), 78–109.

7 Wolfgang Seidel, 'Berlin und die Linke in den 1960ern: Die Entstehung der Ton Steine Scherben', in *Scherben: Musik, Politik und Wirkung der Ton Steine Scherben*, ed. Wolfgang Seidel (Mainz: Ventil Verlag, 2005), 39. Cited in Brown, *West Germany*, 162.

8 Jens Hagen, quoted in Benedikt Geulen and Peter Graf, *Mach mal bitte Platz, wir müssen hier stürmen: Als der Beat nach Deutschland kam. Fotografien von Jens Hagen* (Cologne: M7 Verlag, 2007), 80. Cited in Brown, *West Germany*, 162.

9 On Ton Steine Scherben, see Timothy Brown, 'Music as a Weapon? "Ton Steine Scherben" and the Politics of Rock in Cold War Berlin', *German Studies Review* 32 (2009), Kai Sichtermann, Jens Johler and Christian Stahl, *Keine Macht für Niemand: Die Geschichte der 'Ton Steine Scherben'* (Berlin: Schwarzkopf & Schwarzkopf, 2000).

10 Ton Steine Scherben, 'Macht kaputt was euch kaputt macht', https://www.youtube.com/watch?v=UwE8dlRnsio; 'Keine Macht für Niemand', https://www.youtube.com/watch?v=_UlTvJ2POXM; 'Rauch-Haus-Song', https://www.youtube.com/watch?v=fczGvrfBVUY.

11 See Brown, *West Germany*, 178–82.

12 *Rauchhaus: Das ist unser Haus. Protokoll einer Hausbesetzung in Berlin* (documentary), https://www.youtube.com/watch?v=63Znhap6foI&t=447s (see mins. 4:55–7:27).

13 Ton Steine Scherben, 'Der Traum ist aus', https://www.youtube.com/watch?v=a1vgwHZjoxQ.

14 Bolton, *Worlds of Dissent*, 121. See also Martin Machovec, 'Czech Underground Musicians in Search of Art Innovation', *East Central Europe* 38 (2011). Beyond the Czech case, see Timothy W. Ryback, *Rock Around the Bloc: A History of Rock Music in Eastern Europe and the Soviet Union* (Oxford: Oxford University Press, 1990). See also contributions in Joachim C. Häberlen, Mark Keck-Szajbel and Kate Mahoney, eds., *The Politics of Authenticity: Countercultures and Radical Movements across*

the Iron Curtain, 1968–1989 (New York: Berghahn, 2018), Juliane Fürst and Josie McLellan, eds., *Dropping Out of Socialism: The Creation of Alternative Spheres in the Soviet Bloc* (Lanham, Boulder, New York, London: Lexington Books, 2017). Václav Havel, 'The Power of the Powerless', in *From Stalinism to Pluralism: A Documentary History of Eastern Europe Since 1945*, ed. Gale Stokes (Oxford: Oxford University Press, 1991).

15 Bolton, *Worlds of Dissent*, 118.

16 Ibid., 119.

17 Ivan Martin Jirous, 'Zpráva o třetím českém hudebním obrození', in *Magorův zápisník*, ed. Michael Špirit (Prague: Torst, 1997), 182. Cited in Bolton, *Worlds of Dissent*, 307 n37.

18 For an intriguing discussion of the underground rock scene, its concerts and happenings, see Machovec, *Writing Underground*, 104–30.

19 Bolton, *Worlds of Dissent*, 121.

20 Václav Havel, *Disturbing the Peace: A Conversation with Karel Hvížďala*, trans. Paul Wilson (New York: Vintage, 1997), 128. Cited in Bolton, *Worlds of Dissent*, 138.

21 Bolton, *Worlds of Dissent*, 138.

22 Ibid., 125. On the politics of the underground scene, also Machovec, *Writing Underground*, 63–84.

23 Bolton, *Worlds of Dissent*, 124, 139.

24 See, for example, footage of a Plastic People of the Universe concert in the documentary https://www.youtube.com/watch?v=YjWzA_kxNq Q&t=3205s, or a 1973 concert in Prague, https://www.youtube.com/watch?v=woTjq7akZxk. Compare with the socialist 'Warszawianka', https://www.youtube.com/watch?v=txaW9O7N-F4. Originally composed in Polish before the First World War, the 'Warszawianka' was translated into many languages (and amended) in subsequent years and was frequently performed in socialist states.

25 The Sex Pistols, 'Anarchy in the UK', https://www.youtube.com/watch?v=cBojbjoMttI (not the live concert).

26 Quoted in Greil Marcus, *Lipstick Traces: A Secret History of the Twentieth Century* (London: Faber, 2001), 1. For a history of punk in the UK, see for example Jon Savage, *England's Dreaming: Anarchy,*

Sex Pistols, Punk Rock, and Beyond (New York: St Martin's Griffin, 2002).

27 For a recording of the interview, see https://www.youtube.com/watch?v=OC16gG5Rtzs. See also Matthew Worley, *No Future: Punk, Politics and British Youth Culture, 1976–1984* (Cambridge: Cambridge University Press, 2017), 6.

28 Quoted in Marcus, *Lipstick Traces*, 2.

29 Worley, *No Future*, 3.

30 For the famous slogans, see ibid., 4.

31 On punk in France and Germany, both East and West, see Briggs, *Sounds French*, 144–77, Jeff Hayton, *Culture from the Slums: Punk Rock in East and West Germany* (Oxford: Oxford University Press, 2022). Material, including photos, on the Mont-de-Marsan festival can be found online at https://underground-england.com/punk-at-the-plumacon-the-first-european-punk-festival/.

32 See, for example, Oskar Mulej, 'A Place Called Johnny Rotten Square: The Ljubljana Punk Scene and the Subversion of Socialist Yugoslavia', in *A European Youth Revolt: European Perspectives on Youth Protest and Social Movements in the 1980s*, ed. Knud Andresen and Bart van der Steen (Basingstoke: Palgrave Macmillan, 2016), Grzegorz Piotrowski, 'Punk against Communism: The Jarocin Rock Festival and Revolting Youth in 1980s Poland', in *A European Youth Revolt: European Perspectives on Youth Protest and Social Movements in the 1980s*, ed. Knud Andresen and Bart van der Steen (Basingstoke: Palgrave Macmillan, 2016), Jeff Hayton, 'Härte gegen Punk: Popular Music, Western Media, and State Response in the German Democratic Republic', *German History* 31 (2015). For footage from the Jarocin festival, see https://www.youtube.com/watch?v=zq6d920FMRg.

33 See Craig O'Hara, *The Philosophy of Punk: More Than Noise!!* (Edinburgh: AK Press, 1995), Marcus, *Lipstick Traces*.

34 Worley, *No Future*, Chapter 5.

35 Slime, 'Deutschland muss sterben', https://www.youtube.com/watch?v=ID4lstARKow. On Slime, see Hayton, *Culture from the Slums*, 228–32.

36 See BVerfG, Beschluss der 2. Kammer des Ersten Senats vom 03. November 2000 - I BvR 581/00 -, Rn. (1–33), http://www.bverfg.de/e/rk20001103_1bvr058100.html.

37 Worley, *No Future*, 164.

38 See Matthew Worley, 'Shot By Both Sides: Punk, Politics and the End of "Consensus"', *Contemporary British History* 26 (2012).

39 See the accounts in Grauwacke, *Autonome*.

40 Worley, *No Future*, 96.

41 Abrasive Wheels, 'Vicious Circle', https://www.youtube.com/watch?v=fq2CE5XeHIQ.

42 Worley, *No Future*, 96.

43 Schleimkeim, 'In der Kneipe zur trockenen Kehle', https://www.youtube.com/watch?v=LPHR9i1UUss.

44 Worley, *No Future*, 112. The Clash, 'London's Burning', https://www.youtube.com/watch?v=TCw9_avTlYs; the Adverts, 'Bored Teenagers', https://www.youtube.com/watch?v=dWApeBRj1Zw; the Slits, 'A Boring Life', https://www.youtube.com/watch?v=7f7Iwj1geqQ.

45 Worley, *No Future*, 120.

46 Ibid., 114. The Members, 'The Sound of the Suburbs', https://www.youtube.com/watch?v=NsHGnw1txLY.

47 Worley, *No Future*, 191.

48 Ibid., 180–82. See, for example, the Raincoats, 'Off Duty Trip', https://www.youtube.com/watch?v=Gry6-VLmO_8; Ludus, 'My Cherry Is in Sherry', https://www.youtube.com/watch?v=rvryKnzZtZE; the Slits, 'Typical Girls', https://www.youtube.com/watch?v=QCk8tEOcwqU.

49 Worley, *No Future*, 194.

50 Ibid., 195.

51 The Sex Pistols, 'God Save the Queen', https://www.youtube.com/watch?v=yqrAPOZxgzU.

52 Worley, *No Future*, Chapter 8.

53 See, for example, the punk cult film by Derek Jarman, *Jubilee* (United Kingdom: 1978). For a discussion of the film, see Worley, *No Future*, 222.

54 Worley, *No Future*, 242.

55 See in general Felix Denk and Sven von Thülen, *Der Klang der Familie: Berlin, Techno und die Wende* (Berlin: Suhrkamp, 2012). See also the impressive documentary *Party auf dem Todesstreifen*, https://www.youtube.com/watch?v=_1aLyy38wuI&t=49s.

56 Falko Blask and Michael Fuchs-Gamböck, *Techno – Eine Generation in Ekstase* (Bergisch-Gladbach: Lübbe, 1995), 159–60. This section draws on material discussed in Leonie Karwath and Joachim C. Häberlen, 'Mit der Technik tanzen: Technokörper im Berlin der frühen Neunziger Jahre', *Body Politics: Zeitschrift für Körpergeschichte* 6 (2018).

57 Michael Pilz, 'Objekt von Sensation und Spekulation: Techno in all seinen Spielarten ist eine folgerichtige Zeiterscheinung', *Neue Zeit*, 21 January 1992, 14.

58 Wolfram Neugebauer, Tekknozid: Technik, http://tekknozid.de/ (last accessed 19 January 2020). For some rare video footage of the events, see https://www.youtube.com/watch?v=CfVN7iX_KPc&list=PLvLcQbZsvT5nVy3XZFqb2F5KOYS2aHMMc; without footage for the sound, listen to https://www.youtube.com/watch?v=LlyFEhQ4xVg, or https://www.youtube.com/watch?v=haVW2t4HEjU&t=2475s. For a history of the party, see www.tekknozid.de.

59 Cited in Denk and Thülen, *Klang der Familie*, 163.

60 Cited in ibid., 251.

61 Cited in ibid., 178.

62 Sven Röhrig, 'Wie man Techno macht: 5 Statements by 3-Phase', in Robert Klanten and Gestalten, *Localizer 1.0: The Techno House Book* (Berlin: Die Gestalten Verlag, 1995), LOC 1.0. FEA 1.9. 3PH.

63 Denk and Thülen, *Klang der Familie*, 193.

64 See our discussion in Karwath and Häberlen, 'Mit der Technik tanzen', 120–22.

65 Denk and Thülen, *Klang der Familie*, 46–7.

66 Ibid., 246.

67 See the festival's self-description at https://www.fusion-festival.de/de/x/festival/was-ist-die-fusion (relying on the German version, last accessed 19 January 2020). See also the documentary about the festival, at https://kulturkosmos.de/#, and Anja Schwanhäußer,

Kosmonauten des Underground: Ethnografie einer Berliner Szene (Frankfurt am Main: Campus, 2008).

68 Advanced Chemistry, 'Fremd im eigenen Land', https://www.you tube.com/watch?v=yHe3xIQQpKU&t=149s.

69 On hip hop in Germany, see Timothy Brown, '"Keeping It Real" in a Different 'Hood: (African-)Americanization and Hip Hop in Germany', in *The Vinyl Ain't Final: Hip Hop and the Globalization of Black Popular Culture*, ed. Dipannita Basu and Sidney J. Lemelle (London: Pluto, 2006), Murat Güngör and Hannes Loh, *Fear of a Kanak Planet: HipHop zwischen Weltkultur und Nazi-Rap* (Höfen: Hannibal, 2002), Sascha Verlan and Hannes Loh, *35 Jahre HipHop in Deutschland* (Höfen: Hannibal, 2015).

70 On the history and politics of hip hop in the US, see only Tricia Rose, *Black Noise: Rap Music and Black Culture in Contemporary America* (Hanover, NH: University Press of New England, 1994), Jeff Chang, *Can't Stop Won't Stop: A History of the Hip-Hop Generation* (London: Ebury, 2007), Lester K. Spence, *Stare in the Darkness: The Limits of Hip-Hop and Black Politics* (Minneapolis: University of Minnesota Press, 2011).

71 On hip hop in France, see Dietmar Hüser, '"Vive la RAPublique" – Botschaften und Bilder einer "anderen Banlieue"', *Historische Anthropologie* 7 (1999), Dietmar Hüser, *RAPublikanische Synthese: Eine französische Zeitgeschichte populärer Musik und politischer Kultur* (Cologne: Böhlau, 2004), Eva Kimminich, *'Légal ou illégal?': Anthologie du rap français* (Stuttgart: Reclam, 2002), Eva Kimminich, 'Citoyen oder Fremder? Ausgrenzung und kulturelle Autonomie in der französischen banlieue', *Archiv für Sozialgeschichte* 46 (2006), Alain-Philippe Durand, *Black, Blanc, Beur: Rap Music and Hip-Hop Culture in the Francophone World* (Lanham: Scarecrow Press, 2001).

72 Hüser, 'RAPublique', 275–7.

73 See, for example, NAP, 'Je viens des quartiers', https://www.you tube.com/watch?v=bzFKS4SvPTo. See also Kimminich, 'Citoyen oder Fremder?', 521.

74 Hüser, 'RAPublique', 285–6.

75 KDD, 'Masque de fer', https://www.youtube.com/watch?v=fTow1 W6yddw. See Kimminich, 'Citoyen oder Fremder?', 521.

76 See NTM, 'Laisse pas traîner ton fils', https://www.youtube.com/watch?v=biYdUZXfz9I, and IAM, 'Petit frère', https://www.youtube.com/watch?v=INuD2D7R8bk. See Hüser, 'RAPublique', 283.

77 See for example Mafia K'1 Fry, 'Pour Ceux', https://www.youtube.com/watch?v=Qz0BB9NO9Dc.

78 See Kimminich, 'Citoyen oder Fremder?', 531–2.

79 For an account of the affair, see Hüser, 'RAPublique', 271–5.

80 Advanced Chemistry, 'Operation Artikel 3', https://www.youtube.com/watch?v=zpKh49WWEco.

81 Kimminich, 'Citoyen oder Fremder?', 528.

82 Kery James, 'Lettre à la République', https://www.youtube.com/watch?v=gp3XZDK7Lw4.

83 Tunisiano, 'Je porte plainte', https://www.youtube.com/watch?v=sliRVVTZg1E.

84 Assassin, featuring Wise Intelligent, 'Wake up', https://www.youtube.com/watch?v=23navzmGPow. See Kimminich, 'Citoyen oder Fremder?', 524.

85 Ibid., 533.

86 YouTube videos provide a sense of the emotional intensity of such gatherings; see, for example, https://www.youtube.com/watch?v=xCS8SsFOBAI&t=90s (Hama), https://www.youtube.com/watch?v=32WLn_-8Deo (Beirut), https://www.youtube.com/watch?v=9T6MwHiQUSI (Modena).

Chapter 7: From International Solidarity to Humanitarian Help

1 Christoph Kalter, 'A Shared Space of Imagination, Communication, and Action: Perspectives on the History of the "Third World"', in *The Third World and the Global 1960s*, ed. Samantha Christiansen and Zachary Scarlett (New York: Berghahn, 2012).

2 On the refugee crisis and the support movement, see Patrick Kingsley, *The New Odyssey: The Story of Europe's Refugee Crisis* (London: Guardian Books, 2016), Charlotte McDonald-Gibson, *Cast Away: Stories of Survival from Europe's Refugee Crisis* (London: Portobello Books, 2016), Jan-Jonathan Bock and Sharon Macdonald, eds., *Refugees Welcome? Difference and Diversity in a Changing Germany* (New York: Berghahn, 2019).

3 See Rebecca Adler-Nissen, Katerine Emilie Andersen and Lene Hansen, 'Images, Emotions, and International Politics: The Death of Alan Kurdi', *Review of International Studies* 10 (2019).

4 See Hannah Arendt, *On Revolution* (New York: Penguin, 1990), 2. I take this point from Lasse Heerten, *The Biafran War and Postcolonial Humanitarianism* (Cambridge: Cambridge University Press, 2017), 10.

5 Jean-Philippe Talbo, 'À propos de la génération algérienne', *Partisans* 1 (September–October 1961), 146–8, quoted in Christoph Kalter, *The Discovery of the Third World: Decolonization and the Rise of the New Left in France, c. 1950–1976* (Cambridge: Cambridge University Press, 2016), 201. Bernigaud used Talbo as a pseudonym.

6 See ibid., 90–94, 258–62.

7 Frantz Fanon, *Les Damnés de la terre. Préface de Jean-Paul Sartre* (Paris: Éditions Maspero, 1961). English translation *The Wretched of the Earth. With a Foreword by Homi K. Bhaba and a Preface by Jean-Paul Sartre* (New York: Grove Press, 2004).

8 Kalter, *Discovery of the Third World*, 214–16. The following discussion of Fanon also draws on Kalter's insightful work.

9 On the Algerian War and its importance for anti-colonial struggles around the globe, see, for example, Mokhtefi Elaine, *Algiers, Third World Capital: Freedom Fighters, Revolutionaries, Black Panthers* (London: Verso, 2018), Jeffrey James Byrne, *Mecca of Revolution: Algeria, Decolonization, and the Third World Order* (Oxford: Oxford University Press, 2016), Mathilde von Bulow, *West Germany, Cold War Europe and the Algerian War* (Cambridge: Cambridge University Press, 2016), Alistair Horne, *A Savage War of Peace: Algeria, 1954–1962* (London: Palgrave, 1977).

10 In a way, this anticipated arguments by Dipesh Chakrabarty, *Provincializing Europe: Postcolonial Thought and Historical Difference* (Princeton: Princeton University Press, 2000).

11 Sartre in Fanon, *The Wretched of the Earth*, xliv–xlvi. Quoted in Kalter, *Discovery of the Third World*, 226.

12 On the West German scene, see Dorothee Weitbrecht, *Aufbruch in die Dritte Welt: Der Internationalismus der Studentenbewegung von 1968 in der Bundesrepublik Deutschland* (Göttingen: V & R unipress, 2012), 73–113.

13 The following account is based on Slobodian, *Foreign Front*, 61–4.

14 On the infamous history of colonialism in Congo, see, for example, Georges Nzongola-Ntalaja, *The Congo from Leopold to Kabila: A People's History* (London: Zed Books, 2002).

15 Slobodian, *Foreign Front*, 63.

16 I take that list of protests from ibid., 62.

17 For an account of the protest, see ibid., 64–70.

18 Ibid., 70.

19 On protests against the Shah's visit, see the insightful discussion in ibid., 101–34. For a more German perspective, see Michels, *Schahbesuch*.

20 See, for the West German case, Weitbrecht, *Aufbruch*, 156–60, Slobodian, *Foreign Front*, 78–100.

21 For examples, see Weitbrecht, *Aufbruch*, Frank Bösch, Caroline Moine and Stefanie Senger, eds., *Internationale Solidarität: Globales Engagement in der Bundesrepublik und der DDR* (Göttingen: Wallstein, 2017).

22 See, with reference to travels to Nicaragua, Werner Balsen and Karl Rössel, *Hoch die Internationale Solidarität: Zur Geschichte der Dritte Welt-Bewegung in der Bundesrepublik* (Cologne: Kölner Volksblatt Verlag, 1986), 440. See also Eleanor Davey, 'French Adventures in Solidarity: Revolutionary Tourists and Radical Humanitarians', *European Review of History* 21 (2014).

23 Weitbrecht, *Aufbruch*, 110.

24 On support for the ANC, see Anja Schade, 'Solidarität und Alltag in der DDR aus der Sicht exilierter Mitglieder des African National Congress', in *Internationale Solidarität: Globales Engagement in der Bundesrepublik und der DDR*, ed. Frank Bösch, Caroline Moine and Stefanie Senger (Göttingen: Wallstein, 2017).

25 Detlev Brunner, 'DDR "transnational": Die "internationale Solidarität" der DDR', in *Deutsche Zeitgeschichte – transnational*, ed. Alexander Gallus, Axel Schildt and Detlef Siegfried (Göttingen: Wallstein, 2015), 66.

26 On the campaign for Angela Davis, see Sophie Lorenz, '"Schwarze Schwester Angela": "Rot-Schwarze" Verbundenheitsvorstellungen und die DDR-Solidaritätskampagne für Angela Davis', in *Internationalale Solidarität: Globales Engagement in der Bundesrepublik und der DDR*, ed. Frank Bösch, Caroline Moine and Stefanie Senger (Göttingen: Wallstein, 2017). On friendship brigades, see Eric Burton, 'Solidarität und ihre Grenzen: Die "Brigaden der Freundschaft" der DDR', in *Internationale Solidarität: Globales Engagement in der Bundesrepublik und der DDR*, ed. Frank Bösch, Caroline Moine and Stefanie Senger (Göttingen: Wallstein, 2017), Hubertus Büschel, *Hilfe zur Selbsthilfe: Deutsche Entwicklungsarbeit in Afrika 1960–1975* (Frankfurt a.M.: Campus, 2014), 326–33.

27 Stefanie Senger, 'Getrennte Solidarität? West- und ostdeutsches Engagement für Nicaragua Sandinista in den 1980er Jahren', in *Internationale Solidarität: Globales Engagement in der Bundesrepublik und der DDR*, ed. Frank Bösch, Caroline Moine and Stefanie Senger (Göttingen: Wallstein, 2017), 69f. See also Claudia Olejniczak, *Die Dritte-Welt-Bewegung in Deutschland* (Wiesbaden: Deutscher UniversitätsVerlag, 1999), 195–231.

28 See Gerd Koenen, 'Phantasmagorien einer Weltrevolution: Die "Neue Linke" von 1968', in *'Ein Gespenst geht um in Europa': Das Erbe kommunistischer Ideologien*, ed. Stéphane Courtois and Uwe Backes (Cologne: Böhlau Verlag, 2002), Bastian Hein, *Die Westdeutschen und die Dritte Welt: Entwicklungspolitik und Entwicklungsdienste zwischen Reform und Revolte, 1959–1974* (Munich: Oldenbourg, 2006). For a critical discussion, see Slobodian, *Foreign Front*, 5–12.

29 Nassehi, *Gab es 1968?*, 70.

30 See, for example, Varon, *Bringing the War Home*, Colvin, *Meinhof*.

31 Carlos Marighella, *Minimanual of the Urban Guerrilla* (1969). There are multiple editions of the text circulating: see, for example, https://www.marxists.org/archive/marighella-carlos/1969/06/minimanual-urban-guerrilla/index.htm. On RAF contacts with Palestinian groups, see Thomas Skelton-Robinson, 'Im Netz verheddert: Die Beziehungen des bundesdeutschen Linksterrorismus zur Volksfront für die

Befreiung Palästinas (1969–1980)', in *Die RAF und der linke Terrorismus*, ed. Wolfgang Kraushaar (Hamburg: Hamburger Edition, 2006).

32 See the discussion in Balsen and Rössel, *Internationale Solidarität*, 532–46.

33 Pascal Bruckner, *The Tears of the White Man: Compassion as Contempt*, trans. William R. Beer (New York: Free Press, 1986). For a trenchant critique, see Ross, *May '68*, 162–3.

34 See, for example, Moritz Ege, 'Becoming-Black: Patterns and Politics of West-German "Afro-Americanophilia" in the Late 1960s', *PORTAL Journal of Multidisciplinary International Studies* 12 (2015).

35 Jürgen Habermas, 'Die Scheinrevolution und ihre Kinder', in *Die Linke antwortet Jürgen Habermas*, ed. Oskar Negt (Frankfurt a.M.: Europäische Verlagsanstalt, 1968).

36 Anonymous, 'Vietnam: notre guerre de trente ans', *Partisans* 68 (November–December 1972), 2–4, quoted in Kalter, *Discovery of the Third World*, 279.

37 Ibid.

38 On the following discussion, see Samuel Moyn, *The Last Utopia: Human Rights in History* (Cambridge, MA: Belknap Press of Harvard University Press, 2010), Michael Barnett, *Empire of Humanity: A History of Humanitarianism* (Ithaca and London: Cornell University Press, 2011).

39 For such a long-term perspective, see Lynn Hunt, *Inventing Human Rights: A History* (New York: W.W. Norton, 2007).

40 See Sarah Snyder, *Human Rights Activism and the End of the Cold War* (Cambridge: Cambridge University Press, 2011).

41 On Biafra and the origins of modern humanitarianism, see the excellent study by Heerten, *Biafran War*.

42 Lasse Herten, 'The Dystopia of Postcolonial Catastrophe: Self-Determination, the Biafran War of Secession, and the 1970s Human Rights Moment', in *The Breakthrough: Human Rights in the 1970s*, ed. Jan Eckel and Samuel Moyn (Philadelphia: University of Pennsylvania Press, 2014), 17.

43 Ibid., 18.

44 On the Biafra campaigns in the West, see Heerten, *Biafran War*, 205–64.

45 Ibid., 207, 235.

46 Heerten, 'Dystopia', 19; see also the more detailed discussion of photos showing Biafran infants in Heerten, *Biafran War*, 152–6.

47 Ross, *May '68*, 157.

48 See Heerten, *Biafran War*, 321–7.

49 Account based on Barnett, *Empire of Humanity*, 143–4, Kalter, *Discovery of the Third World*, 100.

50 Ross, *May '68*, 158–69. On the French left's reaction to Biafra, see also Heerten, *Biafran War*, 247–60, Davey, 'Adventures', 586f.

51 Jacques Julliard, 'Le Tiers Monde et la gauche', *Nouvel Observateur*, 5 June 1978, quoted in Ross, *May '68*, 160.

52 Ibid., 161.

53 Juilliard, 'Le Tiers Monde', quoted in ibid., 161.

54 Bruckner, *Tears*, 142–3. Quoted in Ross, *May '68*, 162.

55 Quoted in Barnett, *Empire of Humanity*, 37–8.

56 Benjamin Möckel, 'Humanitarianism on Stage: Live Aid and the Origins of Humanitarian Pop Music', in *The Politics of Authenticity: Countercultures and Radical Movements across the Iron Curtain, 1968–1989*, ed. Joachim C. Häberlen, Mark Keck-Szajbel and Kate Mahoney (New York: Berghahn, 2018), 233.

57 Bob Geldof, *Is That It? The Autobiography* (London: Grove Press, 1986), 215–16, quoted in ibid., 236–7.

58 Peter Hilmore, *Live Aid* (London: Sidgwick & Jackson, 1985), 40. Quoted in Möckel, 'Humanitarianism on Stage', 239.

59 On Amnesty International, see Jan Eckel, *Die Ambivalenz des Guten: Menschenrechte in der internationalen Politik seit den 1940ern* (Göttingen: Vandenhoeck & Ruprecht, 2014), 347–434, Stephen Hopgood, *Keepers of the Flame: Understanding Amnesty International* (Ithaca: Cornell University Press, 2006).

60 Moyn, *Utopia*, 148.

61 Quoted in ibid., 132.

62 See ibid., 147.

63 Eckel, *Ambivalenz*, 378f.

64 Quoted in Moyn, *Utopia*, 148. On pain, see Elaine Scarry, *The Body in Pain: The Making and Unmaking of the World* (Oxford: Oxford University Press, 1985).

65 Eckel, *Ambivalenz*, 380f.

66 Moyn, *Utopia*, 175.

67 See the discussion of 'corpse polemics' by Quinn Slobodian, 'Corpse Polemics: The Third World and the Politics of Gore in 1960s West Germany', in *Between the Avant-Garde and the Everyday: Subversive Politics in Europe from 1957 to the Present*, ed. Timothy Brown and Lorena Anton (New York: Berghahn, 2011). See also Heerten, *Biafran War*, 140–74.

68 See Ross, *May '68*, 168. She quotes Claude Liauzu, *L'Enjeu tiersmondiste: Débats et combats* (Paris: L'Harmattan, 1988).

69 See, for example, Lila Abu-Lughod, *Do Muslim Women Need Saving?* (Cambridge, MA: Harvard University Press, 2013), 4 et passim.

70 Didier Fassin, *Humanitarian Reason: A Moral History of the Present* (Berkeley: University of California Press, 2011), 254.

71 For equally personal and political reflections on my own involvement in the refugee support movement, see Joachim C. Häberlen, *Wie aus Fremden Freunde werden: Ein politisches Essay über Begegnungen mit Flüchtlingen* (Berlin: Neofelis, 2018). See also Joachim C. Häberlen, *Citizens and Refugees: Stories from Afghanistan and Syria to Germany* (London, New York: Routledge, 2022).

72 See only Bock and Macdonald, eds., *Refugees Welcome?*, Larissa Fleischmann, *Contested Solidarity: Practices of Refugee Support between Humanitarian Help and Political Activism* (Bielefeld: transcript, 2020).

73 Lena Bopp, 'Proteste in Beirut: Zurück in die Moderne', *Frankfurter Allgemeine Zeitung*, 11 November 2019 (online).

74 See Yassin al-Haj Saleh, 'A Letter to the Progressive International', *Al Jumhuriya*, 21 September 2020, available at https://aljumhuriya.net/en/2020/09/21/letter-progressive-international/.

75 Robin Yassin-Kassab and Leila Al-Shami, *Burning Country: Syrians in Revolution and War* (London: Pluto Press, 2016), 35.

Chapter 8: Solidarity in the Backyard and the Struggle for Citizenship: Anti-Racism and Migrant Activism

1 See Daniel A. Gordon, *Immigrants & Intellectuals: May '68 and the Rise of Anti-Racism in France* (London: Merlin Press, 2012), 101–4, 111–19, Vincent Lemire, 'Nanterre, les bidonvilles et les étudiants', in *68, une histoire collective (1962–1981)*, ed. Philippe Artières and Michelle Zancarini-Fournel (Paris: La Découverte, 2008).

2 Rudi Dutschke, 'Die geschichtlichen Bedingungen für den internationalen Emanzipationskampf (Rede auf dem Internationalen Vietnam-Kongreß in West-Berlin, Februar 1968)', reprinted in *Rudi Dutschke: Geschichte ist machbar. Texte über das herrschende Falsche und die Radikalität des Friedens*, ed. Jürgen Miermeister (Berlin: Klaus Wagenbach, 1980), 105–21, quote 114–15. For the efforts of both German and foreign, mostly Italian, leftists to agitate among foreign workers in the 1970s, see also Manuela Bojadžijev, *Die windige Internationale: Rassismus und Kämpfe der Migration* (Münster: Westfälisches Dampfboot, 2008), 173–96.

3 Gordon, *Immigrants*, 101–4, 111–19.

4 Ibid., 120–26, quote 125. On the neighbourhood, see also Abdellali Hajjat, 'Alliances inattendues à la Goutte d'or', in *68, une histoire collective (1962–1981)*, ed. Philippe Artières and Michelle Zancarini-Fournel (Paris: La Découverte, 2008).

5 Niels Seibert, *Vergessene Proteste: Internationalismus und Antirassismus, 1964–1983* (Münster: Unrast, 2008). Recent work on protest cultures has begun to pay more attention to migrant struggles.

6 On the history of 'guest workers', see Rita Chin, *The Guest Worker Question in Postwar Germany* (Cambridge: Cambridge University Press, 2007), Jennifer A. Miller, *Turkish Guest Workers in Germany: Hidden Lives and Contested Borders, 1960s to 1980s* (Toronto: University of Toronto Press, 2018), Sarah Thomsen Vierra, *Turkish Germans in the Federal Republic of Germany: Immigration, Space, and Belonging, 1961–1990* (Cambridge: Cambridge University Press, 2018), Karin Hunn, *'Nächstes Jahr kehren wir zurück . . .': Die Geschichte der türkischen 'Gastarbeiter' in der Bundesrepublik* (Göttingen: Wallstein, 2005). For a general background

of migration policies, see Ulrich Herbert, *Geschichte der Ausländerpolitik in Deutschland: Saisonarbeiter, Zwangsarbeiter, Gastarbeiter, Flüchtlinge* (Munich: C. H. Beck, 2001). From a non-state perspective, see Serhat Karakayali, *Gespenster der Migration: Zur Genealogie illegaler Einwanderung in der Bundesrepublik Deutschland* (Bielefeld: transcript, 2015). The most important works on migrant workers' struggles in the Federal Republic are Bojadžijev, *Windige Internationale*, Simon Goeke, *'Wir sind alle Fremdarbeiter!' Gewerkschaften, migrantische Kämpfe und soziale Bewegungen in der Bundesrepublik Deutschland der 1960er und 1970er Jahre* (Paderborn: Ferdinand Schöningh, 2020).

7 On Pierburg, see Bojadžijev, *Windige Internationale*, 162–73, Goeke, *Fremdarbeiter*, 99–112, Regina Heine, 'Kontrollverlust der Gewerkschaften? Der "Pierburg-Streik" 1973 in historischer Perspektive', in *Der Betrieb als sozialer und politischer Ort: Studien zu Praktiken und Diskursen in den Arbeitswelten des 20. Jahrhunderts*, ed. Knud Andersen et al. (Bonn: Dietz, 2015). For the broader context of 'wild strikes', see Peter Birke, *Wilde Streiks im Wirtschaftswunder: Arbeitskämpfe, Gewerkschaften und soziale Bewegungen in der Bundesrepublik und Dänemark* (Frankfurt a.M.: Campus, 2007), 275–304.

8 See Bojadžijev, *Windige Internationale*, 151–62, Goeke, *Fremdarbeiter*, 49–94.

9 Bojadžijev, *Windige Internationale*, 166–7.

10 Ibid., 168.

11 Ibid., 169.

12 The following account draws on Goeke, *Fremdarbeiter*, 112–25. See also Jörg Huwer, '"Gastarbeiter" im Streik: Die spontane Arbeitsniederlegung bei Ford Köln im August 1973', *Geschichte im Westen* 22 (2007), Betriebszelle Ford der Gruppe Arbeiterkampf, ed., *Streik bei Ford Köln* (Cologne: Rosa Luxemburg Verlag, 1973). An online documentation of the strike is available at http://ford73.blogsport.de/.

13 See also Günter Hinken, 'Vom "Gastarbeiter" aus der Türkei zum gestaltenden Akteur: Mitbestimmung und Integration von Arbeitsmigranten bei Ford in Köln', in *Geschichte und Gedächtnis in der Einwanderungsgesellschaft*, ed. Jan Motte and Rainer Ohliger (Essen: Klartext, 2004).

14 Goeke, *Fremdarbeiter*, 114.

15 Ibid., 114–15.

16 Ibid., 115.

17 Ibid., 116–17.

18 See the contributions in *Arbeit – Bewegung – Geschichte 15 (1): Schwerpunkt Linke Betriebsintervention, wilde Streiks und operaistische Politik 1968 bis 1988* (2016).

19 Goeke, *Fremdarbeiter*, 117–24.

20 Thomas Deltombe, *L'Islam imaginaire: La construction médiatique de l'Islamophobie en France 1975–2005* (Paris: La Découverte, 2005), 232, quoted in Joan W. Scott, *Politics of the Veil* (Princeton: Princeton University Press, 2007), 61–2. It should be noted that the original source of the quote is Peyrefitte's 1994 biography of de Gaulle, *Ainsi parlait de Gaulle*. On migration in France and migrant struggles, see in general Gérard Noiriel, *The French Melting Pot: Immigration, Citizenship, and National Identity*, trans. Geoffroy de Laforcade (Minneapolis: University of Minnesota Press, 1996), Gérard Noiriel, *Immigration, antisémitisme et racisme en France, XIXe–XXe siècle: Discours publics, humiliations privées* (Paris: Fayard, 2007), Ahmed Boubeker and Abdellali Hajjat, eds., *Histoire politique des immigrations (post)coloniales: France, 1920–2008* (Paris: Éditions Amsterdam, 2008), Benjamin Stora and Émile Temime, eds., *Immigrances: L'immigration en France au XXe siècle* (Paris: Hachette Littératures, 2007), Jane Freedman, *Immigration and Insecurity in France* (Aldershot: Ashgate, 2008).

21 For a brief account in the context of 1968, see Ross, *May '68*, 42–4. See more generally Jim House and Neil MacMaster, *Paris 1961: Algerians, State Terror, and Memory* (Oxford: Oxford University Press, 2006), Linda Amiri, *La Bataille de France: La guerre d'Algérie en métropole* (Paris: Robert Laffont, 2004). For a history of the Algerian War and its impact on France, see Benjamin Stora, *Histoire de la guerre d'Algérie (1954–1962)* (Paris: La Découverte, 2004), Martin Evans, *Algeria: France's Undeclared War* (Oxford: Oxford University Press, 2012), Todd Shepard, *The Invention of Decolonization: The Algerian War and the Remaking of France* (Ithaca: Cornell University Press, 2006).

22 See Peter Gatrell, *The Unsettling of Europe: The Great Migration, 1945 to the Present* (London: Allen Lane, 2019), 132–3.

23 Gordon, *Immigrants*, 126–7.

24 Quoted in ibid., 130.

25 See ibid., 129–30, Johanna Siméant, *La Cause des sans-papiers* (Paris: Presse de Science Po, 1998), 15–17, Jane Freedman, 'The French "Sans-Papiers" Movement: An Unfinished Struggle', in *Migration and Activism in Europe since 1945*, ed. Wendy Pojmann (New York: Palgrave Macmillan, 2008), 82.

26 The account draws on Madjiguène Cissé, *Papiere für alle*, trans. Nicola Schieweck-Rajeswaran (Berlin: Assoziation A, 2002), 7, 11f., 35–9, 79–81. On the 1996 *sans papiers* movement, see also Freedman, 'The French "Sans-Papiers" Movement', Catherine Raissiguier, *Reinventing the Republic: Gender, Migration, and Citizenship in France* (Stanford: Stanford University Press, 2010), 14–31, Nena Löw, *Wir leben hier und wir bleiben hier! Die Sans Papiers im Kampf um ihre Rechte* (Münster: Westfälisches Dampfboot, 2013), Siméant, *La Cause*.

27 Cissé, *Papiere*, 33.

28 See, from a theoretical perspective, Engin F. Isin and Greg M. Nielsen, eds., *Acts of Citizenship* (London: Zed Books, 2008), Jacques Rancière, *Disagreement: Politics and Philosophy*, trans. Julie Rose (Minneapolis: University of Minnesota Press, 1999).

29 Cissé, *Papiere*, 77–8. See also Freedman, 'The French "Sans-Papiers" Movement', 93–4, Raissiguier, *Reinventing*, 29.

30 Cissé, *Papiere*, 111.

31 Freedman, 'The French "Sans-Papiers" Movement', 83.

32 Quoted in Gatrell, *Unsettling*, 164.

33 Ibid., 172.

34 Ibid., 167.

35 David Renton, *Never Again: Rock Against Racism and the Anti-Nazi League 1976–1982* (London: Routledge, 2019), 15. On Rock Against Racism, see also Ian Goodyer, *Crisis Music: The Cultural Politics of Rock Against Racism* (Manchester: Manchester University Press, 2009).

36 Gatrell, *Unsettling*, 168.

37 Renton, *Never Again*, 26.

38 Ibid.

39 Ibid., 39.

40 See ibid., 37–44.

41 Ibid., 45.

42 Ibid., 46.

43 Ibid., 44. The quote is from Winston James, 'Reflections on Radical History', *Radical History Review*, no. 79 (2001), 99.

44 Quoted in Renton, *Never Again*, 47.

45 Ibid., 41-2.

46 Ibid., 51–2.

47 Ibid., 63. See also Goodyer, *Crisis Music*, 11.

48 Renton, *Never Again*, 104–5.

49 Ibid., 78.

50 Ibid., 83.

51 Quoted in ibid., 118.

52 See Bernd Langer, *Antifaschistische Aktion: Geschichte einer linksradikalen Bewegung* (Münster: Unrast Verlag, 2018), 180–81.

53 See https://semraertaninitiative.wordpress.com/. For her work, see Semra Ertan, *Mein Name ist Ausländer. Benim Adım Yabancı*, ed. Zühal Bilir-Meier and Cana Bilir-Meier (Münster: edition assemblage, 2020).

54 Renton, *Never Again*, 109.

55 See Jan Plamper, *Das neue Wir: Warum Migration dazugehört. Eine andere Geschichte der Deutschen* (Frankfurt a.M.: S. Fischer, 2019), 296–302. See also Christian Jakob, *Die Bleibenden: Wie Flüchtlinge Deutschland seit 20 Jahren verändern* (Berlin: Ch. Links, 2016).

Chapter 9: Camps: The Better World of Peace and Environmental Movements

1 Gudrun Pausewang, *Etwas lässt sich doch bewirken: Ein Roman aus der Friedensbewegung* (Ravensburg: Otto Maier Verlag, 1984), 5–6, 42. This was not her only novel on questions of peace, nuclear power and nuclear armament. More famous are two widely read children's books dealing with the aftermath of nuclear warfare and a nuclear catastrophe: Gudrun Pausewang, *Die letzten Kinder von Schewenborn oder . . . sieht so unsere Zukunft aus?* (Ravensburg: Maier, 1983), Gudrun

Pausewang, *Die Wolke* (Ravensburg: Maier, 1987). See also my discussion in Joachim C. Häberlen, 'Ingrid's Boredom', in *Learning How to Feel: Children's Literature and Emotional Socialization, 1870–1970*, ed. Ute Frevert et al. (Oxford: Oxford University Press, 2014).

2 See the classical studies by Karl-Werner Brand, Detlef Büsser and Dieter Rucht, *Aufbruch in eine andere Gesellschaft: Neue soziale Bewegungen in der Bundesrepublik* (Frankfurt a.M.: Campus, 1983), Roland Roth and Dieter Rucht, *Neue soziale Bewegungen in der Bundesrepublik Deutschland* (Bonn: Bundeszentrale für Politische Bildung, 1987). For a critical discussion, with a focus on West Germany, see Belinda Davis, Friederike Brühöfener and Stephen Milder, eds., *Rethinking Social Movements after '68: Selves and Solidarities in West Germany and Beyond* (New York: Berghahn, 2022).

3 Robert Gildea and Andrew Tompkins, 'The Transnational in the Local: The Larzac Plateau as a Site of Transnational Activism since 1970', *Journal of Contemporary History* 50 (2015), 583.

4 On the struggle at Larzac, see in general Michel Le Bris, *Les Fous du Larzac* (Paris: Presses d'aujourd'hui, 1975), Didier Martin, *Larzac: Utopies et réalités* (Paris: L'Harmattan, 1987), Herman Lebovics, *Bringing the Empire Back Home: France in the Global Age* (Durham: Duke University Press, 2004), 13–57, Pierre-Marie Terral, *Larzac: De la lutte paysanne à l'altermondialisme* (Toulouse: Éditions Privat, 2011), Chris Pearson, *Mobilizing Nature: The Environmental History of War and Militarization in Modern France* (Manchester: Manchester University Press, 2012), 236–72.

5 Gildea and Tompkins, 'Transnational in the Local', 584, Terral, *Larzac*, 41–4.

6 Gildea and Tompkins, 'Transnational in the Local', 585.

7 See also Martin, *Larzac*, 43, Terral, *Larzac*, 56–7.

8 Gildea and Tompkins, 'Transnational in the Local', 584–5, Lebovics, *Empire Back Home*, 36, Terral, *Larzac*, 57–8.

9 On peasant struggles in the context of the years around 1968, see more generally Jean-Philippe Martin, *Des 'Mai 68' dans les campagnes françaises? Les contestations paysannes dans les années 1968* (Paris: L'Harmattan, 2017).

10 See Gildea and Tompkins, 'Transnational in the Local', 588–9, Lebovics, *Empire Back Home*, 15–21, Martin, *Larzac*, 61–2, Terral, *Larzac*, 66–8.

11 See Bernard Lacroix, *L'Utopie communautaire: Histoire sociale d'une révolte* (Paris: Presses universitaires de France, 1981).

12 Martin, *Larzac*, 35–7, Terral, *Larzac*, 339–40.

13 Gildea and Tompkins, 'Transnational in the Local', 591. See also Terral, *Larzac*, 72–3.

14 Gildea and Tompkins, 'Transnational in the Local', 589, Terral, *Larzac*, 87–8.

15 See Xavier Vigna, 'Lip et Larzac: Conflits locaux et mobilisations nationales', in *68, une histoire collective (1962–1981)*, ed. Philippe Artières and Michelle Zancarini-Fournel (Paris: La Découverte, 2008).

16 See Gildea and Tompkins, 'Transnational in the Local', 589–90, Lebovics, *Empire Back Home*, 13–15, Martin, *Larzac*, 57–8, Terral, *Larzac*, 73–4, 78–9.

17 See Terral, *Larzac*, 85–92.

18 Pearson, *Mobilizing Nature*, 254–7, Gildea and Tompkins, 'Transnational in the Local', 591, Martin, *Larzac*, 77–81.

19 Gildea and Tompkins, 'Transnational in the Local', 592, Lebovics, *Empire Back Home*, 45–8.

20 See in general Martin, *Larzac*, 100–103, Terral, *Larzac*, 105–9.

21 Lebovics, *Empire Back Home*, 34.

22 Ibid., 50–51. See also Terral, *Larzac*, 101–2.

23 Martin, *Larzac*, 66–8, 70–71.

24 Quoted in ibid., 102–3. See also Pearson, *Mobilizing Nature*, 250–54.

25 See Stephen Milder, *Greening Democracy: The Anti-Nuclear Movement and Political Environmentalism in West Germany and Beyond, 1968–1983* (Cambridge: Cambridge University Press, 2017), 22–36. On environmental politics and the struggle against nuclear energy in (West) Germany, see also Jens Ivo Engels, *Naturpolitik in der Bundesrepublik: Ideenwelt und politische Verhaltensstile in Naturschutz und Umweltbewegung, 1950–1980* (Paderborn: Schöningh, 2006), Andrew Tompkins, *Better Active than Radioactive! Anti-Nuclear Protest in 1970s France and West Germany* (Oxford: Oxford University Press, 2016), Dolores L. Augustine, *Taking on Technocracy: Nuclear Power in Germany, 1945 to the Present* (New York: Berghahn, 2018).

26 Milder, *Greening Democracy*, 19–20, 36–42, 94. On the protests in Wyhl, see in addition to the literature mentioned above, Nina Gladitz, ed., *Lieber heute aktiv als morgen radioaktiv. Wyhl: Bauern erzählen, warum Kernkraftwerke schädlich sind, wie man eine Bürgerinitiative macht, und wie man sich dabei verändert* (Berlin: Verlag Klaus Wagenbach, 1976), Bernd Nössler and Margret de Witt, eds., *Wyhl – kein Kernkraftwerk in Wyhl und auch sonst nirgends: betroffene Bürger berichten* (Freiburg: Dreisam-Verlag, 1976).

27 For an account, see Milder, *Greening Democracy*, 95, Gerd Auer, 'Hier wird ein Platz besetzt', in *Wyhl – kein Kernkraftwerk in Wyhl und auch sonst nirgends: betroffene Bürger berichten*, ed. Bernd Nössler and Margret de Witt (Freiburg: Dreisam-Verlag, 1976).

28 Auer, 'Ein Platz', 86, quoted in Milder, *Greening Democracy*, 97.

29 Erasmus Schöfer, 'Die Platzbesetzung', in *Erzählungen von Kämpfen, Zärtlichkeit und Hoffnung*, ed. Erasmus Schöfer (Frankfurt a.M.: Fischer, 1979), 135.

30 Quoted in Milder, *Greening Democracy*, 99.

31 Ibid., 99–103.

32 Ibid., 107.

33 For an account of the occupation, see ibid., 106–9, quote 108, Christian Kern and Gerd Auer, 'Die zweite Besetzung in Wyhl', in *Wyhl – kein Kernkraftwerk in Wyhl und auch sonst nirgends: betroffene Bürger berichten*, ed. Bernd Nössler and Margret de Witt (Freiburg: Dreisam-Verlag, 1976).

34 Milder, *Greening Democracy*, 119.

35 Eva Quistorp, *Handbuch Leben: Frauen gegen Umweltzerstörung* (Gelnhausen: Burckhardthaus-Laetare Verlag, 1981), 61.

36 Wolfgang Beer, *Lernen im Widerstand: Politisches Lernen und politische Sozialisation in Bürgerinitiativen* (Hamburg: Association, 1978), 99, quoted in Milder, *Greening Democracy*, 123.

37 See also Wolfgang Beer, 'Volkshochschule Wyhler Wald', in *Wyhl – kein Kernkraftwerk in Wyhl und auch sonst nirgends: betroffene Bürger berichten*, ed. Bernd Nössler and Margret de Witt (Freiburg: Dreisam-Verlag, 1976).

38 See Eine Platzbesetzerin, 'Das Leben auf dem Platz', in *Wyhl – kein Kernkraftwerk in Wyhl und auch sonst nirgends: betroffene Bürger berichten*, ed. Bernd Nössler and Margret de Witt (Freiburg: Dreisam-Verlag, 1976).

39 Roland Burkhart, 'G'hert dä aü zu däne do?', in *Wyhl – kein Kernkraftwerk in Wyhl und auch sonst nirgends: betroffene Bürger berichten*, ed. Bernd Nössler and Margret de Witt (Freiburg: Dreisam-Verlag, 1976).

40 Platzbesetzerin, 'Leben auf dem Platz', 150. See also Beer, *Lernen im Widerstand*, 83–6.

41 On Wackersdorf, see Janine Gaumer, *Wackersdorf: Atomkraft und Demokratie in der Bundesrepublik 1980–1989* (Munich: oekom, 2018).

42 See Günter Zint, ed., *Republik Freies Wendland: Eine Dokumentation* (Frankfurt a.M.: Zweitausendeins, 1980), Klaus Poggendorf, *Gorleben: Der Streit um die nukleare Entsorgung und die Zukunft einer Region* (Lüneburg: nordlanddruck, 2008).

43 See in general Frank Biess, *German Angst: Fear and Democracy in the Federal Republic of Germany* (Oxford: Oxford University Press, 2020), 291–330.

44 See Tim Geiger, 'The Nato Double-Track Decision: Genesis and Implementation', in *The Nuclear Crisis: The Arms Race, Cold War Anxiety, and the German Peace Movement of the 1980s*, ed. Christoph Becker-Schaum et al. (New York: Berghahn, 2016). See also the contributions in Leopoldo Nuti et al., eds., *The Euromissile Crisis and the End of the Cold War* (Stanford: Stanford University Press, 2015).

45 Eckart Conze, Martin Klimke and Jeremy Varon, 'Introduction. Between Accidental Armageddons and Winnable Wars: Nuclear Threats and Nuclear Fears in the 1980s', in *Nuclear Threats, Nuclear Fear, and the Cold War of the 1980s*, ed. Eckart Conze, Martin Klimke and Jeremy Varon (Cambridge: Cambridge University Press, 2017), 5. On the peace movements in 1980s Europe, see, with many more references, Claudia Kemper, ed., *Gespannte Verhältnisse: Frieden und Protest in Europa während der 1970er und 1980er Jahre* (Essen: Klartext, 2017), Eckart Conze, Martin Klimke and Jeremy Varon, eds., *Nuclear Threats, Nuclear Fear, and the Cold War of the 1980s* (Cambridge: Cambridge University Press, 2017), Benjamin Ziemann, 'A Quantum of

Solace? European Peace Movements during the Cold War and Their Elective Affinities', *Archiv für Sozialgeschichte* 49 (2009).

46 See Susanne Schregel, *Der Atomkrieg vor der Wohnungstür: Eine Politik-geschichte der neuen Friedensbewegung in der Bundesrepublik, 1970–1985* (Frankfurt a.M.: Campus, 2011). On the connection between the peace and environmental movements, see Silke Mende and Birgit Metzger, 'Eco-Pacifism: The Environmental Movement as a Source for the Peace Movement', in *The Nuclear Crisis: The Arms Race, Cold War Anxiety, and the German Peace Movement of the 1980s*, ed. Christoph Becker-Schaum et al. (New York: Berghahn, 2016), Janine Gaumer, '"Was hat die Wiederaufbereitungsanlage mit Frieden zu tun?" Atomkraftgegnerinnen, Friedensaktivistinnen und der gemeinsame "Widerstand" gegen nukleare Bedrohungsszenarien in den 1980er Jahren', in *Gespannte Verhältnisse: Frieden und Protest in Europa während der 1970er und 1980er Jahre*, ed. Claudia Kemper (Essen: Klartext, 2017). On the peace movement in West Germany more generally, see, with many more references, Christoph Becker-Schaum, ed., *'Entrüstet Euch!': Nuklearkrise, NATO-Doppelbeschluss und Friedensbewegung* (Paderborn: Schöningh, 2012), Christoph Becker-Schaum et al., eds., *The Nuclear Crisis: The Arms Race, Cold War Anxiety, and the German Peace Movement of the 1980s* (New York: Berghahn, 2016).

47 Clive Rose, *Campaigns against Western Defence: NATO's Adversaries and Critics* (New York: St Martin's Press, 1985), 178.

48 See David Fairhall, *Common Ground: The Story of Greenham* (London: I. B. Tauris, 2006), 9–11.

49 Ibid., 7.

50 Ibid., 8.

51 For an account, see Jill Liddington, *The Long Road to Greenham: Feminism and Anti-Militarism in Britain since 1820* (London: Virago, 1989), 221–33, Sasha Roseneil, *Disarming Patriarchy: Feminism and Political Action at Greenham* (Buckingham: Open University Press, 1995), 14–38, Barbara Harford and Sarah Hopkins, eds., *Greenham Common: Women at the Wire* (London: Women's Press, 1984), 9–18. For other peace camps inspired by Greenham, such as the camps at Comiso, Sicily or Reckershausen, West Germany, see Laura Branciforte, 'The

Women's Peace Camp at Comiso, 1983: Transnational Feminism and the Anti-Nuclear Movement', *Women's History Review* 31, no. 2 (2022).

52 On the decision for a women-only camp, see Fairhall, *Common Ground*, 24–8, Harford and Hopkins, eds., *Greenham*, 32–5. On feminism at Greenham, see also the works by Sasha Roseneil, *Disarming Patriarchy*, and *Common Women, Uncommon Practices: The Queer Feminism of Greenham* (London: Cassell, 2000).

53 Roseneil, *Common Women*, 81.

54 Ibid., 80.

55 Ibid., 78.

56 Harford and Hopkins, eds., *Greenham*, 27.

57 Liddington, *Long Road*, 236–9.

58 Quoted in ibid., 241–2.

59 Fairhall, *Common Ground*, 41.

60 Quoted in Liddington, *Long Road*, 245.

61 For an account, see ibid., 242–5, Harford and Hopkins, eds., *Greenham*, 89–95.

62 Liddington, *Long Road*, 248.

63 Ibid., 247.

64 See Harford and Hopkins, eds., *Greenham*, 96–103, quote 100.

65 Fairhall, *Common Ground*, 58–9.

66 Roseneil, *Common Women*, 102.

67 Ibid., 106–8.

68 Ibid., 107.

69 Ibid., 283.

70 See Marianne Zepp, 'Rationality of Fear: The Intellectual Foundations of the Peace Movement', in *The Nuclear Crisis: The Arms Race, Cold War Anxiety, and the German Peace Movement of the 1980s*, ed. Christoph Becker-Schaum et al. (New York: Berghahn, 2016), Susanne Schregel, 'Konjunktur der Angst: "Politik der Subjektivität" und "neue Friedensbewegung"', in *Angst im Kalten Krieg*, ed. Bernd Greiner, Christian Th. Müller and Walter Dierk (Hamburg: Hamburger Edition, 2009), Biess, *German Angst*, 314–30.

71 Roseneil, *Common Women*, 131. See also Ziemann, 'Quantum', 382–7. On gender politics in the West German peace movement, see Belinda

Davis, 'The Gender of War and Peace: Rhetoric in the West German Peace Movement of the Early 1980s', *Mitteilungsblatt des Instituts für soziale Bewegungen* 32 (2004).

72 On the Protestant Church in the GDR and the role it played for the opposition, see Mary Fulbrook, *Anatomy of a Dictatorship: Inside the GDR, 1949–1989* (Oxford: Oxford University Press, 1995), 115–25, 201–36, Ilko-Sascha Kowalczuk, *Endspiel: Die Revolution von 1989 in der DDR* (Munich: C. H. Beck, 2009), 198–215, David Doellinger, *Turning Prayers into Protests: Religious-Based Activism and Its Challenge to State Power in Socialist Slovakia and East Germany* (Budapest: Central European University Press, 2013).

73 Stefan Wolle, *Die heile Welt der Diktatur: Alltag und Herrschaft in der DDR, 1971–1989* (Berlin: Ch. Links Verlag, 1998), 261–6.

74 On the peace movement in the GDR, see in general Detlef Pollack, *Politischer Protest: Politisch alternative Gruppen in der DDR* (Opladen: Leske + Budrich, 2000), 77–96, Patrick von zur Mühlen, *Aufbruch und Umbruch in der DDR: Bürgerbewegung, kritische Öffentlichkeit und Niedergang der SED Herrschaft* (Bonn: Dietz, 2000), 48–61, Rainer Eckert, 'The Independent Peace Movement in East Germany', in *The Nuclear Crisis: The Arms Race, Cold War Anxiety, and the German Peace Movement of the 1980s*, ed. Christoph Becker-Schaum et al. (New York: Berghahn, 2016). For a detailed study on East Berlin, see Thomas Klein, *'Frieden und Gerechtigkeit!' Die Politisierung der Unabhängigen Friedensbewegung in Ost-Berlin während der 80er Jahre* (Cologne: Böhlau, 2007).

75 Quoted in Reinhard Henkys, 'Zwischen Militarismus und Pazifismus: Friedensarbeit der evangelischen Kirchen', in *Friedensbewegung in der DDR: Texte 1978–1982*, ed. Wolfgang Büscher, Peter Wensierski and Klaus Wolschner (Hattingen: Scandica Verlag, 1982), 15.

76 See Klaus Ehring and Marin Dallwitz, *Schwerter zu Pflugscharen: Friedensbewegung in der DDR* (Reinbek bei Hamburg: Rowohlt, 1982), 12–32.

77 Wolle, *Heile Welt*, 257–61.

78 See Pollack, *Politischer Protest*, 82. See also the discussion in Ehring and Dallwitz, *Schwerter zu Pflugscharen*, 156–81, quote from the ESG Naumburg 166.

79 See the detailed study by Anke Silomon, *'Schwerter zu Pflugscharen' und die DDR: Die Friedensarbeit der evangelischen Kirchen in der DDR im Rahmen der Friedensdekaden 1980 bis 1982* (Göttingen: Vandenhoeck & Ruprecht, 1999).

80 Ehrhart Neubert, *Geschichte der Opposition in der DDR, 1949–1989* (Berlin: Ch. Links, 1997), 383–4.

81 Ibid., 398–404.

82 Pollack, *Politischer Protest*, 83.

83 Neubert, *Geschichte der Opposition*, 389–95.

84 Ibid., 405–12.

85 Ibid., 396–8.

86 Ehring and Dallwitz, *Schwerter zu Pflugscharen*, 76–87, quote 86.

87 See Pollack, *Politischer Protest*, 99–102, zur Mühlen, *Aufbruch*, 126–55, Ned Richardson-Little, *The Human Rights Dictatorship: Socialism, Global Solidarity and Revolution in East Germany* (Cambridge: Cambridge University Press, 2020), 180–221.

88 On environmental protests in the GDR, see in general Christian Möller, *Umwelt und Herrschaft in der DDR: Politik, Protest und die Grenzen der Partizipation in der Diktatur* (Göttingen: Vandenhoeck & Ruprecht, 2020), 250–319, Julia E. Ault, *Saving Nature under Socialism: Transnational Environmentalism in East Germany, 1968–1990* (Cambridge: Cambridge University Press, 2021).

89 See Möller, *Umwelt und Herrschaft*, 316. He refers to Wolfgang Rüddenklau, *Störenfried: DDR-Opposition 1986–1989, mit Texten aus den 'Umweltblättern'* (Berlin: BasisDruck, 1992), 61–2.

90 Quoted in Pollack, *Politischer Protest*, 92, see more generally 165–78. On the Kirchliche Forschungsheim Wittenberg, see also Neubert, *Geschichte der Opposition*, 449–51, Michael Beleites, *Dicke Luft: Zwischen Ruß und Revolte. Die unabhängige Umweltbewegung in der DDR* (Leipzig: Evangelische Verlagsanstalt, 2016), 75–90, zur Mühlen, *Aufbruch*, 65–7.

91 Ault, *Saving Nature*, 168–73.

92 See Klein, *'Frieden und Gerechtigkeit!'*, 286, Astrid Mignon Kirchhof, '"For a Decent Quality of Life": Environmental Groups in East and West Berlin', *Journal of Urban History* 41 (2015), Neubert, *Geschichte der Opposition*, 746, Ault, *Saving Nature*, 193–4.

93 On November 1987, see Wolle, *Heile Welt*, 297. In general, see Neubert, *Geschichte der Opposition*, 629–32, Pollack, *Politischer Protest*, 104–7, Beleites, *Dicke Luft*, 186–210. On the role of environmental protests in the end of communism, see Ault, *Saving Nature*, 197–227.

94 See Eva von Redecker, *Revolution für das Leben: Philosophie der neuen Protestformen* (Frankfurt a.M.: Fischer, 2020).

95 Anna Feigenbaum, Fabian Frenzel and Patrick McCurdy, *Protest Camps* (London: Zed Books, 2013), Stephen Milder, 'From Wyhl to Wall Street: Occupation and the Many Meanings of "Single-Issue" Protest', *Moving the Social* 56 (2016).

96 Feigenbaum, Frenzel and McCurdy, *Protest Camps*, 35.

97 Donatella della Porta and Gianni Piazza, *Voices of the Valley, Voices of the Straits: How Protest Creates Community* (New York: Berghahn, 2008), 92–4.

Chapter 10: *Taking the City: Urban Activism*

1 The French original is Henri Lefebvre, *Le Droit à la ville* (Paris: Éditions Anthropos, 1968). An English translation is published in Eleonore Kofman and Elizabeth Lebas, eds., *Henri Lefebvre: Writings on Cities* (Cambridge, MA: Blackwell Publishers, 1996). For a discussion, see David Harvey, 'The Right to the City', *New Left Review* 53 (2008), Dirk Gebhardt and Andrej Holm, 'Initiativen für ein Recht auf Stadt', in *Initiativen für ein Recht auf Stadt: Theorie und Praxis städtischer Aneignungen*, ed. Dirk Gebhardt and Andrej Holm (Hamburg: VSA, 2009), Mark Purcell, 'Excavating Lefebvre: The Right to the City and Its Urban Politics of the Inhabitant', *GeoJournal* 58 (2002).

2 On gentrification and struggles against it, see, with a global perspective, Loretta Lees and Martin Phillips, eds., *Handbook of Gentrification Studies* (Cheltenham: Edward Elgar, 2018), John R. Short, *The Unequal City: Urban Resurgence, Displacement and the Making of Inequality in Global Cities* (London: Routledge, 2018), Jerome Krase and Judith N. DeSena, eds., *Gentrification around the World* (Cham: Palgrave Macmillan, 2020), Eleonora Pasotti, *Resisting Redevelopment:*

Protest in Aspiring Global Cities (Cambridge: Cambridge University Press, 2020).

3 Jenny Künkel, *Sex, Drugs & Control: Das Regieren von Sexarbeit in der neoliberalen Stadt* (Münster: Westfälisches Dampfboot, 2020).

4 Detlef Hartmann, 'Stadtknast – Knaststadt', *Große Freiheit* 43 (March 1981), 10–13.

5 Marco Soresina, 'The Housing Struggle in Milan in the 1970s: Influences and Particularities', *Journal of Urban History* 46 (2020): 1391.

6 Heigl, *Rom*, 52–3.

7 Ibid., 54.

8 Ibid., 55.

9 Ibid., 56.

10 Ibid., 61–7.

11 Ibid., 68.

12 On practices of self-reduction, see Lumley, *States of Emergency*, 262–5, 299–306, Heigl, *Rom*, 70–78.

13 Heigl, *Rom*, 72.

14 Ibid., 76–8.

15 Ibid., 92–4.

16 Ibid., 150–70.

17 Ibid., 81–8.

18 See the detailed account in ibid., 180–229.

19 Quoted in ibid., 66.

20 Ibid., 78–81.

21 Ibid., 89.

22 Ibid., 97–101.

23 Ibid., 233–6.

24 Ibid., 128–30.

25 Quoted in Christiane Reinecke, 'Into the Cold: Neighborliness, Class, and the Emotional Landscape of Urban Modernism in France and West Germany', *Journal of Urban History* 48 (2020), 170.

26 Quoted in ibid., 168.

27 Alexander Mitscherlich, *Thesen zur Stadt der Zukunft* (Frankfurt a.M.: Suhrkamp, 1974), ix–x. See also Alexander Mitscherlich, *Die Unwirtlichkeit unserer Städte: Anstiftung zum Unfrieden* (Frankfurt a.M.:

Suhrkamp, 1965), Wolf Jobst Siedler, Elisabeth Niggemeyer and Gina Angreß, *Die gemordete Stadt: Abgesang auf Putte und Straße, Platz und Baum* (Berlin: Herbig, 1964). For a discussion, see Martin Baumeister, Bruno Bonomo and Dieter Schott, 'Introduction: Contested Cities in an Era of Crisis', in *Cities Contested: Urban Politics, Heritage, and Social Movements in Italy and West Germany in the 1970s*, ed. Martin Baumeister, Bruno Bonomo and Dieter Schott (Frankfurt a.M.: Campus, 2017).

28 Ault, *Saving Nature*, 150.

29 Hartmann, 'Stadtknast'.

30 'Back Side', *Info Nürnberg*, 7 September 1976. Also cited in Häberlen, *Emotional Politics*, 151.

31 Frauenkollektiv, 'So, so, einen Frauenasta habt ihr – Ach ja, einen Frauenasta?', *diskus* 5 (20 October 1976), 18–27. Also cited in Häberlen, *Emotional Politics*.

32 On such critiques of urban life across the political spectrum, see Christiane Reinecke, *Die Ungleichheit der Städte: Urbane Problemzonen im postkolonialen Frankreich und der Bundesrepublik* (Göttingen: Vandenhoeck & Ruprecht, 2021), 144–60, Häberlen, *Emotional Politics*, 145–55.

33 Anon., 'Neues vom Bohnenviertel', *s 'Blättle*, 11 October 1976, 5. Also cited in Häberlen, *Emotional Politics*, 149.

34 Hartmann, 'Stadtknast'.

35 Peter Blum, 'Straße und Straßenmusik', *Großstadtpflaster* 1 (n.d., probably winter 1976/7), 1–4. See also Anon., 'Wer hat uns die Straße geklaut?', *Pflasterstrand* 5 (2–15 March 1977), 22. Also cited in Häberlen, *Emotional Politics*, 204.

36 Klaus Bernd Vollmar, 'Wandmalereien', *Ulcus Molle* 1/2 (1980), 20. Also cited in Häberlen, *Emotional Politics*, 204.

37 *Wandmalereien & Texte: Nehmt der Langeweile ihren Sinn* (Berlin: Kramer, 1979), 92–3, 102–3.

38 Arvid Bengtsson, *Ein Platz für Kinder: Plädoyer für eine kindgemäße Umwelt. Entwurf, Ausführung, Ausstattung von Spielanlagen, Tummelplätzen und Abenteuerspielplätzen in Städtebau und Umweltplanung* (Wiesbaden: Bauverlag, 1971), 13. For a similar argument, see an interview with Prof. Dr Gerhard Biermann, head of the Institut für Psychohygiene, Cologne, in *Garten und Landschaft* 1 (1973), 3–4.

39 Uli Edel, *Christiane F. – Wir Kinder vom Bahnhof Zoo* (West Germany: 1981). For a discussion of the scene and social housing projects in West Berlin, see Christiane Reinecke, 'Am Rande der Gesellschaft? Das Märkische Viertel – eine West-Berliner Großsiedlung und ihre Darstellung als urbane Problemzone', *Zeithistorische Forschungen* 11 (2014), 229.

40 Hartmann, 'Stadtknast'. For similar arguments, see also the discussions in *Garten und Landschaft* 1 (1973), and Bengtsson, *Platz für Kinder*, 5, Hans Mayrhofer and Wolfgang Zacharias, *Aktion Spielbus: Spielräume in der Stadt – mobile Spielplatzbenutzung* (Weinheim: Beltz Verlag, 1973), 28. See also my discussion in Häberlen, *Emotional Politics*, 153–4.

41 See Ning de Coninck-Smith, 'Natural Play in Natural Surroundings: Urban Childhood and Playground Planning in Denmark, c. 1930–1950', in *Working Paper 6. Child and Youth Culture*, ed. Odense University (Odense: 1999), Roy Kozlovsky, 'Adventure Playgrounds and Postwar Reconstruction', in *Designing Modern Childhoods: History, Space, and the Material Culture of Children*, ed. Marta Gutman and Ning de Coninck-Smith (New Brunswick: Rutgers University Press, 2008).

42 On adventure playgrounds in Germany, see Autorengruppe Abenteuerspielplatz Märkisches Viertel, *Abenteuerspielplatz – wo verbieten verboten ist: Experiment und Erfahrung* (Reinbek bei Hamburg: Rowohlt, 1973), Jürgen Schmitz, *Abenteuer Spielplatz: 10 Jahre Erziehungsarbeit. Eine Zwischenbilanz* (Dormagen: Zenk Verlag, 1986), Ursula Schulz-Dornburg, *Abenteuerspielplätze: Ein Plädoyer für wilde Spiele* (Düsseldorf: Econ-Verlag, 1972). For a similar experiment in Frankfurt, see Karin Günther-Thomas, Regina Henze and Linette Schönegge, *Kinderplanet, oder: Das Elend der Kinder in der Großstadt* (Reinbek bei Hamburg: Rowohlt, 1972).

43 Cited Basak Tanulku and Jens Kaae Fisker, 'Alternative Spaces Emerging from the Gezi Protests: From Resistance to Alternatives', in *The Production of Alternative Urban Spaces: An International Dialogue*, ed. Jens Kaae Fisker et al. (London: Routledge, 2019), 201. On Istanbul and the Gezi Protests, see Pelin Tan, 'Istanbul: Widerstand im Staddteil und gegenkulturelle Räume', in *Initiativen für ein Recht auf Stadt:*

Theorie und Praxis städtischer Aneignungen, ed. Dirk Gebhardt and Andrej Holm (Hamburg: VSA, 2011), Isabel David and Kumru F. Toktamış, eds., *'Everywhere Taksim': Sowing the Seeds for a New Turkey at Gezi* (Amsterdam: Amsterdam University Press, 2015), Oscar Hemer and Hans-Åke Persson, eds., *In the Aftermath of Gezi: From Social Movement to Social Change?* (Cham: Palgrave Macmillan, 2017).

44 For press reports about Istanbul's rainbow stairs, see https://www. huffingtonpost.co.uk/chloe-gunning/istanbul_b_7440890.html, https://www.sueddeutsche.de/panorama/aufregung-um-bunte-treppe-in-istanbul-kein-ende-des-regenbogens–1.1761376, https://www.jebiga.com/rainbow-stairs-in-istanbul-huseyin-cetinel/.

45 Tina Steiger, 'Cycles of the Copenhagen Squatter Movement: From Slumstormer to BZ Brigades and the Autonomous Movement', in *The Urban Politics of Squatters' Movements*, ed. Miguel A. Martínez López (New York: Palgrave Macmillan, 2018), René Karpantschof and Flemming Mikkelsen, 'Youth, Space, and Autonomy in Copenhagen: The Squatters' and Autonomous Movement, 1963–2012', in *The City Is Ours: Squatting and Autonomous Movements in Europe from the 1970s to the Present*, ed. Bart van der Steen et al. (Oakland: PM Press, 2014). See also Peter Birke, ed., *Besetze deine Stadt! – BZ din by! Häuserkämpfe und Stadtentwicklung in Kopenhagen* (Berlin: Assoziation A, 2007).

46 See James Hinton, 'Self-Help and Socialism the Squatters' Movement of 1946', *History Workshop Journal* 25 (1988), Minayo Nasiali, 'Citizens, Squatters, and Asocials: The Right to Housing and the Politics of Difference in Post-Liberation France', *American Historical Review* 119 (2014).

47 See Alex Vasudevan, *Metropolitan Preoccupations: The Spatial Politics of Squatting in Berlin* (Chichester: Wiley and Sons, 2016), 89–91. For the early squatting movement in the Federal Republic, see *Häuserkampf I: Wir wollen alles – Der Beginn einer Bewegung*. (Hamburg: LAIKA Verlag, 2012).

48 See Wolf Wetzel, 'Die Geschichte des "Blocks" ist auch die Geschichte eines Frankfurter Stadtteils', in *Häuserkampf I: Wir wollen alles – Der Beginn einer Bewegung* (Hamburg: LAIKA Verlag, 2012), Goeke,

Fremdarbeiter, 330–37, Bojadžijev, *Windige Internationale*, 205–13, Sarah Jacobson, 'Redefining Urban Citizenship: Italian Migrants and Housing Occupations in 1970s Frankfurt am Main', *Contemporary European History* (2022).

49 On squatting movements in Europe and the urban revolts of the early 1980s, see in general van der Steen and Andresen, eds., *Youth Revolt*, Bart van der Steen et al., eds., *The City Is Ours: Squatting and Autonomous Movements in Europe from the 1970s to the Present* (Oakland: PM Press, 2014), Miguel A. Martínez López, ed., *The Urban Politics of Squatters' Movements* (New York: Palgrave Macmillan, 2018), Squatting Europe Kollective, ed., *Squatters' Movement in Europe: Commons and Autonomy as Alternatives to Capitalism* (London: Pluto Press, 2014), Balz and Friedrichs, eds., *'All we ever wanted . . .'*.

50 Linus Owens, 'Amsterdam Squatters on the Road: A Case Study in Territorial and Relational Urban Politics', in *A European Youth Revolt: European Perspectives on Youth Protest and Social Movements in the 1980s*, ed. Bart van der Steen and Knud Andresen (Basingstoke: Palgrave Macmillan, 2016), 55.

51 Hans Pruijt, 'The Power of the Magic Key: The Scalability of Squatting in the Netherlands and the United States', in *Squatters' Movement in Europe: Commons and Autonomy as Alternatives to Capitalism*, ed. Squatting Europe Kollective (London: Pluto Press, 2014), 114–15.

52 Hans Pruijt, 'Squatting in the Netherlands: The Social and Political Institutionalization of a Movement', in *Public Goods versus Economic Interests: Global Perspectives on the History of Squatting*, ed. Freia Anders and Alexander Sedlmaier (New York: Routledge, 2017), 263–5.

53 Ibid., 265, Owens, 'Amsterdam Squatters', 56.

54 Pruijt, 'Squatting', 265–7, Owens, 'Amsterdam Squatters', 56–7. On the Dutch squatting movement, see also Nazima Kadir, 'Myth and Reality in the Amsterdam Squatters' Movement, 1975–2012', in *The City Is Ours: Squatting and Autonomous Movements in Europe from the 1970s to the Present*, ed. Bart van der Steen, et al. (Oakland: PM Press, 2014), Lynn Owens, *Cracking under Pressure: Narrating the Decline of the Amsterdam Squatters' Movement* (University Park: Pennsylvania State

University Press, 2009), Eric Duivenvoorden, *Een voet tussen de deur: Geschiedenis van de kraakbeweging, 1964–1999* (Amsterdam: Arbeiderspers, 2000). A brilliant discussion by participants of the squatting movement itself is Agentur BILWET, *Bewegungslehre: Botschaften aus einer autonomen Wirklichkeit* (Berlin: Edition ID-Archiv, 1991).

55 On the squatting movement in West Berlin, see, for example, Vasudevan, *Metropolitan Preoccupations*, 86–132, Häberlen, *Emotional Politics*, 222–64, Carla MacDougall, '"We too are Berliners": Protest, Symbolism and the City in Cold War Germany', in *Changing the World, Changing Oneself: Political Protest and Collective Identities in West Germany and the U.S. in the 1960s and 1970s*, ed. Belinda Davis et al. (New York: Berghahn, 2010), Carla MacDougall, 'In the Shadow of the Wall: Urban Space and Everyday life in Berlin Kreuzberg', in *Between the Avant-Garde and the Everyday: Subversive Politics in Europe from 1957 to the Present*, ed. Timothy Brown and Lorena Anton (New York: Berghahn, 2011), Suttner, *'Beton brennt'*. On Zurich, see Kriesi, *Zürcher Bewegung*, Nigg, ed., *Wir wollen alles*, Thomas Stahel, *Wo-Wo-Wonige: Stadt- und wohnpolitische Bewegungen in Zürich nach 1968* (Zurich: Paranoia City, 2006), Vogel and Schultze-Kossack, eds., *Zür(e)ich brennt*, Mischa Brutschin, 'Züri brännt', in *Häuserkampf I: Wir wollen alles – Der Beginn einer Bewegung* (Hamburg: LAIKA Verlag, 2012). Beyond these cities, see, for example, David Templin, *Freizeit ohne Kontrollen: Die Jugendzentrumsbewegung in der Bundesrepublik der 1970er Jahre* (Göttingen: Wallstein, 2015), Volkhart Schönberg, 'Freiburg: Bewegungen in den besetzten Häusern', in *Häuserkampf I: Wir wollen alles – Der Beginn einer Bewegung* (Hamburg: LAIKA Verlag, 2012), amantine, ed., *'Die Häuser denen, die drin wohnen!': Kleine Geschichte der Häuserkämpfe in Deutschland* (Münster: Unrast, 2012).

56 For a chronological overview of squatting in Berlin, including the histories of individual houses, see https://www.berlin-besetzt.de/.

57 Vasudevan, *Metropolitan Preoccupations*, 98–105.

58 Schöneberger Besetzerrat, 'Offener Brief an die Bürger Berlins', 12 December 1981, found in Ordner Häuserkämpfe, Papiertiger Archiv Berlin. Also cited in Häberlen, *Emotional Politics*, 244.

59 Vasudevan, *Metropolitan Preoccupations*, 109–15, Reinhild Kreis, 'Heim-werken als Protest: Instandbesetzer und Wohnungsbaupolitik in West-Berlin während der 1980er-Jahre', *Zeithistorische Forschungen* 14 (2017). See also the partially fictional, partially autobiographical account by Heinz Bude, Bettina Munk and Karin Wieland, *Aufprall* (Munich: Hanser, 2020).

60 Häberlen, *Emotional Politics*, 243–9.

61 Vasudevan, *Metropolitan Preoccupations*, 123–9, Häberlen, *Emotional Politics*, 259–63.

62 On Kreuzberg, see Hanno Hochmuth, *Kiezgeschichte: Friedrichshain und Kreuzberg im geteilten Berlin* (Göttingen: Wallstein, 2017), Barbara Lang, *Mythos Kreuzberg: Ethnographie eines Stadtteils (1961–1995)* (Frankfurt a.M.: Campus, 1998), Andrej Holm, *Wir bleiben alle! Gentrifizierung – Städtische Konflikte um Aufwertung und Verdrängung* (Münster: Unrast Verlag, 2010).

63 On Hamburg's Hafenstraße, see Jake P. Smith, 'Embedded Abstractions: Authenticity, Aura, and Abject Domesticity in Hamburg's Hafenstraße', in *The Politics of Authenticity: Countercultures and Radical Movements across the Iron Curtain, 1968–1989*, ed. Joachim C. Häberlen, Mark Keck-Szajbel and Kate Mahoney (New York: Berghahn, 2018), Carl-Heinz Mallet, *Die Leute von der Hafenstraße: Über eine andere Art zu leben* (Hamburg: Edition Nautilus, 2000).

64 Vasudevan, *Metropolitan Preoccupations*, 133–63, Andrej Holm and Armin Kuhn, 'Squatting and Gentrification in East Germany since 1989', in *Public Goods versus Economic Interests: Global Perspectives on the History of Squatting*, ed. Freia Anders and Alexander Sedlmaier (New York: Routledge, 2016).

65 On squatting in the GDR, see Udo Grashoff, *Schwarzwohnen: Die Unterwanderung der staatlichen Wohnraumlenkung in der DDR* (Göttingen: V&R Unipress, 2011).

66 Untitled Flyer, Die Besetzer Scheinerstr. 47 (29.12.1989), Robert Havemann Gesellschaft: Archiv der DDR Opposition, RTc09. The flyer is cited in the unpublished Ph.D. thesis by Jake P. Smith, 'Strangers in the Dead Land: Redemption and Regeneration in the European Counterculture'. I'm grateful to him for sharing the draft with me.

67 See Vasudevan, *Metropolitan Preoccupations*, 146–59, Andrej Holm and Armin Kuhn, 'Squatting and Urban Renewal: The Interaction of Squatter Movements and Strategies of Urban Restructuring in Berlin', *International Journal of Urban and Regional Research* 35 (2011).

68 For studies of recent urban protests, see, for example, Holm, *Wir bleiben alle*, Dirk Gebhardt and Andrej Holm, eds., *Initiativen für ein Recht auf Stadt: Theorie und Praxis städtischer Aneignungen* (Hamburg: VSA, 2011), Miguel A. Martínez López, *Squatters in the Capitalist City: Housing, Justice, and Urban Politics* (London: Routledge, 2020), Neil Brenner, Peter Marcuse and Margit Mayer, eds., *Cities for People, Not for Profit: Critical Urban Theory and the Right to the City* (London: Routledge, 2012), Mark Purcell, *Recapturing Democracy: Neoliberalization and the Struggle for Alternative Urban Futures* (New York: Routledge, 2008).

Chapter 11: The Personal Is Political: Women and Gay Movements

1 On the role of women in the French May 1968, see Michelle Zancarini-Fournel, 'Genre et politique: Les années 1968', *Vingtième Siècle: Revue d'histoire* 75 (2002).

2 Carla Lonzi, 'Let's Spit on Hegel', in *Italian Feminist Thought: A Reader*, ed. Paola Bono and Sandra Kemp (Oxford: Basil Blackwell, 1991 [1970]), 51.

3 On the marginalization of positions that sought to question gender roles, see, with regard to Italy, Maud Anne Bracke, *Women and the Reinvention of the Political: Feminism in Italy, 1968–1983* (New York: Routledge, 2014), 50–51. Her argument might well be extended to the rest of Western Europe. See only, on France and West Germany, Bantigny, *1968*, 259–78, Christina von Hodenberg, 'Writing Women's Agency into the History of the Federal Republic: "1968", Historians, and Gender', *Central European History* 52 (2019), 92–4.

4 The speech is reprinted in Ann Anders, ed., *Schlüsseltexte der neuen Frauenbewegung seit 1968* (Frankfurt a.M.: Athenäum, 1988), 39–47. It

can be found at https://www.1000dokumente.de/index.html?c=
dokument_de&dokument=0022_san&object=translation.

5 The story has been told many times; see, for example, Kristina Schulz,
   *Der lange Atem der Provokation: Die Frauenbewegung in der Bundesrepublik
   und in Frankreich* (Frankfurt a.M.: Campus, 2002), 79–82, Brown, *West
   Germany*, 286–7, Belinda Davis, 'The Personal Is Political: Gender, Politics, and Political Activism in Modern German History', in *Gendering
   Modern German History: Rewriting Historiography*, ed. Karen Hagemann
   and Jean H. Quataert (New York: Berghahn Books, 2007), 208–13.

6 On the early women's movement in West Berlin, see Annett Gröschner, *Berolinas zornige Töchter: 50 Jahre Berliner Frauenbewegung* (Berlin:
   FFBIZ, 2018), 43–60.

7 The historiography on the women's movement in Europe is vast, see
   for example Kristina Schulz, ed., *The Women's Liberation Movement:
   Impacts and Outcomes* (New York: Berghahn, 2017), Schulz, *Atem*, Ilse
   Lenz, *Die Neue Frauenbewegung in Deutschland: Abschied vom kleinen
   Unterschied* (Wiesbaden: Verlag für Sozialwissenschaften, 2008),
   Katharina Karcher, *Sisters in Arms: Militant Feminisms in the Federal
   Republic of Germany since 1968* (New York: Berghahn, 2017), Jessica
   Bock, *Frauenbewegung in Ostdeutschland: Aufbruch, Revolte und Trans-
   formation in Leipzig 1980–2000* (Halle (Saale): Mitteldeutscher Verlag,
   2020), Andrea Bührmann, *Das authentische Geschlecht: Die Sexual-
   itätsdebatte der neuen Frauenbewegung und die Foucaultsche Machtanalyse*
   (Münster: Westfälisches Dampfboot, 1995), Andrea Trumann, *Femi-
   nistische Theorie: Frauenbewegung und weibliche Subjektbildung im
   Spätkapitalismus* (Stuttgart: Schmetterlingsverlag, 2002), Lisa Green-
   wald, *Daughters of 1968: Redefining French Feminism and the Women's
   Liberation Movement* (Lincoln: University of Nebraska Press, 2018),
   Christine Bard, ed., *Les Féministes de la deuxième vague* (Rennes: Presses
   universitaire de Rennes, 2012), Claire Duchen, *Feminism in France:
   From May '68 to Mitterrand* (London: Routledge, 1986), Claire
   Duchen, ed., *French Connections: Voices from the Women's Movement in
   France* (Amherst: University of Massachusetts Press, 1987), Marga-
   retta Jolly, *Sisterhood and After: An Oral History of the UK Women's
   Liberation Movement, 1968–Present* (Oxford: Oxford University Press,

2019), Martin Pugh, *Women and the Women's Movement in Britain since 1914*, 3rd edn (London: Palgrave, 2015), 260–307, Barbara Caine, *English Feminism, 1780–1980* (Oxford: Oxford University Press, 1997), 255–71, Bracke, *Women*, Maud Anne Bracke, 'Building a "Counter-Community of Emotions": Feminist Encounters and Socio-Cultural Difference in 1970s Turin', *Modern Italy* 17 (2012), Zsófia Lóránd, *The Feminist Challenge to the Socialist State in Yugoslavia* (Cham: Palgrave, 2018).

8 On the US Women's Movement, see Christine Stansell, *The Feminist Promise: 1792 to the Present* (New York: Modern Library, 2010), 219–72, Alice Echols, *Daring to Be Bad: Radical Feminism in America, 1967–1975* (Minneapolis: University of Minnesota Press, 1989), Dawn Keetley and John Pettegrew, eds., *Public Women, Public Words: A Documentary History of American Feminism* (Lanham: Rowman & Littlefield, 2002).

9 Betty Friedan, *The Feminine Mystique* (New York: Dell, 1963), Anne Koedt, 'The Myth of the Vaginal Orgasm (1970)', in *Public Women, Public Words: A Documentary History of American Feminism*, ed. Dawn Keetley and John Pettegrew (Lanham: Rowman & Littlefield, 2002), Shulamit Firestone, *The Dialectic of Sex: The Case for Feminist Revolution* (New York: Morrow, 1970), Kate Millett, *Sexual Politics* (Garden City: Doubleday, 1970), Pamela Allen, 'Free Space (1970)', in *Radical Feminism*, ed. Anne Koedt, Ellen Levine and Anita Rapone (New York: Quadrangle Books, 1973).

10 See Lucy Delap, *Feminisms: A Global History* (Chicago: University of Chicago Press, 2020), 224–7.

11 Allen, 'Free Space', 272.

12 Ibid., quotes 273, 276, 278.

13 Koedt, 'Myth', quotes 133–4, 138.

14 For Italy, see Bracke, *Women*. For West Germany, see for example Bührmann, *Geschlecht*, Imke Schmincke, 'Von der Politisierung des Privatlebens zum neuen Frauenbewusstsein: Körperpolitik und Subjektivierung von Weiblichkeit in der Neuen Frauenbewegung Westdeutschlands', in *Zeitgeschichte als Geschlechtergeschichte: Neue Perspektiven auf die Bundesrepublik*, ed. Julia Paulus, Eva-Maria Silies and

Kerstin Wolff (Frankfurt a.M.: Campus, 2012), Imke Schmincke, 'Sexualität als "Angelpunkt" der Frauenfrage? Zum Verhältnis von sexueller Revolution und Frauenbewegung', in *Sexuelle Revolution? Zur Geschichte der Sexualität im deutschsprachigen Raum seit den 1960er Jahren*, ed. Peter-Paul Bänziger et al. (Bielefeld: transcript, 2015).

15 Schulz, *Atem*, 102.

16 See, with reference to West Germany and the UK, Häberlen, *Emotional Politics*, 172–85, Reichardt, *Authentizität*, 699–711, Till Kadritzke, 'Bewegte Männer: Men's Liberation und Autonome Männergruppen in den USA und Deutschland, 1970–1995', in *Feminismus in historischer Perspektive: Eine Reaktualisierung*, ed. Feminismus Seminar (Bielefeld: transcript, 2014), Lucy Delap, 'Uneasy Solidarity: The British Men's Movement and Feminism', in *The Women's Liberation Movement: Impacts and Outcomes*, ed. Kristina Schulz (New York: Berghahn, 2017), Kate Mahoney, '"Finding Our Own Solutions": The Women's Movement and Mental Health Activism in Late Twentieth-Century England' (University of Warwick, 2017), 213–16.

17 Cited in Greenwald, *Daughters*, 108.

18 Cited in Brown, *West Germany*, 290.

19 Cited in ibid., 294. Translation amended. The full text is available online at http://www.glasnost.de/hist/apo/weiber.html. See also Karcher, *Sisters*, 23–4.

20 Quotes, with amended translations, from Greenwald, *Daughters*, 158. See also Schulz, *Atem*, 107–8.

21 Schulz, *Atem*, 122–43, Greenwald, *Daughters*, 153–83.

22 Schulz, *Atem*, 143–61, Karcher, *Sisters*, 71–6. On similar campaigns in the UK, see Jolly, *Sisterhood*, 101–12.

23 Bracke, *Women*, 85–6.

24 In the UK, an outlier in this regard, the 1967 Abortion Act had made free and legal abortions relatively easy. Abortion rights were hence no major rallying cause for the British women's movement. See Dorothy McBride Stetson, 'Women's Movements' Defence of Legal Abortion in Great Britain', in *Abortion Politics, Women's Movements, and the Democratic State: A Comparative Study of State Feminism*, ed. Dorothy McBride Stetson (Oxford: Oxford University Press, 2001).

25 See Schulz, *Atem*, 148–9. On discussions within the West German women's movement about contraception and especially the pill, see also Eva-Maria Silies, *Liebe, Lust und Last: Die Pille als weibliche Generationserfahrung in der Bundesrepublik 1960–1980* (Göttingen: Wallstein Verlag, 2010), 385–412, Eva-Maria Silies, 'Taking the Pill after the "Sexual Revolution": Female Contraceptive Decisions in England and West Germany in the 1970s', *European Review of History* 22 (2015).

26 Quotes from Frauke Lippens, 'Die sanfte Geburt', *Courage* 4, February 1979, 46–7; Sonja, 'Hausgeburt', *Das Blatt* 88a (18 February–3 March 1977), 11; Ein Medizinstudent, 'An alle Frauen, die nicht die Möglichkeit haben, eine Hausgeburt zu machen', *Das Blatt* 98 (1–14 July 1977), 19. All quoted in Häberlen, *Emotional Politics*, 190.

27 On West Germany, see for example Gröschner, *Zornige Töchter*, 92–4, Schulz, *Atem*, 204–5. For a detailed study of a feminist self-help and support centre in San Lorenzo, Rome, see also Heigl, *Rom*, 407–36. See also Bracke, *Women*, 108.

28 Cited in Sue O'Sullivan, 'Passionate Beginnings: Ideological Politics 1969–72', *Feminist Review* 11 (1982), 81. See also Jolly, *Sisterhood*, 93–4.

29 The pamphlet can be found online at https://frauenmediaturm.de/neue-frauenbewegung/chronik–1973/. For a brief reference on a similar protest, see Schulz, *Atem*, 163.

30 On the origins and spread of Reclaim the Night protests in Europe and beyond, see Finn Mackay, *Radical Feminism: Feminist Activism in Movement* (Basingstoke: Palgrave, 2015), 71–3. On Italy, see Bracke, *Women*, 118.

31 On Reclaim the Night protests in West Germany, see Karcher, *Sisters*, 95–9, Häberlen, *Emotional Politics*, 213–14.

32 See Mackay, *Radical Feminism*, 73–81. On the slogan see https://ayewellhmm.wordpress.com/2020/11/12/remembering-reclaim-the-night–1977/.

33 Jonathan Dean, *Rethinking Contemporary Feminist Politics* (Basingstoke: Palgrave, 2010), 102. See also Mackay, *Radical Feminism*, 84–9.

34 Jane Freeland, 'Domestic Abuse and Women's Lives: East and West Policies during the 1960s and 1970s', in *Gendering Post-1945 German History: Entanglements*, ed. Karen Hagemann, Donna Harsch and Friederike Brühöfener (New York: Berghahn, 2019), 264–5, Jane Freeland, *Feminist*

Transformations and Domestic Violence in Divided Berlin, 1968–2002 (Oxford: Oxford University Press, 2022), Gröschner, *Zornige Töchter*, 94–8.

35 Lóránd, *Feminist Challenge*, 193–5.

36 On consciousness-raising, see, for example, Ursula Krechel, *Selbsterfahrung und Fremdbestimmung: Bericht aus der neuen Frauenbewegung* (Darmstadt, Neuwied: Luchterhand, 1975), 13–16, Mackay, *Radical Feminism*, 45–6, Jolly, *Sisterhood*, 99–101, Bracke, *Women*, 66–79, Maria Bühner, 'The Rise of a New Consciousness: Lesbian Activism in East Germany in the 1980s', in *The Politics of Authenticity: Countercultures and Radical Movements across the Iron Curtain, 1968–1989*, ed. Joachim C. Häberlen, Mark Keck-Szajbel and Kate Mahoney (New York: Berghahn, 2018).

37 Frauen aus der Frauengruppe Freiburg, 'Kleingruppen – Erfahrungen und Regeln', in *Frauenjahrbuch 1975*, 184–98.

38 Alice Schwarzer, cited in Jane Freeland, 'Women's Bodies and Feminist Subjectivities in West Germany', in *The Politics of Authenticity: Countercultures and Radical Movements across the Iron Curtain, 1968–1989*, ed. Joachim C. Häberlen, Mark Keck-Szajbel and Kate Mahoney (New York: Berghahn, 2018), 134.

39 Cited in Bracke, *Women*, 107. See also Heigl, *Rom*, 413.

40 Gisela S., 'Frauen malen Frauen', *Andere Zeitung*, 8 October 1976, 15.

41 Cited in Kate Mahoney, 'The Political, Emotional, and Therapeutic: Narratives of Consciousness-Raising and Authenticity in the English Women's Liberation Movement', in *The Politics of Authenticity: Countercultures and Radical Movements across the Iron Curtain, 1968–1989*, ed. Joachim C. Häberlen, Mark Keck-Szajbel and Kate Mahoney (New York: Berghahn, 2018), 72. See also, based on oral history interviews, Jolly, *Sisterhood*, 99–101.

42 Ulla, Birgit, Susan, Sabine and Barbara, '"Ich möchte lernen, ich selbst zu sein." Siebzehnjährige Oberschülerinnen schreiben über sich', *Kursbuch 47* (March 1977), 143–58. See the extended discussion in Häberlen, *Emotional Politics*, 167–9. See also, for an ambivalent assessment of CR groups in Munich, Elisabeth Zellmer, *Töchter der Revolte? Frauenbewegung und Feminismus der 1970er Jahre in München* (Munich: Oldenbourg, 2011), 164–72.

43 Cited in Bühner, 'Rise', 163.

44 Ulla et al., '"Ich möchte lernen"'.

45 Bracke, *Women*, 68.

46 Ibid., 77.

47 'Körperbewusstsein: Erfahrungen einer Selbsthilfe-Gruppe', in *Frauenjahrbuch* 1976, 135–51.

48 Greenwald, *Daughters*, 172–81.

49 Jeska Rees, 'A Look Back at Anger: The Women's Liberation Movement in 1978', *Women's History Review* 19 (2010).

50 Bracke, *Women*, 187.

51 See, with reference to Italy, ibid., 190–96. On Europe more broadly, see Schulz, ed., *Women's Liberation Movement*.

52 See for example Kathrin Stern, *Die 'Frauen für den Frieden/Ostberlin' – Widerstand oder Opposition?* (Oldenburg: BIS-Verlag, 2009), Davis, 'Gender of War and Peace', Astrid Mignon Kirchhof, 'Frauen in der Antiatomkraftbewegung: Das Beispiel der Mütter gegen Atomkraft', *Ariadne* 64 (2013). For Italy, see Branciforte, 'Women's Peace Camp'.

53 On lesbian political activism, see, for example, Gabriele Dennert, Christiane Leidinger and Franziska Rauchut, eds., *In Bewegung bleiben: 100 Jahre Politik, Kultur und Geschichte von Lesben* (Berlin: Querverlag, 2007), Sheila Jeffreys, *The Lesbian Revolution: Lesbian Feminism in the UK, 1970–1990* (New York: Routledge, 2018).

54 Cited in Christine Bard, 'Lesbianism as Political Construction in the French Feminist Movement', in *The Women's Liberation Movement: Impacts and Outcomes*, ed. Kristina Schulz (New York: Berghahn, 2017), 165. For earlier debates about homosexuality in the French women's movement, see Frédéric Martel, *The Pink and the Black: Homosexuals in France since 1968*, trans. Jane Marie Todd (Stanford: Stanford University Press, 1999), 32–47.

55 Monika Sauer, 'Bericht aus einer Frauenwohngemeinschaft', *Lesbenpresse* 3 (March 1976), 23.

56 See *Hamburger Frauenzeitung* 16 (December 1977). Interestingly, such debates within the women's movement have received very little attention in the historical literature on the women's movement. See, with reference to more recent debates, Mackay, *Radical Feminism*, 226–38,

Jolly, *Sisterhood*, 185–9. For a feminist position critical of 'transgenderism', see Jeffreys, *Lesbian Revolution*, 189–92, Sheila Jeffreys, *Gender Hurts: A Feminist Analysis of the Politics of Transgenderism* (London: Routledge, 2014). For such debates in gay circles, see Benno Gammerl, *anders fühlen: Schwules und lesbisches Leben in der Bundesrepublik. Eine Emotionsgeschichte* (Munich: Carl Hanser, 2021), 186–7.

57 Cited in Tiffany N. Florvil, *Mobilizing Black Germany: Afro-German Women and the Making of a Transnational Movement* (Urbana: University of Illinois Press, 2020), 26.

58 Cited in Natalie Thomlinson, *Race, Ethnicity and the Women's Movement in England, 1968–1993* (Houndmills, Basingstoke: Palgrave Macmillan, 2016), 164. On black feminism in Europe, see the contributions in Akwugo Emejulu and Francesca Sobande, eds., *To Exist is to Resist: Black Feminism in Europe* (London: Pluto Press, 2019).

59 Dagmar Schultz, *Audre Lorde – The Berlin Years 1984 to 1992* (Germany: 2012). See also Florvil, *Black Germany*, 35–57.

60 Thomlinson, *Race*, 57.

61 Ibid., 169–70. See also, refuting charges of racism in the context of Reclaim the Night marches, Mackay, *Radical Feminism*, 89–102.

62 Quoted in Thomlinson, *Race*, 168.

63 For an account of the event, including quotes, see Martel, *Pink and the Black*, 18–19, Jacques Girard, *Le Mouvement homosexuel en France 1945–1980* (Paris: Syros, 1981), 81–111, Michael Sibalis, 'L'Arrivée de la libération gay en France: Le Front Homosexuel d'Action Révolutionnaire (FHAR)', *Genre, Sexualité, Société* 3 (2010), Julian Jackson, *Living in Arcadia: Homosexuality, Politics, and Morality in France from the Liberation to AIDS* (Chicago: University of Chicago Press, 2009), 183–4.

64 See Martel, *Pink and the Black*, 24–6.

65 See Antoine Idier, 'A Genealogy of a Politics of Subjectivity: Guy Hocquenghem, Homosexuality, and the Radical Left in Post-1968 France', in *The Politics of Authenticity: Countercultures and Radical Movements across the Iron Curtain, 1968–1989*, ed. Joachim C. Häberlen, Mark Keck-Szajbel and Kate Mahoney (New York: Berghahn, 2018), 89–90, Antoine Idier, *Les Vies de Guy Hocquenghem: Politique, sexualité, culture* (Paris:

Fayard, 2017). On the FHAR, see also Girard, *Le Mouvement*, 81–111, Michael Sibalis, 'The Spirit of May '68 and the Origins of the Gay Liberation Movement in France', in *Gender and Sexuality in 1968: Transformative Politics in the Cultural Imagination*, ed. Lessie Jo Frazier and Deborah Cohen (Houndmills: Palgrave Macmillan, 2009).

66 On gay liberation movements in Europe beyond France, see, for example, Gert Hekma, Harry Oosterhuis and James Steakley, 'Leftist Sexual Politics and Homosexuality: A Historical Overview', *Journal of Homosexuality* 29 (1995), Lucy Robinson, *Gay Men and the Left in Post-War Britain: How the Personal Got Political* (Manchester: Manchester University Press, 2008), Craig Griffiths, *The Ambivalence of Gay Liberation: Male Homosexual Politics in 1970s West Germany* (Oxford: Oxford University Press, 2021), Patrick Henze, *Schwule Emanzipation und ihre Konflikte: Zur Westdeutschen Schwulenbewegung der 1970er Jahre* (Berlin: Querverlag, 2019), Josie McLellan, 'Glad to Be Gay Behind the Wall: Gay and Lesbian Activism in 1970s East Germany', *History Workshop Journal* 74 (2012), Dario Pasquini, '"This Will Be the Love of the Future": Italian LGBT People and Their Emotions in Letters from the Fuori! and Massimo Consoli Archives, 1970–1984', *Journal for the History of Sexuality* 29 (2020).

67 On Arcadie, see Jackson, *Arcadia*. On the same period in West Germany, see Clayton J. Whisnant, *Male Homosexuality in West Germany: Between Persecution and Freedom, 1945–69* (Basingstoke: Palgrave, 2012).

68 *Rapport contre la normalité* (Paris: Éditions Champs Libre), 72, quoted in Michael Sibalis, 'The Gay Liberation Movement in France', in *Sexual Revolutions*, ed. Gert Hekma and Alain Giami (Basingstoke: Palgrave Macmillan, 2014).

69 Idier, *Les Vies*, 73–4, 87–8, Sibalis, 'Spirit of May '68', 244. See also Craig Griffiths, 'The International Effects of the Stonewall Riots', in *Global Encyclopedia of Lesbian, Gay, Bisexual, Transgender, and Queer (LGBTQ) History*, ed. Howard Chiang (Farmington Hills: Charles Scribner's Sons, 2019).

70 Idier, *Les Vies*, 85–7.

71 Jackson, *Arcadia*, 188–9, Griffiths, *Ambivalence*, 100–101, Henze, *Emanzipation*, 321–35.

72 For activism in France and Homolulu, see, respectively, Sibalis, 'Gay Liberation', 192, Griffiths, *Ambivalence*, 208–11. On gay activism in general, see the literature mentioned above.

73 On these debates, see for example Griffiths, *Ambivalence*, 163–98.

74 Guy Hocquenghem, *Homosexual Desire*, trans. Daniella Dangoor (Durham: Duke University Press, 1993) (first published as *Le Désir homosexuel* (Paris: Éditions universitaires, 1972)).

75 Ibid., 50.

76 Ibid., 130.

77 See Lukas Betzler and Hauke Branding, 'Guy Hocquenghems radikale Theorie des Begehrens: Nachwort zur Neuherausgabe', in *Guy Hocquenghem: Das homosexuelle Begehren*, ed. Lukas Betzler and Hauke Branding (Hamburg: Edition Nautilus, 2019), 166–8.

78 Hocquenghem, *Desire*, 131–2.

79 Griffiths, *Ambivalence*, 166–76, Henze, *Emanzipation*, 300–321.

80 Griffiths, *Ambivalence*, 196.

81 Gammerl, *anders fühlen*, 195–203.

82 Cited in Robinson, *Gay Men*, 78.

83 These are the words of one gay man interviewed by Gammerl, *anders fühlen*, 276.

84 On France, see Martel, *Pink and the Black*, 259–81.

85 See in general Gammerl, *anders fühlen*, 273–82, Magdalena Beljan, *Rosa Zeiten? Eine Geschichte der Subjektivierung männlicher Homosexualität in den 1970er und 1980er Jahren der BRD* (Bielefeld: transcript, 2014), 173–231. On homophobia in the French right, see Martel, *Pink and the Black*, 245–58.

86 Beljan, *Rosa Zeiten?*, 193–6, Griffiths, *Ambivalence*, 164–5.

87 See, with regard to West Germany, Gammerl, *anders fühlen*, 277–81. On Aids activism, see also Martel, *Pink and the Black*, 216–44, 285–309, Deborah Gould, *Moving Politics: Emotion and ACT UP's Fight against AIDS* (Chicago: University of Chicago Press, 2009).

88 For some of these debates in different national contexts see Mackay, *Radical Feminism*, 209–27, Jolly, *Sisterhood*, 236–41, Scott, *Politics*,

Gröschner, *Zornige Töchter*, 263–7, Patsy l'Amour laLove, ed., *Beiss-reflexe: Kritik an queerem Aktivismus, autoritären Sehnsüchten, Sprechverboten* (Berlin: Querverlag, 2017), Susan Rottmann and Myra Marx Ferree, 'Citizenship and Intersectionality: German Feminist Debates about Headscarf and Anti-Discrimination Laws', *Social Politics: International Studies in Gender, State & Society* 15 (2008), 481–513, Joyce Marie Musha-ben, '"Die Freiheit, die ich meine . . ." An American View of the Kopftuch Debate', *Femina Politica* 13 (2004). Such debates happen, for example, in queer-feminist online magazines such as *F Word* (London) or *Missy Magazine* (Germany).

89 Patrick Greenfield, 'Pride Organisers Say Sorry After Anti-Trans Group Leads March', *Guardian*, 8 July 2018, https://www.theguard ian.com/world/2018/jul/08/london-pride-organisers-say-sorry-after-anti-trans-group-leads-march.

90 'Trans Activist Allegedly Tries to Burn Lesbians at French Pride March', online at *Fourth Wave – For Women*, 12 September 2021, https://4w.pub/trans-identified-male-allegedly-attempts-to-burn-lesb ians-in-french-pride-march/. It should be noted that the platform is 'gender-critical', that is, critical of queer conceptions of gender fluidity.

Chapter 12: Living Differently: Dwelling, Working, Travelling

1 Printed in *radikal* 50/51 (December 1978/January 1979), 8. Reprinted in Häberlen, *Emotional Politics*, 9.

2 Harald Schenk, *Wir leben zusammen, nicht allein: Wohngemeinschaften heute* (Cologne: Kiepenheuer und Witsch, 1984). I have discussed this movement in Joachim C. Häberlen, 'Feeling at Home in Lonely Cities: An Emotional History of the West German Urban Commune Move-ment during the Long 1970s', *Urban History* 48 (2021). On communes in West Germany, see with much detail Reichardt, *Authentizität*, 351–459, Detlef Siegfried, '"Einstürzende Neubauten": Wohngemeinschaften, Jugendzentren und private Präferenzen kommunistischer "Kader"

als Formen jugendlicher Subkultur', *Archiv für Sozialgeschichte* 44 (2004). Beyond West Germany, see John Davis and Anette Warring, 'Living Utopia: Communal Living in Denmark and Britain', *Cultural and Social History* 8 (2011).

3 On rural communes in France, see Lacroix, *L'Utopie*.

4 Davis and Warring, 'Utopia', 515.

5 Rudi H. P. Damme, *Zur Stabilität von Wohngruppen: Ein Modell aktivierender Sozialforschung zur Theorie und Praxis des kollektiven Alltags* (Bonn: SOAK Druck- & Verlagskooperative, 1980), 14.

6 On rural communes in West Germany, see Reichardt, *Authentizität*, 459–98.

7 Davis and Warring, 'Utopia', 515. On France, see Lacroix, *L'Utopie*.

8 Heidi Dann and Knut Heydolph, *Alltag in Wohngemeinschaften* (Bonn: Eigendruck, 1979), 5.

9 Davis and Warring, 'Utopia', 516–17.

10 G. Blankenburg and E. Wesche, 'Wohngemeinschaft kontra Kleinfamilie', *Blickpunkt* 104 (1970), reprinted in *Humanes Wohnen Materialien* 1 (November 1973), 1–6.

11 G. Meyer-Ehlers, M. Haußknecht and S. Rughöft, *Kollektive Wohnformen: Erfahrungen – Vorstellungen – Raumbedürfnisse in Wohngemeinschaften, Wohngruppen und Wohnverbänden* (Wiesbaden: Bauverlag, 1973), 188.

12 Cited in Lacroix, *L'Utopie*, 24. The source dates from April 1971.

13 Cited in Davis and Warring, 'Utopia', 520.

14 Reichardt, *Authentizität*, 420–22.

15 Davis and Warring, 'Utopia', 521.

16 On gender questions in communes, see also Belinda Davis, 'Radical Change Close to Home: Transforming the Self and Relations in West German Alternative Politics', in *Social Movements After '68: West Germany and Beyond*, ed. Friederike Brühöfener, Belinda Davis and Stephen Milder (New York: Berghahn, 2022).

17 For a contemporary study of children in communes, see Ute Straub and Barbara Schröder, *Kinder in Wohngemeinschaften* (Herford: Zündhölzchen, 1978). See also Davis and Warring, 'Utopia', 523, Häberlen, 'Feeling at Home', 10–11.

18 Wildfried Goldhorn, 'Bürgerkrieg Arndtstr. 30, 1. Stock, oder: wie verschlafe ich die Revolution!', *Andere Zeitung*, 11 January 1977, 4, cited in Häberlen, *Emotional Politics*, 201.

19 Lacroix, *L'Utopie*, 31.

20 Rüdiger Pohl, ed., *Mittlere Wohndauer: 18 Monate. Berichte, Daten und Meinungen über Wohngemeinschaften in der Stadt* (Bonn: SOAK Druck- & Verlagskooperative, 1978).

21 For the various difficulties rural communes encountered, see in general Lacroix, *L'Utopie*.

22 Schenk, *Wir leben zusammen*, 33, 36–7.

23 Dieter Korczak, *Neue Formen des Zusammenlebens: Erfolge und Schwierigkeiten des Experiments 'Wohngemeinschaft'* (Frankfurt a.M.: Fischer, 1979), 84.

24 Schenk, *Wir leben zusammen*, 23.

25 Gudrun Cyprian, *Sozialisation in Wohngemeinschaften: Eine empirische Untersuchung ihrer strukturellen Bedingungen* (Stuttgart: Ferdinand Enke Verlag, 1978), 78–9, Davis and Warring, 'Utopia', 524.

26 See the detailed account in 'Bericht der Wohngemeinschaft aus Posemuckel', in . . . *vor uns die Mühen der Ebenen: Alltagsprobleme und Perspektiven von Wohngemeinschaften*, ed. Johann August Schülein (Giessen: Focus-Verlag, 1980).

27 Dann and Heydolph, *Alltag*, 67.

28 *Humanes Wohnen Materialien 6* (n.d., probably 1974), 52.

29 R. von Schweitzer, 'Die Wohngruppe als Alternative zur Lebensform in der Kleinfamilie', *Hauswirtschaft und Wissenschaft* 6 (1972), 270–75. The text is reprinted in *Humanes Wohnen Materialien 1* (November 1973), 7–16, here 12.

30 Richard Meng and Wolfgang Thiel, 'Schöner Wohnen? Über die Gestaltung der Räume in Wohngemeinschaften', in . . . *vor uns die Mühen der Ebenen: Alltagsprobleme und Perspektiven von Wohngemeinschaften*, ed. Johann August Schülein (Giessen: Focus-Verlag, 1980), 170.

31 Hans-Dieter Bahr, *Missgestalten: Über bürgerliches Leben* (Lollar: Achenbach, 1976), 105, quoted in Meng and Thiel, 'Schöner Wohnen?', 170.

32 Meng and Thiel, 'Schöner Wohnen?', quotes 172, 178–9, 182, 184–5.

33 See, for example, Rüdiger Pohl, 'Probleme einer (ganz normalen) Wohngemeinschaft', in *Mittlere Wohndauer: 18 Monate. Berichte, Daten und Meinungen über Wohngemeinschaften in der Stadt*, ed. Rüdiger Pohl (Bonn: SOAK Druck- & Verlagskooperative, 1978).

34 Barbara, 'Leserbrief', *Info Hannoverscher Wohngemeinschaften* 4/5 (June 1974), 12–14.

35 Korczak, *Neue Formen*, 111.

36 For a comedy depicting this development, see Ralf Westhoff, *Wir sind die Neuen* (Germany: 2014).

37 See Frank Georgi, 'Selbstverwaltung: Aufstieg und Niedergang einer politischen Utopie in Frankreich von den 1968er bis zu den 80er Jahren', in *1968 und die Arbeiter: Studien zum 'proletarischen Mai' in Europa*, ed. Bernd Gehrke and Gerd-Rainer Horn (Hamburg: VSA-Verlag, 2007), 256–7.

38 Ibid., 253. See also the discussion in Chapter 9.

39 Ibid., in particular 253–9.

40 For a compendium of such alternative projects from all across Western Europe, see Walter Hollstein and Boris Penth, eds., *Alternativ-Projekte: Beispiele gegen die Resignation* (Reinbek bei Hamburg: Rowohlt, 1980). For France see the contributions in Frank Georgi, ed., *Autogestion, la dernière utopie?* (Paris: Publications de la Sorbonne, 2003).

41 See the discussion in Reichardt, *Authentizität*, 319–50.

42 On LIP, see, with many more references, Jens Beckmann, *Selbstverwaltung zwischen Management und 'Communauté': Arbeitskampf und Unternehmensentwicklung bei LIP in Besançon 1973–1987* (Bielefeld: transcript, 2019), Donald Reid, *Opening the Gates: The Lip Affair, 1968–1981* (London: Verso, 2018).

43 Reid, *Opening*, 47–58, quote 51.

44 Beckmann, *Selbstverwaltung*, 61–2, Reid, *Opening*, 66–79.

45 Reid, *Opening*, 96–7.

46 Beckmann, *Selbstverwaltung*, 73, 77.

47 Quoted in Reid, *Opening*, 129.

48 Monique Piton, *Anders leben. Chronik eines Arbeitskampfes: Lip, Besançon*, trans. David Wittenberg (Frankfurt a.M.: Suhrkamp, 1976), 52–60,

quote 59. For attempts to organize life and work differently, see also the contributions in Georgi, ed., *Autogestion*.

49 See only Julian Jackson, *The Popular Front in France: Defending Democracy, 1934–38* (Cambridge: Cambridge University Press, 1988), 85–103, Antoine Prost, *Autour du Front populaire: Aspects du mouvement social au XXe siècle* (Paris: Seuil, 2006), Stéphane Sirot, 'La Vague de grèves du Front Populaire: Des interprétations divergentes et incertaines', in *Les Deux France du Front populaire: Chocs et contre-chocs*, ed. Gilles Morin and Gilles Richard (Paris: L'Harmattan, 2008).

50 Beckmann, *Selbstverwaltung*, 76.

51 Ibid., 68.

52 Ibid., 88–9.

53 Ibid., 93.

54 Ibid., 94.

55 Reid, *Opening*, 279.

56 Ibid., 326–8.

57 Beckmann, *Selbstverwaltung*, 222.

58 Ibid., 232.

59 Ibid., 240–41.

60 Ibid., 240.

61 Ibid., 246.

62 For an example of a dense network of self-managed neighbourhood projects, see Mimmo Pucciarelli, 'L'Autogestion au quotidien dans un quartier "alternatif": La Croix-Rousse, Lyon, 1975–2001', in *Autogestion, la dernière utopie?*, ed. Frank Georgi (Paris: Publications de la Sorbonne, 2003).

63 Reichardt, *Authentizität*, 321.

64 See Boltanski and Chiapello, *Spirit*, du Gay and Morgan, eds., *New Spirits?* For a similar argument in a West German context, see Ulrich Bröckling, *The Entrepreneurial Self: Fabricating a New Type of Subject* (Los Angeles: Sage, 2016).

65 Bernward Vesper, *Die Reise: Romanessay* (West Berlin: März, 1977).

66 Kerouac, *On the Road*. The book was originally published in 1957. On Kerouac and his novel, see also Chandarlapaty, *Beat Generation*, Wilson, 'Author'.

67 Christiane Rochefort, *Encore heureux qu'on va vers l'été* (Paris: Grasset, 1975). Published in German as *Zum Glück gehts dem Sommer entgegen* (Frankfurt a.M.: Suhrkamp, 1977). For reviews of the book in West Germany's leftist press, see *Pflasterstrand* 24 (23 February–8 March 1978), 20–21; *Traumstadt* 1 (March 1978), 7–9; *Lesbenpresse* 7 (May 1978), 7; *BUG Info* 1026, 16.

68 Quoted in Richard Ivan Jobs, *Backpack Ambassadors: How Youth Travel Integrated Europe* (Chicago: University of Chicago Press, 2017), 153.

69 Anja Bertsch, 'Alternative (in) Bewegung: Distinktion und transnationale Vergemeinschaftung im alternativen Tourismus', in *Das Alternative Milieu: Antibürgerlicher Lebensstil und linke Politik in der Bundesrepublik Deutschland und Europa 1968–1983*, ed. Sven Reichardt and Detlef Siegfried (Göttingen: Wallstein, 2010), 116–17.

70 Jobs, *Backpack Ambassadors*, 165.

71 Ibid., 175.

72 Ibid., 214–15.

73 Ibid., 214–19.

74 Juliane Fürst, *Flowers through Concrete: Explorations in Soviet Hippieland* (Oxford: Oxford University Press, 2021), 171.

75 Cited in ibid., 172.

76 Ibid., 173.

77 Cited in Jobs, *Backpack Ambassadors*, 209.

78 Ibid., 210.

79 Ibid., 211–12.

80 Bertsch, 'Alternative (in) Bewegung', 124–5.

81 Ibid., 119–20.

Chapter 13: Emotional Politics: Changing the Self, Changing the World

1 The phrase is from a West German context, see Haunss, *Identität*, 115, Reichardt, *Authentizität*, 55–6, Häberlen, *Emotional Politics*, 104–13. However, Italian radical activists developed a similar understanding of the political in the context of the 1977 movement, see for example

Heigl, *Rom*, 251–2, 368–9, Moroni and Balestrini, *Goldene Horde*, 303–15. See also, written somewhat in the spirit of a subjective politics, Luisa Passerini, *Autobiography of a Generation: Italy, 1968* (Hanover, NH: University Press of New England, 1996).

2 See my discussion in Häberlen, *Emotional Politics*, 123–66.

3 Edwards, *More Work!*, 75–6, Lumley, *States of Emergency*, 300.

4 I've discussed this material in more detail in Häberlen, *Emotional Politics*.

5 Anon., 'Psychisches Elend und Politische Praxis', *Hundert Blumen* 9 (n.d., probably summer 1973), 6–7.

6 Duhm, *Angst*. See, with many more examples, Häberlen, '(Not) Narrating', 126–35. On broader discourses of fear, see also Frank Biess, *German Angst: Fear and Democracy in the Federal Republic of Germany* (Oxford: Oxford University Press, 2020), 242–89.

7 Anon., 'Grüne Liste – Natur als Politik', *Pflasterstrand* 18 (3–16 November 1977), 30–32.

8 Rainer Klassen, 'Aphorismus zur Vernunft', *Ulcus Molle* 3/4 (1979), 7.

9 Herbert Röttgen, 'Kinderrevolution', *Das Blatt*, 22 April–5 May 1977, 14–16.

10 Cover page of *Pflasterstrand*, 20 December 1977, reproduced in Häberlen, *Emotional Politics*, 97.

11 Christiane Matties, 'Penthesilea, Annie und die anderen Frauen', *Konkursbuch: Zeitschrift für Vernunftkritik* 2 (1978), 189–204.

12 Lucy Körner, 'Bioenergetik', *Ulcus Molle* 9/10 (1979), 21–3.

13 Matthias Beltz, 'Abenteuer in der Fabrik: Geschichten aus der Beziehung zwischen Linksradikalen und Arbeiterbewegung', *Autonomie: Materialien gegen die Fabrikgesellschaft*, 9 October 1977, 9–22, quote 17.

14 Gerd-Gustl Müller, *Der Job: Roman* (Munich: Weismann Verlag, 1977), 74.

15 On discourses about sexuality on the left, see my discussion in Joachim C. Häberlen, 'Feeling Like a Child: Visions and Practices of Sexuality in the West German Alternative Left during the Long 1970s', *Journal for the History of Sexuality* 25 (2016).

16 Männergruppe Frankfurt, 'Tod dem Patriarschismus [*sic*]: Es lebe der Mann!', *diskus*, 3 November 1975, 26–8.

17 Sylvia, 'Die Last meiner Lust', *Erotik und Umbruch: Zeitung zu Sexualität*, mid-summer 1978, 32–3.

18 Anon., 'Lesben und Orgasmuß', *Hamburger Frauenzeitung*, July 1976, 17–18.

19 Pamphlet by Liberale Schüleraktion der Deutschen Jungdemokraten, probably early 1970s, Ordner Schulkämpfe, Papiertiger Archiv Berlin.

20 W. S., 'Ich scheiß auf die Gesellschaft . . . aber sie gibt's mir ganz schön zurück', *Carlo Sponti*, 4 May 1974, 1.

21 Anon., 'Torschlusspanik um 10 (Discotheken)', *ABBLDIBABBLDI-BIBBLDIBABBLDIBU: Schülerzeitung der HCO*, 2 December 1973, 8–10. See similarly Patricia von Böckmann, 'Traumfabrik', *Rumpelstielzchen*, May 1974. See also Alexa Geisthövel, 'Anpassung: Disco und Jugendbeobachtung in Westdeutschland, 1975–1981', in *Zeitgeschichte des Selbst: Therapeutisierung – Politisierung – Emotionalisierung*, ed. Pascal Eitler and Jens Elberfeld (Bielefeld: transcript, 2015), 251.

22 See for example Anon., 'statt eines Forums: subjektiver Mischmasch', *radikal 74* (11 January–1 February 1980), 16.

23 On men's groups, see Rebecca Clifford, Robert Gildea, and Anette Warring, 'Gender and Sexuality', in *Europe's 1968: Voices of Revolt*, ed. Robert Gildea, Mark James and Anette Warring (Oxford: Oxford University Press, 2013), 248–50, Kadritzke, 'Männer'.

24 See Maik Tändler, 'Therapeutische Vergemeinschaftung: Demokratie, Emanzipation und Emotionalisierung in der "Gruppe", 1963–1976', in *Das Selbst zwischen Anpassung und Befreiung: Psychowissen und Politik im 20. Jahrhundert*, ed. Maik Tändler and Uffa Jensen (Göttingen: Wallstein, 2012), 143, Maik Tändler, *Das therapeutische Jahrzehnt: Der Psychoboom in den siebziger Jahren* (Göttingen: Wallstein, 2016), Reichardt, *Authentizität*, 782–806, Barbara Sutter, '"Selbstveränderung und Sozialveränderung": Von der Selbsthilfegruppe und ihren Verheißungen zum Bürgerschaftlichen Engagement und seinen Zumutungen', in *Das beratene Selbst: Zur Genealogie der Therapeutisierung in den 'langen' Siebzigern*, ed. Sabine Maasen et al. (Bielefeld: transcript, 2011).

25 Micha, 'Warum ich in die Männergruppe gegangen bin', *Mann-o-Mann*, February 1975, 11–12.

26 Delap, 'Solidarity', 226.

27 *Carlo Sponti*, 26/27 January 1977.

28 Die verbliebenen fünf aus der Männergruppe, 'Männer – ohne Männlichkeit ratlos?', *Carlo Sponti*, 20/21 May 1976, 8–9.

29 Ibid.

30 Delap, 'Solidarity', 224.

31 See Häberlen, *Emotional Politics*, 182.

32 Patrick, 'Zaghafte Antwort eines "Softies" (Ende)', *Info BUG* 94 (16 February 1976), 3–4. For a discussion see Häberlen, *Emotional Politics*, 164.

33 For a rather critical discussion, see Reichardt, *Authentizität*, 703–11.

34 Manfred et al., 'Hickhack', *Mannsbild* 1976, 5–9.

35 Foucault, 'Subject', 785.

36 Patrick, 'Zaghafte Antwort eines "Softies"', *Info BUG* 92 (2 February 1976), 7–8. See also the discussion in Häberlen, *Emotional Politics*, 161–5, Reichardt, *Authentizität*, 699–703.

37 Claudia Rößler, 'Der Mythos von der Ausnahme, oder: Auch der "softe Mann" ist keine Alternative', *Frauenoffensive*, 3 January 1976.

38 Quotes from Reimar Lenz, 'Der neue Typ', Parts I and II, *Das Blatt* 136 (22 December 1978–11 January 1979), 30, and *Das Blatt* 137 (12–25 January 1979), 30–31.

39 All quotes from Benno Gammerl, 'Frau Muskeltyp, Herr Hexe und Fräulein Butch? Geschlechtlichkeiten und Homosexualitäten in der zweiten Hälfte des 20. Jahrhunderts', in *Zeitgeschichte als Geschlechtergeschichte: Neue Perspektiven auf die Bundesrepublik*, ed. Julia Paulus, Eva-Maria Silies and Kerstin Wolff (Frankfurt a.M.: Campus, 2012), 128–36.

40 Autorengruppe, *Männerbilder: Geschichten und Protokolle von Männern* (Munich: Trikont Verlag, 1976), 56–8.

41 Anon., 'SE-Panik', *HAW-Info* 21 (March/April 1976), 15–56.

42 See Häberlen, *Emotional Politics*, 181.

43 On troubling discussions about paedophilia, see David Paternotte, 'Pedophilia, Homosexuality and Gay and Lesbian Activism', in *Sexual Revolutions*, ed. Gert Hekma and Alain Giami (Basingstoke: Palgrave Macmillan, 2014), Julian Bourg, 'Boy Trouble: French Pedophiliac Discourse of the 1970s', in *Between Marx and Coca-Cola: Youth Cultures in Changing European Societies, 1960–1980*, ed. Axel Schildt and Detlef Siegfried (New York: Berghahn, 2006), Franz Walter, Stephan Klecha and

Alexander Hensel, eds., *Die Grünen und die Pädosexualität: Eine bundes-deutsche Geschichte* (Göttingen: Vandenhoeck & Ruprecht, 2015).

44 See Stansell, *Promise*, 345–7. The most famous (and controversially discussed) anti-pornography text is Andrea Dworkin, *Pornography: Men Possessing Women* (London: Women's Press, 1981).

45 'The Erogenous Zones of Man and Woman', *HAW-Info* 11, July 1973, 9, reproduced in Häberlen, 'Feeling Like a Child', 231.

46 Anon., 'Lesben und Orgasmuß'.

47 Heiner, 'Männersolidarität', *Mannsbild*, n.d. [1976], 20–25.

48 Martel, *Pink and the Black*, 38.

49 For an argument that the sexual liberation around 1968 actually changed both men's and women's sex lives, see Anne-Claire Rebreyend, *Intimités amoureuses: France 1920–1975* (Toulouse: Presses Universitaire du Mirail, 2008), 239–82.

50 Manfred, untitled report, *Mannsbild*, n.d. [1976], 5–6.

51 Ulla et al., '"Ich möchte lernen"', 156.

52 Rainer, Jürgen and Joachim, 'Sterilisationsgruppe', *Mannsbild*, n.d. [probably 1976], 53.

53 Anon., 'Zeit, Verbindlichkeit, Sexualität', *Carlo Sponti*, March 1977, 4.

54 (ein schwuler), 'Zum Vorwort und Artikel: Pilgrim, der verunsicherte Mann, aus Info 110', *Info BUG* 111 (28 June 1976), 7.

55 Günter Amendt, 'Nur die Sau rauslassen?', *konkret Sexualität*, 1980, 23–30.

56 See Lisa Duggan and Nan D. Hunter, eds., *Sex Wars: Essays on Sexual Dissent and Political Culture* (New York: Routledge, 1995), Thomas Foster, Carol Siegel and Ellen E. Berry, eds., *Sex Positives? The Cultural Politics of Dissident Sexualities* (New York: New York University Press, 1997), B. Ruby Rich, 'Review: Feminism and Sexuality in the 1980s', *Feminist Studies* 12 (1986), Echols, *Daring*, 289–91. On similar conflicts in the UK, see Emma Healey, *Lesbian Sex Wars* (London: Virago, 1996).

57 Cited in Rich, 'Review', 528–9.

58 Flyer is reproduced in Susan Ardill and Sue O'Sullivan, 'upsetting an applecart: difference, desire and lesbian sadomasochism', *Feminist Review* 80 (2005): 117. See also the discussion in Jeffreys, *Lesbian Revolu-*

tion, 115–34. It should be noted that Jeffreys was a member of LASM, hence her perspective is critical of sadomasochism. See critically Margaret Hunt, 'The De-Eroticization of Women's Liberation: Social Purity Movements and the Revolutionary Feminism of Sheila Jeffreys', *Feminist Review* 34 (1990).

59 All quotes in Ardill and O'Sullivan, 'upsetting', 118.

60 See, with a focus on the US and, to a lesser extent, Great Britain, the discussion in Astrid Henry, *Not My Mother's Sister: Generational Conflict and Third-Wave Feminism* (Bloomington: Indiana University Press, 2004), 88–114.

61 See, for example, the Porn Film Festival, Berlin, founded in 2006, https://pornfilmfestivalberlin.de/en/about-the-festival/. With a focus on the US, see Tristan Taormino et al., eds., *The Feminist Porn Book: The Politics of Producing Pleasure* (New York: Feminist Press at the City University of New York, 2012). Any quick search on Google for feminist sex shops in cities like London or Berlin will point to places such as Other Nature (Berlin, founded in 2011), Sexclusivitäten (Berlin, founded in 2001), or Sh! (London, founded in 1992). See also, for the UK, Jolly, *Sisterhood*, 145–7.

62 Cherry Smyth, 'The Pleasure Threshold: Looking at Lesbian Pornography on Film', *Feminist Review* 34 (1990), 157.

63 Ardill and O'Sullivan, 'upsetting', 119, 120.

64 See with many examples Häberlen, *Emotional Politics*, 186–94.

65 Anon., 'Nacktbadeaktion', *s'Blättle: Stadtzeitung für Stuttgart und umgebung*, 20 September 1977, 16–17.

Chapter 14: In Search of a Different Reality: Alternative Spirituality

1 Eribon, *Foucault*, 500–501.

2 Dieter Duhm, *Der Mensch ist anders: Besinnung auf verspottete, aber notwendige Inhalte einer ganzheitlichen Theorie der Befreiung. Kritik am Marxismus. Beiträge zur Korrektur.* (Lampertheim: Kübler, 1975), 91.

3 Carlos Castañeda, *The Teachings of Don Juan: A Yaqui Way of Knowledge* (New York: Ballantine Books, 1968), Carlos Castañeda, *A Separate Reality: Further Conversations with Don Juan* (New York: Simon and Schuster, 1971), Carlos Castañeda, *Journey to Ixtlan: The Lessons of Don Juan* (New York: Simon and Schuster, 1972).

4 See, in a West German context, for example, Vine Deloria, *Nur Stämme werden überleben: Indianische Vorschläge für eine Radikalkur des wildgewordenen Westens* (Munich: Trikont, 1976), William Willoya and Vinson Brown, *Im Zeichen des Regenbogens: Träume und Visionen des indianischen Volkes*, trans. Sylvia Luetjohann (Obernhain: Iris-Verlag, 1976), Doug Boyd, *Rolling Thunder: Erfahrungen mit einem Schamanen der neuen Indianerbewegung*, trans. Janet Woolverton (Munich: Trikont Verlag, 1978), Stan Steiner, *Der Untergang des weißen Mannes?* (Munich: Trikont-Dianus Buchverlag, 1980).

5 Duhm, *Der Mensch ist anders*, 99–100.

6 On Germany, see Reichardt, *Authentizität*, 824, Michael Mildenberger, *Die religiöse Revolte: Jugend zwischen Flucht und Aufbruch* (Frankfurt a.M.: Fischer Verlag, 1979), Pascal Eitler, 'Körper – Kosmos – Kybernetik: Transformationen der Religion im "New Age" (Westdeutschland 1970–1990)', *Zeithistorische Forschungen* 4 (2007), Pascal Eitler, '"Alternative" Religion: Subjektivierungspraktiken und Politisierungsstrategien im "New Age" (Westdeutschland 1970–1990)', in *Das alternative Milieu: Antibürgerlicher Lebensstil und linke Politik in der Bundesrepublik Deutschland und Europa, 1968–1983*, ed. Sven Reichardt and Detlef Siegfried (Göttingen: Wallstein, 2010), Pascal Eitler, 'Privatisierung und Subjektivierung: Religiöse Selbstverhältnisse im "New Age"', in *Privatisierung: Idee und Praxis seit den 1970er Jahren*, ed. Norbert Frei and Dietmar Süß (Göttingen: Wallstein, 2012). I've discussed alternative spirituality in more detail in Joachim C. Häberlen, 'Spiritual Politics: New Age and New Left in West Germany around 1980', *European History Quarterly* 51 (2021). For an impressionistic view of the UK, see Paul Heelas, *The New Age Movement: The Celebration of the Self and the Sacralization of Modernity* (Oxford: Blackwell, 1996), 49–57, 106–115. On Italy, see Isotta Poggi, 'Alternative Spirituality in Italy', in *Perspectives on the New Age*, ed. James R. Lewis and J. Gordon Melton (Albany: State University of

New York Press, 1992). Beyond the Iron Curtain, see Terje Toomistu, 'The Imaginary Elsewhere of the Hippies in Soviet Estonia', in *Dropping Out of Socialism: The Creation of Alternative Spheres in the Soviet Bloc*, ed. Juliane Fürst and Josie McLellan (Lanham, Boulder, New York, London: Lexington Books, 2017), Irina Costache, 'The Biography of a Scandal: Experimenting with Yoga during Romanian Late Socialism', in *Dropping Out of Socialism: The Creation of Alternative Spheres in the Soviet Bloc*, ed. Juliane Fürst and Josie McLellan (Lanham, Boulder, New York, London: Lexington Books, 2017).

7 See, for example, Sergius Golowin, *Hexen, Hippies, Rosenkreuzer: 500 Jahre magische Morgenlandfahrt* (Hamburg: Merlin-Verlag, 1977), Sergius Golowin, *Magische Gegenwart: Forschungsfahrt durch eine Zivilisation in Wandlung* (Munich: Trikont-Dianus Buchverlag, 1980), Hans Peter Duerr, *Traumzeit: Über die Grenze zwischen Wildnis und Zivilisation* (Frankfurt a.M.: Syndikat, 1978), Yann Daniel, *Das Nebelpferd: Geschichten aus der Bretagne*, trans. Angela Wicharz-Lindner (Munich: Trikont-Dianus Buchverlag, 1980), Harold A. Hansen, *Der Hexengarten*, trans. Elke Herzog (Munich: Trikont-Dianus Buchverlag, 1980). More popular books, originally published in the United States, are Marilyn Ferguson, *The Aquarian Conspiracy: Personal and Social Transformation in the 1980s* (Los Angeles: J. P. Tarcher, 1980), Fritjof Capra, *The Turning Point: Science, Society, and the Rising Culture* (New York: Simon and Schuster, 1982). German editions: Marilyn Ferguson, *Die sanfte Verschwörung: Persönliche und gesellschaftliche Transformation im Zeitalter des Wassermanns*, trans. Thomas Reichau (Basel: Sphinx-Verlag, 1982), Fritjof Capra, *Wendezeit: Bausteine für ein neues Weltbild*, trans. Erwin Schuhmacher (Bern: Scherz, 1983).

8 Sonnenberg, *Von Marx zum Maulwurf*, 58–62, 313–15.

9 Herbert Röttgen and Florian Rabe, *Vulkantänze: Linke und alternative Ausgänge* (Munich: Trikont-Verlag, 1978). See my discussion of the book in Häberlen, *Emotional Politics*, 84–6.

10 Christiane Thurn and Herbert Röttgen, 'Eine notwendige Einleitung', in *Die Rückkehr des Imaginären: Märchen, Magie, Mystik, Mythos, Anfänge einer anderen Politik*, ed. Christiane Thurn and Herbert Röttgen (Munich: Trikont-Dianus Buchverlag, 1981), 17.

11 Ibid.

12 See only Michael Casey, *Che's Afterlife: The Legacy of an Image* (New York: Vintage Books, 2009).

13 See my discussion in Häberlen, *Emotional Politics*, 76–122. For similar critiques in Italy, see Angelo Ventrone, 'Revolution as a Quest for an Authentic Life: The 1960s and 1970s in Italy', in *The Politics of Authenticity: Countercultures and Radical Movements across the Iron Curtain, 1968–1989*, ed. Joachim C. Häberlen, Mark Keck-Szajbel and Kate Mahoney (New York: Berghahn, 2018).

14 Capra, *Turning Point*, 23.

15 Boyd, *Rolling Thunder*, 97.

16 Capra, *Turning Point*, 21.

17 Ferguson, *Conspiracy*, 371.

18 Steiner, *Untergang*, 33.

19 Boyd, *Rolling Thunder*, 62–3.

20 Quoted by Thurn and Röttgen, 'Einleitung', 15–16. See also Heelas, *New Age Movement*, 84–8.

21 Castañeda, *Separate Reality*, 106–8. On Casteñeda's influence in the United States, see Philip Jenkins, *Dream Catchers: How Mainstream America Discovered Native Spirituality* (Oxford: Oxford University Press, 2004), 169–72.

22 Duerr, *Traumzeit*, 26, 40, 67.

23 Ibid., 58–60, 108, 159.

24 Capra, *Turning Point*, 21.

25 Ibid., 462, see also 23–5.

26 Ferguson, *Conspiracy*, 226.

27 Quoted in Charlene Spretnak, ed., *The Politics of Women's Spirituality: Essays on the Rise of Spiritual Power within the Feminist Movement* (New York: Anchor Press, 1982), 382–3. The book contains numerous texts about feminist spirituality and politics from a North American context. The original book is Anne Kent Rush, *Moon, Moon* (New York: Random House, 1976). It was also published in German as *Mond, Mond*, trans. Anita Eichholz (Munich: Verlag Frauenoffensive, 1978). For the German context, see also Lutz von Padberg, *New Age und Feminismus: Die neue Spiritualität* (Frankfurt a.M.: Ullstein, 1990).

28 Fürst, *Flowers*, 147, 266–74. See also William Jay Risch, 'Soviet "Flower Children": Hippies and the Youth Counter-Culture in 1970s L'viv', *Journal of Contemporary History* 40 (2005), 578–9.

29 Fürst, *Flowers*, 269.

30 Nicola Schulz and Karl Heinz Albers, *Nicht nur Bäume haben Wurzeln: Eine Streitschrift für einen Rückschritt zum Fortschritt* (Munich: Trikont-Dianus Verlag, 1982), 75, 117–18.

31 Ibid., 31–2. On conservative positions in the environmental movement, specifically the emerging Green Party, see also Silke Mende, *'Nicht rechts, nicht links, sondern vorn': Eine Geschichte der Gründungsgrünen* (Munich: Oldenbourg, 2011), 72–93.

32 Thurn and Röttgen, 'Einleitung', 15.

33 On New Age politics, see Eitler, '"Alternative" Religion', 342–50, Ferguson, *Conspiracy*, 189–240.

34 Ferguson, *Conspiracy*, 411.

35 Heelas, *New Age Movement*, 75.

36 Cited in Pascal Eitler, '"Selbstheilung": Zur Somatisierung und Sakralisierung von Selbstverhältnissen im New Age (Westdeutschland 1970–1990)', in *Das beratene Selbst: Zur Genealogie der Therapeutisierung in den 'langen' Siebzigern*, ed. Sabine Maasen et al. (Bielefeld: transcript, 2011), 164.

37 'Gespräch mit Robert Jungk', in *Die Rückkehr des Imaginären: Märchen, Magie, Mystik, Mythos, Anfänge einer anderen Politik*, ed. Christiane Thurn and Herbert Röttgen (Munich: Trikont-Dianus Verlag, 1981), 59.

38 Ibid., 61–2.

39 See Eitler, '"Alternative" Religion', 344.

40 See, for example, Alois Zuchtriegel, 'Psychotherapie aus spiritueller Sicht', *Hologramm* 29 (March 1982), 4–9. For a similar argument, see Boyd, *Rolling Thunder*. See also Eitler, '"Selbstheilung"', 260. On healing in the New Age, see Catherine L. Albanese, 'The Magical Stuff: Quantum Healing in the New Age', in *Perspectives on the New Age*, ed. James R. Lewis and J. Gordon Melton (Albany: State University of New York Press, 1992), 77–81.

41 Quoted in Eitler, '"Selbstheilung"', 172.

42 Costache, 'Biography of a Scandal', 32.

43 Eitler, '"Selbstheilung"', 173.

44 Quoted in Eitler, 'Körper', 126.

45 Quoted in ibid., 127.

46 Quoted in Eitler, '"Selbstheilung"', 175.

47 Corinne McLaughlin, 'Gruppenbewusstsein und feminine Energie', *Hologramm* 9 (May 1978), 3–4.

48 'Denn die Weisheit ist beweglicher als alle Bewegung: Ein Gespräch mit Dagmar von Garnier über Tanz, Frauen und Spiritualität. Zusammengestellt von Marianne Oehlmann-van Nes', in *Hologramm* 28 (January 1982), 18–20.

49 This is the perspective Pascal Eitler takes, see Eitler, '"Alternative" Religion', '"Selbstheilung"', 'Privatisierung'.

50 Swami Satyananda, *Ganz entspannt im Hier und Jetzt: Tagebuch über mein Leben mit Bhagwan in Poona* (Reinbek bei Hamburg: Rowohlt, 1982), back cover. The book was first published in 1979.

51 See Philip Goldberg, *American Veda: From Emerson and the Beatles to Yoga and Meditation. How Indian Spirituality Changed the West* (New York: Harmony Books, 2010), 151–61.

52 Hugh B. Urban, *Zorba the Buddha: Sex, Spirituality, and Capitalism in the Global Osho Movement* (Oakland: University of California Press, 2015), 88.

53 On Bhagwan and his followers, see Maik Tändler, 'Ausstieg und Erleuchtung: Die Bhagwan-Bewegung in der Bundesrepublik in den 1970er und 1980er Jahren', in *Exit: Ausstieg und Verweigerungen in 'offenen' Gesellschaften nach 1945*, ed. Petra Terhoeven and Tobias Weidner (Göttingen: Wallstein, 2020), Urban, *Zorba*, Joachim Süss, *Zur Erleuchtung unterwegs: Neo-Sannyasin in Deutschland und ihre Religion* (Berlin: Dietrich Reimer Verlag, 1994).

54 Tändler, 'Ausstieg', 268, Urban, *Zorba*, 104.

55 Cited in Tändler, 'Ausstieg', 275. See also Süss, *Erleuchtung*, 252–5.

56 Heelas, *New Age Movement*, 68.

57 Tändler, 'Ausstieg', 276–7. On the perception of the movement as fascist, see also Süss, *Erleuchtung*, 209–11.

58 Swami Satyananda, *Im Grunde ist alles ganz einfach: Gespräche mit sieben Bhagwan-Jüngern über ihre Beziehung zum Meister und zur Kommune*,

über Liebe und Sex, über Politik und Drogen, über Wiedergeburt und Erleuchtung, über Freunde und Eltern (Frankfurt a.M.: Ullstein, 1981), 6f. Quoted in Tändler, 'Ausstieg', 277–8.

59 See, for example, Familie Wierpsek, 'Bumerang Nr. 3', *Ulcus Molle* 3/4 (1979), 16–19; Achim Bergmann, 'Reise nach Irland', in *Die Rückkehr des Imaginären: Märchen, Magie, Mystik, Mythos, Anfänge einer anderen Politik*, ed. Christiane Thurn and Herbert Röttgen (Munich: Trikont-Dianus Buchverlag, 1981), Peter M. Michels, 'Rasta & Reggae', in *Die Rückkehr des Imaginären: Märchen, Magie, Mystik, Mythos, Anfänge einer anderen Politik*, ed. Christiane Thurn and Herbert Röttgen (Munich: Trikont-Dianus Buchverlag, 1981), Süss, *Erleuchtung*, 256. On West German leftist fascination with Afro-Americans, see also Moritz Ege, *Schwarz werden: 'Afroamerikanophilie' in den 1960er und 1970er Jahren* (Bielefeld: transcript, 2007).

60 Fürst, *Flowers*, 159–66, 269–75.

61 Costache, 'Biography of a Scandal'.

62 Toomistu, 'Imaginary Elsewhere'.

63 Satyananda, *Ganz entspannt*, 103.

64 Heelas, *New Age Movement*, 65. See also Lisbeth Mikaelsson, 'New Age and the Spirit of Capitalism: Energy as Cognitive Currency', in *New Age Spirituality: Rethinking Religion*, ed. Steven J. Sutcliffe and Ingvild Sælid Gilhus (London: Routledge, 2014), Kimberley J. Lau, *New Age Capitalism: Making Money East of Eden* (Philadelphia: University of Pennsylvania Press, 2000).

65 Satyananda, *Ganz entspannt*, 103.

66 Heelas, *New Age Movement*, 95f., 126–8.

67 Joachim Bruhn, 'Unter den Zwischenmenschen', in *Diktatur der Freundlichkeit: Über Bhagwan, die kommende Psychokratie und Lieferanteneingänge zum wohltätigen Wahnsinn*, ed. Initiative Sozialistisches Forum (Freiburg: Ça-Ira-Verlag, 1984), quote 9.

68 Tändler, 'Ausstieg', 276–7.

69 For a balanced and ultimately optimistic view, see Paul Heelas, *Spiritualities of Life: New Age Romanticism and Consumptive Capitalism* (Oxford: Blackwell Publishing, 2008).

Chapter 15: Bringing Down Communism in Eastern Europe: The Revolutions of 1989

1 A recording of the famous press conference can be found at https://www.youtube.com/watch?v=JbzhHGcEz-E&t=9s.

2 For an account of these events, see Kowalczuk, *Endspiel*, 457–62, Gareth Dale, *The East German Revolution of 1989* (Manchester: Manchester University Press, 2006), 90–96, Mary Elise Sarotte, *The Collapse: The Accidental Opening of the Berlin Wall* (New York: Basic Books, 2014), 105–53.

3 See, for example, Charles S. Maier, *Dissolution: The Crisis of Communism and the End of East Germany* (Princeton: Princeton University Press, 1997), Vladimir Tismaneanu, 'The Revolutions of 1989: Causes, Meanings, Consequences', *Contemporary European History* 18 (2009), Vladimir Tismaneanu, ed., *The End and the Beginning: The Revolutions of 1989 and the Resurgence of History* (Budapest: Central European University Press, 2012), Steven Kotkin, *Uncivil Society: 1989 and the Implosion of the Communist Establishment* (New York: Modern Library, 2010).

4 While there is a massive historiography on the fall of communism in the GDR, the historiography on the revolutions in Poland and Czechoslovakia is much less developed. For transnational perspectives, see, in addition to the literature mentioned below, Sorin Antohi and Vladimir Tismaneanu, eds., *Between Past and Future: The Revolutions of 1989 and Their Aftermath* (Budapest: Central European University Press, 2000), Joachim von Puttkamer, Włodzimierz Borodziej and Stanislav Holubec, eds., *From Revolution to Uncertainty: The Year 1990 in Central and Eastern Europe* (London: Routledge, 2019).

5 See Kenney, *Carnival*, 4–5, James Krapfl, *Revolution with a Human Face: Politics, Culture, and Community in Czechoslovakia, 1989–1992* (Ithaca: Cornell University Press, 2013), 53–65, Kowalczuk, *Endspiel*, 462–74, Dale, *Revolution*, 43–5, Ehrhart Neubert, *Unsere Revolution: Die Geschichte der Jahre 1989/90* (Munich: Piper, 2008), 223–4.

6 Timothy Garton Ash, *The Magic Lantern: The Revolution of '89, Witnessed in Warsaw, Budapest, Berlin and Prague.* Updated Version (London:

Atlantic Books, 2019), 73. For a general account of the long end of communism in Poland, see John Connelly, *From Peoples into Nations: A History of Eastern Europe* (Princeton: Princeton University Press, 2020), 687–704, Włodzimierz Borodziej, *Geschichte Polens im 20. Jahrhundert* (Munich: C. H. Beck, 2010), 360–83. I take the term 'negotiated revolution' from Nigel Swain, 'Negotiated Revolution in Poland and Hungary, 1989', in *Revolution and Resistance in Eastern Europe*, ed. Kevin McDermott and Matthew Stibbe (New York: Berg, 2006).

7 On Wojtyła's famous visit to Poland, see Jan Kubik, *The Power of Symbols against the Symbols of Power: The Rise of Solidarity and the Fall of State Socialism in Poland* (University Park: Pennsylvania State University Press, 1994), 129–52.

8 See, for example, the detailed discussion of the December 1970 strikes in Laba, *Roots*, 15–82.

9 Connelly, *Peoples into Nations*, 689–91, Bloom, *Seeing through the Eyes*, 81–124.

10 Bloom, *Seeing through the Eyes*, 145–8.

11 Connelly, *Peoples into Nations*, 700–701.

12 On such monuments during the August 1980 strikes, see Laba, *Roots*, 135–40.

13 On the strikes, see Szymanski, *Protest*, 53–155, Bloom, *Seeing through the Eyes*, 145–81, Szporer, *Solidarity*, Connelly, *Peoples into Nations*, 700–702. On Solidarność, see Laba, *Roots*.

14 Connelly, *Peoples into Nations*, 702–4, Bloom, *Seeing through the Eyes*, 287–322.

15 See with many examples Szymanski, *Protest*, 168–95.

16 Kenney, *Carnival*, 26. On underground Solidarność after 1981, see Bloom, *Seeing through the Eyes*, 323–43.

17 Kenney, *Carnival*, 32.

18 On WiP, see Bloom, *Seeing through the Eyes*, 357–60.

19 On environmental campaigns, see Piotr Żuk, 'Anti-Military Protests and Campaigns against Nuclear Power Plants: The Peace Movement in the Shadow of the Warsaw Pact in Poland in the 1980s', *Journal of Contemporary Central and Eastern Europe* 25 (2017), 371–2.

20 See Kenney, *Carnival*, 49–51 (on sobriety societies), 57–90 (WiP), 168–75 (underground youth movements). On oppositional youth movements in Poland, see Kirsten Gerland, *Politische Jugend im Umbruch von 1988/89: Generationelle Dynamik in der DDR und der Volks-republik Polen* (Göttingen: Wallstein, 2016), 235–61.

21 Kenney, *Carnival*, 218.

22 Ibid., 220. On the festive character of the 1980 strikes, see also Bloom, *Seeing through the Eyes*, 167.

23 Kenney, *Carnival*, 221.

24 Ibid., 222.

25 Ibid., 223–4.

26 Ibid., 233–5.

27 Ibid., 250.

28 Ibid., 258–61.

29 Garton Ash, *Magic Lantern*, 22.

30 On these negotiations, see also Connelly, *Peoples into Nations*, 720–21, Bloom, *Seeing through the Eyes*, 363–73.

31 On opposition in the GDR, see in general Mary Fulbrook, 'Popular Discontent and Political Activism in the GDR', *Contemporary European History* 2 (1993), Neubert, *Geschichte der Opposition*, Pollack, *Politischer Protest*, zur Mühlen, *Aufbruch*.

32 Kowalczuk, *Endspiel*, 75, Gareth Dale, *Popular Protest in East Germany, 1945–1989* (London: Routledge, 2005), 122–3.

33 Kowalczuk, *Endspiel*, Dale, *Protest*, 123–4.

34 Kowalczuk, *Endspiel*, 309–13, Dale, *Protest*, 129–34.

35 All quotes in Dale, *Protest*, 138.

36 On the elections, see Kowalczuk, *Endspiel*, 320–35, numbers 329, Dale, *Protest*, 139.

37 Kowalczuk, *Endspiel*, 333–5.

38 For a vivid description of the situation in the embassy, including photos, see https://www.planet-wissen.de/geschichte/ddr/die_berliner_mauer/pwiezufluchtpragerbotschaft100.html#Lage-spitzt-sich-zu.

39 Kowalczuk, *Endspiel*, 349–56, 379–85, Dale, *Protest*, 140–45.

40 Kowalczuk, *Endspiel*, 370.

41 Ibid., 386–8, Dale, *Protest*, 152–3, Dale, *Revolution*, 12–17.

42 Kowalczuk, *Endspiel*, 387. See also Neubert, *Unsere Revolution*, 78–94.

43 See Maier, *Dissolution*, 175–7.

44 Cited in ibid., 133.

45 Cited in Kowalczuk, *Endspiel*, 364–5. See also Steven Pfaff, *Exit-Voice Dynamics and the Collapse of East Germany: The Crisis of Leninism and the Revolution of 1989* (Durham: Duke University Press, 2006), 193–6.

46 Kowalczuk, *Endspiel*, 366, Neubert, *Unsere Revolution*, 85–6.

47 For an impressive personal account of the day, see Stefan Wolle, 'Seltsame Nacht: Ein Nachtrag zum Revolutionstagebuch von 1989', in *Revolution und Vereinigung 1989/90*, ed. Klaus-Dietmar Henke (Munich: Deutscher Taschenbuch Verlag, 2009). See also Kowalczuk, *Endspiel*, 388–95, Dale, *Protest*, 154, Dale, *Revolution*, 18–20, Pfaff, *Dynamics*, 114–16.

48 Cited in Richardson-Little, *Human Rights Dictatorship*, 238, Kowalczuk, *Endspiel*, 404.

49 For a detailed account of the events in Leipzig, see Maier, *Dissolution*, 135–46. See also Kowalczuk, *Endspiel*, 403–6, Dale, *Protest*, 155–6, Dale, *Revolution*, 22–33, Neubert, *Unsere Revolution*, 132–9.

50 Dale, *Revolution*, 50.

51 Cited in Pfaff, *Dynamics*, 178. See also Richardson-Little, *Human Rights Dictatorship*, 239. See also the documentary Gerd Kroske and Andreas Voigt, *Leipzig im Herbst: 16.10.–7.11.1989* (Germany: 1989), https://www.bpb.de/mediathek/236044/leipzig-im-herbst.

52 Kowalczuk, *Endspiel*, 439–47.

53 Ibid., 447–50. For an analysis of street demonstrations, see also Dale, *Revolution*, 35–55.

54 Kowalczuk, *Endspiel*, 474–7.

55 See Dale, *Revolution*, 78–83.

56 Kowalczuk, *Endspiel*, 415–17.

57 For an account, see ibid., 423–6. The account, including the quote, is based on politburo member Gerhard Schürer's personal recollections, published in Hans-Hermann Hertle, *Der Fall der Mauer: Die unbeabsichtigte Selbstauflösung des SED-Staates* (Opladen: Westdeutscher Verlag, 1996).

58 Kowalczuk, *Endspiel*, 463–4, 467–9.

59 Cited in Dale, *Revolution*, 98. See also Pfaff, *Dynamics*, 197.

60 Dale, *Protest*, 165. See also Richardson-Little, *Human Rights Dictatorship*, 244–5, Pfaff, *Dynamics*, 200–206, Andreas Rödder, *Deutschland einig Vaterland: Die Geschichte der Wiedervereinigung* (Munich: C. H. Beck, 2009), 118–27.

61 See Marc Dietrich Ohse, '"Wir sind ein Volk!" Die Wende in der "Wende"', in *Revolution und Vereinigung 1989/90*, ed. Klaus-Dietmar Henke (Munich: Deutscher Taschenbuch Verlag, 2009).

62 For histories of the unification, see Konrad H. Jarausch, *The Rush to German Unity* (Oxford: Oxford University Press, 1994), Rödder, *Deutschland*.

63 See Kowalczuk, *Endspiel*, 496–551, election results 534, Dale, *Protest*, 149–50, 156–60, Pfaff, *Dynamics*, 239–53.

64 Cited in Rödder, *Deutschland*, 121.

65 See, in addition to the literature mentioned above, Charles S. Maier, 'Essay: Die ostdeutsche Revolution', in *Revolution und Vereinigung 1989/90*, ed. Klaus-Dietmar Henke (Munich: Deutscher Taschenbuch Verlag, 2009).

66 Kowalczuk, *Endspiel*, 471–3. He is referring to Vera-Maria Baehr, ed., *Wir denken erst seit Gorbatschow: Protokolle von Jugendlichen aus der DDR* (Recklinghausen: Ritter, 1990). On the role of the youth during the end of the GDR, see also Gerland, *Jugend*, 85–140.

67 See Barış Yörümez, 'Authenticity through Transgression: Small Acts of Resentment in Post-1968 Czechoslovakia', in *The Politics of Authenticity: Countercultures and Radical Movements across the Iron Curtain, 1968–1989*, ed. Joachim C. Häberlen, Mark Keck-Szajbel and Kate Mahoney (New York: Berghahn, 2018), 54.

68 Kenney, *Carnival*, 121.

69 See ibid., 145–50, 166–8, 266–7.

70 On these events, see ibid., 215–17, 238–41, 244–8, 254–7. The best account of the Velvet Revolution in Czechoslovakia is Krapfl, *Revolution*. See also Miroslav Vaněk and Pavel Mücke, *Velvet Revolutions: An Oral History of Czech Society* (Oxford: Oxford University Press, 2016), Beáta Blehová, *Der Fall des Kommunismus in der Tschechoslowakei*

(Vienna: Lit Verlag, 2006), Bernard Wheaton and Zdenek Kavan, *The Velvet Revolution: Czechoslovakia, 1988–1991* (Boulder: Westview Press, 1992).

71 See Blehová, *Fall des Kommunismus*, 205–8.

72 Kenney, *Carnival*, 285–6.

73 Ibid., 286–7.

74 Quoted in ibid., 281.

75 Krapfl, *Revolution*, 14–15, 46–7. For an account of the events of 17 November 1989, see also Blehová, *Fall des Kommunismus*, 208–19.

76 Krapfl, *Revolution*, 16.

77 Ibid., 54.

78 Ibid., 56.

79 Ibid., 20–21, 57–8.

80 Both quoted in ibid., 105.

81 On the 'Ideals of November', see ibid., 76–110. I take the translation from Krapfl.

82 Quoted in ibid., 86.

83 Quoted in ibid., 53–4.

84 Quoted in ibid., 91–2.

85 Quoted in ibid., 18.

86 Ibid., 23.

87 Ibid., 104.

88 Ibid., 31.

89 Ibid., 29, 208–9.

90 On the neo-liberal transformations after 1989, see Philipp Ther, *Europe since 1989: A History*, trans. Charlotte Hughes-Kreutzmüller (Princeton: Princeton University Press, 2016).

91 Quoted in Krapfl, *Revolution*, 31.

92 On the question of what, if anything, happened in 1968, see Ross, *May '68*, in particular 19–20, Nassehi, *Gab es 1968?*

Index